The Patricians of Nishapur

Harvard Middle Eastern Studies, 16

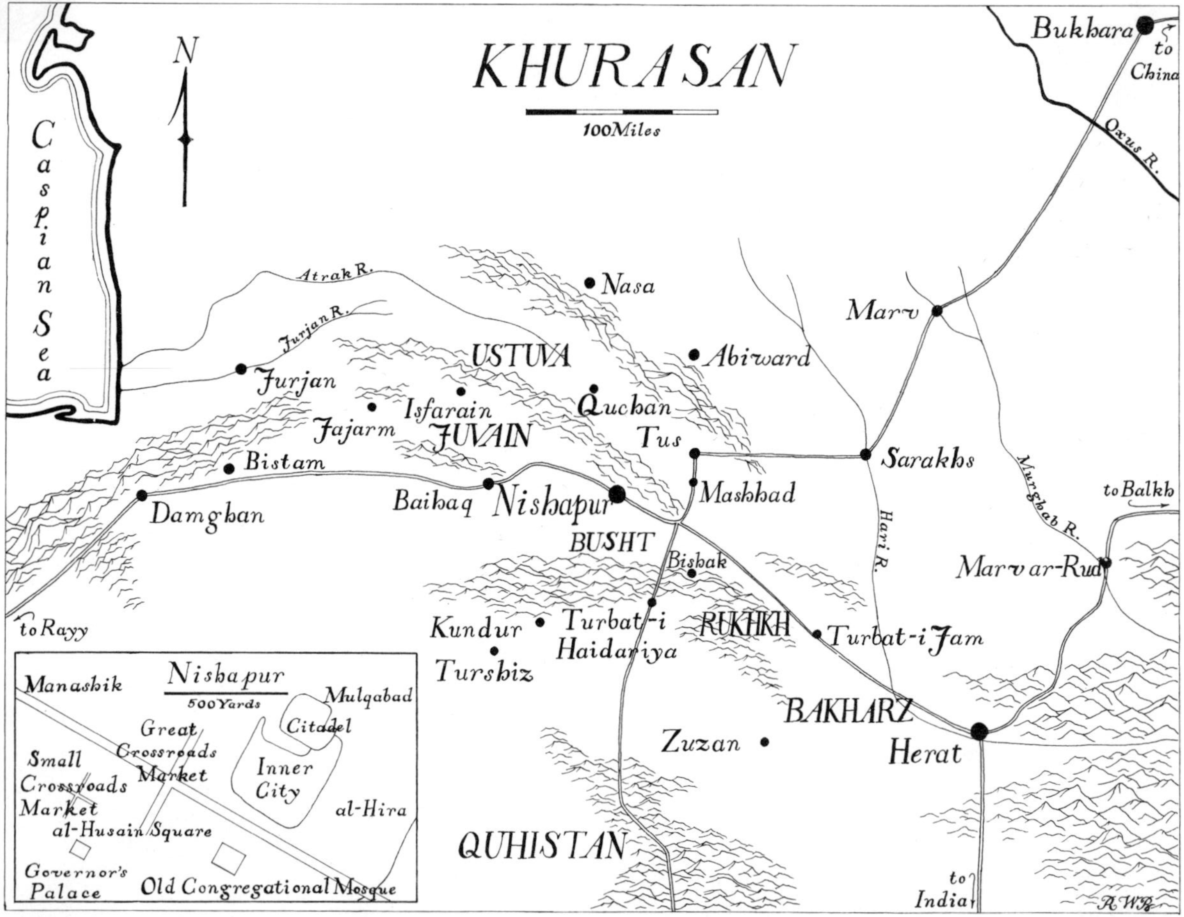
KHURASAN
100 Miles
N
Caspian Sea
Atrak R.
Jurjan R.
Jurjan
Nasa
USTUVA
Abiward
Marv
Bukhara
to China
Oxus R.
Isfarain
Quchan
Jajarm
JUVAIN
Tus
Sarakhs
Murghab R.
to Balkh
Bistam
Baihaq
Nishapur
Mashhad
Damghan
BUSHT
Hari R.
Bishak
Marv ar-Rud
to Rayy
Kundur
Turbat-i Haidariya
RUKHKH
Turbat-i Jam
Turshiz
BAKHARZ
Zuzan
Herat
QUHISTAN
to India
A.W.B.
Nishapur
500 Yards
Manashik
Mulqabad
Great Crossroads Market
Citadel
Small Crossroads Market
Inner City
al-Husain Square
al-Hira
Governor's Palace
Old Congregational Mosque

The Patricians of Nishapur

A Study in Medieval Islamic Social History

Richard W. Bulliet

Harvard University Press
Cambridge, Massachusetts / 1972

Library of Congress Catalog Card Number 70-173413
SBN 674-65792-6
Printed in the United States of America

For my mother and father

Acknowledgments

This book began as a doctoral dissertation which I wrote under the direction of Professor George Makdisi, and I happily acknowledge my debt to him for the assistance he gave me in penetrating the intricate history of the medieval Muslim law schools. Likewise I wish to thank Professor Richard N. Frye for making accessible to me before their publication the manuscript materials upon which this book is based and for his willingness to share his wealth of lore on the history of Iran. Yet I would never have gotten to the point of beginning my dissertation were it not for the brilliant teaching of Professor H. A. R. Gibb who inspired in me the desire to study medieval Islamic society and drummed enough Arabic into me to enable me to do it.

Invaluable assistance of another kind was rendered me by a number of people who had the patience and the kindness to sit for hours and endure my recital of Nishapuri history as I attempted to unravel its mysteries by thinking aloud and who not infrequently contributed important insights. Chief among this group I must single out for special thanks L. C. Bulliet, Roy P. Mottahedeh, Paul V. Smith, and my parents. To Barbara Henson and Brenda Sens who typed the manuscript I would also like to extend my thanks.

Financial support during the period of preparing my dissertation was afforded me by the Woodrow Wilson Foundation and by the United States government through an NDFL-Fulbright-Hays Fellowship; and I especially want to thank the taxpayers of the United States who, willy-nilly, contributed so much to my graduate education.

Contents

Note on Transliteration and Dates

The Arabic transliteration system used is that of *Webster's Seventh New Collegiate Dictionary* with the one exception that the silent *h* of the feminine ending is not written. Well-known place-names have been left in their familiar form, and Persian place-names have been transliterated according to modern Persian usage. This presents occasional anomalies, as when a man from Juvain is surnamed al-Juwainī, but hopefully none serious enough to be confusing.

Double dates are used throughout since *hijra* dates are easier for the specialist to work with and Christian dates more palatable to the general reader. The difficulty in adopting this procedure is that the lunar Muslim year is somewhat shorter than the solar Christian year; hence the two overlap in an irregular fashion. Since the dates given in the sources are all hijra dates, the Christian equivalent should, strictly speaking, be the span of two years in which the Muslim year falls, for example, 1050–51/442. This makes reading terribly awkward, however, so here only one Christian year is given as the equivalent of each hijra year, that one being the Christian year in which the greater part of the hijra year falls. It should always be borne in mind, therefore, that it is the hijra year that is accurate while the Christian year may be off by one.

A person's age computed with hijra dates is influenced by shortness of the Muslim year. As the Muslim century is three years shorter than the Christian, a Muslim centenarian would be only ninety-seven years old by the Christian calendar. Accordingly, since Muslim ages are used throughout, seemingly undue longevity may be reduced by subtracting two from the age of anyone in his seventies.

Introduction

This is a book about a city, a book about a social class, and above all, perhaps, a book about a book. The city of Nishapur was one of the great metropolises of the Middle East, indeed of the world, from the tenth/fourth to the twelfth/sixth century. Compared with the effort modern historians have put into the study of comparable cities, this book is a very modest beginning. Much, much more can be done, and it is the hope and intention of the author someday to do some of it. Here, however, the city serves primarily as milieu for a group of people, the patricians of Nishapur. The singularity of the city—its specific size, location, industries, ethnic complexion, and so forth—conditioned the thoughts and actions of this group of people. This is unquestionably so albeit difficult to verify. Yet in another medieval city the same social group might be readily identifiable once allowance is made for the different specific conditions of that city. Thus, in some ways what is true of the patricians of Nishapur is true of the patricians of other cities, and in some ways it is not. A world of controversy is contained in the judgment of these similarities and dissimilarities.

The particular conceptual foundation underlying what is said in this book about the patricians of Nishapur is surely debatable and should be set forth clearly, not for the purposes of debate but to inform the reader of the author's biases and prejudgments. The notion of "the Islamic city" will never be called into use. The arguments adduced by various defenders of the concept of a city type defined by the Islamic religion have not, in the author's opinion, been convincing. Nishapur was an Islamic city in the sense that most of its inhabitants adhered to that faith, but an understanding of its character and composition will be little more advanced by a study of Islamic Fez than by an equivalent study of Christian Toulouse or Montpellier. The corollary that "the Western city" is not *sui generis* logically follows.

The word "patrician" has been chosen, and its use justified at length in chapter 2, with this lack of clear differentiation between Islam and the West in mind. The words "notables" and "dignitaries" are not only without significant content, but they have a vaguely non-Western ring to them, as if the implied dignity and note were formal or ceremonial and not based upon real functions in society. The word *ᶜulamāʾ*, meaning "the learned in the religious sciences," is better than "notables" or "dignitaries"; but the stress that it puts upon learning and scholarship is misleading unless properly understood. Education played a crucial role in the lives of the patriciate, but to the degree that it actually defined the group, it defined its membership rather than the prerequisites for membership. Patrician status was confirmed more than achieved through education.

Thus, the word "patrician" was arrived at by the elimination of the usual alternatives and by the desire to denote high social rank combined with local identification and loyalty. Hopefully, it will prove a not unwise coinage.

If the word "patrician" is adopted, however, can the word "burgher" be far behind? At the present stage of development of medieval Islamic social history, changes over time in the balance of power and prestige among land owners, merchants, artisans, and government officials are difficult to make out. There was no lack of conflict within the patriciate, but the roots of the conflict are still buried. Since source materials are not lacking, time and effort are bound to elucidate the situation more. But for now, questions of patrician vs. burgher or merchant vs. artisan must remain suspended.

All this being said, the original question still remains of how far one can extrapolate from the patriciate of Nishapur a broad pattern of social functioning applicable to a wider area. Only additional studies made of other cities from a similar viewpoint can really determine the answer to this. Tentatively, however, the thesis may be advanced that the type range of the Nishapur patriciate is Khurasan and Transoxania. The shared historical tradition of these two areas in pre-Islamic times, in particular the heritage of weak or nonexistent imperial rule and correspondingly strong local political authorities, combined with such economic and geographic factors as flourishing long distance trade, interspersed settled and desert areas, and labor intensive but essentially local irrigation systems, seems to have created an urban environment in the area that fostered the development of local patriciates.

Of course, the existence of a similar class in the cities of western Iran, Iraq, Syria, Egypt, and North Africa has been abundantly demonstrated. The positing of Nishapuri-type patrician development exclusively for the eastern Iranian area is done with reference not to the class per se but to the particular role that it played in society. It would take an extensive comparative study to show just how the Nishapur patriciate differed in composition and function from the Damascus patriciate, if the use of that term could be justified in Damascus; but there seems to be sufficient evidence that important differences did exist. Universal "Islamic" social types are as little to be sought for as a universal "Islamic" city type.

Compounding the problem of comparing the patriciate of Nishapur with the corresponding group in cities at any great remove geographically is the specificity of the political-historical situation of Khurasan in the period with which this book is primarily concerned, the tenth/fourth through twelfth/sixth centuries. The ᶜAbbāsid caliphate in

Baghdad which had been at least nominally ruling the Islamic world since 750/132, was in a state of such decline as to have little tangible influence upon political events in the provinces. Khurasan and Transoxania were as far distant from Egypt and Syria in political experience as they were in space, and as the period wore on the divergence in historical experience only became deeper.

As the tenth/fourth century began, Khurasan and Transoxania were under the domination of an Iranian dynasty known as the Sāmānids whose capital was at Bukhara just beyond the Oxus River. Loyal, if not really subordinate, to the ᶜAbbāsid caliph, the Sāmānid princes were not unlike their predecessors the Ṭāhirids or certain independent and semi-independent dynasties in other parts of the caliphate. By the year 1000/390, however, the history of the eastern provinces of the caliphate was clearly following a distinctive course; the Ghaznavids had succeeded the Sāmānids in most of their domains and thus had become the first ruling dynasty of Turkish origin. Within another thirty years the advent of the Turkish Seljuqs inaugurated a new chapter in Middle Eastern history. Their steady expansion westward engulfed the ᶜAbbāsid caliphate and rejoined the western and eastern provinces. Suddenly the effect of almost two centuries of comparative isolation of one half of the caliphate from the other became quite evident. The Seljuqs brought with them to the western provinces social and institutional forms that now appeared distinctively eastern, notably the institution of the *madrasa* or religious college, and it is an open question, as stated before, to what extent these eastern forms, emanating more often than not from the patrician class, found genuine counterparts in the society of Iraq, Syria, and Egypt.

However, as remarked at the outset, city and social class are not necessarily the most important subjects of this book. It is also a book about the *History of Nishapur* (Taʾrīkh Naisābūr) by al-Ḥākim an-Naisābūrī (d. 1015/405) and its continuation, known as the *Sequel to the History of Nishapur* (as-Siyāq li-Taʾrīkh Naisābūr), by ᶜAbd al-Ghāfir al-Fārisī (d. 1135/529). For all intents and purposes, these two may be considered one single work. They are compilations of patrician biographies, and the means and ends of compiling were the same for both authors.[1] Al-Ḥākim's work is preserved in a single, drastically abbreviated manuscript which contains little more than the name of each individual. It was used extensively by other authors, however, so that many full

1. For a discussion of the validity of considering these two works as one see Richard Bulliet, "A Quantitative Approach to Medieval Muslim Biographical Dictionaries," *Journal of the Economic and Social History of the Orient*, 13 (1970), 195–211.

biographies can be gleaned from other sources. Al-Fārisī's continuation is preserved in two manuscripts, one containing a selection of complete biographies and beginning half-way through the alphabet and the other containing virtually all of the biographies in abbreviated form. It was also used extensively by other authors. All three manuscripts have been published in facsimile form by Richard N. Frye in the volume *The Histories of Nishapur*, and detailed information concerning their provenance and condition is contained in his introduction.

The compilation of biographical dictionaries is one of the more unusual culture traits of medieval Islamic society. Many other cities had their histories written in this form, but the genre also includes collections based upon other unifying categories, such as occupation or religious faction. In addition, there are pure reference compilations, such as dictionaries that list surnames alphabetically with biographical examples and dictionaries devoted to differentiating between similar or identical names. Even with multiple repetitions in different works, there must be several hundred thousand biographies of separate individuals contained in dictionaries still extant.

The author's fervent hope is that by writing a work of social history based to a very great extent on the biographical dictionaries of Nishapur, the feasibility and value of intensive study of such works may be demonstrated and further researches into them stimulated. Progress in understanding the social history of medieval Islamic society depends upon better utilization of these sources. The tapping of their great potential has hardly begun.

The reason for this slowness to utilize valuable materials is not hard to find. Extracting usable information from a very large number of brief, general, religiously-oriented biographies presents a formidable methodological problem. Quantitative or statistical approaches are feasible, particularly in a case such as that of Nishapur where there are some forty-four hundred biographies restricted to a single locale. The author has examined one such approach elsewhere.[2] These approaches do not play a significant part in this book, however. Instead, a technique of family reconstitution has been heavily relied upon. Part II is devoted to detailed histories of nine of Nishapur's patrician families on the premise that the quite meager concrete data recorded for any individual takes on fuller significance when pooled with the data recorded for that individual's brothers, cousins, forebears, and offspring. The result is a portrait of a family as a func-

2. Bulliet, "A Quantitative Approach," pp. 195–211.

tioning social unit that is more complete and informative than the portrait of any individual in the family. Since the patriciate was made up of a limited number of such families monopolizing honor and prestige within the community generation after generation, this approach has proved to be a fruitful one.

Part II is devoted to family histories, but Part I is an analysis of the composition and functions of the patriciate within the city and in the broader political and social context as well. The degree to which this analysis relies upon and is distilled from patrician family portraits, of which the ones contained in Part II are only a selection, cannot be exaggerated. A coherent understanding of Nishapur's social structure would be impossible without a thorough knowledge of family ties and relationships. That is why the sometimes tedious narrations of cousins, uncles, and brothers-in-law have been included in the text. The analysis in Part I is a fleshless skeleton without them.

Finally, a few words must be said about the sources used. The works of al-Ḥākim and al-Fārisī have already been discussed, but a few details about the facsimile edition should be clarified. In the first of the two manuscripts of al-Fārisī (the manuscript in the middle of the book which is cited here as Fārisī I) several folios are mislocated but consecutively numbered in their incorrect locations. The correct order of the affected portion of the text is as follows: folio 30 should be followed by folio 82, then f86, f87, f83, f84, f80, f81, f85, and back to f31; folio 79 consequently should be followed by folio 88.

The other manuscript of al-Fārisī, which follows the book's introduction and is cited as Fārisī II, is also erratically paged. Folio 40 has been numbered so as to have three sides. After the third page numbered 40, a "folio," that is to say a sequence of two pages bearing the same number, switches from being the verso of one leaf and the recto of the next to the normal pattern of recto and verso of the same leaf. To circumvent this bit of confusion, the page with the number at the top (when it has not been chopped off by the photography), which is always a recto, will be uniformly cited as the *a* side of the folio and its verso as the *b* side, regardless of the number at the bottom of the verso. Furthermore, f68a is incorrectly numbered f69a, and f107b–108a are missing entirely with f99b–100a being reprinted in their place. Figure 1 is a facsimile of these two missing pages.

Of the other biographical dictionaries consulted, most derive their information on Nishapur ultimately from al-Ḥākim and al-Fārisī. Subkī's *Ṭabaqāt ash-Shāfiᶜiya al-Kubrā* and Samᶜānī's *Kitāb al-Ansāb* have been particularly useful, however, because of their authors' habit of quoting directly and extensively from these sources. Both have

Figure 1. Folio 107b–108a from Fārisī II (manuscript of al-Fārisī, *As-Siyāq li Ta'rīkh Naisābūr*).

ابي منصور بن ابي سعد توفي في حد الكهولة **عبد الغفور** بن خليفة

الطبري ابو بكر مستور صالح **عبد السلام** بن عبد الصمد

البزاز الهروي المحتسب ابو الفضل صالح مستور سمع بمرو ونيسابور **عبد السلام**

ابن الحاكم ابي عبد الله محمد بن الهيصم التميمي ابو محمد ابن اخت محمد بن احمد الكاسدري

عبد المنعم بن عبد الكريم بن هوازن القشيري ابو المظفر سبط الائمة اصغر

اولاد زين الاسلام [illegible] سمع اصحاب الخليلي والخفاف وسمع بالعراق مشايخ بغداد **عبد

الماجد** بن عبد الواحد بن عبد الكريم بن هوازن القشيري ابو المحاسن اخذ عن

والده الاصول ودرس عليه الفقه والتفسير عبد الخالق **عبد الخالق** بن

زاهر بن طاهر الشحامي ابو منصور المستملي **عبد الخالق** بن احمد بن عبد

القادر بن محمد بن يوسف البغدادي ابو الفرج فاضل دخل نيسابور تاجرا وكتب

عن المتاخرين وخرج في جمادى الاخرة سنة سبع وعشرين وخمس مائة وسمع منا واستجازنا

لنفسه ولاولاده رواية احاديث عنا وقرانا احاديث من فوائده التي جمعها

من اسمه عمر من الطبقات الثلث فمن

الطبقة الاولى عمر بن احمد بن ابرهيم بن عبدويه بن سدوس بن

علي بن عبد الله بن عبيد الله بن عبد الله بن عتبة بن مسعود الهذلي العبدوي

ابو حازم الحافظ الامام في صنعة الحديث الثقة الاثبت كثير

السماع حسن الاصول سمعه ابوه مع جماعة من المتقدمين مثل ابي

اسحق وابي علي الرفا الهروي وغيرهما فلم يحدث عنهم تورعا وقال لست اذكرهم

فلما روى عنهم وحدث عمن سمع منهم بخراسان والعراق والحجاز بعد الخمسين والثلثمائة

فروى عن والده ابي الحسن العبدوي وعن عمه ابي عبد الله وابن نجيد وابن مطر وابي بكر

الاسماعيلي وابي الفضل بن خميرويه وابي الحسن السراج وابي احمد الغطريفي وابي الحسين

الحجاجي وبشر الاسفرايني وابي محمد الشيباني وابي عبد الله الهمي والحسين بن

احمد الصفار وابي حامد الوراق وابي عبد الخلال وابي بكر بن قريش وابي الحسن الكارزي

been used of necessity in two editions. Only the first six volumes of the new Cairo edition of Subkī, all published through 1968, were available to the author. It is cited as Subkī. For the remainder, the old Cairo edition was used and is cited as Old Subkī. For Samᶜānī, the first six volumes of the new Hyderabad edition, all published through 1966, were used. The old facsimile edition in the E. J. W. Gibb Memorial Series was used for the remainder. Both are cited as Samᶜānī, but references to the former include volume and page numbers and to the latter folio numbers. Details on these various editions may be found in the bibliography.

The fourth most useful source has been the Ḥanafī biographical dictionary of Ibn Abī al-Wafāʾ called *al-Jawāhir al-Muḍiya fī Ṭabaqāt al-Ḥanafiya*. The available Hyderabad edition is unfortunately ridden with errors.

Part I | *The Patrician City*

Abbreviations

EI^{1}, EI^{2}	*Encyclopaedia of Islam*
Fārisī I, Fārisī II	al-Fārisī
GAL	Brockelmann
Ḥākim	al-Ḥākim an-Naisābūrī
Ḥuffāẓ	adh-Dhahabī, *Kitāb Tadhkira al-Ḥuffāẓ*
I. Athīr	Ibn al-Athīr, *Al-Kāmil fī at-Taᵓrīkh*
IAW	Ibn Abī al-Wafāᵓ
ᶜIbar	adh-Dhahabī, *Al-ᶜIbar fī Khabar man Ghabar*
I. Funduq	Ibn Funduq
I. Jauzī	Ibn al-Jauzī, *Al-Muntaẓam fī Taᵓrīkh al-Mulūk wa al-Umam*
I. Khallikān	Ibn Khallikān
Mushtabah	adh-Dhahabī, *Al-Mushtabah fī ar-Rijāl*
Lubāb	Ibn al-Athīr, *Al-Lubāb fī Taḥdhīb al-Ansāb*
Samᶜānī	as-Samᶜānī
Shadharāt	Ibn al-ᶜImād, *Shadharāt adh-Dhahab fī Akhbār man Dhahab*
Subkī, Old Subkī	as-Subkī (1964–1968 edition and 1905–1906 edition respectively)
T. Baghdād	al-Khaṭīb al-Baghdādī
T. Islām	adh-Dhahabī, *Taᵓrīkh al-Islām*
T. Jurjān	as-Sahmī

1 / Nishapur

In winter the land looks like desert. There are no bushes, no trees save for a few poplars around the small villages spotted every couple of miles across the flat plain. The mountains just a few miles away to the north are covered with winter snow; the plain, in the dry shadow of the mountains, is snowless. Low mountains visible to the east, west and, quite distant, to the south make the plain into a bowl. Its color is a uniform beige. Nor is this desert impression erroneous. There is desert in the bowl; and were it not for irrigation, almost the entire plain would be barren. Only dry stream beds testify to the fact that melted snow for a brief time each spring waters the land naturally. Perennial streams are rare.

But there is extensive irrigation.[1] Above ground low dikes can be seen separating each field from the one next to it so that each can be flooded in turn with the carefully rationed water. Visible, too, are long rows of circular mounds, sometimes miles in length, each mound marking the mouth of a well that descends to an underground *qanāt* stream. Every twenty or thirty yards the man-made stream is tapped by a well which lets light and air in to the diggers and gives them a way to dispose of the spoil from their excavation. Some rows of mounds are old with low, gently sloping sides; the channel beneath is no longer usable, although the mounds still afford a track between fields for donkeys and pedestrians. Perhaps the slope, calculated with greater accuracy than one would expect from primitive instruments, was too shallow; and the channel silted up. Perhaps it was too steep, and the fast flowing water gouged so large a tunnel that the roof collapsed. Most likely normal erosion finally did such damage that it was cheaper to build a new qanāt than to continue repairing the old one.

Thus the rain and snow on the mountains are tapped as groundwater by this ancient Iranian system to irrigate the farmland below. Although expensive and labor intensive in construction, the qanāt tunnels keep the water from evaporating in the hot summer sun and eliminate any need to lift the water to the fields as it flows forth from the tunnel mouth in a small stream above every village. Qanāt irrigation has its natural limits, however. On the mountainside the mother well is dug down to the water table, and the slope of the tunnel cannot deviate far from an optimum one- or two-foot fall in every thousand. As a result, areas near the mountains cannot be watered without the water flowing uphill or at too shallow a slope. A mile or more before the mountains

1. On qanāt irrigation see H. E. Wulff, "The Qanats of Iran," *Scientific American*, 218 (1968), 94–105; Henri Goblot, "Dans l'ancien Iran, les techniques de l'eau et la grande histoire," *Annales: Économies, sociétés, civilisations*, 18 (1963), 499–520.

are reached, the dike ridges between fields stop. There is desert between this northern limit of fields and the mountains. Likewise, there is a maximum distance, varying no doubt with economic conditions, longer than which it is not feasible to dig a qanāt. Therefore, there is desert to the south as well, beyond the reach of the artificially channeled flow from the mountains.

Almost at the northern edge of this band of irrigated farmland delimited by qanāt technology, there is a highway. Today an unnecessary bend takes it a half mile south of the route it followed fifty years ago so that traffic is brought within sight of the shrine of Muḥammad Maḥrūq and the elegant, modern concrete and tile monument to Omar Khayyam situated in a garden beside it which is incongruously luxuriant, but the more lovely for its incongruity. A thousand years ago the highway passed a bit farther still to the south, but the modern highway cannot follow its barely discernible route because between the highway and the monuments to Muḥammad Maḥrūq and Omar Khayyam cuts the railroad from Tehran to Mashhad following a straight northwest to southeast path across the plain.

Today, as a thousand years ago, the highway, with the railroad which now parallels it, is the more important of the two routes from Tehran, the modern successor of the important medieval city of Rayy, to the east. The modern eastern terminus of the route is the large city of Mashhad, one of the most important pilgrimage sites for Shiᶜite Muslims. Beyond, the Soviet border is closed and the Afghan frontier laborious to cross. However, in medieval times the highway went much further. The shrine at Mashhad was not yet a popular pilgrimage site although the ᶜAlid *imām* who is buried there, ᶜAlī ar-Riḍā, died in 818/203. The large town of Ṭūs, now an expanse of ruins to the north of Mashhad was there instead, a double town whose two parts, Nauqān and Ṭābarān, varied in relative size and importance. Northeastward from Ṭūs the road went to Sarakhs, now on the border of Soviet Turkmenistan, and on to Marv, Bukhara, Samarqand, and eventually China.

Ṭūs and Mashhad are situated around the corner from the plain of Nishapur. To go northward, the highway that crosses the Nishapur plain in a southeasterly direction first crosses the low pass at the eastern end of the bowl and rounds the end of the high, water-bearing mountains, the eastern extremity of the Elburz range, that make up its northern rim. Mashhad or Ṭūs is the first town to greet the traveller, modern or medieval, after rounding the mountain spur and turning north. This is a natural invasion route for intruders from Central Asia. But the traveller need not turn northward.

Just after crossing the pass there is an equally important highway that turns off to the southeast. The first important city it reaches, now as then, is Herat in Afghanistan. There the route branches, one road going north of the mountainous spine of Afghanistan to reach Balkh, an important medieval city but today a ruin, like so many others, near the shrine city of Mazar-i Sharif, the other road turning south to Qandahar, Ghazni, Kabul, and eventually India.

In medieval times, with China and India as eastward terminals, this highway, or system of highways, was one of the world's most important trade routes. Not only did the rarities of the lands to the east pass along it to the Islamic countries and Europe beyond, but the flow of trade stimulated the production for export of a great variety of goods, cloth predominating, in all of the cities already mentioned. The focus of this group of highways was the pass at the eastern end of the Nishapur bowl. From there westward, disregarding the substantially less important route leading northwest from Ṭūs on the north side of the mountains, there was one main road, called after the province the Khurasan Highway, passing through Baihaq, Semnan, and Damghan to Rayy. At Rayy it forked, but the main route passed directly on to Baghdad, the seat of the ʿAbbāsid caliphate and hence the central metropolis of the Muslim world.

The route is a natural one following the irrigable corridor between mountain and desert. The junction east of Nishapur is natural, too. It seems almost geographically determined that somewhere near the road junction there should be a city, an entrepôt. But whether a city will be sited in one location or in another location perhaps a few miles away cannot be set down to geographical determinism. Today, holy death and devotion have combined to make Mashhad the eastern terminal city, and logically so, since closed or difficult borders and the decline of Asiatic inland trade in general have made pilgrimage traffic more important than the east-west transit trade. In the Middle Ages, Ṭūs was a secondary town; and Nishapur, in the fertile, sheltered plain south of the mountains, was the entrepôt, a junction city rather than a terminal city.

About thirty thousand people live in Nishapur at the present time. It is an unprepossessing provincial town. From a mile away, although clearly in sight in the crisp, clear air, it seems to be invisible, lost in the uniform beige of winter. Most of the houses are of sun-dried brick plastered over with mud and straw. Their color is the same as the earth. Only when the green returns in early spring does the city stand out in the landscape, and even then the omnipresent mud brick and the low domed roofs, built that way because of the lack of wood for rafters, lend it an organic quality that harmonizes with the fields and the villages.

As spring approaches, the farmers plow and see to their narrow irrigation channels and dikes. The channels continue the direction of flow of the qanāts from which they issue; the rise of the land toward the north-northeast where it abruptly meets the mountains would be imperceptible but for the water. The dikes separating the fields are perpendicular to the water flow, dividing the land into what look from the air like tier after tier of terraces. Two or three kilometers east of Nishapur the aerial view changes, however.[2] Instead of rows of terraces, the dikes look like strips of contour plowing on hillsides or elevation lines on a map. Sets of concentric circles and more irregular closed figures appear over a broad area. This is the medieval city of Nishapur.

Standing on the dirt road south of the shrine of Muḥammad Maḥrūq, the view in the direction of the mountains is unbroken by any building; only on the visual periphery to the right is there a glimpse of bright green, the pennant waving atop a minor local shrine. A thousand years earlier there would have been 100,000 people or more between that spot on the dirt road and the mountains. One of the world's greatest metropolises then, only a farmer on a donkey now. Walking forward across the fields one begins to encounter the remains of the city, bits of broken brick underfoot, undulations in the land betraying ruins buried twenty feet or so underground. This southern part of the medieval city was a prosperous area of villas and gardens. Many qanāts that ran beneath the heart of the city came to the surface here providing plentiful water for irrigation.

Further on the land becomes rougher. Odd knolls and depressions, their slopes genuinely terraced by the diked fields, signify that one is approaching the center of the city. So, too, do increasing traces of excavation, holes dug by farmers searching for illicit gold and finding only the different kinds of pottery that find their way in such quantity to the antique stores of Tehran. The same technique is used here that is used for digging qanāt wells. One man works below filling a leather bucket with spoil which the top man hauls up by means of a sturdy wooden windlass straddling the hole. The spoil is thrown out on the ground around, and one cannot avoid trampling in the excavation areas on the myriad of medieval potsherds brought up this way.

In the very center of the city, where the biggest buildings should have left the highest mounds, the landscape is relatively flat. Mounds that were thirty or forty feet high fifty

2. The aerial photographs which were used were taken in 1956 for the Iranian government by Huntington Aerial Surveys, Ltd., and obtained through the Iranian National Cartographic Society.

years ago have been transformed into depressions six feet deep by the treasure hunters. Standing in one such depression, which looks like a pre-Apollo artist's imagining of a moonscape, full of odd angled, sculptured chunks of earth for some reason left undug, the beige studded with potsherds of white, tenth-century, slip-painted ware, thirteenth-century turquoise glaze, and many others, one can see a line of white running at a uniform level around the bordering walls. It is a line of plaster, an old ceiling or floor; it testifies that the excavation was once a single building. It is a hundred yards square. Allowing ten square feet per person, the medieval building might have accommodated a thousand people. Perhaps it was a mosque.

The heart of medieval Nishapur has been gutted, unscientifically and unsystematically, by farmers' plows and treasure hunters' spades. The few spots excavated in the late thirties by an expedition from the Metropolitan Museum of Art led by Charles Wilkinson are hard now to locate.[3] Only from the air can some idea be gained of the old city. Two rows of mounds are seen to intersect at right angles. This is doubtless the Great Crossroads Market (al-Murabbaᶜa al-Kabīra) mentioned by the medieval geographers. A faint smaller crossing can be made out as well. It is probably the Small Crossroads Market. South of it is a building excavated by the Wilkinson expedition. It has many rooms, and wall paintings of noblemen were discovered in some of them. The geographers' descriptions of the topography of the city raise the possibility that this is the governor's palace or seat of government (Dār al-Imāra). Southeast of the Great Crossroads Market there is a suspiciously regular square, extensively potholed. The location is right for the Congregational Mosque, known after the building of the Congregational Mosque of al-Manīᶜī in the middle of the eleventh/fifth century as the Old Congregational Mosque.

But this is to ignore the most conspicuous part of the ruins. Directly east of the Great Crossroads Market is a flat mound some twelve or fifteen feet high. It is almost square and covers an area of about thirty-five acres. Butting against it to the north is a smaller (nine acres), taller (forty feet) mound. These mounds are the remains of the inner city (*shahrastān*) of Nishapur and of the citadel (*quhandiz*) respectively. What is implied by the term inner city as used by the geographers is vague. It contained neither seat of government nor congregational mosque nor central market. All of these were located in the *rabaḍ*, which is often translated suburbs but which is better translated outer city

3. For a map of the Wilkinson excavations see C. K. Wilkinson, "The Īrānian Expedition 1937," *Bulletin of the Metropolitan Museum of Art*, 33 (1938), section II, p. 4.

as it denotes a completely urbanized area—in fact, the heart of the city. By the time Nishapur had flowered into a great metropolis in the tenth/fourth century, the inner city was no more than a residential area, and probably not a particularly desirable one as its elevation must have made water supply a problem.

The building of the inner city probably goes back to the very early days of Nishapur after the Sasanian emperor Shapur I (reigned A.D. 240–272?) founded it as a fortress for the protection of the road to the east.[4] An isolated fortress city on what was then a frontier, Nishapur stood in need of protection; hence the building of a high fortified town in the shadow of an even higher and more imposing citadel. Around this secure nucleus in which refuge could be taken in time of trouble, agriculture prospered. Many villages were built and qanāts dug.

Then with the invasion of the Muslim Arabs in the seventh/first century came a long period of turmoil followed by great prosperity. Nishapur by the end of the eighth/second century was safely removed from the frontier, which had moved east to the Oxus river and then beyond. It was the western point of a long flat diamond of cities that served as metropolitan centers for the enormous province of Khurasan. To the southeast was Herat; to the northeast around the tip of the mountain range was Marv; far to the east of either of these, and sometimes not even included in Khurasan, was Balkh. The trade of these cities and of the cities beyond the Oxus, such as Bukhara and Samarqand, as well as the overland trade from India and China, funneled through Nishapur once security returned. It became an obvious site for a capital and was used as a primary or secondary governing center by each successive dynasty in the region until its destruction between 1153/548 and 1161/556.

The villages that had grown up around the Sasanian fortress were engulfed in the expanding metropolis.[5] The names of some remained as the names of city quarters, and

4. For the legendary account of Nishapur's origin see Ḥākim, f57a–58a; for a modern scholar's discussion of the subject see A. V. W. Jackson, *From Constantinople to the Home of Omar Khayyam* (New York, 1911), pp. 246–250. The Wilkinson expedition (C. K. Wilkinson, "The Īrānian Expedition, 1936," *Bulletin of the Metropolitan Museum of Art*, 32 [1937], section II) was unable to confirm by excavation the identification of the Sasanian city with some part of the Islamic period ruins although on the evidence of literary sources the identification seems indisputable. The identification of the Sasanian city with three mounds twenty-four miles southeast of the present ruins made by P. M. Sykes ("A Sixth Journey in Persia," *The Geographical Journal*, 37 [1911], 154) is based upon hearsay, the remains of two walls, two pieces of unidentified pottery, broken bricks, a red bead, and one coin. The argument cannot be seriously maintained on such evidence.

5. Ḥākim, f58a–59b, contains two lists, one of villages incorporated into the city and the other of

the whole process doubtless influenced the multiplication of cemeteries and internal gates which is abundantly evident in medieval sources. Thus, the outer city came into being by the coalescence of old farming villages and new settlements around the fortified Sasanian city after the Arab conquest. Gradually, trade, government, and religion converted the part of this semiurban amalgam that lay nearest the Sasanian city and along the highway which skirted its south side into a true city heart. The Great Crossroads Market spread along the highway and a crossing street; the Old Congregational Mosque and the governor's palace were just off the highway to the south.

How large the city was at its peak is hard to say. There is no circuit wall that can be used to determine its physical extent, and the overlapping of ruins from later periods confuses ground observations. A very approximate estimate based on the presence or absence of brick and sherd underfoot and on the area of irregular irrigation dikes seen on aerial photographs would be roughly six and a half square miles of built up land. Depending on the density multiplier adopted,[6] which ultimately depends upon the number of people in an averge household, an unknown and probably incalculable number for this part of the world during the medieval period, these six and a half square miles may have held anywhere from one to five hundred thousand inhabitants.

There are good reasons besides natural caution for preferring the lower end of this range, however. Overlapping ruins may have distorted the area estimate, and large areas on the outskirts of the city may have been semirural and less densely settled than the city core. But more important than these considerations is the fact that except for one perennial stream of sufficient force to turn a few mills, Nishapur was not situated on any body of water.[7] Therefore, all products of the land consumed by its residents—food, firewood, fodder, and so forth—had to be brought to the city by means of land transport, that is to say, on the backs of camels and donkeys. The fame and importance of the Khurasan Highway, unlike that of some modern superhighways, stemmed from

---

city quarters. Approximately one-third of the names of quarters can be found on the village list as well. Some names on the village list, such as al-Ḥīra, are unquestionably Arab in origin, proving that the city grew out of new Arab settlements as well as older Persian villages.

6. A multiplier of 100 per hectare is suggested by J. C. Russell, "Late Ancient and Medieval Population," *Transactions of the American Philosophical Society*, n.s. 48 (1958), 89. Leopoldo Torres Balbás arrives at higher estimates in "Extension y demografia de las ciudades hispanomusulmanas," *Studia Islamica*, 3 (1955), 35–59.

7. Al-Maqdisī, *Aḥsan at-taqāsīm fī maʿrifa al-aqālīm*, ed. M. J. de Goeje, in *Bibliotheca Geographorum Arabicorum*, III[1] (Leiden, 1906), p. 329.

the traffic that passed along it rather than from its own physical impressiveness. It was not paved. There was no reason for it to be, for there was no wheeled traffic. Animals travelled more comfortably on a broad beaten dirt path than they could have on a Roman style stone pavement. Only wheeled vehicles would have benefited from pavement, but wheeled vehicles could not compete in economy with camel transport.[8]

Thus, if an average inhabitant consumed in a year a ton of hauled-in goods, a population of half a million at the upper end of the range would require the daily passage of well over five thousand loaded camels into the city. Moreover, the density of population and cultivation in the surrounding countryside would have to have been much greater than at present to supply this vast cargo, for the expense of this slow overland transport would have made it out of the question to bring in foodstuffs and firewood on a regular basis from too far away. In short, the logistical problems of keeping a large city supplied without access to water transportation are so formidable that an estimate of maximum population in the one hundred thousand range is much more plausible than an estimate in the five hundred thousand range.[9]

However, although the subject of this book is the medieval city of Nishapur, to stress urban considerations in this way is to put the cart before the horse, to use an idiom that would have been meaningless to the medieval Nishapuris. The point of departure was a desert plain made fruitful by water ingeniously channeled from nearby mountains, and emphasis must be placed on this starting point. It is a simple fact of agricultural efficiency that medieval society, in northeastern Iran or anywhere else, was predominantly agricultural. The great city of Nishapur represents the agricultural surplus, centralized by rent, taxation, and the market, of hundreds of farming villages. It was more than that, too, of course. There was trade, manufacture, and a small amount of mining; but above all the city lived on the surplus of the countryside. Only in the twentieth century has agricultural technology made it possible for the majority of the population of a country to live in the city.

The rural area administratively and economically dependent on Nishapur stretched beyond the bowl in which the city was situated to include the nether side of the sur-

8. Richard Bulliet, "Le Chameau et la roue au Moyen Orient," *Annales: Économies, sociétés, civilisations*, 24 (1969), 1092–1103.

9. There seems to be no concrete basis for Bosworth's estimate of thirty or forty thousand (C. E. Bosworth, *The Ghaznavids: Their Empire in Afghanistan and Eastern Iran 994–1040* (Edinburgh, 1963), p. 162.

rounding mountains and an appreciable stretch of the highway leading to Herat.[10] It amounted to some 12,728 square miles (33,250 square kilometers) and contained between 1671 and 1871 villages. The same area today numbers 1763 villages with a population, excluding Nishapur itself and the large town of Turbat-i Haidariya, of 594,635.[11] Assuming that average village size, as opposed to total number of villages, has remained roughly the same through the centuries at approximately 350[12] because of such naturally limiting factors as distance from fields and amount of capital necessary to dig a qanāt, the medieval population of the area must also have been on the order of a half million souls. If the area dependent on Baihaq, which was not always considered to be separate from Nishapur, is added to the above, the pertinent figures become 18,800 square miles (48,700 square kilometers), 2284 modern villages, and, excluding Sabzavar, 829,391 people. The average village size for this larger area is 361 compared with 337 for the smaller area.

The intimate relationship between the people of Nishapur and this agricultural hinterland appears over and over again. Families that have survived in the historical record because of their religious or cultural distinction frequently can be traced to a rural origin. They commonly owned country estates which are only occasionally mentioned but from which they derived their leisure-supporting wealth. The income from agricultural lands also financed the religious endowments (*waqf*, pl. *awqāf*) which paid for the building and upkeep of all kinds of religious edifices and public works, not to mention special funds to buy such things as ink for religious scholars.[13] When the land failed to produce abundantly because of drought, cold, or political turmoil, the city felt the

10. Determination of the districts dependent upon Nishapur was made from Ḥākim, f65b–66b; Abū ᶜAbd Allāh Yāqūt, *Muᶜjam al-Buldān* (Beirut, 1955–1957); and Maqdisī, *Aḥsan*, pp. 316–319. The area judged from these sources to have been dependent upon Nishapur runs from Turbat-i Jam in the east southwest to Zuzan, northwest to Kundur, north to Sultanabad, northeast to Quchan, and southeast along the north side of the mountains to the intersection with the road from Nishapur to Turbat-i-Jam. The Baihaq area was judged to comprise a triangle on the west side of the area just described with its points at Quchan, Kundur, and Jajarm.

11. Population figures are taken from the *Farhang-i Jughrāfiyā-yi Irān* and are not highly accurate.

12. J. Behnam, "Population," in *The Land of Iran*, The Cambridge History of Iran, I (Cambridge, Cambridge University Press, 1968), p. 479, suggests two ranges of village size, a larger village of around 350 and a smaller one of around 160. Many villages in the latter category may have been excluded in the crude data upon which the estimates for the Nishapur area are based. The effect of such an exclusion would be to raise the total population figures for the area.

13. Fārisī II, f31b.

effects immediately. The wealthy, of course, could import food from distant, undistressed markets; but the less wealthy suffered. There was an acute famine in 1011/401 which took thousands of lives, yet the death rate for that and adjacent years among the wealthy families of the patriciate shows no significant increase.[14] Evidently, famine did not reach them, at least not a famine of only one year. But their ability to ride out such agricultural crises does not mean that they did not feel them at all. Their leadership in communal prayers for rain as well as the condition of their own estates kept them close to the people and the land.[15]

Beyond this general distinction between rich and poor, those who could survive a famine and those who could not, the social makeup of a city like Nishapur is hard to ascertain from the sources available. It was a huge city by contemporary standards, and its inhabitants pursued many different trades. The products of some of its tradesmen survive, but all trace of the tradesmen themselves is gone. From sun-dried brick to the highest quality pottery, Nishapur had an extensive clay fabricating industry as well as a small industry exporting clay for consumption as food.[16] The variety of pottery styles abundantly evident on a tour of the ruins is remarkable, but not a single potter's or brickmaker's name has survived. The same holds true for glass makers, wall painters, and stucco workers. The only common trade about which information is preserved in literary sources is weaving.[17] Weaving is depicted as a rural cottage industry and the weavers as an oppressed lot ripe for proselytization by the ascetic, fundamentalist preaching of the Karrāmiya, an Islamic sect which from time to time accumulated enough power to engage in violent riots with the adherents of the dominant religious factions.

Undoubtedly the poor lived everywhere in Nishapur since the menials of the wealthy must be included among them, but they were concentrated in the northwestern part of

14. I. Funduq, 175–176; ᶜUtbī, *Kitab-i Yamini*, tr. James Reynolds (London, 1858), pp. 365–371. The number of deaths recorded in the biographical dictionaries which happen to fall in any given year do not constitute anything like a reliable calculation of death rate, even for the patriciate, because for too many individuals no date at all is given. Nevertheless, a truly democratic famine should have left some mark.

15. Fārisī I, f47b; II, f14a.

16. Clay has been eaten as a food by various societies for various reasons, but the clay of Nishapur was known in particular as a gourmet's delight. Berthold Laufer, "Geophagy," *Field Museum of Natural History Anthropological Series*, 18 (1930), 150–152.

17. ᶜAbd al-Qāhir al-Baghdādī, *Al-Farq bain al-firaq*, II, tr. A. S. Halkin (Tel Aviv, 1935), p. 19.

the city.[18] As pointed out earlier, qanāt irrigation sets its own limits. The water cannot be made to flow to an exit point too near the mother well, and it is economically unfeasible to dig and maintain too long a tunnel. The highway passed along the northern edge of the broad band of irrigable land defined by these limits, but it passed through the center of the city. Consequently, the northern parts of the city encroached on the desert land between the farmland and the mountains. No qanāts exist today in the most northerly parts of the ruins, and few, if any, did then.[19] To get water in this part of the city one had to descend long flights of stairs to a qanāt stream flowing beneath the city and then carry the water back up.[20] The stream would eventually exit on the southern side of town, where the rich had villas and gardens, or in the fields beyond. This burdensome method of getting water particularly affected the northwest; hence that is where the poor lived and where the militancy of the Karrāmiya found fertile ground. The northeast did not share this physical defect of the northwest because through it ran Nishapur's only perennial stream.[21] Along the banks of this stream in the quarters of al-Ḥīra and Mūlqābād, not too far from the business district of the center of town, were built the houses of the wealthiest patricians. Thus Nishapur's wealthier families lived either in the garden areas of the south and southwest or along the stream flowing through the east side of town while the poor clustered in the northwest. Through the middle from west to east ran the highway lined, along with its cross-streets, with stores, businesses, and public buildings.

Our inability to make precise statements about social strata must not obscure, however, the normal preponderance, which must have obtained in Nishapur as in every other city of comparable size and heterogeneity, of the lower social orders. Just as the city lay in a much more populous but less well known countryside and benefited from its fruits, the upper stratum of Nishapuri society with which this book is concerned was the top of a social pyramid whose lower levels are almost completely

18. The name of the quarter was Manāshik; see Maqdisī, *Aḥsan*, p. 336; Ḥākim, f59a.

19. Maqdisī mentions four qanāt streams that ran through town on the surface. At least one of them was on the western fringe of the city, but the location of the others cannot be pinned down (Maqdisī, *Aḥsan*, p. 329).

20. Maqdisī, *Aḥsan*, p. 329; Old Subkī IV, 281–282. Presumably the reason stairsteps were used instead of a well was that the flow of water in the qanāt stream would wash the bucket into the tunnel where it could easily become lodged.

21. Maqdisī, *Aḥsan*, p. 329; Abū al-Faḍl Baihaqī, *Tārīkh-i Baihaqī*, ed. Q. Ghanī and ᶜA. A. Fayyāḍ (Tehran, 1945), p. 413.

unknown. Those lower levels, however, supplied the service and labor which enabled the people on top to live in leisure. The cloth merchant prospering from the production of poor rural weavers, who, as today, were probably dependent upon him for both loom and raw fiber, and spending his leisure time in the study of religious traditions and in the company of learned divines is the type, along with the owner of country estates, of the patrician of Nishapur.

This simple abstraction of Nishapur's social classes, dwelt upon here to counterbalance in anticipation the narrow focus upon the top four or five percent of the population of what is to follow, says nothing of the relations between common folk and patriciate outside the sphere of economics. The appeal among the poor of Karrāmiya propaganda enabled that sect to muster turbulent mobs, but these mobs were always met by equally violent mobs rallying to the support of the patrician religious factions. Perhaps these latter mobs came from less depressed groups than did the Karrāmīs; they obviously felt that they would suffer some kind of loss in the event of a Karrāmī political victory. But whatever their motivation, their willingness to fight and even die for the leaders of their religious faction bespeaks some kind of sincere bond, whether economic, political, or purely religious, between them and the few patrician families whose domination of positions of religious leadership was almost complete. As desirable as it would be to define more precisely this bond between the elite (*khāṣṣ*) and the common people (*ᶜāmm*), concrete evidence upon which to base such a definition is lacking for Nishapur, and differing local situations make evidence of this sort from other cities essentially nontransferable.[22]

Uncertainty about the economic and social characteristics of the mass of the population is echoed in the areas of language and religion. Today Nishapur is quite obviously Persian in language and Shiᶜite Muslim in faith. But it is equally obvious that this was not true in the tenth/fourth century. There is nothing to be added here to the debate on the roots of Persian Shiᶜism, which became the country's official religion under the Safavids in the sixteenth/eleventh century, except a note that the names ᶜAlī, al-Ḥasan, and al-Ḥusain were becoming increasingly popular in non-Shiᶜite circles throughout the tenth/fourth and eleventh/fifth centuries.[23] There were certainly Shiᶜites of various

22. The best study of such relationships is Ira Lapidus's *Muslim Cities in the Later Middle Ages*, but both time and place are too far removed from Nishapur in the eleventh/fifth century to make his work applicable.

23. At the beginning of the period, these three names account for 17 percent of all *ism's* in the biographical dictionaries, and at the end of the period they account for 58 percent.

types living in the city at that earlier period, but how many and who remain mysteries. The geographer al-Maqdisī, who visited Nishapur in the tenth/fourth century, indicates substantial Shiᶜite strength;[24] but he could well have been misled by the proclivity of the Karrāmīs to tar all their opponents with the black name of Ismāᶜīlī Shiᶜism.[25]

Muslim sectarian differences are not all that is at issue, however. When the conquering Arabs reached Nishapur, the people of the city were all either Zoroastrian, Christian, Jewish, or possibly even Buddhist. Conversion to Islam doubtless began almost immediately. There was much to be gained from being friends with the new rulers. The fire temple in the citadel was converted into a mosque as a symbol of the new order and for the use of the Arabs and those early converts,[26] but large scale conversion surely came much later. No timetable can be given for this process, and this is particularly unfortunate, for the role and importance of religious leaders must be keyed to it. A Muslim religious leader could not have a popular following if there were not a substantial number of Muslims in the populace, and his political weight would be at least in part a reflection of the weight of his following in the city as a whole. The same applies to the countryside, which presumably was slower to adopt the new faith than was the city. When a religious notable led an armed band of his rural retainers on an expedition to free members of his faction from prison,[27] did they follow him by virtue of his religious eminence or because he filled for them the traditional Persian role, long antedating the coming of the Arabs, of aristocratic estate owner, *dihqān*? Important as questions of this sort are for understanding the function in society of the group of people being studied in this book, they are unanswerable insofar as they depend upon the degree to which Islam was spread amongst the populace at any particular time. The simple generalization must suffice that by the end of the eleventh/fifth century the bulk of at least the urban population of the Nishapur area was Muslim, although Christian, Jewish, and Zoroastrian communities continued to exist.[28]

24. Maqdisī, *Aḥsan*, p. 336.
25. ᶜUtbī, *Kitab-i Yamini*, pp. 471–484.
26. Ḥākim, f66b.
27. See chapter 9.
28. Two villages of Jews were incorporated into Nishapur during its growth (Ḥākim, f58b), and in the eleventh/fifth century individual Jews are known to have been living in the city (Fārisī II, f141a). References to the Nestorian see of Nishapur are given by A. V. W. Jackson, *From Constantinople*, 250–251; and after the destruction of the city in the twelfth/sixth century the quarter of Ramjār apparently survived as a separate town and became a diocesan see dependent on Antioch;

The linguistic and ethnic situation is only slightly clearer. Broadly speaking, there were Arabs, Persians, and Turks in the medieval city speaking Arabic, Persian, and Turkish; but the balance and social significance of these three is indefinable in any concrete way. Most numerous among the Arab tribal contingents that settled in Khurasan after the initial conquests were Tamīm of the North Arab group or confederation, Bakr of the Rabīᶜa group, and coming appreciably later Azd of the South Arabs. Other tribes were represented, however, including Muḥammad's tribe, the Quraish, and the Anṣār tribes of Medina. These Arabs were initially an occupying army of nomadic origin with no particular attachment to the conquered land, but eventually they settled into and became a part of the country in a pattern that is largely unknown. Around Nishapur, settlement is definitely known to have taken place in two areas, Ustuvā, northwest of Nishapur on the other side of the mountains, and Busht, the more or less desert country southwest of the city, which as a result became known as the ᶜArabistān of Khurasan.[29] But even if areas such as these which were heavily populated by Arabs retained a distinctive feeling and perhaps even colloquial use of the Arabic language for several centuries after the conquest, the Arabs who settled in the city or migrated there later became in the course of time almost entirely assimilated to the indigenous population. Arabic continued to be spoken, but only because of its artificial retention as a vehicle of religious instruction, and it seems to have been spoken with a Persian accent.[30]

By the eleventh/fifth century the only way families of Arab descent can be identified is by last names deriving from old tribal affiliations.[31] Names of North Arab origin, such as Tamīmī and Shaibānī, occur most frequently among the relatively small total number of individuals with tribal names, as would be expected in light of the large role the tribe of Tamīm (Shaibān is a subtribe of Tamīm) played in the early Arab settlement.

Ernst Honigmann, "Nīshāpūr," in *Encyclopaedia of Islam*, 1st ed., III, 928–929; W. E. D. Allen, *A History of the Georgian People* (London, 1932), p. 108. Less trace remains of the Zoroastrians, but there still seems to have been a fire temple in Baihaq in the eleventh/fifth century (I. Funduq, 253) and possibly a quarter in Nishapur named for Zoroaster (Fārisī II, f50b).

29. See Fārisī I, f49b; II, f97a, for Ustuvā and Ḥākim, f66b, for Busht.

30. IAW, I, p. 358. The Persian accent is revealed by an anecdote which relies on a pun in which the long *a* in *atān*, "she-ass," is pronounced as a long *u* as in *atūn*, "bath-house furnace." In the text the long *a* is written as a long *u*. This pun must have been based upon the vowel change of long *a* to long *u* that is characteristic of the Persian spoken in Nishapur to this day.

31. Throughout the tenth/fourth and eleventh/fifth centuries the percentage of nisbas of Arab tribal derivation remains fairly constant at the low level of 7–8 percent.

Also prominent is the name Sulamī which relates to a branch of the Bakr tribe, the other important group of early settlers. Curiously, the third group of Arabs in Khurasan, the South Arab Azd tribe, which came appreciably later than the Tamīm and Bakr, has almost disappeared from the city's onomasticon by the eleventh/fifth century. Possibly the circumstance of their coming as a unit in support of their tribal leader Muhallab b. Abī Ṣufra when he was appointed governor of Khurasan in 697/78 led to their settlement in cities rather than on the land and hence to their quicker absorption and loss of identity. Be that as it may, there is much less trace of them by the eleventh/fifth century than there is of the Arabs of Quraish and of the Anṣār whose numerical strength was very much smaller. Undoubtedly the retention of tribal names among descendants of the latter group was prolonged because of the religious prestige accruing to members of these tribes which had first supported the Prophet; but if some people persisted for one reason or another in using the tribal names inherited from their ancestors, there is no suggestion that Arab descent was felt to be either a social credit or a liability. Intermarriage, the acid test of social discrimination, was common between indigenous families and families of Arab descent.

There do not at first sight appear to be many questions to be raised about the Persian element in the population. Nishapur was a Persian city with a majority Persian population in which Persian was the normal language of everyday discourse. But this broad generalization may well conceal important distinctions within the Persian population. In addition to any religious and class distinctions surviving from the Sasanian empire, there is the question of regional differences within the lands of the Persians. The idea of the Persian speaking people all sharing a single political entity which is the embodiment of their national identity is a relatively modern one and one that is to this day not entirely felt in the hearts of many Iranian subjects. In medieval times local dialect, history, and customs constituted the core of an individual's identity which was overlain by a veneer, of varying thickness, of cosmopolitan religious practices and imperial administrative procedures. The forces that kept people isolated, such as slow and expensive communications, were much stronger than such forces as allegiance to a common ruler which served to bring them together. Unfortunately, this dimension of life is largely invisible in the literary works surviving from the period, for these works are an integral part of the cosmopolitan veneer of society. They reflect a culture which if not artificial, was at least confined to society's upper crust. Evidence of the local cultures and allegiances which were the rule among the mass of the populace appears only sporadically. In Nishapur, for example, there was a special residential quarter for people from Kirmān and another for people from Rayy.[32] Likewise, there was a trade depot (*khān*) reserved for merchants from Fārs and regulated by them, an institution reminiscent of the factories established by the Italian city-states in foreign territories.[33] And in nearby Baihaq, a smaller and more vulnerable city or urbanized area than Nishapur, there are several recorded instances of small scale wars between the local residents and rival towns such as Juvain and Isfarā'in.[34] Yet in spite of these strongly felt local allegiances, immigration did not bar an individual from full acceptance in the patriciate of Nishapur. Acceptance by the masses of such a foreigner from another province may well have been a different story; if it was, it was a story that was not written down.

The inhabitants of Nishapur were unquestionably thoroughly familiar with the Turks long before they surrendered their city to the first unequivocally Turkish dynasty, the Seljuqs, in 1037/428.[35] They knew the Turks primarily as soldiers, for a large part of the Ghaznavid and Sāmānid armies was composed of Turkish *mamlūks*, and as Nishapur was the headquarters of the military governor of Khurasan under those dynasties, Turkish troops were frequently quartered in the city. They knew them also as governors, sometimes as ephemeral appointees of the Sāmānid and Ghaznavid courts in Bukhara and Ghazna but also as locally based, land-holding governing families. The Sīmjūrids were such a family. Descended from a Turkish mamlūk who served the Sāmānids early in the tenth/fourth century, they became hereditary governors of the province of Quhistān south of Nishapur and on several occasions extended their governorship, with or without Sāmānid authorization, to include Nishapur as well.[36] Unlike less permanent governors, they played the part of patron of local interests, particularly those of the Shāfiʿī faction, and in so doing assimilated the traditional pattern of the Persian landed families. Finally, Nishapur was familiar with Turks visiting or passing through town on educational or commercial journeys. Just as visitors are reported from places as far west as Spain, others passed through the city from

32. Ḥākim, f59b.
33. See chapter 11.
34. I. Funduq, p. 267.
35. The traditional date of the Seljuq occupation of Nishapur, 1038/429, is brought into question by a Seljuq dinar from the Nishapur mint with the date 1037/428 in the collection of the American Numismatic Society.
36. Wilhelm Barthold, *Turkestan Down to the Mongol Invasion* (London, 1968), pp. 238–239, 246ff.

as far east as Kashgar, the gateway to China. In short, Turks were in no way strange or unusual in Nishapur although they comprised a small and not on the whole highly respected segment of the community.[37]

This, then, gives at least some idea of what the city of Nishapur was like in the eleventh/fifth century. Standing in the fields full of odd mounds and holes near the shrine of Muḥammad Maḥrūq, one needs a great deal of imagination to fill the empty stage in front of the mountain backdrop with the appropriate props: a huge beige fortress rising above a small, walled inner town and fairly towering over the low roofs of a sprawling, disorganized metropolis strung out along a crowded highway below the walled town; a scattering of impressive religious buildings, their portals and minarets decorated with intricate brickwork designs, ornate calligraphic carvings, and occasional vivid ceramic tiles; intimate, winding streets and alleys named after notable men who once lived on them or after the trade carried on in them in small, open, alcove shops; expensive villas with walls enclosing carefully groomed and irrigated gardens full of fruit trees and flowers around a polygonal central basin. In the same way it is difficult to populate the stage in the mind's eye with the endless variety of common folk plying their trades, scholars and government clerks in their distinctive costumes, mystics wearing the patched cloaks of their holy indigence, heavily laden camel trains plodding deliberately along to the dull bong of the lead camel's bell, mounted soldiers with their short Turkish bows resting unstrung and retroflexively bent in saddle holsters, and perhaps on rare occasions early in the century one of the Ghaznavid sultan's caparisoned war elephants with its Indian mahout. But this setting of the stage is for background effect only. Its sole purpose is to provide a physical and human context which will lend verisimilitude to the lives and deeds of the principal characters, the patricians of Nishapur.

37. Locations associated with Turks appear to be in the less well watered parts of the city (Ḥākim, f18b; Fārisī II, f49b).

2 | *The Patriciate*

It is only with great trepidation that the word patrician is introduced here to denote the dominating group of upper-class families in medieval Nishapur. The study of medieval Islamic society has been led astray and distorted too often in the past by the unconsidered borrowing of terms proper to medieval Christian society in Europe. The applicability of the word Pope to the person of the Caliph has been so thoroughly refuted that it is no longer the problem it once was; but the words feudal and fief still engender protracted debates about their proper definition when used in an Islamic context, as, in fact, does the word city whenever it implies similarity between the medieval European city, often considered to be "the city" par excellence, and the medieval Muslim city.[1] But the same considerations that prompted the borrowing of these other terms apply to the word patrician. If one wishes to write about a complex of phenomena, functions or institutions perceived to be in some sense unitary, one must have a single word or phrase by which to designate that complex. "Feudalism" is used thus to describe a medieval Islamic complex relating landholding to government service even though that complex bears only a rudimentary resemblance to the medieval European institution that the word originally denoted.

In Nishapur and other medieval Iranian cities the top rung of local society, exclusive, that is, of transient imperial agents and governors merely stationed in the city for a longer or shorter period of time, was made up of a limited number of wealthy extended families whose dominance remained relatively stable over a period of many generations. The prestige and power of these families derived from one or more of three sources: landholding, trade, or religion. Clearly, several terms might be employed to describe this group of families; but because of the nuances surrounding these various terms, patriciate seems to be the most satisfactory. Aristocracy, for example, has too secular an overtone to fit well the predominantly religious families which were in many ways the most important component of the group. Elite, on the other hand, does not convey the important element of heredity that characterized the group. "Religious class," which I used on previous occasions before hitting upon the word patriciate, mirrors the difficulty of aristocracy by excluding the secular dimension. In short, as is so often the case when the vocabulary of the languages proper to the time and place in question does not furnish a term for a particular concept, there is no term that fits the situation perfectly. Patrician and patriciate are the best of a bad lot.

1. Max Weber puts the case for the European city being the only "full urban community" in *The City*, tr. Don Martingale and Gertrude Neuwirth (New York, 1962), pp. 88–96.

The virtues of the word patriciate stem primarily from its application to somewhat analogous groups of families that held power in many European cities in the twelfth and thirteenth centuries, but its earlier use to designate a class of urban notables in Rome is also important. Specifically, the connotations that can most usefully be transferred to the eastern Iranian setting are those of a wealthy, hereditary, urban aristocracy controlling a city through an oligarchic distribution of offices and perquisites but also feeling a loyalty and concern for the city which they visualize in many ways as being indistinguishable from their own corporate group. The emphasis here is on heredity, oligarchic control, and a very real identification with the city itself.

Yet if the word is valuable to the extent that it connotes precisely this kind of civic social body, it can easily lead one astray if it calls to mind a closer and more concrete European meaning and context. Nishapur is not Montpellier; eastern Iran is not Tuscany. This truism must be uttered because it can too easily be lost sight of. The level of technology common to most of the eastern hemisphere in the eleventh century was such that superficial descriptions of medieval European and Middle Eastern cities sometimes seem quite similar. Everywhere artisans and craftsmen worked with the fruits of the soil. They tanned, spun, wove, dyed, milled, baked, and butchered. Food and clothing were the primary products. To a lesser extent they smelted and hammered metal, baked and decorated ceramics. Transportation was everywhere slow and expensive, but water transport was somewhat faster and somewhat cheaper. This margin led to the burgeoning of port and river cities. Warfare was devoted for the most part to cutting and piercing, which made city walls the natural answer to local insecurity. But to the same degree that this common stage of technological evolution focused people's attention and effort on the same general set of occupations and procedures, it made people all the more aware of and jealous of the minutiae of those occupations and procedures. Differences between fabrics, arms, pots, and so forth that now make up the lore of antiquarians were then signal and vital. Even places quite close to each other would have their own styles of weaving or their own characteristic recipes to accompany their local dialect. The similarities between a medieval European town and a medieval Iranian town are abundant at the general level, but at the human level there are vast differences.

When talking about the patriciate, however, even this general similarity becomes tenuous. It is not as if the Italian patrician in his haughty town tower having his portrait painted with egg yolk and pigment and the Iranian patrician in the walled garden of his town villa listening to two theologian guests trying to stump one another with tricky questions about what the Prophet may at one time have said fill exactly the same niche in society. Far from it. The generalizable patterns of world social history are both less precise and less useful than those of technological history. That is why the use of the word patrician to describe both men must be adopted with the greatest caution. The specific differences between the general social role of these two are most clearly seen by looking separately at the three groups which in both cases can sometimes be included under the term patrician: the landholders, the merchants, and the clerics.

Eastern Iran, more than any of the other lands of the Islamic caliphate, was distinguished by its vigorous, powerful, well entrenched country estate owners known as *dihqāns*. More or less on the eastern border of the Sasanian empire before Islam, the dihqāns of this area were particularly self-reliant and confident of their position in the overall scheme of things. The most powerful of them were lords of cities and small principalities and made their separate peace with the invading Arabs, often most advantageously.[2] For the most part they retained their land and their revenues after the Arabs had clearly won, and they even managed on occasion to maneuver the ruling Muslims into paying higher taxes than they, the conquered infidels. Few Arabs settled in their country to challenge their aristocratic position. But despite appearances, the early centuries of Islam were for them a long, soft, steadily deepening twilight. The dihqāns never regained the undisputed dominance of society they lost with the coming of the Arabs. Central government administration weakened their governmental prerogatives; their prestige had to be increasingly shared with the men of religion; their military prowess was superceded by that of the Turks. By the eleventh/fifth century they were no longer at the peak of the social pyramid except in a sentimental way. Their last important act was the bequeathing to world literature of their epic poetry in the form of Firdausī's *Shāhnāmeh*.

By comparison, the landed aristocracy of twelfth century Europe was in a twilight, too; but it was one punctuated by the clanging of swords and the moans of the wounded. The cities of Europe had to fight, both figuratively and at times with sword and mace, to secure one right or privilege after another from their lords. Whether it was administration of justice, levying of tolls, regulation of trade, or whatever, the lords resisted either directly or obliquely the aspirations of the citizens. Strong central

2. Daniel C. Dennett, *Conversion and the Poll Tax in Early Islam* (Cambridge, Mass., 1950), pp. 126–128.

governments had not yet brought their governing prerogatives to an end. The church was a rival, but it was not clearly ahead in the competition. Except for occasional town militias, there was no important alternative to aristocratic military strength, only recently tested and proven in the crusades. In a sense, the Iranian dihqāns had already experienced under the caliphate the emasculation that Europe's local lords would not meet until the rise of the strong central monarchies.

The situation of the merchants reveals the same sort of dissimilarity. Although never integrated into the apparatus of government, merchants had occupied an important niche in Middle Eastern society uninterruptedly for many centuries prior to the advent of Islam. Geography had made the area a natural junction for trade routes from many places, and local manufactures had always been added to the flow of goods from other lands. The economy of the Middle East was monetized as early as that of any other region, and its monetary history was never broken. The merchant, as the controller of the flow of goods and, with his natural associate the money-changer, of money, was a natural and integral part of the Middle Eastern economy; just as the trading economy focused on cities like Nishapur, so it was in the entrepôt cities that the merchant was most important and respected. Warehouses of goods and bags of silver dirhams could not buy the sort of status that was the dihqān's by virtue of inherited property, but they could buy land in imitation of the dihqāns, or more importantly they could endow religious foundations and subsidize scholars and thereby buy the acceptance of the religious branch of the patriciate. The merchants did not have to fight for recognition and respect as merchants; that was theirs automatically because a certain respect for trade was traditional and normal in their society. It was only if they wanted to be truly part of the patriciate that they had to trade a part of their wealth one way or another for an additional measure of respect and acceptance. As a result, it is not unusual to read about the scion of a wealthy merchant family distributing the entire family fortune for religious ends and gaining for it great respect which he was then able to pass on to his children.[3] What this amounted to was a partial trade of mercantile wealth for acceptance as a religious patrician, a position with a different economic base.

In Europe, on the other hand, the fall of Rome and the Germanic invasions had

3. The Ashᶜarī theologian ᶜAbd al-Qāhir al-Baghdādī, for one, exhausted his father's fortune on scholarship and refused to use his learning to make a living; Fārisī I, f55a; II, f105a. Another man from Nishapur claimed to have spent over 30,000 dirhams subsidizing religious scholars while on an educational sojourn in Baghdad (I. Jauzī, VII, 62).

caused a hiatus in trade and a lapse from the monetized economy of Rome back to something more like a natural economy. The merchants who begin to rise in the eleventh century and to claim the privileges of wealth in the twelfth, providing in the process much of the drive behind the rise of Europe's cities, were not favored by a social position resting upon centuries of unbroken trading history. Just as the dihqāns can be said to have lost with the Arab conquest the battle that the European landed aristocracy had not yet begun to fight, so the twelfth century European merchants can be seen as fighting for the kind of basic respect as an important and integral segment of society that had been accorded their Middle Eastern counterparts as a matter of course for many centuries. The resulting difference in the goals and motivation of the two groups cannot be ignored. The merchants of Nishapur were, on a smaller scale, more like the banking families of renaissance Italy or the industrialist families of early twentieth century America than they were like the merchants of the medieval European cities: they were trying to trade commercial status for status of a higher kind rather than simply to force society to grant status to commerce because of its wealth producing power where no such status had previously been recognized.

The third category, that of the clerics or men of religion, exhibits differences between the European and the Islamic contexts of much greater magnitude and more far-reaching implications than obtain for the landed aristocracy or the merchants. First and foremost, Islam has no tradition of clerical celibacy. Therefore, the employment of an entire family in religious pursuits for several generations is no more unusual than would be the continuance of a single family in the same trade for an equal length of time. There was a time in the earliest days of Islam when nepotism was looked at askance, but by the eleventh/fifth century it was the rule. To a certain degree the absence of familial continuity in medieval Christianity was offset by the operation of a collegiate principle. Monks, nuns, canons and so forth were grouped into various kinds of bodies capable of providing corporate continuity and self-protection without hereditary membership. Not even the seemingly analogous development of mystic fraternities from the thirteenth/sixth century onward provides a true functional parallel of this kind of institution in Islam. The role of religious corporations in Islam was taken up by religious dynasties. But even if Christian religious groups and Islamic religious families bear some functional similarities, their social positions were dramatically different. While an aristocratic European family would often place a son in the church hierarchy in order to strengthen its own position, religious position in Islam could be sufficient in and of itself to guarantee the eminence of a family. Muslim religious patricians had sons and daughters to marry off which made it possible for an ambitious family of, say, merchant background to marry into and eventually become a part of this most eminent social group. This was an asset that made the social role of a religious dignitary much more like that of a landed aristocrat in the European context than a bishop or an abbot.

Second in importance only to this potentiality for dynastic succession is the judicial power of the Muslim men of religion. The history of urban constitutional development in medieval Europe is largely the story of conflicting legal jurisdictions. The lord had great judicial powers and the church somewhat more modest ones, but gradually both lost ground to a new and growing jurisdiction, that of the town itself as embodied in its consuls, chaptermen, and so forth. Some have seen this constitutional development of a jurisdiction proper to the town itself as the most crucial aspect of European urban history in the Middle Ages. Some have considered this kind of autonomy to be part of the very definition of the word city and, looking in vain for it outside the European context, have pronounced European urban development to be something unique and of inestimable value in the formation of a Western civilization. To argue these ideas would be to digress, but this viewpoint cannot be ignored in looking at a medieval Islamic city from the legal and religious standpoint.

The legal jurisdiction within and about Nishapur or any other Islamic city of the time was essentially as described below. Whatever jurisdiction the dihqān may have exercised at one time, there is no trace of its continued existence as late as the eleventh/fifth century. On his own domain he probably still judged disputes between peasants as a matter of tradition and convenience, but evidence is lacking even for this. Legally he bears no comparison with the European lord of the same period. The religious courts, on the other hand, had unchallenged jurisdiction over virtually everything. Islamic law covers everything that Western law covers and a lot more besides, and the religious judge, the *qāḍī*, was the upholder of Islamic law. There was no recognized right of appeal from the qāḍī's court, for the law that he applied was the law of God. There was, however, one other jurisdiction. That was the jurisdiction of the civil court of the central government called the *maẓālim* court. The actual function of this court is not always clear, and it no doubt varied with the power and pretensions of the central government; but it was in large part a criminal court exercising what amounted to a residual jurisdiction, since one area in which Islamic law is not particularly developed is criminal law. In no way that can be seen from surviving documents did the maẓālim court infringe or try to infringe upon the jurisdiction of the qāḍī's court in Nishapur. Except for the times when it was actually situated in the city, the central government interfered little in the internal affairs of Nishapur. As long as taxes were collected and the ruler's name put on the coins and mentioned in the noon prayer on Friday, it seemed best to leave well enough alone; the ruler needed the cities more than the cities needed the ruler.[4]

From this it is obvious that the constitutional fights over jurisdiction engaged in by the European towns have no place in the medieval Islamic context. But to infer from this that Islamic towns lacked something vital is not justified. If the office of qāḍī remained in the hands of patrician families for generations and those families identified with the town and were the bulwark of the town's society, then that town was effectively autonomous in jurisdiction. There was no appeal from the qāḍī's court nor was there anybody authorized to tell him what the law was. Advisory legal opinions were frequently sought from jurisconsults known as muftīs, but these were the personal opinions of the men issuing them, and the men were almost invariably from the same group of patrician families as the qāḍī himself. The actual decisions rendered by the qāḍī were based on legal concepts that were not indigenous to the local community, although local traditions may well have crept in via spurious traditions of the Prophet; but then so were the decisions made by the judges in medieval European cities. The important question is that of jurisdiction, and in that regard, what Europe's towns had to struggle for existed de facto in Islamic cities like Nishapur. Through the religious courts the patriciate of Nishapur was as autonomous, though not as constitutionally distinct, as the consulate of Toulouse. It is more than just symbolic that the prime sources for the study of European towns are cartularies full of legal documents while those for Islamic cities are biographical dictionaries full of biographies of patricians.

The purpose of this entire discussion has been to qualify and explain the use of precisely this term patrician in a medieval Islamic context. By now consideration of what is not intended by the term may have occluded those connotations of the term that are intended, and a restatement of the intended connotations is in order. The patricians of Nishapur were a group of families, often intermarried, with landowning, merchant, or religious backgrounds, and not infrequently all three, who monopolized political and religious power in the city with scarcely an intermission throughout a

4. See chapter 11.

period of at least a hundred and fifty years terminating with the destruction of the city in the twelfth/sixth century. As will be seen in the studies of separate families, these families are not easily interchangeable. Each is quite distinctive; the various sources of power in and around the city could be combined in a multitude of ways. Yet they all share a local base and a local allegiance; none is the agent of the central government. Even if only half conscious of the fact, this semiconsciousness being indicated by the fact that their collected biographies could be entitled *The History of Nishapur*, they were the city of Nishapur. The stage set in the last chapter and filled with supernumeraries was theirs to act upon.

This being the case, it seems strange that the patriciate was divided into two contending parties and even stranger that their rivalry from time to time took on the proportions of an intraurban war, either hot or cold, which took scores of lives and contributed in the end to the death of the city. These two parties were the Ḥanafīs and the Shāfiʿīs.

3 / Ḥanafī and Shāfiʿī

It is the job of the social historian to discover the social content of historical events or, more properly, of descriptions of historical events. If a chronicler records that the A's fought the B's, he may mean either that the A-ness of the A's vitally conflicted with the B-ness of the B's or that A and B are more or less superficial and irrelevant labels used out of convenience or habit to describe a conflict that was based upon something entirely different. It is almost routine to find economic conflict concealed beneath racial labels, racial conflict described in religious terms, religious conflict confused with linguistic differences, and so forth. Never, unfortunately, is the truth of the matter clear-cut. However much effort is spent stripping away the veneer of misleading words and descriptions, the possibility always remains that the veneer was not as superficial as it appeared and that in fact it contained more than a grain of truth.

Middle Eastern society from the tenth/fourth century to the twelfth/sixth century presents a puzzle of this kind as vast in scope as it is deep in mystery. This puzzle is the apparent bitter conflict between the several interpretations of Islamic religious law. This conflict, or rather the violence and bitterness of this conflict, is neither permanent nor ubiquitous in Islamic history. By the time of the Ottoman Empire it had died out in most areas, and even during its period of greatest virulence North Africa was relatively immune from it.[1] When a chronicler states that partisans of one legal interpretation fought to the death with partisans of another legal interpretation in the streets of one of the great cities of Iran or Iraq, what does he actually mean? A general answer to this question cannot even be contemplated at this time; the study of the problem has scarcely begun for places other than Baghdad.[2] Here, only the situation in Nishapur will be explored, and even in this limited context the answers arrived at must be unsatisfactorily tentative and imprecise.

Clearly, the place to start is with the interpretations of Islamic law. It cannot be said too often that the law, the *sharīʿa*, is the fullest expression of Islam. The heart of Islam is the Qurʾan, God's word, and the messenger through whom it was transmitted to mankind, Muḥammad. The sharīʿa is the interpretation of the Qurʾan and of Muḥammad's personal statements, the *ḥadīth*, as they apply to the life of the believer in this world and the next. All aspects of law as the term is understood in Western society are encompassed in the sharīʿa as well as everything that pertains to ritual religious ob-

1. Maqdisī, *Aḥsan*, p. 236.

2. See George Makdisi, *Ibn ʿAqīl et la résurgence de l'Islam traditionaliste au XIe siècle* (Damascus, 1963).

servance: how to pray, how to perform ablutions, how to bury the dead, and so on. Never has a law of such scope been developed from so small a corpus of positive legislation. For every verse of explicit legislation in the Qurᵓan and every unequivocal commandment in the *ḥadīth*, there are dozens of verses and sayings whose relevance to the practical life of the believer can be discovered only by some kind of interpretation; similarly, for every practical situation whose legal status is explicitly established by the Qurᵓan or ḥadīth, there are hundreds of situations that can be covered only by interpretation. The interpretation of the law, in other words, is of potentially greater consequence in Islam than is the interpretation of the Constitution in the history of the United States.

This being the case, there would seem to be no particular reason why differences in interpretation could not lead in the course of time to widespread bloodshed and bitter animosities. In practice, however, the concrete law arrived at by the various modes of interpretation has never differed radically. As marked as have been the disagreements over such things as the permissibility of analogical reasoning and of personal judgment in interpreting the law, all different schools of interpretation are in basic agreement on the nature of the state, the relations between Muslims and non-Muslims, and the general ordering of Muslim society. This excepts, of course, the Shiᶜites, whose legal code, while similar in details, reflects fundamental differences on such questions as the nature of the state. But within Sunni Islam, which in the period under examination can perhaps best be defined as the residual category of all Muslims who do not consider themselves to be Shiᶜites or members of some other separatist sect, the various paths of legal interpretation tend to converge at the level of practical law.

In view of this convergence, it is difficult to see how differences in legal interpretation alone could have generated so much social conflict and violence. Even minor differences in religious or legal observance, of course, can rouse people's wrath if they become symbolic of much greater differences, not necessarily confined to religion or law, at a more abstract level. The history of Christian schisms gives ample proof of this. But the abstract differences which were admittedly great and which definitely did exist between the Sunni law schools in medieval times did not have much capacity for emotional involvement. A legal specialist might possibly have considered the precise sense of the word *ijmāᶜ*, "consensus," in its legal application an issue worth fighting over; but it is hard to imagine how he could have explained and conveyed his rage to a mass of illiterate followers. The points at issue were far more cerebral than such parallel issues as the nature of God and the humanity of Christ in the early Christian church. Nor did any of the law schools ever officially declare the others to be beyond the pale; for the record, they all recognized each other as legitimately Muslim.[3] Thus the interpretation of minor legal differences as symbols of fundamental ones and hence as sufficient immediate causes for social conflict does not appear to be a fruitful way of approaching the violence between the law schools. When Shiᶜites rioted against Sunnis, each side would signify in its battlecry the crux of the conflict. The Shiᶜites would cry out the names of ᶜAlī and his descendants and the Sunnis the names of the three caliphs, Abū Bakr, ᶜUmar, and ᶜUthmān, who ruled—illegitimately in Shiᶜite eyes—between the Prophet and his son-in-law. However, when partisans of the Sunni law schools clashed, there are no such battle cries reported either of an abstract or a concrete kind. As much as anything, it is the lack of reference to disputed points of law in descriptions of strife between law schools that gives the impression that hidden beneath the labels of the law schools some other conflict was being played out.

In Nishapur two law schools engaged in rioting. These were the Ḥanafīs and the Shāfiᶜīs. Other schools of legal interpretation had small numbers of adherents in the city, notably the Mālikīs, Ẓāhirīs, and Ḥanbalīs, but they played no known part in the Ḥanafī-Shāfiᶜī struggle. There is nothing to be gained here by discussing in any detail the history of these two schools; however, a brief summary is in order.[4] The Ḥanafī school is named for a jurist named Abū Ḥanīfa who worked in Iraq and died in 767/150. His followers, who developed in his name the Ḥanafī school of interpretation, following the principles that he himself apparently taught, allowed somewhat more leeway for the operation of individual interpretation of Qurᵓanic analogies than did the legal schools that were formed later; the school is therefore frequently characterized as being more "liberal" or "rational" than the other schools. Muḥammad ash-Shāfiᶜī died in 820/208 and was thus able to study both under an immediate disciple of Abū Ḥanīfa and under the founder of the Mālikī law school, Mālik b. Anas. The school of interpretation that he established aimed at compensating for the weaknesses he observed in the Ḥanafī and Mālikī approaches. He attempted to weld together the techniques of ana-

3. Off the record is a different story. A Ḥanafī from Transoxania is quoted as saying: "If I had my way, I'd collect the *jizya* from the Shāfiᶜīs" (IAW, II, 136). The *jizya* was a tax levied only upon non-Muslims.

4. For a fuller history see Joseph Schacht, *An Introduction to Islamic Law* (Oxford, 1964), chaps. 6–7.

logical reasoning and consensus of legal scholars so as to add rigor to the Ḥanafī interpretative method and flexibility to the Mālikī.

The upshot of this legal ferment in eighth/second century Iraq and Arabia was that the Mālikī, Ḥanafī, and Shāfiʿī schools developed along quite similar lines. The Mālikī school spread westward and for reasons that are not altogether clear soon became supreme in Islamic North Africa. The Ḥanafī and Shāfiʿī schools, on the other hand, expanded in the central areas of the ʿAbbāsid caliphate and eastward into Iran and Transoxania. It was in these latter areas for the most part that they became warring factions, not, interestingly enough, in Iraq where they initially developed and where their early intellectual clashes about legal interpretation took place.

The situation in Nishapur was fairly typical, then, of the general situation in eastern Iran and Transoxania.[5] Most cities accommodated two warring factions, and more often than not they bore the labels Ḥanafī and Shāfiʿī. The word used in describing the situation is *ʿaṣabiya*. Ibn Khaldūn's famous usage of this word to denote the fundamental bond of social solidarity among kindred individuals is well-known, and it is therefore regarded as having an essentially positive connotation. But in the vocabulary of writers familiar with the eastern Islamic world of the tenth/fourth and eleventh/fifth centuries it had both a different meaning and a different value connotation. ʿAṣabiya meant factional strife, and it had an ominous, wild ring to it. It stood for the force that bound men together, to be sure; but it bound them together in factions so hostile to one another that the fabric of society was rent. *Taʿaṣṣub*, the quality of engaging in or fomenting ʿaṣabiya, is not badly translated by the word fanaticism, which is, in fact, one of its meanings in modern Arabic.

The origins of the factional struggle in Nishapur are unknown. It antedates the specific struggle between the Ḥanafīs and Shāfiʿīs, for it existed in the late ninth/third century when the protagonists were the people who followed the legal tradition of the city of Kufa and those who followed that of Medina.[6] By the beginning of the tenth/fourth century there are biographical notations of people characterized as *mutaʿaṣṣib* or "fanatic."[7] Yet there is little evidence of genuine factional violence until the latter part

5. Maqdisī, *Aḥsan*, p. 336.

6. This early factional division was politically important at the time of the revolt of Ḥaikān (see chapter 5 and I. Athīr, VII, 300). Any continued importance it might have had in the tenth/fourth century is not apparent in the sources, but as late as the end of that century a qāḍī could still be identified as the last of the qāḍīs in Khurasan of the Kufan tradition (IAW, I, 343).

7. Ḥākim, f29b.

of the century. Sometime around 990/380 a prominent preacher named ᶜAbd ar-Raḥmān aṣ-Ṣābūnī, the father of Shaikh al-Islām Abū ᶜUthmān Ismāᶜīl aṣ-Ṣābūnī, was assassinated "on account of fanaticism (taᶜaṣṣub) and faction (*madhhab*)." [8] Although the word madhhab commonly refers to law school, it is also used for other types of factions and therefore does not tie this murder down conclusively to the Ḥanafī-Shāfiᶜī struggle. However, it was around the same time that Nishapur became the center of political maneuvering between the ruling Sāmānid dynasty in Bukhara and two subordinate dynasties in Khurasan, the Sīmjūrids and the Ghaznavids. The legal factions in Nishapur became involved in turn in that political maneuvering, and key posts in the city were often awarded to the faction favoring the dynasty temporarily in power.[9] This favoritism must surely have exacerbated the existing animosity between the law schools, and ᶜAbd ar-Raḥmān aṣ-Ṣābūnī's murder is an index of the level of violence that was reached.

The story of escalation of factional discord through the next century and a half from aṣ-Ṣābūnī's assassination to all out intraurban warfare and the destruction and abandonment of the city is told in full in chapters 5 and 6. It is a dismal tale and one that is simply unbelievable when looked at as the product of differences in the theory of legal interpretation and in the minutiae of legal practice. These differences could not have been the sole bones of contention between the factions which took their names from them. There must have been more to it.

Getting at the deeper dimensions of the conflict presents problems, however. The hypothetical approaches that come to mind—economics, race, language, class—founder upon two obstacles. The first is the restricted nature of the available quantitative data. If the underlying cleavage represented by the law schools was based upon one of these factors—for instance, if the real source of conflict was animosity between the Arab immigrants and the native Persians—it cannot be substantiated from the available data. Within the patriciate there is no perceptible difference between Ḥanafīs and Shāfiᶜīs in economic status, class, race, or language.

The second obstacle is the uncertainty whether the causes of the original splitting of the Nishapuri patriciate into two law schools are the same as those which raised the differences between the schools to a fever pitch. It is entirely possible that the differen-

8. See chapter 10 and Subkī III, 274.
9. See chapter 5.

tiating principle operative in the origin of the schools had become inoperative by the end of the tenth/fourth century when the rivalry became bitter. Ethnic background or spoken language, for example, could conceivably have prompted the first formation of the schools as social groups and subsequently have been lost sight of as the amalgamation of the Arab minority and the Persian majority both genetically and linguistically became an accomplished fact. The development of the schools along increasingly bitter and violent lines would thus, presumably, be a product of some inner logic of factional relations divorced from the original bases of factional formation.

The prospect that the true nature of factional conflict in Nishapur may, in fact, be unascertainable without some new kind of data is naturally cold comfort at the present moment when the nature of the factions is precisely what is under discussion. The airing of unsubstantiable hypotheses, intriguing though they might be, concerning the origin of the factions would be out of place here; and the question of possible relationships between initial causes of factional formation and what appear as proximate causes of factional violence in the late tenth/fourth and eleventh/fifth centuries must be left hanging. The only generalities that might be hazarded for the presumed formative period of the factions in the ninth/third and early tenth/fourth centuries are that the Ḥanafīs preceded the Shāfiᶜīs in Khurasan and that from early times intermarriage of families of one school with families of the other was a rare occurrence. The bar on intermarriage seems to be constant in the history of the factions and bespeaks their deep, if elusive, social significance.

Leaving behind the unanswered question of the origins of the factions and proceeding to differences between the factions at the height of their rivalry in the eleventh/fifth century, there is an important lead offered by the historical narrative itself. The persecution of the Shāfiᶜīs carried out by ᶜAmīd al-Mulk al-Kundurī and his Ḥanafī allies in the mid-eleventh/fifth century was ostensibly based upon theology. It was not Shāfiᶜī law that was proscribed; it was Ashᶜarī theology.[10]

Just as the detailed legal differences between the law schools do not seem to have been responsible for or even too closely linked to the political differences between the social factions named for the schools, so the theological distinctions between the Ashᶜarīs and the rival Muᶜtazilīs do not seem to be at the bottom of the rivalry between the two factions that adhered to them. Before outlining these theological distinctions

10. See chapter 5.

and their historical emergence, however, there is something that must be clearly understood. Schools of legal interpretation and schools of theological interpretation do not coincide. The former are formally constituted and recognized by the state; the boundaries between them are clear-cut and rarely crossed. The latter exist as intellectual currents without concrete form or official recognition. No law school adheres as a point of doctrine to a specific brand of theology, nor does any theological scheme include a belief in the propriety of any one law school to the exclusion of all others. The position of Ḥanbalism, which might be considered simultaneously a school of law and a school of theology, is exceptional and unique; but since there were few Ḥanbalis in eleventh/fifth century Nishapur, their special characteristics need not be considered here.

In Nishapur only the Muʿtazilīs and the Ashʿarīs matter when dealing with theology. The Muʿtazilīs rose to prominence early in the ninth/third century with a doctrinal formulation derived in large part from Greek philosophical principles. Theirs was the first methodical effort to confront the theological problems posed by the Qurʾan and the ḥadīth of the Prophet. The particularly thorny problem of determinism they explicated in such a way as to preserve for mankind a modicum of free will. The problem of the eternity of the Qurʾan, which conflicted in their minds with the Greek definition of God as the first cause of everything, they resolved in favor of the Qurʾan's creation by God in time.

The political impact of the Muʿtazilīs was unquestionably great. During the second quarter of the ninth/third century an inquisition was instituted by the ʿAbbāsid caliphate on their behalf with the object of making Muʿtazilī doctrine truly orthodox and of extirpating other theological views. Socially they seem to have been important as well. However fruitless the abortive inquisition may have been in the long run in establishing an Islamic orthodoxy, the Muʿtazilīs did introduce a higher order of rigor and rationality to Muslim thinking on both theological and other subjects, and they may have saved Islam by their Hellenistic approach from dangerous schisms born of incomplete assimilation of sophisticated, Hellenized, pre-Islamic theologies.[11] By the end of the ninth/third century, however, the impact of Muʿtazilī ideas had been felt. Although Muʿtazilīs continued to exist in substantial numbers, they continued as a school of

11. H. A. R. Gibb, *Studies on the Civilization of Islam* (Boston, 1962), "The Social Significance of the Shuʿubiya," pp. 70–71.

theology which could no longer be a powerful political and social influence by the force of its ideas alone.

What had broken the strength of the Muʿtazilīs was the rise in the second half of the ninth/third century and first half of the tenth/fourth of the diametrically opposed theological doctrine of the Ḥanbalīs. The Ḥanbalīs, whose influence was felt much more strongly in Baghdad than anywhere else, believed firmly in the unqualified omnipotence of God and in the uncreatedness of his Word, the Qurʾan. They maintained that if the Qurʾan declared that God sat on a throne and if that declaration conflicted with the Greek notion that to ascribe the act of sitting to God is somehow to limit Him and bring Him down to human level, then so much the worse for Greek philosophy. The Qurʾan was God's word and as such was to be believed in detail and without question.

Although the Ḥanbalīs had no role to play in eleventh/fifth century Nishapur, they were instrumental in the development of the second of the theological schools that figure in Nishapur's factional history, that of the Ashʿarīs. Abū al-Ḥasan al-Ashʿarī died in Baghdad in 936/324. The path of his personal intellectual development was a tortuous one and need not be explored for present purposes. It is sufficient to note that he lived during a period of intellectual ferment and debate between the Muʿtazilīs and Ḥanbalīs in Iraq. The theology that he developed, or that his disciples developed in his name, was a compromise between those two polar positions. On point after point they granted the Ḥanbalīs the substance of their position while devising rationalistic arguments to satisfy the criticisms of the Muʿtazilīs. God's sitting became in Ashʿarī doctrine a real sitting but one inconceivably different from human sitting; the Qurʾan became an eternal attribute of God and therefore uncreated; and so forth. As with most compromising positions, however, the immediate net effect was not to bring about the uniting of the opposing positions but simply to create a third doctrine unacceptable to the militants at either extreme.

It must be borne in mind that, as in the case of the schools of legal interpretation, most of this theological development grew out of the intellectual cockpit of the great Iraqi cities of Basra, Kufa, and Baghdad. Through the ninth/third century, Khurasan did not bear comparison with Iraq. It produced taxes and commercial products, and it also produced bright young men who went to Iraq and became part of the intellectual culture at the center of the caliphate, but it was not itself a paramount center of Muslim intellectual endeavour. Only in the tenth/fourth century did it begin to achieve this status, which in the eleventh/fifth century it enjoyed to a greater degree than any other province in the Islamic world with the possible exception of Iraq.

The only one of the legal and theological developments previously described which was geographically centered to any degree in Khurasan was chronologically the latest of them, Ashᶜarī theology. Abū al-Ḥasan al-Ashᶜarī's first important disciples lived as he did in Iraq, and important members of later generations continued to do so.[12] But beginning in the second half of the tenth/fourth century, the school became increasingly centered in Nishapur. Some of the movement occurred through the immigration of scholars from the west; some of it occurred through Khurasanian scholars travelling to Iraq, becoming indoctrinated in the new theology, and returning home to teach. Whatever the method, the result was that in comparison with Muᶜtazilī theology which had become common in Khurasan at an earlier date in a more or less passive and unproductive fashion, Ashᶜarī theology came as a dynamic new doctrine promulgated by some of the most outstanding thinkers and writers the school was ever to produce, men like Ibn Fūrak and Abū Sahl aṣ-Ṣuᶜlūkī.[13]

While the warning given earlier against drawing equations between schools of law and schools of theology must not be taken lightly, it is necessary nonetheless to investigate what relationships short of one to one equations existed between these two types of factions. The tempting generalization and the one against which the warning was intended is that all Muᶜtazilīs were Ḥanafīs and all Ashᶜarīs Shāfiᶜīs. This is demonstrably untrue if it is applied to medieval Islam in general, for there are abundant exceptions to it. But in the case of the patricians of Nishapur and the local cleavage between Ḥanafī and Shāfiᶜī it is tempting indeed. There is no obvious exception to it. On the other hand, the theological beliefs and legal affiliations of a great number of patricians whose biographies have been preserved are not given. All of the known or presumed Ashᶜarīs are Shāfiᶜīs, and all of the known or presumed Muᶜtazilīs are Ḥanafīs; but this does not come close to accounting for all of the known patricians. For the most part, if anything is recorded about a man's religious affiliations it is his law school. References to theology are much rarer. In fact, the likelihood is great that many, if not most, patricians never considered themselves members of any theological camp.

12. The history of al-Ashᶜarī's disciples is best told by Michel Allard, *Le Problème des attributs divins dans la doctrine d'al-Ashᶜarī et de ses premiers grands disciples* (Beirut, 1965).

13. See chapter 11 and Qushairī genealogical key #28; chapter 9 and Basṭāmī genealogical key #1.

Legal affiliation was a practical necessity; a patrician could not lead a normal life without reference to it, and normally he would be born to it. Theology, on the other hand, was for those who had a taste for such things. The educational system stressed the learning of ḥadīth but not of theology. Therefore, the most that can be said about the relationship between law and theology at the local human level in Nishapur is that by and large those people to whom Ashᶜarī theology appealed were Shāfiᶜīs and those who adhered to the Muᶜtazilī dogma were Ḥanafīs but that an indeterminate number of people forewent the dubious pleasures of theological speculation entirely or preferred the headier wine of Sufi mysticism.

What, then, of the persecution of the Ashᶜarīs by ᶜAmīd al-Mulk al-Kundurī and the Ḥanafīs? It has already been implied that this was in reality an episode in the continuing rivalry between the Shāfiᶜīs and the Ḥanafīs rather than a theological heresy hunt in the narrowest sense. If many or most Shāfiᶜīs were innocent of the Ashᶜarī stigma, how could a persecution of the Ashᶜarīs so strongly affect them? The answer to this question in detail may be found in the histories of the Qushairī family and the Basṭāmī family.[14] Briefly, the migration of the Ashᶜarī school to Nishapur in the tenth/fourth century introduced into the city a number of brilliant and dynamic individuals who happened to belong to the Shāfiᶜī law school. They seem to have served as a kind of catalyst in the Shāfiᶜī community which had been somewhat moribund before their arrival. Their children became prize matches for the Shāfiᶜī leaders who themselves studied under them. Within a generation the newcomers had become an integral part of the top echelon of Shāfiᶜī patricians and had in the process spread their Ashᶜarī doctrines among the older patrician families. Ibn Fūrak became linked to the Sufi family of Abū al-Qāsim al-Qushairī and Abū ᶜAlī ad-Daqqāq. Abū Sahl aṣ-Ṣuᶜlūkī made alliance with the aristocratic ᶜAlids and with the Basṭāmī family which soon acquired hereditary leadership of the Shāfiᶜī law school and which later combined through marriage with the family of one of the greatest Ashᶜarīs Imām al-Ḥaramain al-Juwainī. In short, by the middle of the eleventh/fifth century when the persecution of the Ashᶜarīs commenced, the top leadership of the Shāfiᶜī law school had become predominantly Ashᶜarī and hence on theological grounds vulnerable to a trumped up charge of heresy to which it was invulnerable on legal grounds. Thus, the blow struck by al-Kundurī and his Ḥanafī cohorts was meant to decapitate the Shāfiᶜīs by discrediting the Ashᶜarī

14. See chapter 11 and chapter 9.

leadership and consequently leaving the bulk of theologically disinterested Shāfiʿīs leaderless. That this is exactly what happened is indicated by the remark in the biography of the Ḥanafī rabble rouser aṣ-Ṣandalī that the Shāfiʿīs were split into smaller factions (*iftirāq*) while the Ashʿarīs were annihilated (*īdāʾ*).[15]

Unfortunately, this exposition has not really brought the original questions much closer to solution. As stated at the outset, there were rival factions within the patriciate of Nishapur, described most commonly by the names of law schools, whose enmity grew from simple rivalry to open bloodshed and suicidal destruction of the city. There appears to have been no mundane basis for their rivalry nor do the legal differences between the law schools appear to have been sufficiently serious to have caused it. Theology was unquestionably involved, but an examination of the exact nature of the involvement suggests that it was at least as much tactical as strategic. Only one source even identifies al-Kundurī as being himself a Muʿtazilī and thus understandably an enemy of the Ashʿarīs, and that source is the much later Ashʿarī zealot Subkī.[16] Earlier and less biased sources show him to be intellectually more inclined toward the Ashʿarī/Shāfiʿī camp.[17] Nor is it absolutely certain that all of al-Kundurī's Ḥanafī allies were strenuously Muʿtazilī.[18] Nothing, in fact, points to Ashʿarī theology being very much more than a pretense for attacking the Shāfiʿī faction. Why the Shāfiʿī faction was considered a target of attack is still in question.

Having thus far proceeded by a negative route in this discussion, belittling first the legal and then the theological components of the conflict and declaring economic, ethnic, and linguistic approaches to be unprofitable both because of insufficient data and because of strong indications that there was parity between the factions in these areas, I must know turn to the constructive task of building a case for the general answer which will be proposed. In preview, that general answer is that the terms Ḥanafī and Shāfiʿī have a consistent double meaning. On the one hand, they denote modes of legal interpretation, as already explained, and, on the other, they stand for two political

15. Fārisī I, f68a.

16. Subkī, III, 390. He calls al-Kundurī not just a Muʿtazilī but a Shiʿite and a Karrāmī as well for good measure.

17. Al-Kundurī began his career as a protégé of the head of the Shāfiʿī faction in Nishapur, Imām al-Muwaffaq al-Basṭāmī (Fārisī I, f88a). He is also reported in one source to have had Sufi inclinations (Ibn al-Qaisarānī, *Ziyāda ʿalā Kitāb al-Ansāb al-Muttafaqa* [Leiden, 1865], p. 132.)

18. Subkī says that "he sought the aid of a group of Muʿtazilīs who claimed that they followed the *madhhab* of Abū Ḥanīfa," (III, 391), but Subkī is biased. Aṣ-Ṣandalī, however, one of his closest allies, seems definitely to have been a Muʿtazilī (see chapter 15 and Ḥasanī genealogical key #11).

parties within the patriciate, vying for possession of key political posts within the city and ultimately for the city itself. The term political party is intended here to denote a political action group bound together by an essentially political ideology, a vision of the right ordering of society. The vision ascribed here to the Ḥanafīs, understanding that word in its second meaning of political party, is a conservative one. Intellectually anchored upon the oldest of the law schools and theological systems, it conceived of a social order dominated by law and by rationality and crowned by a patrician class which merited its preeminence by its monopoly of legal and religious knowledge, a monopoly preserved by the educational system and by the continued use of the Arabic language for religious and legal matters. The Ḥanafī vision was aristocratic as well as conservative; it harked back to an earlier period before the bulk of the population had converted when Muslims were relatively few and quite understandably felt themselves to be a superior class. It should be noted, however, that this vision did not exclude the Shāfiʿīs. As fellow patricians and fellow initiates into the arcana of Arabic religious treatises, they merited the same prominence as the Ḥanafīs—as long as they did not act to destroy the vision. In particular, whenever a threat came from the direction of the populist Karrāmiya, there could be no question but that the Shāfiʿīs were to be considered as allies against a common enemy.

The Shāfiʿī ideology, on the other hand, can be characterized, at least after the fact, as a progressive one. It was not progressive in the modern sense which implies rationality and a belief in the betterment of society—such ideas would have been more at home among the Ḥanafīs—but in the literal sense of supporting those trends which were comparatively new in society and which became dominant throughout Muslim society in the course of the succeeding two centuries. This meant mysticism and semideterminism instead of rationality and free will, but it also meant a more human and emotional religious experience that was more accessible to the general populace. To this end the use of Persian as a written language in religious and legal affairs was tolerated.[19] As the newer party, its vision had been formed in a predominantly Muslim society, which may explain somewhat its greater openness to the mass of Muslims; but this openness must not be overemphasized. The Shāfiʿī party was as patrician as the Ḥanafī, and it saw the Ḥanafīs basically as equals, particularly in contradistinction to the Karrāmiya.

19. Persian was used in Sufi writings, and as is pointed out further on, most of the Sufis in Nishapur were Shāfiʿīs. Furthermore, there are several concrete examples of Shāfiʿīs in Nishapur writing legal treatises in Persian (Fārisī I, f39a, 80b), and no parallel examples from the Ḥanafī camp.

Again it must be pointed out that these descriptions of the Ḥanafī and Shāfiʿī party ideologies are intended to apply primarily to the eleventh/fifth century and that while they may be the product of some unknown principle of differentiation operative at the time of their initial formation, the mystery of that initial formation makes it impossible to trace any connections between it and the later period. Thus the roots of the conflict still remain buried, and analysis must remain restricted to what is visible on the surface in the eleventh/fifth century.

Presenting the conclusion before the argument, as has been done here, has a way of improving the argument itself and is thus somewhat unfair. The reader knows in advance what the author intends and becomes less aware of alternative conclusions that might be drawn from the same material. It also has the more legitimate advantage, however, of helping to draw together a disjointed argument composed of a number of disparate and not obviously related points. Since the evidence for the conclusions already presented is of precisely this disjointed nature, it was with the intention of assisting rather than deceiving that the device has been employed here. As stated at the beginning of this chapter, the conclusions presented are unsatisfactorily tentative and imprecise, but such is the lot of the social historian.

Four salient points have already been put forward. First, the Ḥanafī party antedated the Shāfiʿī party and hence developed in a somewhat different society, the exact character of which depends upon the crucial, but so far unknown, timetable of conversion in the conquered lands. Second, intermarriage between the parties was rare, at least among the patrician families. Since marriage is a channel for the transfer of wealth and power far more often than it is for the communication of ideas and since there is no legal bar to marriage between law schools, the absence of such alliances strongly indicates the mundanity of what was at stake. Third, even if the law school labels attached to the parties do not stand primarily for competition between modes of legal interpretation, they do point to a major arena of political rivalry, namely the judicial system.[20] The role of law in society being what it was, control of the courts constituted political power whatever the brand of law the courts dispensed. Fourth, the pinpointing of Ashʿarī theology as a focus of contention highlights the fact that the conflict centered on the top patrician families. Since the Ashʿarī position was subsequently to become the dominant theological position in Islam, the emphasis placed upon it also points to what has been called here the progressive orientation of the Shāfiʿī party.

20. See chapter 5.

The additional points to be added to the four above concern Sufism and the institution known as the *futūwa*. First, however, an unequivocal instance of the double meaning of the words Ḥanafī and Shāfiʿī is worth recording. In one biography a man is described as follows: "He was a Ḥanafī in law school [madhhab], but he was a Shāfiʿī in morals [*akhlāq*] and social relations [*muʿāshara*]."[21] The term Shāfiʿī in this sentence can in no way be understood as referring to a law school qua law school; it must stand for a much broader conception, what has been called here a political party or ideology.

In the field of mysticism as in theology there is no formal identification with a specific law school. There is nothing to prevent members of any law school from becoming mystics. In reality, however, the practice of mysticism was almost non-existent among the Ḥanafīs during the period under discussion. Since the legal affiliation of many mystics is uncertain, there may be some unknown exceptions to this generalization, but its overall validity is reinforced by the fact that the one person clearly identified as both a Ḥanafī and a Sufi is the very same man mentioned above whose life style marked him as a Shāfiʿī despite his Ḥanafī legal affiliation.

Mysticism fits into the factional pattern in other ways as well. The three currents that contribute to the formation of Sufism are asceticism, pietism, and mystic speculation. These three currents are denoted by the terms *zuhd* (*zāhid*), *ʿibāda* (*ʿābid*), and *taṣawwuf* (*ṣūfī*) respectively, although the latter term to some extent includes the two former. In Nishapur there is a clear chronological ordering of these three currents.[22] At the

21. Fārisī II, f17a. There is another Ḥanafī who is described as being a Shāfiʿī (Fārisī I, f9b), but the nature of his bipartisanship is not spelled out.

22. The percentage of all individuals in each chronological period bearing any of the three epithets under discussion is:

	Hijra Years						
Epithets	200–270	270–312	314–335	335–388	405–425	425–460	460–525
zāhid, ʿābid, or ṣūfī	3	6.5	6.4	10.1	12.2	17.8	17.1

The percentage distribution of the three epithets within each of these groups is:

	Hijra Years						
Epithets	200–270	270–312	314–335	335–388	405–425	425–460	460–525
zāhid (ascetic)	100	55	35	37	42	26	21
ʿābid (pietist)	0	42	45	20	23	19	11
ṣūfī	0	3	20	43	35	55	68

beginning of the ninth/third century asceticism alone was known, but during the century pietism made its appearance. Around the middle of the tenth/fourth century the mystic Sufi strain became common, and by the end of the eleventh/fifth century it was clearly dominant. It would be incorrect to infer, however, that each new current absorbed the previous ones producing an amalgam at the end known simply as Sufism. This was true to some extent, and the resultant Sufism did encompass all three currents; but there were always ascetics who eschewed pietism and mysticism, mystics who had no truck with asceticism, such as the famous Sufi who sojourned in Nishapur, Abū Saᶜīd b. Abī al-Khair, and so forth.[23]

Usually these three tendencies are distinguished in biographies, and the distinctions made are of interest.[24] In asceticism the Shāfiᶜīs and the Ḥanafīs are roughly balanced, but the Karrāmiya is tremendously overrepresented. Karrāmī overrepresentation appears again in the area of pietism, although it is less marked. The appeal of pietism to the Shāfiᶜīs is noticeably greater than it is to the Ḥanafīs. It is in the third area, mysticism strictly speaking, that the Shāfiᶜī preponderance is truly striking. No Karrāmīs are labeled as Sufis nor are any Ḥanafīs with the one exception noted earlier. There are twenty-three Shāfiᶜīs so identified, however, as well as four members of law schools with only small handfuls of adherents in the city.

From this breakdown of the Sufi movement into component parts it becomes clear that while there was a slow but steady growth in extreme forms of personal religious observance from the ninth/third century to the twelfth/sixth, there was a late starting but extremely rapid growth in the specifically mystic, Sufi current which absorbed to

23. Fārisī I, f74b–75a; II, f120a; and Reynold A. Nicholson, *Studies in Islamic Mysticism* (Cambridge, Eng., 1921), chap. 1. Nicholson's account (pp. 24–36) makes it very clear that Abū Saᶜīd was well received in Nishapur by the Shāfiᶜīs and bitterly opposed by the Ḥanafīs and the Karrāmīs.

24. Of those people whose legal affiliation is ascertainable, the breakdown into ascetic, pietist, and Sufi is as follows:

	Ḥanafī	Shāfiᶜī	Karrāmī	Mālikī	Ẓāhirī
zāhid	8	11	8	1	0
ᶜābid	2	10	5	0	0
ṣūfī	1	23	0	2	2

These figures should be compared to an overall approximate proportional representation of Shāfiᶜīs, Ḥanafīs, and Karrāmīs of 7:3:1. The representation of Mālikīs and Ẓāhirīs is negligible, but their appearance on the Sufi line of the chart highlights the absence of Sufis in the Ḥanafī and Karrāmī columns.

some degree the earlier ascetic and pietist currents. It is this dramatic growth in mysticism that is most directly associated with the Shāfiʿī party. The Ḥanafīs remained sobersided, indulging in asceticism if in anything at all; and the Karrāmīs stressed asceticism and pietism, as befitted their role as leaders of the oppressed poor, while avoiding mysticism, which might well have detracted from the activism and militancy of their message.

In mysticism as in theology, then, the Shāfiʿī party gives the appearance of great growth and vigor from around the middle of the tenth/fourth century. Nor is this merely coincidental. Many of the foremost Sufis in the city were unquestionably Ashʿarīs in theology. Notable examples are Abū ʿAbd ar-Raḥmān as-Sulamī, author of the first Sufi biographical dictionary, and Abū al-Qāsim al-Qushairī,[25] who wrote in addition to his famous *Risāla* on Sufism a treatise in defense of the Ashʿarīs against the charges leveled at them by ʿAmīd al-Mulk al-Kundurī. But more famous than either of these is al-Ghazzālī, who is traditionally considered to have forged a bond between Ashʿarī theology and Sufism on the one hand and the broad middle road of Islamic thinking on the other which was to dominate Muslim religious development for centuries to come. Thus the dynamic development of Ashʿarī theology and rapid growth of Sufism go hand in hand to the extent that one man is represented as being a shaikh of "Ashʿarī Sufism."[26] The Ḥanafī party's rationalist inclinations made them antagonistic to both of these new trends. It is among the antirationalist Ḥanbalīs that Sufism finds its other home, but that does not take place in Nishapur.

The futūwa and related groups present a puzzle whenever and wherever they are encountered.[27] Upon certain points there is agreement: the membership consisted of young men, usually celibate; special ritual and dress were involved; and there was some sort of connection with Sufism. But beyond these points there is disagreement and mystery. Associations have been sought with banditry, chivalry, the upper class, the lower class, artisan guilds, police, and so forth. Geographical diversity and changing forms and functions over time doubtless give rise to much of the confusion, for from the early period of futūwa development, beginning in the tenth/fourth century and

25. Fārisī II, f2b; and chapter 11 and Qushairī genealogical key #3.

26. Fārisī II, f51a.

27. A full bibliography on the subject of futūwa may be found in Friedrich Taeschner, "Futuwwa," *Encyclopaedia of Islam*, new ed., II, pp. 961–969. To it should be added the work of his pupil, D. A. Breebaart, *The Development and Structure of the Turkish Futuwah Guilds*, microfilm (Ann Arbor, 1966).

perhaps even earlier, there is rarely enough information extant for a detailed study of the institution in a restricted time and place.

Nor is the situation much better for Nishapur in the eleventh/fifth century. There is enough information to demonstrate the importance of the futūwa but not really enough to show exactly what it was or what it did. Yet it is important that only information emanating from Nishapur be taken into consideration in evaluating the institution there since there is no reliable benchmark study proximate enough in either time or place to be used to fill in any gaps. It is better to leave the gaps than to hazard possibly misleading comparisons.

Futūwa is the idealized quality of young manliness (*fatā*, pl. *fityān*, means young man) parallel to *murūwa*, the idealized quality of mature adulthood. As an ideal it was discussed and refined by Sufi thinkers in particular, some of whom lived or studied in Nishapur. Indeed, some of these men strove to realize the ideal in the conduct of their own lives, but this alone did not generate the futūwa organization with its special rites and customs.[28] Alongside the ideal expanded upon by the Sufīs, there was a quite different and probably prior tradition of futūwa representing the self image of the militarily inclined landowning dihqāns.[29] Their conception of the ideal young man as a convivial squire as adept at poetry as at archery was not in consonance with the mystic's vision of a chaste and fraternal disciple following his master on the mystic path, but neither was there dissonance between them. They coexisted.

These two components of the institutionalized futūwa of the eleventh/fifth century may well have been conjoined with a third populist or artisan component. In the later futūwa, association with artisan movements is unquestionable, but it cannot be traced in the eleventh/fifth century. Likewise, the ᶜ*ayyārūn*, who appear throughout Iraq and Iran now as bandits, now as irregular affiliates of the government from the ninth/third century onward and who are clearly of lower-class origin, cannot be conclusively identified with or tied to the futūwa as an institution.[30] If this third component was of

28. Traces of the early Sufi development of the futūwa ideal are to be found throughout as-Sulamī's *Ṭabaqāt aṣ-Ṣūfiya*, ed. Nūr ad-Dīn Sharība (Cairo, 1953).

29. This conception of futūwa is reflected in some of the poetry in the Khurasanian section of Thaᶜālibī's *Yatīma ad-Dahr* (Cairo, 1934).

30. The question of the possible relationship between the futūwa and the ᶜayyārūn is treated by Claude Cahen, *Mouvements populaires et autonomisme urbain dans l'Asie musulmane du moyen âge* (Leiden, 1959), pp. 30–56. The paragon of futūwa mentioned by al-Qushairī and others is a Nishapuri named Nūḥ al-ᶜAyyār (Breebart, *Turkish Futuwah*, pp. 15, 25).

significance in the futūwa of Nishapur, the existing sources of information, emanating as they do from the patriciate, scarcely reflect it.

Getting down to the evidence, which is not abundant, concerning the futūwa in Nishapur, two of the earliest known works on the subject of futūwa were written by Nishapuris. One is the *Kitāb al-Futūwa* of Abū ʿAbd ar-Raḥmān as-Sulamī, the other a chapter on the subject in the well-known *Risāla al-Qushairiya* by Abū al-Qāsim al-Qushairī. Both of these men, as mentioned before, were Shāfiʿīs, Ashʿarīs, and Sufis. The latter, moreover, had a direct disciple who was a fatā[31] and a grandson, who was also a great-grandson of the Ashʿarī theologian Ibn Fūrak, who was a fatā "according to the Ashʿarī doctrine" (*ʿalā madhhab al-Ashʿarī*).[32]

Further, the primary agent of Niẓām al-Mulk's pro-Ashʿarī and pro-Shāfiʿī policy in Nishapur, Abū ʿAlī Ḥassān al-Manīʿī, was a man whose rise to prominence in his hometown of Marv ar-Rud was due to the prestige of his dihqān family and his own leadership of the local futūwa.[33] And again there was a member of the Basṭāmī family, hereditary leaders of the Shāfiʿī party, who held the post of *raʾīs* in the town of Isfarāʾin and was a member of the futūwa, although without going along with their asceticism and special customs.[34]

References to the futūwa in Nishapur do not stop with these; other fityān with either dihqān or Sufi connections are known. But these are the most suggestive and important occurrences. Even without the reference to futūwa "according to the Ashʿarī doctrine" the close connection between this institutionalized ideal of young manhood and the Shāfiʿī-Ashʿarī-Sufi nexus already described would be inescapable. Never does a term relating to the futūwa appear in a Ḥanafī biography, even when the biography speaks of military training. What the fityān actually did and what relation they may have had with the common people cannot be determined; but their party affiliation is certain, and it is Shāfiʿī.

In summary, the conflicts that wracked Nishapur for some two centuries and contributed in no small way to its destruction and death as a great city were basically between two political parties, the Ḥanafīs and the Shāfiʿīs. Both were patrician in outlook, though doubtless enjoying support among the less privileged strata of the

31. Fārisī II, f82a.
32. See chapter 11 and Qushairī genealogical key #34.
33. Fārisī I, f15a–17b.
34. See chapter 9 and Basṭāmī genealogical key #22.

population, and both were adamantly opposed to the true lower class movement of the Karrāmiya. What each wanted, it appears, was complete political power within the city, but the true ends of the political struggle were broader than this. The gaining of power was only a step toward their realization; the wielding of power was the realization. Neither party acted as the agent of a greater political power. What each strove for was local supremacy for the purpose of molding the city in a particular image.

For the Ḥanafīs that image was an old one. Old values of order and rationalism were breaking down and required restatement and revival. If possible, the apparent proponents of moral decay, the Ashᶜarī-Sufi clique that guided the Shāfiᶜī party, must be driven out or discredited. Failing that, the old values must be upheld in every way possible and the new ones confronted head-on. For the Shāfiᶜīs, the image was a new one, and ultimately a victorious one. In an increasingly troubled world, it looked to mystic withdrawal, fraternal solidarity, and unquestioning faith in the bases of religion. These were images worth fighting over, for they involved entirely different notions as to what direction the social and moral evolution of Nishapur, considered as an entity in itself and not as a part of a much greater society, should take. They did not prescribe, however, different ways of ordering that society. Ḥanafī and Shāfiᶜī alike believed that the patriciate was one with the city and its rightful and natural leader.

Thus the patriciate was one despite its profound political cleavage. A person born into a Ḥanafī family would grow up in conformance to Ḥanafī ideals, marry the daughter of a fellow Ḥanafī and, if necessary, fight for the Ḥanafī party against the wicked Shāfiᶜīs. But if a matter arose affecting the common interest of the patriciate, whether the matter was clubbing the riff-raff of the Karrāmiya in the streets or determining upon defense or surrender of the city before an approaching invader, he would join with his fellow patricians, Ḥanafī and Shāfiᶜī alike, to put up a solid front.

For the same reason, moreover, that the common interest of the patriciate, regardless of party, was involved, when that Ḥanafī went to school, he went in company with the Shāfiᶜīs he would one day grow up to oppose. As powerful as the political differences between Ḥanafī and Shāfiᶜī were, they did not call into being a dual educational system; and it is to this seeming anomaly that attention must now be turned.

4 / *The Education of a Patrician*

It was not the ability to quote Ciceronian tags or to parse Horace that instilled in generations of Englishmen the confidence that they could run a government office or prescribe for the "civilizing" of a subject people. Rather, it was the high birth and social status and the nexus of friendships and family connections that were implied by a command of Latin grammar and literature. Nor was the English educational system unique in playing a more important role in certifying a person's status than in informing his mind for useful work; the American educational system of today, in which a B.A. degree is increasingly required for profitable employment, is another example. But compared to either of these, the educational system of medieval Islam stands out as a monumental example of social status being outwardly defined by possession of a more or less arbitrary body of knowledge. Medieval Islamic education imparted, in and of itself, little social status. Instead, a proper education was symbolic of good breeding and wealth and was acquired in such a way as to provide the social contacts necessary for a successful career.

This being said, the thorny question that must be faced is how. How did an apparently unrestricted system function in a discriminatory fashion? How did the nature of the education imparted affect the patriciate and the overall role of the educational system in the society? In answering these questions, we will have to make a deeper examination of the history of medieval Muslim education than might appear immediately germane to the subject of Nishapur's patriciate, but the confusion that presently exists on the subject of Islamic educational history leaves no other course.

Most discussions of Islamic education are dominated, one way or another, by the riddle of the *madrasa*. The apparently sudden appearance of this educational institution in Baghdad in the mid-eleventh/fifth century and its subsequent rapid spread to the rest of the Islamic world, all in connection with the portentous name of the Seljuq vizier Niẓām al-Mulk, has quite justifiably excited the curiosity of numerous scholars. What kind of institution was the madrasa? Where did it come from? What part did it play in the grand political designs of Niẓām al-Mulk?

Some of these and related questions have been answered; some have not.[1] Not all

1. The madrasa question has been debated in almost every work on Muslim education. The most recent chapter in the controversy has been written by George Makdisi, "Muslim Institutions of Learning in Eleventh-Century Baghdad," *Bulletin of the School of Oriental and African Studies*, 24

of the answers proposed will stand up under careful scrutiny. Most popular, and least substantiable, of the theories advanced is that the madrasa was a kind of Sunni college designed to produce "orthodox" bureaucrats for a Seljuq crusade against Shiᶜism, dubbed "The Sunni Revival." More sober examination of the relevant sources has established that in Baghdad, at least, the madrasa was first and foremost a college of Islamic law and not in any sense an organ of government. But whatever the answer or theory put forward, preoccupation with madrasa-related questions has served to distort the history of Islamic education in general.

Since the madrasa is commonly viewed as a homogeneous institution and hence a plurality of madrasas as a homogeneous system, the comparative heterogeneity of the educational institutions antedating or coexisting with the madrasa has been interpreted to mean that aside from the madrasa there was no system to education. As one author has put it: "The Muslim system of advanced studies in the pre-madrasa period was remarkable in many ways. Firstly, it was not organized."[2] Naturally, if this is true, then the introduction of the madrasa was truly the turning point in Muslim educational history, for it meant the bringing of order out of chaos. But there are two reasons for believing that such was not the case. There is the common sense reason that medieval Islamic civilization would thus be unique in world history in reaching its greatest peak of scholarship and literary production, both qualitative and quantitative, in a random and haphazard fashion. And then there is the objective reason that ample data exists to prove that systematized education existed long before the madrasa made its appearance in Baghdad.

To be sure, no network or hierarchy of specialized places of learning can be pointed to. A teacher could teach in a mosque or in his home, in a shop or by the riverside. He could even teach in a madrasa, an institution which appeared in Nishapur two centuries or more before Niẓām al-Mulk did and which served a variety of educational purposes.[3] Nor was there any notable systematization in the curriculum. Neither matriculation nor graduation interfered with the students' search for learning. Age restrictions and required courses were similarly absent. Travel for purposes of study was regularly indulged in, but the routes traversed varied greatly with the individual.

(1961), 1–56; and A. L. Tibawi, "Origin and Character of *al-madrasah*," *Bulletin of the School of Oriental and African Studies*, 25 (1962), 225–238.

2. Munir-ud-Din Ahmed, *Muslim Education and the Scholars' Social Status . . .* (Zurich, 1968), p. 52.

3. See appendix I.

It was teaching rather than learning that was the object of systematization. Islamic society, like some other largely illiterate societies, revered the spoken more than the written word. In the legal system, the emphasis upon oral testimony and evidence with the concomitant development of a body of certified public witnesses (*ʿādil* or *shāhid*) in each city bespeaks this reverence. In education, oral transmission of knowledge, not just of Prophetic traditions (ḥadīth), from generation to generation with the concomitant elaboration of chains of authority (*isnād*) and rules for criticizing such chains is evidence of the same feeling. Although serious students normally wrote down what they heard recited and most teachers taught from written texts, still independent study of a written text was not the equivalent of hearing the same text recited by one who had heard it recited by a predecessor and so on back to the original author of the work. For example, the *Ṣaḥīḥ* of Bukhārī, one of the most authoritative ḥadīth collections, was well known in Nishapur in the fourth/tenth century; but those students who aspired to teach it themselves travelled some two hundred miles to the town of Kushmaihan near Marv where there was a man who recited the text from a copy made from a copy made from Bukhārī's own dictation. Unquestionably, this sort of practice served to some degree to minimize the textual corruptions that inevitably cropped up when a work was copied by hand through several generations; but it also meant that a student reading al-Kushmaihanī's autograph text would not be credited with having as reliable a source as a student hearing read a copy of the text made at al-Kushmaihanī's dictation by one of his students.[4]

This does not necessarily mean that a scholar's notes and written works perished with him. In Nishapur they were frequently bequeathed to a library, and one library in particular was endowed for the purpose of preserving such works.[5] Furthermore, they were consulted once they had been deposited in a library. The biographical dictionaries that have made this present book possible were compiled by examining and collating these written remains. It was only as sources for teaching that they became devalued.

Although this seemingly peculiar restriction on the transmittal of the Islamic learned tradition is manifest in the biographical literature, how it worked out in the day to day educational process is not. Biographical literature was written by and for the patriciate,

4. For a biography of al-Kushmaihanī, see Samʿānī, f484a.

5. Two successive custodians of this library in the Baihaqī madrasa are known, Abū Ṣāliḥ Aḥmad al-Muʾadhdhin (Fārisī II, f31a–32a) and his son-in-law Abū al-Qāsim Salmān al-Anṣārī (Fārisī I, f29b–30a).

to whom, since education was one of its defining characteristics, the process of education was too familiar to require being spelled out in detail. Numerous technical phrases clearly related to the educational system recur repeatedly but are nowhere specifically defined. This means that an understanding of the system must depend at several crucial points upon technical definitions that have been deduced from contexts which are seldom unambiguous.

With this cautionary note, a description of the systematization of teaching, as it existed in Nishapur at least, may be attempted. The central concern of the system was certification of teachers. Since teaching was often undertaken as a religious duty without stipend and was not restricted to any particular type of building, the kind of certification inherent in modern educational systems could not exist. Teaching was not a "job"; there was no employer. Whatever the certifying authority, it had to be able to regulate even the teaching a man did without remuneration in his own home. That is, it had to be an authority whose ultimate sanction was of a moral or ethical rather than financial or institutional nature.

At bottom, that certifying authority was the collective will of the learned patricians, but it was an authority that made itself felt in practice through a number of procedures and offices. A person wishing to teach in a specific institution would have to present his credentials to the director of the institution or to an official whose specific function was to examine teachers' qualifications. The credentials presented to this official or to the director may in some instances have taken the form of a text taken down from dictation and certified in writing by the teacher to be genuine and accurate. Such a written certification was known as an *ijāza*, and it eventually became commonplace in Islamic education along with such abuses as bought ijāzas and ijāzas secured for children too young to have gotten them themselves.[6] But in the tenth/fourth and eleventh/fifth centuries the practice seems not to have been widespread.[7] What a man had in his memory counted for more than what he had on paper, even if he had to refresh his

6. For examples of men procuring ijāzas for their children see Fārisī II, f99b, f107b (the latter reference is not contained in the published text; see fig. 1, this volume).

7. There is an interesting story of a man from Nishapur who went to another city and made himself out to be the son of Abū ᶜAbd Allāh Ismāᶜīl al-Fārisī (see chapter 11 and Qushairī genealogical key #50). This enhanced the value of his teaching. His deception was eventually discovered, however, by visitors to Nishapur who asked the historian al-Fārisī, the real son of Abū ᶜAbd Allāh Ismāᶜīl, about his brother. Clearly, if the impostor had been certified to teach on the basis of a written ijāza, he would have been unable to assume a false name, for the *ijāza* would have contained his real name. Therefore, the certification he underwent must have been oral. Fārisī I, f25a–b; II, f69a–b.

memory continually by reference to his notes. The examination he took was an oral inquisition and is apparently signified by the words "so-and-so examined him (*kharraja lahu*) on his points of learning (*al-fawāʾid*)," or "on such-and-such book." Having passed this test, the candidate would be considered "approved" (*qubūl*), whence comes the title "Master of Approval" (*ṣāḥib al-qubūl*) sometimes borne by the official charged with administering the examination, and a class (*majlis*) would be "convened for him" (*ᶜuqida lahu*).[8]

This general pattern applied to teaching outside of specific institutions, as well. A man had to be examined and approved before he could teach, even if he taught in his own home.[9] The certifying authority in these noninstitutional cases was more conspicuously the collective authority of the city's shaikhs; on a number of occasions the familiar passive construction "a class was convened for him" is replaced by "the shaikhs convened a class for him"[10] just as the head of an institution is occasionally quoted as saying "I convened a class for him."[11] Who exactly was authorized to conduct an examination in the city at large, as opposed to in a specific institution, is hard to pin down. In a smaller town such as Isfarāʾin, there could be one office of Master of Approval for the whole town,[12] but a single office would obviously have been out of the question for a city the size of Nishapur. A specific title pertaining to a class of officials charged with this duty is not in evidence in Nishapur although the responsibility was probably divided among a large number of shaikhs. The title of the person situated at the pinnacle of the system is known, however. He was the Shaikh al-Islām.[13]

8. All of these terms occur in a variety of contexts, and their meaning is sometimes far from clear. Distinguishing between technical and nontechnical usages can be particularly difficult. The word *qubūl*, for example, is used frequently for any sort of social approval or acceptance. *ᶜUqida lahu* can be used for convening sessions for preaching and legal disputation, as well as for ḥadīth classes. It is only rarely used for convening a law class (IAW, II, p. 117). There is also an instance of its use to describe the appointment to office of a raʾīs (Ḥamza as-Sahmī, *Taʾrīkh Jurjān* [Hyderabad, 1950], p. 186). *Kharraja lahu al-fawāʾid* occurs in no less debatable contexts. In one example, the text reads "his nephew examined him on his *fawāʾid* and read them to his children" (Fārisī II, f93a). What the last clause means is not at all clear.

9. For an example of this see Fārisī II, f88a.

10. Fārisī II, f88a.

11. Al-Ḥākim convened classes personally for people in the Dār as-Sunna madrasa. Samᶜānī, II, 105; V, 125.

12. Fārisī II, f132b.

13. Known holders of the office of Shaikh al-Islām in Nishapur with the dates of their tenure: (1) ?–449, Abū ᶜUthmān Ismāᶜīl aṣ-Ṣābūnī (Ṣābūnī genealogical key #1); (2) ca. 451–463, Abū ᶜAlī Ḥassān al-Manīᶜī (Fārisī I, f15a–17b; Subkī, IV, 299–302); (3) ca. 465–482, Abū Naṣr Aḥmad

The office of Shaikh al-Islām appeared in the tenth/fourth century in Khurasan[14] and, like the madrasa, was transmitted to the western Islamic countries only a century or two later, by which time it had undergone a transformation which caused some scholars of western origin to misunderstand it when they came upon it in earlier eastern sources. Subkī, in particular, goes astray by assuming that it was the personal honorific title of one man, Abū ᶜUthmān Ismāᶜīl aṣ-Ṣābūnī,[15] holder of the office in Nishapur until his death in 1057/449, and that it was unjustly and scandalously usurped by the Ḥanbalī Abū Ismāᶜīl ᶜAbd Allāh al-Anṣārī of Herat, who died in 1088/481.[16] Consequently, the exact function of the office of Shaikh al-Islām is as difficult to discern as the various other elements of the educational system.

Two of the most explicit statements of the functions of the Shaikh al-Islām come in connection with the holders of the office mentioned above. In his biography of Abū Ismāᶜīl ᶜAbd Allāh al-Anṣārī, al-Fārisī calls him "Shaikh al-Islām in Herat and Master of Approval (Ṣāḥib al-Qubūl) in his time" and goes on to praise him for, among other things, "the ordering of madrasas, teachers (*aṣḥāb*), convents, and the holding (*nuwab* pl. of *nauba*) of classes."[17] Furthermore, he says that "he examined himself (*kharraja li-nafsihi*) on his points of knowledge,"[18] an exceedingly rare locution that makes sense only if he was at the top of the accrediting system and hence beyond being examined by anyone else.

Abū ᶜUthmān Ismāᶜīl aṣ-Ṣābūnī is quoted as saying, "I never recited an account or tradition in class unless I knew it's *isnād* or entered the library without purifying myself [by ritual ablutions]. Nor did I ever recite ḥadīth or convene a class or sit down to teach law without being ritually clean."[19] The convening of a class appears in this quotation to be a process quite distinct from teaching a class oneself and would seem to relate to

---

aṣ-Ṣāᶜidī (Ṣāᶜidī genealogical key #24); (4) 482–527, Abū Saᶜīd Muḥammad aṣ-Ṣāᶜidī (Ṣāᶜidī genealogical key #38); (5) died 551, Abū al-Maᶜālī al-Ḥasan b. ar-Razzāz (I. Athīr, XI, 216).

14. Aṣ-Ṣābūnī and al-Jārūdī mentioned below seem to have been the first to bear the title in Nishapur and Herat respectively. The first in Balkh was Abū al-Qāsim Yūnus an-Naḍrī al-Khīwī who died in 1020/411 (Samᶜānī V, 265; *Faḍāʾil Balkh*, ms. Bibliothèque Nationale, Persian 115, f194b–195a).

15. See chapter 10 and Ṣābūnī genealogical key #1.

16. Subkī, IV, 271–272.

17. Fārisī I, f33b; II, f82b. The texts differ slightly.

18. Fārisī II, f82b.

19. Fārisī II, f38a–b.

his role as Shaikh al-Islām. This special sense of the word "convene" is corroborated by the statement that aṣ-Ṣābūnī's brother, "acted as deputy for the Shaikh al-Islām in convening sessions for preaching (*tadhkīr*) on those occasions when he was prevented from doing so himself by illness or travel."[20] Furthermore, his son Abū Bakr ᶜAbd ar-Raḥmān aṣ-Ṣābūnī, who never held the post, for understandable reasons, is described as his father's successor "in instituting (*nauba*) classes, approval (*qubūl*), and attendance of assemblies."[21]

A third source of enlightenment on the functions of the office is, oddly enough considering its author's ignorance of the office, Subkī's biography of al-Anṣārī's predecessor as Shaikh al-Islām in Herat, Abū al-Faḍl Muḥammad al-Jārūdī. Subkī quotes an anonymous source as saying that "he was the first to establish in Herat the custom of examining credentials (*takhrīj al-fawāʾid*) and investigating (*sharḥ*) and certifying (*taṣḥiḥ*) men."[22] Evidently the practice was known elsewhere before al-Jārūdī, who died in 1022/413, brought it to Herat, but it had undoubtedly been in the process of evolving for some time. Thus, the same constellation of words and phrases appears in connection with al-Anṣārī, aṣ-Ṣābūnī, and al-Jārūdī, and the image takes form of the Shaikh al-Islām as the individual ultimately responsible for the certification of teachers and the convening of classes in a given locality.

Unfortunately, there is too little evidence currently available to flesh out the portrait and show how this ultimate responsibility was delegated or asserted throughout a large city. It is possible that one intermediary figure between the Shaikh al-Islām and the accrediting official in a particular institution was the head (raʾīs) of each separate law school charged with regulating the teaching of his particular legal doctrine throughout the city. Presumably, appointments to subordinate offices of this kind were either made or confirmed by the Shaikh al-Islām in the same way that subordinate posts in the judicial system were under the jurisdiction of the chief qāḍī. The implication of such an educational set up, of course, is that a Shaikh al-Islām belonging to the Shāfiᶜī madhhab, such as aṣ-Ṣābūnī, might have had final jurisdiction over the certification of Ḥanafī teachers. In view of the bitter conflict between the Ḥanafīs and the Shāfiᶜīs, this might seem like an unlikely possibility. It must always be borne in mind, however, that

20. Fārisī II, f46b.
21. Fārisī I, f44b.
22. Subkī, IV, 115–116. The fact that al-Jārūdī held the office of Shaikh al-Islām is conveyed in ᶜIbar, III, 114.

the words Ḥanafī and Shāfiᶜī stand for political parties as well as law schools and that a Shāfiᶜī might be disliked by the Ḥanafīs for his political ideas and affiliations and yet greatly respected for his scholarship, intelligence, and probity in legal and educational matters. Otherwise, it seems inconceivable that the Shāfiᶜīs could have tolerated for so long the Ḥanafī grip on the office of chief qāḍī. In actual practice, they must have known that the incumbent could be depended upon to be just. In one instance, the Ḥanafī holder of the office was actually chosen by a prominent Shāfiᶜī.[23] This clear separation between law and scholarship on the one hand and politics on the other must also be invoked to explain the apparent respect accorded to various Karrāmī leaders in their capacity as scholars.[24] Education was simply too important to the continued existence of the patriciate to become an object of political wrangling.

The educational system of medieval Nishapur, then, was a system of teachers. Where a man taught was beside the point. Madrasa or mosque, home or store, the quality of the education depended upon the teacher, not the place. Whom a man taught was equally irrelevant. Although the use of Arabic as the language of instruction in this Persian speaking locale was a powerful practical limitation upon the potential student body, it was not an institutionalized one. Aside from such relatively restricted subjects as medicine and belles lettres (*adab*), which were probably not comprehended in the system described above at all, all instruction was ultimately religious and not to be refused to any Muslim desirous and capable of receiving it. Again, what a man taught was not closely regulated. A man taught what he knew, and it was upon that that he was examined for permission to teach. Occasionally, a man was certified to teach only one book. Missing, in comparison with other educational systems, is a clear division of learning into disciplines. Different subjects existed within flexible bounds, but the discipline was essentially unitary: oral transmission of knowledge through chains of authority.

The point of control in the system was the determination of who was to get to teach. The certifying apparatus previously outlined, though only dimly perceptible in sources written by men who were too enmeshed in the system ever to describe it, was the very heart of Islamic education of that time. The *ᶜulamāᵓ*, that is to say, those patricians whose careers were devoted to learning, acted through the certifying apparatus headed by the Shaikh al-Islām to preserve the integrity of the oral tradition. In the field of law, the

23. See Appendix II, #13.

24. Al-Fārisī is very moderate in his biographies of Karrāmīs. He gives ample evidence that there was no bar to their attending classes taught by Shāfiᶜīs and Ḥanafīs (Fārisī II, f29a, 45b, 55a, 144b).

other patrician speciality, the concept of ijmāᶜ, or the concensus of those learned in the law, is a direct analogy. What counted for certification was the chain of oral authority. A boor or narcotics addict who had it might teach;[25] an upstanding merchant who did not could not.

In many ways this system of education is very attractive. It emphasizes the essential core of education—knowledge—and it ignores irrelevancies such as age, sex, and test scores, which have barred and continue to bar so many in Western society from the joys and fruits of education. The premise that learning was for whomever wanted it is undeniably attractive, and such sights as the teacher of one class sitting as a student in another or an eight year old child partaking of the same lore as an eighty year old man are lamentably absent from the modern educational scene. But the ultimately petrifying impact on society of a concept of knowledge rooted in oral authority does not seem enviable to a society which no longer esteems petrifaction in education.

Whatever the merits or demerits of the medieval Muslim educational system in its theoretical form, however, it is the practical operation of the system that is of importance here. Despite its theoretical democracy, the system actually served to buttress and maintain the exclusiveness of the patriciate. It is the way it did this that now must be examined.

To begin with, there is an obvious and often exampled equation between permission to teach and social status. Many, many learned men visited Nishapur during the period under consideration; their biographies are often preserved in the city's biographical dictionaries. Only the most important of visitors, however, had classes convened for them, no matter how short their stay, as a mark of honor. One day in 1015/406 an embassy from the Ziyārid ruler Manūchihr b. Qābūs to Maḥmūd of Ghazna came to Nishapur. It stayed for only one day, but that was time enough for each of the three members of it to give a class in ḥadīth with the shaikhs of Nishapur in attendance. First the raʾīs of Jurjan recited, then the *khaṭīb*, who seems to have acted as Shaikh al-Islām there without the title, and finally the prominent scholar and historian of Jurjan, Abū al-Qāsim Ḥamza as-Sahmī. The fact that all three classes were squeezed into one day and that they were ordered by the official status of the teacher clearly indicates the intent of the patricians of Nishapur to honor the visitors.[26] A similar display had been put on six years earlier for an ambassador to Maḥmūd from the Khwārizmshāh.[27]

25. For the patrician narcotics addict see Fārisī II, f31a; for the boor see Fārisī I, f6b.
26. Fārisī I, f12b–13a; II, f3a; as-Sahmī, *Taʾrīkh Jurjān*, pp. 411, 413.
27. Fārisī II, f24b.

That visiting dignitaries had classes convened in their honor does not signify, however, that birth or position alone was sufficient certification to teach. This might seem to be the case from the dozen or so instances in which an individual is said to have "convened a class for himself" (*ᶜuqida li-nafsihi majlis*).[28] Although in most of these cases the individual involved is, in fact, a member of one of the important patrician families, the usual import of the phrase is not that he bypassed the accreditation system but that he convened a class for himself in a specific mosque or madrasa for which he was personally the certifying authority. In at least two cases, the person involved convened the class for himself in a smaller town for which he was the overall certifying authority, equivalent to the Shaikh al-Islām in a large city, as is indicated by the notation in those cases that he also "examined himself" (*kharraja li-nafsihi al-fawāʾid*).[29] Those individuals who convened classes for themselves in Nishapur did not also "examine themselves."

But if high patrician birth alone did not enable a man to teach—and had it done so, the quality of education would surely have plummeted—neither was a good education sufficient either. The way in which the certification of teachers served to maintain the exclusiveness of the patriciate was in denying the honor and privilege of teaching to people of low birth. The common folk, if they had the time, could learn all they wanted; but the honor of teaching, as well as such perquisites as endowed teaching positions and the possibility of marrying the daughter of a genuine patrician scholar, would still be denied them. The social mobility theoretically inherent in the educational system did not exist in practice.

The most obvious proof that this was the case lies in the fact that all teachers were patricians.[30] They were patricians not by educational qualifications but by family background and inherited status. A clear statement that commoners were excluded is not necessary to demonstrate that they were, in fact, excluded. The exception that proves the rule, to use a saw that is not without meaning in the study of

28. For examples see Fārisī I, f11b–12a; II, f59a. Fārisī I, f12a–b; II, f59b; I. Funduq, pp. 235–236. Fārisī I, f44b; II, f92a. Fārisī I, f87b, 83a; II, f75a. Fārisī I, f67a; II, f113b–114a. Fārisī II, f114b. Fārisī II, 122a. Fārisī I, f52a–b; II, f98a–b. Fārisī II, f33a–34b.

29. Fārisī I, f28b–29b; II, f71b. Fārisī I, f92a; II, f136b.

30. Some two hundred teachers who taught more than one known student can be identified, and all of them are patricians. Excluding teachers from other cities, over half of the teachers can be placed on family trees and the status of their entire family ascertained.

history, is Abū Sahl Muḥammad al-Ḥafṣī.[31] He studied the *Ṣaḥīḥ* of Bukhārī under al-Kushmaihanī who studied it under Muḥammad b. Yūsuf al-Farbarī who studied it under Bukhārī himself. Seventy-five years after the death of his master al-Kushmaihanī, Abū Sahl Muḥammad al-Ḥafṣī found himself, not too surprisingly, to be the only man still alive who had studied under him. Because of the principle that oral transmission of knowledge was the only truly valid transmission, al-Ḥafṣī thus became an irreplaceable source of learning. He was brought to Nishapur from Marv and honored personally by Niẓām al-Mulk. Then in the Niẓāmiya madrasa he gave a class in which he dictated the *Ṣaḥīḥ* to a great crowd including the young patrician children who would then be able to say in later life that they had studied under a student of al-Kushmaihanī.

The interesting note in his biography, however, is that "he was from the ranks of the common people (*al-ᶜawāmm*); nevertheless, his learning was sound." A commoner becoming a teacher, which happened in this case because of extraordinary circumstances, was therefore a rare enough phenomenon to call for special, almost astonished, mention. But besides demonstrating the uncommonness of upward social mobility via education, the story of al-Ḥafṣi also underlines the fact that there was no barrier to a commoner attending and being a legitimate student in a class.[32]

If education did not afford a means of scaling the social ladder, the exclusiveness of the teaching profession did serve to confirm an ascent made in some other way. Successful merchant families did succeed in entering the patriciate. They bought land, contrived to become certified public witnesses, and married their children to patrician children. But it was not an easy climb, and it normally took several generations. One of the last barriers to overcome was the exclusiveness of the teaching profession. Yet it, too, could be surmounted by money, as in the case of a money-changer, himself not included in any biographical dictionary, who lavished money upon the famous scholar al-Aṣamm in return for which his son received special attention among the myriad of al-Aṣamm's students. The upshot was that his son became a teacher and a patrician despite the fact that he later lost his notes and was severely limited in what he could teach.[33]

31. Fārisī II, f15a.

32. There is a counter-example, but one that is difficult to interpret, in the case of a patrician who stole teaching notes and used them for educating "the sons of the people" (*awlād an-nās*). Perhaps he used them specifically to coach commoners to become teachers. Fārisī II, f85a.

33. Fārisī II, f4a; ᶜIbar, III, 144.

Whether money always played a part or not, the procedure which gained for one the privilege of even having one's credentials examined appears to have been one of sponsorship. The offspring of established patrician families would naturally require no special sponsorship, but the well-educated son of a wealthy merchant, for example, would be "chosen" (*muntakhab*) by an established scholar and thus sponsored for certification.[34] By this means, the ordered co-optation of the most enterprising and successful commoners into the ranks of the patriciate was assured without either tainting the certification proceedings per se with considerations of status or risking inundation by a mass of educated plebeians.

Thus there was a system of Muslim education aside from, or rather, denying any special place to the institution of the madrasa. It was a system that was intimately related to the structure of the patriciate. Theoretically, and in some ways practically, democratic, it was nevertheless a system that turned in its one controlled dimension upon considerations of birth and position. Commoners found in it elucidation of the religion which informed a greater or lesser part of their lives; patricians found in it a source of honor and prestige which were readily convertible into more worldly benefits.

Yet the description of the system that has been advanced here suffers from two major shortcomings above and beyond the many difficulties inherent in attempting to deduce a system from a tangle of imperfectly understood technical terms. The first defect is that the description is at once too simple and too rigid. The inbred, exclusive character of the patriciate meant that even in a large city most patricians knew personally or knew about most other patricians. The very concept of a biographical dictionary encompassing the entire class testifies to this. Consequently, it must be assumed that many events that would here be defined or categorized according to an almost mechanical system were in actuality informal or only loosely formalized interpersonal actions. "Sponsorship," "examination," "certification," "convening a class": these are broad terms, suggested by textual locutions, that in all probability encompass a range of definitions from formal ceremonies to tacit understandings. Flexibility and variety undoubtedly

34. The word *intikhāb* is almost always ambiguous in educational contexts since it also means making a selection of a teacher's ḥadīth. When it is used in connection with the phrase *kharraja lahu al-fawāʾid*, however, it seems to refer to nomination of a person to sit for examination. Examples of this context may be found in Fārisī II, f24b–f25a, 88a. The latter example is particularly interesting. It reads: "Abū ᶜAmr al-Baḥīrī and ᶜAbd ar-Raḥmān al-ᶜAmmārī nominated him, and Aḥmad b. ᶜAlī al-ᶜAwwālī examined him on the ḥadīth collections on the stipulation of the two shaikhs. The shaikhs [pl.] urged him to teach and eventually they convened a class for him in his house."

existed in the day to day operations of the system, and allowance must be made accordingly.

The second defect in the description of the system is that it is static. One suspects that the patricians of Nishapur themselves would not object to this; adherence to tradition was to them the hallmark of a proper educational system. Nevertheless, the madrasa did eventually work a change in Islamic education, and the patrician class in the Islamic world suffered sorely from the Mongol invasions and the political convulsions preceding and following them. Likewise, the system was not always there. At some early point education doubtless was more democratic and entrance into the patriciate by this route more a reality. But the evolution of the system is beyond reconstruction from exclusively Nishapuri materials. The destruction of the city in the mid-twelfth/sixth century cut short its later educational development, and during the period of early evolution Nishapur was a small outpost rather than a major educational center. All that can be spoken of with regard to the evolution of the system in Nishapur during the tenth/fourth and eleventh/fifth centuries is the increasing role of government officials in the patronage of education, and this will be discussed in the next chapter.

The impact of education on the patriciate was felt in other ways besides the concrete organization of the system. The first question posed at the start of this chapter, how an apparently unrestricted system functioned in a discriminatory fashion, has been adequately elucidated. The other, how the nature of the education imparted affected the patriciate and the social role of the educational system itself, has yet to be dealt with; but the foregoing discussion provides a sound basis for doing so.

Just as the principle of oral transmission of knowledge strongly influenced the organization of education, so it did the social structure and role of the patriciate. It put an emphasis upon men rather than upon the works of men. Honor inhered in the act of teaching rather than in scholarly contributions to knowledge. Indeed, to "contribute" to a ḥadīth was impious. It also put an emphasis upon precocious study and longevity. Most patrician children seem to have begun to hear ḥadīth at the age of eight or less, and ages as low as three are not unheard of. In most cases, they probably failed to comprehend the Arabic in which the lesson was given and were unable to write down the words. However, they still might fix enough of it in their memory to give them at least a claim in later life to being a disciple of a long dead master. The aforementioned al-Ḥafṣī surely must have been a child when he heard the *Ṣaḥīḥ* of Bukhārī from al-Kushmaihanī, for he taught it on his authority seventy-five years after the master's death. The most important educational link was between the child and the old man, for it was the only way to secure a shorter, and therefore more prestigious, chain of authority. As a result, both child and graybeard enjoyed enhanced status, the child because he might bear a "high" chain of authority and the old man because he might be the last link with a bygone, but still revered, generation. The feeling that the patriciate was a single organism continuing from generation to generation was in this way greatly emphasized.

There was no place in this educational system for factional violence between Ḥanafī and Shāfiʿī. Education transcended factional conflict in the same way that a foreign invasion or a Karrāmī uprising did. It involved the entire patriciate; their continued enjoyment of upper class perquisites depended to a large degree upon it. The patriciate stood to lose all if internal rivalries made them blind to their collective interest in times of crisis, and it stood to lose no less if the principles and forms of the educational system were allowed to take second place to factional conflict. Consequently, Ḥanafī and Shāfiʿī sat side by side in the same classes as a matter of course, naturally excepting classes in law. The premier teachers with the "highest" chains of authority were few at any given time, and the value of their teaching was as great for the Ḥanafīs as for the Shāfiʿīs. A member of one party could look with pride upon having studied under a member of the other, but that was no bar to fighting them tooth and nail if the occasion arose. Whatever the roots of the patrician factions were, they were not reflected in the structure and operation of the educational system.

5 / *The Patriciate and the State*

Perhaps the most elusive aspect of the patriciate is its relationship with the state. The patricians of Nishapur were politicians without a polity. As has frequently been observed by others, cities in medieval Islamic countries were not constitutionally autonomous corporate entities.[1] They were parts of larger political entities ranging from petty principalities to enormous empires. Somewhere there was a court; and in that court there was a ruler whose power, when observed from a kind of limbo between theory and practice, was absolute.

In theory, rulers, like other Muslims, were subject to Islamic law, and from time to time there occurred well publicized incidents in which a ruler humbly accepted the judgment of a simple qāḍī against him. But even the theory began to dissolve in the eleventh/fifth and twelfth/sixth centuries before the routine violations of law perpetrated by the plethora of princes and power seekers. Political or legal theory did not serve during this period as any kind of meaningful check upon the absolutism of the ruler. He had, in fact, the leeway to do exactly what he wished insofar as his rivals would allow him. In practice, however, absolutist tyranny was not the predominant mode of government, at least in Iran. Absolutist acts were not uncommon, but neither were they the rule.

With the theoretical restraints upon unjust rule vitiated by neglect and too little relevancy to real political life, a question arises as to what were the practical restraints upon tyranny that were, for the most part, effective. A number of answers might be given to this question, such as governing tradition, moral pressure from the religious community, and fear of provoking a rebellion by a subordinate; and each played its part. Other answers that might come to mind had no part to play. Popular military action, for example, was not a real possibility. One of the strongest restraints upon unjust rule, however, was the political power, as opposed to the less tangible and possibly less real moral power, of the local patriciates.

What lent political power to the patriciates was the fact that given the desire on the part of the rulers to preserve the commercial, urban character of Islamic society, the cities were more important to the ruler than the ruler was to the cities.[2] Insofar as an

1. The case against urban autonomy has been most recently restated by S. Stern, "The Constitution of the Islamic City," in *The Islamic City*, Papers on Islamic History, I, ed. S. M. Stern and A. H. Hourani (Oxford, 1970), pp. 25–50.

2. It was the absence of this desire on the part of the Mongols that made their invasion of the Middle East so shattering.

urban patriciate was able to dispose the allegiance of a city according to its own inclination, to deny a city to one ruler and surrender it to another, that patriciate was possessed of tremendous political leverage vis-à-vis the state which ruled it. The patriciate did not govern the city, nor was the city formally autonomous; but the patriciate was capable of acting as if it governed the city and of considering the city as an independent political unit. The evidence for this statement can be seen both in policies adopted by the state with regard to the patriciate and in actions taken by the patriciate with regard to the state.

As has been pointed out earlier, the legal status of the city is not a point of departure as it is in the study of medieval European towns.[3] The city was not subject to the ruler's law nor the ruler to the city's; both were subject to God's law. What is a point of departure is the question of who was empowered to apply God's law. In theory the selection of qāḍīs was the prerogative of the ruler, but in practice it was largely under the control of the patriciate. The circumstances surrounding judicial appointments in Nishapur are rarely reported; but when they are, they tend to reinforce this impression conveyed by the list of appointees.[4]

When the Sāmānids took over Nishapur from the Ṣaffārids in 899/286, they did not appoint a qāḍī of proven loyalty from Bukhara or some other part of their domain. Instead the Sāmānid amir asked Muḥammad b. Isḥāq b. Khuzaima,[5] who was at that time the most prominent Shāfiᶜī in Nishapur, to choose a qāḍī for him. After considering several candidates, all of them apparently Ḥanafīs, Ibn Khuzaima made his choice, and it was approved without question.[6] The importance of staying on the good side of Ibn Khuzaima and of deferring to him in matters of local interest is further underscored by an anecdote in which the Sāmānid amir on his ceremonial first visit to Nishapur commits a grave social faux pas by mistakenly greeting someone else before Ibn Khuzaima.[7]

Later on, the concern shown by the Sāmānids for preserving local good will in the appointment of a qāḍī is reflected in a somewhat different way by the appointments made by Sīmjūrid governors. Whereas the Sāmānids were inclined to support the Ḥanafī faction, the Sīmjūrids, for reasons that were probably as much political as

3. See chapter 2.
4. See Appendix II.
5. Subkī, III, 109–119.
6. IAW, I, 276; II, 55; Samᶜānī, II, 207.
7. Subkī, III, 117.

religious, were patrons of the Shāfiᶜīs, even in territories beyond immediate Sīmjūrid control.[8] Not only did they bring to Nishapur at the behest of the Shāfiᶜīs the famous theologian Ibn Fūrak and establish for him a madrasa,[9] but they made it a point to select a local Shāfiᶜī as qāḍī whenever feasible. Thus, Abū Bakr Aḥmad al-Ḥīrī al-Ḥarashī was almost certainly a Sīmjūrid appointee; and there is even less question that Abū ᶜAmr Muḥammad al-Basṭāmī was.[10] These are the only two Shāfiᶜī qāḍīs in Nishapur from the beginning of the tenth/fourth century to the destruction of the city. The way the Sīmjūrids dealt with the patriciate on the question of the qāḍī-ship, then, was to elevate the recognized leader of the faction they supported into the position. This was certainly not as politic an approach as that taken by the first Sāmānid ruler of the city, but once the office had become a bastion of Ḥanafī strength, it was the best way of assuring their Shāfiᶜī supporters of their good will.

As Sīmjūrid support for the Shāfiᶜīs became more firm and their pretentions to independent power more obvious, the Sāmānids began to see the Ḥanafīs as their best hope for retaining the allegiance of the city. The appointment of Abū al-ᶜAlāᵓ Ṣāᶜid,[11] a singularly able and strong-minded Ḥanafī, to the office of qāḍī was forced upon a Sīmjūrid governor by the Sāmānid ruler in Bukhara even though the man he replaced was also a Ḥanafī. The early Sāmānid policy of letting the patriciate go its own way in return for according political allegiance had given way to a new policy, parallel to that of the Sīmjūrids, of backing one patrician party and hoping that it would promote Sāmānid interests in the city.

The choice of Abū al-ᶜAlāᵓ Ṣāᶜid was a wise one from the Sāmānid point of view. Nishapur did not come out strongly for any of the rebels that began to plague the declining dynasty. When the Sāmānids finally did go down, however, Abū al-ᶜAlāᵓ Ṣāᶜid went with them. Maḥmūd of Ghazna, who came out on top in the struggle to succeed the Sāmānids in Khurasan, was pro-Ḥanafī because his rivals were the pro-Shāfiᶜī Sīmjūrids; but he deposed Abū al-ᶜAlāᵓ nevertheless and replaced him with another Ḥanafī.

Abū al-ᶜAlāᵓ was not to be denied so easily, however, particularly after he had

8. One beneficiary of Sīmjūrid patronage singled out by Ibn al-Athīr (Lubāb, I, 589) is Abū Bakr Muḥammad al-Qaffāl ash-Shāshī, a convert from Muᶜtazilī to Ashᶜarī theological doctrines who led the way in spreading Shāfiᶜī and Ashᶜarī views in Transoxania, well outside Sīmjūrid home territories. For a biography of al-Qaffāl see Subkī, III, 200–222.

9. See chapter 11 and Qushairī genealogical key #28.

10. See chapter 7 and Maḥmī genealogical key #19; chapter 9 and Basṭāmī genealogical key #5.

11. See chapter 13 and Ṣāᶜidī genealogical key #1.

shattered by his determined opposition Maḥmūd's effort to subvert patrician power completely by backing the nonpatrician Karrāmiya.[12] The exact succession of qāḍīs is uncertain, and there is one instance of the patricians electing their own qāḍī, thus arrogating to themselves entirely the ruler's prerogative; but it is quite certain that before Ghaznavid rule in Nishapur had run its course, the family of Abū al-ᶜAlā Ṣāᶜid had regained the office of qāḍī never to relinquish it until the destruction of the city.

Until the rise of the Ṣāᶜidī family, the office of qāḍī, the main point of tangency between the state and the patriciate, had been regarded as a possible tool for the imposition of state authority. But it had always been used with care. No outsider had been thrust upon the patriciate although it was well within the ruler's power to do so.[13] The object of policy had been either to placate the patriciate by leaving the office to be filled by them or to bind one of the patrician parties to the support of the state by favoring it with the appointment. Throughout the Seljuq period, however, no effort was made to influence the patriciate by the manipulation of this office. It was hereditary in the Ṣāᶜidī family, and it seems fairly certain that whoever might have tried to alter the situation would have been faced with such implacable Ḥanafī opposition as to make peaceful government impossible.

No other offices are quite comparable to that of qāḍī. Some offices were entirely within the sphere of the state, namely, those dealing with taxation, the military, the minting of coins, and the postal system.[14] The top echelon of officials in these areas, including the governor, were almost invariably outsiders, frequently Turks, who came, served, and departed without making much lasting impress upon the local society. There were exceptions to this, of course, such as the Sīmjūrid governors who seem to have desired to make Nishapur the capital of an independent principality; but they were few in number. The lower echelons of the purely state bureaucracy were recruited

12. See below.

13. This does not mean that outsiders were never thrust upon local patriciates anywhere. Several members of the Ṣāᶜidī family alone held judicial posts in cities other than Nishapur. However, without a separate examination of the local political situations in cities where such appointments were made, no general conclusions on the subject can be drawn.

14. Of the one chief of the postal service who is given a biography it is remarked that after leaving government service, "he occupied himself with drunkenness, nakedness, and lust" (Fārisī II, f27a–b). Whether an editorial comment upon government officials was intended by the compiler is a matter of conjecture.

from local families with a tradition of such service, but these families were not really a part of the patriciate. Secretarial skills rather than the religious sciences comprised their educational background; and if one of their number chanced to become famous, it usually came about through service in some place other than Nishapur. Intermarriage between patrician families and secretarial families was not impossible nor was there any insuperable barrier keeping a secretary from becoming a religious scholar. However, the patricians and the secretaries embodied two different traditions and two different ways of life, and there can be no question but that within the sphere of local politics and customs, the patrician commanded infinitely greater respect and allegiance than did the secretary. The son of a secretary might rise to become a vizier, but he was never likely to be looked upon as a pillar of society in his home town.

The patriciate, too, had its offices in which the state played no part. The office of Shaikh al-Islām was the exclusive preserve of the patriciate, for educational matters were a vital concern to them and outside both the interest and the competence of the state.[15] Only Niẓām al-Mulk interfered with the office of Shaikh al-Islām by bringing one of his lieutenants, Abū ᶜAlī Ḥassān al-Maniᶜī, from Marv ar-Rud to take over the position in Nishapur.[16] But this was part of Niẓām al-Mulk's extraordinary policy toward the patriciate which went far beyond anything that had been envisioned by his predecessors and which will be discussed in detail below.

This leaves two offices besides that of qāḍī that were the concern both of the state and of the patriciate, the offices of khaṭīb and raᵓīs.[17] The emblems of sovereignty in medieval Islam were coinage and the *khuṭba*. If a ruler's name is on the coins of a given mint in a given year, it means that in that year, either directly or indirectly, he enjoyed sovereign power over that mint. Similarly, if in the sermon (khuṭba) given by the khaṭīb in a congregational mosque at the noon prayer on Friday blessings were invoked upon the name of a ruler, that ruler may be considered to have been the recognized

15. See chapter 4.

16. Fārisī I, f15a–17b; II, f61b–62a. On the Maniᶜī family see ᶜAbbās Iqbāl, "Jāmiᶜ-yi Maniᶜīyi Nīshābūr," *Mihr*, 3 (1936), 1089–94.

17. The office of *muḥtasib* which was of considerable importance in Islamic countries further west seems to have been almost inconsequential in the east. The functional if not literal correspondence between the muḥtasib and the Greek *agoranomos* suggests that the incorporation of the former office into Muslim legal and political theory did not have too great practical effect in previously Sasanian territories. The office of raᵓīs, on the other hand, is uncommon outside of the Iranian area and may be similarly linked to a pre-Islamic Persian office.

sovereign in that community on that particular Friday. Furthermore, anything else the khaṭīb might say in the khuṭba was regarded as an official declaration on the part of the ruler. Accordingly, the khaṭīb was looked upon by the populace, as a figure of great authority, but he was greatly restricted in his disposition of that authority. When the patricians of Nishapur surrendered their city to the Seljuqs, the populace did not really believe it until they heard it from the lips of Abū ᶜUthmān Ismāᶜīl aṣ-Ṣābūnī in the khuṭba days after the surrender had been effected.[18] It is quite evident, however, that if Abū ᶜUthmān had been unwilling to proclaim the change of allegiance from the Ghaznavids to the Seljuqs, he would have been replaced with the full acquiescence of the patriciate by someone who was.[19]

Thus, the office of khaṭīb, for all its prestige and potential for mobilizing public opinion, was not normally a political plum to be fought over. The sovereign's right to have the khuṭba said in his name was uncontested, and the khaṭīb was expected by everyone to be obedient in this respect. At the time of the persecution of the Ashᶜarīs, however, the potential power of the office was realized in a way that it had not been before. The khaṭībs of Khurasan were ordered by the vizier al-Kundurī to anathematize in the khuṭba all believers in the theological doctrines of al-Ashᶜarī. Abū ᶜUthmān Ismāᶜīl aṣ-Ṣābūnī, who was a steadfast Ashᶜarī, resigned to avoid carrying out the order. This left a vacancy that had to be filled, and filling it seems to have proved difficult.[20] What the leaders of the persecution were seeking was not just a dignified official mouthpiece but someone to lead a crusade. When they finally found their man in a rabble-rousing fanatic named ᶜAlī aṣ-Ṣandalī, the persecution was able to move forward with a strong base of popular support.[21] This extraordinary use of the office of khaṭīb was never repeated. By ordering his lieutenant al-Manīᶜī to build a new congregational mosque and turn it over to the Shāfiᶜīs, Niẓām al-Mulk tacitly recognized the right of the khaṭīb to uphold the views of his own patrician party and to confine his state duties to mentioning the name of the ruler.

The functions of the raᵓīs are as intangible as those of the khaṭīb are concrete. A careful sifting of the sources can uncover many examples of what holders of the office

18. See chapter 10 and Ṣābūnī genealogical key #1.

19. In the time of al-Khujistānī (see below) the khaṭīb who had served under several previous regimes was imprisoned. (Samᶜānī, V, 167.)

20. Fārisī I, f28b.

21. See chapter 15 and Ḥasanī genealogical key #11.

did, but its exact nature still escapes definition.[22] In Nishapur, a strange assortment of families filled the office. For most of the tenth/fourth century the Mīkālī family dominated the post.[23] The richest and most powerful family in the area with a lineage reaching back to the pre-Islamic Sasanian emperors, the Mīkālīs were too lofty to be considered patricians in the sense in which the word is being used here. They did not intermarry with any of the patrician families; they did not pursue the religious sciences; they served in various capacities at the court of the ruler; in short, they were a family of aristocratic courtiers.

Another raʾīs, Abū Naṣr Manṣūr b. Rāmish, who held the office twice and was noted, at least during his first term, for his justice and his "protection of the common folk and the poor from tyranny and from the state bureaucrats," was much more clearly a patrician.[24] Both of his sons were Sufis, and one of them taught ḥadīth in the Niẓāmiya madrasa.[25] Even more unquestionably a patrician was Abū Naṣr Aḥmad aṣ-Ṣāᶜidī,[26] grandson of the qāḍī Abū al-ᶜAlāʾ Ṣāᶜid, who became raʾīs during the persecution of the Ashᶜarīs. The Shāfiᶜī raʾīs he supplanted, however, Abū al-Faḍl Aḥmad al-Furātī,[27] seems to have been in a slightly ambiguous position. Although imprisoned as an Ashᶜarī during the persecution, he was attached by marriage to both the Shāfiᶜī Ṣābūnī and Ḥanafī Ṣāᶜidī families. This is most extraordinary for a member of the patriciate. Intermarriage between the factions took place only rarely. Furthermore his religious education was not what it might have been. It is explicitly stated that it was

22. On the office of raʾīs see A. K. S. Lambton, "The Internal Structure of the Seljuq Empire," in *The Cambridge History of Iran* (Cambridge, Eng., 1968), vol. 5, *The Saljuq and Mongol Periods*, ed. J. A. Boyle, pp. 279–280; and Cahen, *Mouvements populaire, passim.*

23. An extensive history of the Mīkālī family has been written by Saᶜīd Nafīsī (Baihaqī, *Tārīkh-i Baihaqī*, ed. Saᶜīd Nafīsī III, 969–1008). However, there are several family members mentioned by al-Fārisī who are not included on Nafīsī's family tree. Their biographical references and their genealogies back to Abū al-ᶜAbbās Ismāᶜīl are as follows: (1) Abū ᶜAbd Allāh Jaᶜfar b. Muḥammad b. ᶜAbd Allāh b. Ismāᶜīl, Fārisī II, f50b; (2) Abū Aḥmad al-Ḥasan b. Muḥammad b. Ismāᶜīl, Fārisī I, f3b; II, f52b; (3) Abū Shujāᶜ al-Muẓaffar b. Muḥammad b. ᶜAlī b. Ismāᶜīl, Fārisī I, f89b; II, f132a; (4) Abū Ibrāhīm Naṣr b. Aḥmad b. ᶜAlī b. Ismāᶜīl, Fārisī I, f92a; II, f136b; (5) Abū ᶜAlī Ṭāhir b. ᶜUbaid Allāh b. Aḥmad b. ᶜAlī b. Ismāᶜīl, Fārisī II, f77a; (6) Abū Manṣūr ᶜAbd Allāh b. Ṭāhir b. ᶜUbaid Allāh b. Aḥmad b. ᶜAlī b. Ismāᶜīl, Fārisī I, f35b; II, f84a. Finally there is a biography of a female member of the family (Fārisī II, f51b) whose place on the family tree is hard to determine.

24. Fārisī I, f79a; II, f128b.

25. Fārisī I, f43a–b, 45a–b; II, f91a, 93b.

26. See chapter 13 and Ṣāᶜidī genealogical key #24.

27. See chapter 10 and Ṣābūnī genealogical key #3.

the dignity of his office that recommended him as a teacher rather than the quality of his learning. Finally, he led the funeral prayers for the leader of the Karrāmiya whose father had held the office of raʾīs under Maḥmūd of Ghazna.[28] This was an honor customarily reserved for a relative (the person in question was survived by a brother and a son) or a close friend, and it seems almost unimaginable that a dyed in the wool patrician could have enjoyed such a close relationship with the leader of the patriciate's most constant enemies. To complete the confusing picture, Abū ᶜAlī Ḥassān al-Manīᶜī, the non-Nishapuri who was planted in the office of Shaikh al-Islām by Niẓām al-Mulk, was also given the office of raʾīs.

All in all, no clear pattern emerges in the office of raʾīs. It was obviously an important office, and various rulers thought of the raʾīs as a possible instrument for executing state policy in the city. But exactly how the raʾīs exerted his influence remains a mystery which is only deepened by the diversity of the individuals known to have held the post. Undoubtedly there was some way in which the raʾīs acted as an intermediary between the state and the patriciate, sometimes being more in tune with the former, as was the case with the Mīkālīs and al-Manīᶜī, and sometimes with the latter, as was the case with Ibn Rāmish and aṣ-Ṣāᶜidī. But the mechanism of his mediation, although it might possibly have been military, defies concrete definition.[29]

However, official appointments were by no means the only way in which the patriciate and the state came into contact. Concrete political actions taken by the patriciate and the state toward each other are less frequently reported than official appointments but are often more indicative of the political relationship between the two.

The earliest and most dramatic recorded action taken by Nishapur's patriciate toward a ruler took place in 880/266–881/267.[30] The Ṭāhirid dynasty, which had ruled Khurasan as a semi-independent governorship under the suzereignty of the ᶜAbbāsid caliph for more than half a century, was at its end, and it was as yet unclear as to which of several pretenders to power would inherit the Ṭāhirid capital of Nishapur. The Ṣaffārids, who were already established in southern Iran, loomed as the most powerful contender and eventually emerged victorious; but both Aḥmad b. ᶜAbd Allāh al-

28. Fārisī II, f29a.

29. Ibn Rāmish is given the title *sālār* which is also borne by one of the figures instrumental in the surrender of the city to the Seljuqs. This was apparently a military title. It is possible that command of some sort of local militia or police was vested in the raʾīs.

30. I. Athīr, VII, 296–301; T. Baghdād, XIV, 217–219; IAW, II, 217; ᶜIbar, II, 36.

Khujistānī, a former lieutenant of the Ṭāhirids, and the Sharkab family were well entrenched in the area before the Ṣaffārids came on the scene.

The complicated three-way fight between the Ṣaffārids, the Sharkabs, and al-Khujistānī provides the backdrop for what happened in Nishapur. Al-Khujistānī was in possession of the city, and for one reason or another he had roused the opposition of the patriciate. The leader of the patrician opposition was Yaḥyā b. Muḥammad b. Yaḥyā adh-Dhuhlī, known as Ḥaikān, a noted scholar in his own right and the son of an equally noted scholar.[31] Ḥaikān favored the Ṣaffārid, ᶜAmr b. al-Laith; but rather than wait for a possible Ṣaffārid victory, he raised the city in a full-scale military revolt against al-Khujistānī. Armed with a wooden sword, he is reported in one source to have passed in review ten thousand troops in his urban militia.

Whatever arguments Ḥaikān had mustered to gain unanimous patrician acquiescence in his revolutionary plans soon began to wear thin, however. Al-Khujistānī knew of the factional rivalry between the Kufan madhhab and the Medinan madhhab that at that time split the patriciate, and he managed to entice the leaders of the Kufan madhhab into opposition to Ḥaikān. As a result, the early success of the revolt was reversed, and its leader was forced into flight. Eventually he was captured and put to death by al-Khujistānī.

Never again did the patricians of Nishapur express their political power in the form of an armed revolt against a ruler, but at times of political crisis they did manage to make their will felt. There are no detailed accounts of patrician reactions to the unrest that marked the decline of the Sāmānid dynasty in the latter part of the tenth/fourth century, but evidence of strong factional support for the various parties has already been presented. When the Ghaznavids were being challenged by the Seljuqs, on the other hand, the patriciate was unanimous in expressing its will.

Nishapur surrendered to the Turks without putting up even token resistance.[32] The leaders of the Hanafī and Shāfiᶜī factions, the *naqīb* or official head of the ᶜAlid family, the khaṭīb, and a person with the title *sālār* who was probably in command of the local troops all concurred, not without reluctance on the part of some, in the surrender. The document sent to the Ghaznavid court reporting the surrender stated that the city was indefensible and observed that Maḥmūd of Ghazna, the reigning sultan's father, had

31. ᶜIbar, II, 17.

32. The surrender account from the *Taʾrīkh-i Baihaqī* is translated by Bosworth, *The Ghaznavids*, pp. 252–257.

never punished a subject for leaving the conduct of a war to the central government; but this was surely disingenuous. A century and a half earlier the patricians had raised an army of 10,000 men in an attempt to assure the accession to power in the city of the ruler of their choice. More pertinently, sixty years after the surrender to the Seljuqs the city successfully withstood a siege of forty days rather than surrender to a Turkish army that was probably no weaker than the original Seljuq force. The conclusion that the surrender of the city to the Seljuqs was a deliberate political action taken by the city's patriciate is inescapable. Ghaznavid rule had profited Nishapur little as the dynasty had become increasingly involved in India, and the memory of Maḥmūd's effort to attack the patriciate by giving power to the Karrāmiya was still warm. The unsophisticated Seljuqs gave promise of being less intrusive in city affairs and more malleable to patrician desires. A change of government was unanimously seen to be a good risk, and action was taken accordingly.

The actions, or more the policies, taken by the state with regard to the patriciate vary greatly but clearly demonstrate a realization on the part of various rulers of both the real and the potential political power of that class. When, previously, appointments to the office of qāḍī were spoken of, two different policies were adumbrated, one a kind of laissez-faire policy adopted at the beginning of Sāmānid rule in Nishapur and the other a divide and conquer policy in which the ruler essentially bought the allegiance of one of the patrician parties. Both of these policies recur from time to time, but of much greater importance for an understanding of the relationship between state and patriciate are three unusual policies each associated with an outstanding political figure. These are the policies of Maḥmūd of Ghazna, ᶜAmīd al-Mulk al-Kundurī, and Niẓām al-Mulk.

For the most part, Maḥmūd was content to use patronage of the Ḥanafī party as his instrument for maintaining his authority in Nishapur. At the beginning of his reign when he was still quite insecure, he took the extraordinary step of officially endorsing by means of his coinage the Muᶜtazilī theology propounded by the Ḥanafī leadership.[33] His Sīmjūrid rivals had supported the Shāfiᶜīs by building a madrasa for the Ashᶜarī theologian Ibn Fūrak, and Maḥmūd was only going one step further by stamping a Muᶜtazilī slogan on his coins. When the initial Sīmjūrid threat had been countered, a further act of patronage was taken by Maḥmūd's brother Naṣr, who was his governor

33. Richard Bulliet, "A Muᶜtazilite Coin of Maḥmūd of Ghazna," *American Numismatic Society Museum Notes*, 15 (1969), 119–129.

in Nishapur, in building a madrasa for the Ḥanafī leader Abū al-ᶜAlāᵓ Ṣāᶜid. Then came further troubles with the Sāmānids which resulted in Maḥmūd's securing his position in Nishapur once and for all and in the dismissal of Abū al-ᶜAlāᵓ Ṣāᶜid from the post of qāḍī, almost certainly because of some inclination he had shown to favor the Sāmānids who were his original patrons.

This left Maḥmūd in a quandary. The Shāfiᶜīs opposed him because of his favoritism toward the Ḥanafīs, and now the unchallenged leader of the Ḥanafīs had turned out to be politically unreliable. Moreover, the absolute allegiance of the city could not be assumed as long as the enemy Ilek Khans were ruling in Transoxania. In 1006/396, four years after Abū al-ᶜAlāᵓ's deposition, the Ilek Khans did in fact capture the city and hold it for a time.[34] What he did was to abandon all hope of ruling through the patriciate. He appointed the head of the Karrāmī sect to the office of raᵓīs and gave him carte blanche to establish his authority by whatever means he wished.

Extortion, intimidation, assassination, and eventually failure were the results of this policy. Exactly why Maḥmūd allowed his Karrāmī protégé to be humiliated and disgraced in a legal fight with Abū al-ᶜAlāᵓ Ṣāᶜid is hard to tell from the sources. The judge was clearly a supporter of Abū al-ᶜAlāᵓ,[35] and Maḥmūd may have been unable to prevail upon him to render a decision contrary to his party allegiance. Then again, Maḥmūd's brother Naṣr may have backed the man he founded a madrasa for so strongly that Maḥmūd did not dare risk a rift in his family. But above considerations of this nature, Maḥmūd must have realized that he could not resist the patriciates in all of the cities under his control without instituting a genuine reign of terror and that to allow a tremendously respected Ḥanafī to be convicted of heresy on the accusation of a Karrāmī would be to declare war on all the patriciates in his empire. Maḥmūd had little choice but to abandon his support for the Karrāmiya in Nishapur and his policy of subverting patrician domination of the city.

The policy of ᶜAmīd al-Mulk al-Kundurī, the vizier of Ṭughril Beg, was to carry the notion of divide and conquer to its logical conclusion. Previous applications of the principle had merely resulted in the establishment of an intransigent opposition party ready and willing to support any opponent of the existing regime. The reason for this is that the power and influence of any patrician was based far more upon local factors

34. A. K. Markow, *Inventarny Katalog Musulmanskich Monet* (St. Petersburg, 1896), p. 202, coin #49.

35. See chapter 13 and Ṣāᶜidī genealogical key #8.

such as wealth, reputation, and family connections than upon state patronage. Thus, the removal of state patronage from one patrician party did not deprive that party to any great degree of its power and influence in the community. It merely antagonized it.

The only way to make a policy of divide and conquer work was to destroy completely the capacity of the unfavored party to act as a fifth column without at the same time frightening the favored party so much that they might see the common interest of the entire patriciate threatened. This is what al-Kundurī attempted to do.[36] For reasons that had more to do with expediency than religion, he picked the Ḥanafīs as the favored party and entered into an understanding with their leader Abū Naṣr Aḥmad aṣ-Ṣāᶜidī. In his capacity as vizier he ordered the theological doctrines of al-Ashᶜarī anathematized in the khuṭba and declared a prohibition upon any Ashᶜarī holding an official religious or educational post anywhere in the empire. Never since the early days of the ᶜAbbāsid caliphate had such a theological persecution been set in motion.

The target was clearly Nishapur since it was the very heart of the Ashᶜarī movement. Every possible means of destroying Shāfiᶜī-Ashᶜarī power in the city was utilized: the mass mobilization power of the khaṭīb, exclusion from positions of authority, arrests, forced self-exile, mob action. Inside of a few years the Shāfiᶜī party was for all intents and purposes dead in the city of Nishapur. This does not mean necessarily that al-Kundurī's policy was truly a successful one, for the Ashᶜarīs were still alive in exile and were not without their supporters in the empire as a whole. But a change in rulers brought a reversal of al-Kundurī's policy before its ultimate effects could really be known. Conceivably, had fate permitted, al-Kundurī might have succeeded in destroying the Ashᶜarīs and establishing the state as the arbiter of Islamic orthodoxy. If so, the whole later history of Islam would have been changed as well as the political position of the patriciate which depended so much upon religious autonomy. But such did not come to pass, for al-Kundurī was succeeded by an even more ambitious and astute politician, Niẓām al-Mulk.

Nishapur holds a special place in Niẓām al-Mulk's personal political history. It was one of the largest and most important cities of the empire he set out to govern, as it had been for Maḥmūd of Ghazna and ᶜAmīd al-Mulk al-Kundurī, but it was in addition the first large metropolis to come under Niẓām al-Mulk's control. Alp Arslān, the

36. For al-Kundurī's biography see Fārisī I, f88a–b; II, f129b.

nephew of Ṭughril Beg, succeeded to his father's position as governor of Nishapur in 1058/450. In 1063/455 he succeeded his uncle as sultan. During the intervening five years, his vizier, Niẓām al-Mulk, had an opportunity to come to grips locally with the problems of state-patriciate relations and to work out policies for solving them that could later be applied to the empire as a whole. But al-Kundurī, as the vizier of the sultan, was not without influence in the city during those five years even though Alp Arslān appears to have governed much more actively than his father. Thus, to a certain extent, Niẓām al-Mulk was constricted in his choice of policy alternatives. The old policy of divide and conquer, which al-Kunduri had carried to an extreme, could not be adopted without risking a rupture between the sultan and his nephew.

The policy that Niẓām al-Mulk hit upon was brilliant and original. Although never fully developed during his lifetime, it eventually transformed the shape of government in the Middle East. The observed situation was that local patriciates had such political power in the cities upon which the empire depended that the state was forced into acceding to their wishes in such things as appointments or else playing the game of factional politics with all the risks of creating an entrenched opposition inherent therein. What the state was unable to do was control the patriciate; it had the brute force to do so, but it could not afford the disruption strong-arm methods would inevitably produce. The solution begun by Niẓām al-Mulk and brought to its ultimate expression under the Ottoman Empire was to control the patriciate by making it dependent upon the state. The primary, but not the only, instrument of this policy under Niẓām al-Mulk was the Niẓāmiya madrasa; the eventual result under the Ottomans was the absorption of the religious establishment into the state bureaucracy.

Patronage through the building of madrasas was not new with Niẓām al-Mulk. The Sīmjūrids had built a madrasa for Ibn Fūrak, and the Ghaznavids had built the Ṣāᶜidiya madrasa for Abū al-ᶜAlā᾿ Ṣāᶜid. These were undoubtedly the models Niẓām al-Mulk had in mind when he commissioned the building of the first Niẓāmiya in Nishapur in 1058/450.[37] What made the Niẓāmiya different from the Ṣāᶜidiya and from most other earlier madrasas was the retention in the hands of the builder of the power of appoint-

37. The Niẓāmiya in Nishapur was founded during the governorship of Alp Arslān which lasted from 1058/450 to 1063/455 and Imām al-Ḥaramain al-Juwainī is reported to have been its director for almost thirty years at the time of his death in 1085/478 (Fārisī I, f48b). Hence its establishment must have come in the first or, at the latest, the second year of Alp Arslān's governorship. It thus antedates the Niẓāmiya in Baghdad by five or six years.

ment. This may not have been an innovation since Ṭughril Beg had built a madrasa in Nishapur fifteen years earlier that had always retained the name The Madrasa of the Sultan, but the Niẓāmiya set an example by its lavish scale and by the fact that a sister institution of the same name was eventually built in every major city of the empire.

All of Niẓām al-Mulk's madrasas were Shāfiᶜī institutions, but none of them was allowed to become a bastion of militant Shāfiᶜī politics. Niẓām al-Mulk was a patron of the Shāfiᶜīs because they were the underdogs at the time of his accession to power, and bipartisan patronage would not have been acceptable in the overheated climate of patrician politics. He was not, however, a Shāfiᶜī fanatic. If al-Kundurī had backed the Shāfiᶜīs who had given him his start in life,[38] Niẓām al-Mulk would have created his Niẓāmiyas for the Ḥanafīs. His object was to restore and maintain a balance between patrician factions of every stripe, but he was constrained to work through one faction only. He patronized the Shāfiᶜīs, but the price of his patronage was relaxation on their part of factional political tension. This is the opposite of earlier divide and conquer policies. When Shāfiᶜīs clashed with Ḥanafīs or Ḥanbalīs, Niẓām al-Mulk refused to support them and tried to defuse the situation.[39]

Niẓām al-Mulk did not indulge in the wishful thinking that led some other rulers to ignore the problem of patrician factionalism entirely. He worked actively to lever at least one faction into political quiescence. Nor did he hold the short-sighted view that all out patronage of one faction would provide political control. He patronized the Shāfiᶜīs with his Niẓāmiyas, but he did not hesitate to appoint Ḥanafīs to official posts. In Nishapur he also attempted to encroach upon the true heart of the educational system by installing his agent al-Manīᶜī in the post of Shaikh al-Islām. That attempt seems not to have been repeated elsewhere, and on al-Manīᶜī's death the position went to the local Ḥanafī leader of the earlier persecution of the Ashᶜarīs, Abū Naṣr Aḥmad aṣ-Ṣāᶜidī.

During Niẓām al-Mulk's lifetime, his policy was not marked by notable success. Factional riots and animosity continued long after his death. But he had planted the seed of state patronage of the patriciate. The Niẓāmiyas had been personal endowments of their founder, but their utility in calming political passions was not lost upon rulers

38. The young al-Kundurī was brought to the attention of Ṭughril Beg by the Shāfiᶜī leader Imām al-Muwaffaq al-Basṭāmī. On him see chapter 9 and Basṭāmī genealogical key #9.

39. One such situation arose in Baghdad in 1078/470, and Niẓām al-Mulk's neutral position is shown by a letter he wrote to the leader of the Shāfiᶜīs (I. Jauzī, VIII, 312). A second incident occurred in Herat in 1067/459. Niẓām al-Mulk again refused to support the militant Shāfiᶜīs (Serge de Beaurecueil, *Khwādja ᶜAbdullāh Anṣārī* [Beirut, 1965], pp. 109–110).

themselves. Increasingly, viziers, rulers, and members of ruling families established madrasas throughout Islamic territories. Education was still essentially under patrician control, but the influence of the state grew steadily. Finally, the independence of the local patriciates was sapped completely, and the entire educational system became an adjunct of the state apparatus. The office of Shaikh al-Islām, its functions entirely transformed, became the pinnacle of a state religious bureaucracy.

These later developments which have been so broadly sketched are beyond the scope of the present subject; they serve only to illuminate the particular role of Nishapur and its patriciate in certain aspects of the late medieval transformation of Islamic society. The true subject of this chapter has been the relations between the state and the patriciate, of which the policy of Niẓām al-Mulk was only the latest phase. What has been in question throughout is the nature and degree of the political independence of the patriciate. Nishapur was no more constitutionally autonomous than any other medieval Middle Eastern city; but its patriciate, which identified itself with the city, wielded substantial political power. Aside from such explicit state functions as tax administration, the internal life of the city was almost completely under the control of the patriciate. Whether the state ignored the patrician factions or attempted to split them, it was forced to accede to their wishes. The external affairs of the city came under patrician control only in times of crisis. The choice between resistance and surrender, obedience and revolt, lay with the patriciate; and they reached their decisions collectively on the basis of the self-interest of their city and their class. Niẓām al-Mulk began the process that eventually ended the quasi-autonomy of the patriciate, but before that process had gone far, the patriciate of Nishapur had destroyed both itself and its city.

6 / *The End of the Patriciate*

The destruction of Nishapur can be described in some detail; yet ultimately it defies logical explanation. The city was sacked and pillaged by Turkish tribesmen at least three times in a brief span of years; and the period of military action and counteraction, raid and counterraid, inaugurated by the first tribal victory must surely have increased the capacity of the general populace for accepting death and destruction as a normal condition of existence while at the same time seriously interfering with the production and exchange of goods and bringing many people into distressed circumstances thereby. Still, distressed circumstances and an atmosphere of violence are insufficient explanation for the fantastic, self-destructive wave of factional riot and warfare that followed upon the tribal eruption.

What the patriciate had achieved in Nishapur was a locally controlled, semiautonomous polity from which they themselves received the greatest benefit. Deep running as the current of hostility between their factions was, in previous times of crisis their common interest had induced them to act together. This time factional feelings triumphed over the common interest. Instead of uniting to rebuild the city, the Ḥanafīs and Shāfiʿīs fought over its ruins. Both sides lost. The city was abandoned; the patriciate was broken. Whether the two sides miscalculated each other's strength and risked all in the mistaken hope that a quick and final victory would be forthcoming, or whether the history of bitterness and hatred between the factions had simply reached a point where renewed cooperation was impossible regardless of the magnitude of the outside threat cannot be determined from the remaining sources. The course of events, however, can.

In the year 1153/548, a representative of the Seljuq sultan Sanjar was sent to collect a tribute payment of 30,000 sheep from the Ghuzz nomads newly entered into Khurasan.[1] Payment was refused on the pretext that only the sultan himself had authority over the tribes. Sanjar, hearing of the refusal to pay, decided to teach the Ghuzz the unwisdom of their rebellious act. He called together his amirs and marched upon the Ghuzz with the full strength of his army. The Ghuzz chieftains were terrified and tried to placate the

1. The events recounted in this chapter are contained primarily in accounts by Muḥammad ar-Rāwandī, *Rāḥat aṣ-ṣudūr wa āyat as-surūr*, ed. M. Iqbāl (London, 1921); and I. Athīr. Rāwandī's account (pp. 177–182) deals for the most part with the events of 1153/548. Events after that date are compressed into a single passage on p. 182. That passage evidently describes events occurring in different years and has been treated accordingly; it will be re-cited for each occasion to which it seems relevant. I. Athīr's account of the events of 1153/548 is to be found in vol. XI, pp. 176–184. See also ʿIbar, IV, 128–129.

sultan with offers of money and slaves, but it was too late. Seeing that there was no way of averting the sultan's wrath, the chieftains mustered their forces to resist. Miraculously, when the two forces met, the Ghuzz put to flight the imperial field army and succeeded in capturing Sanjar himself.

All of Khurasan lay open and virtually unprotected before the victorious Ghuzz. After plundering Marv, Sanjar's capital, and Ṭūs, they decended upon Nishapur. There was only a brief resistance, and then the city was sacked. The Manīʿī Congregational Mosque was defended, and its defenders were slaughtered. The Muṭarriz Mosque, a Shāfiʿī landmark capable of holding two thousand men at prayer, was set ablaze, and the towering flames illuminated the sky throughout the night. Bodies piled in heaps in the streets; in two quarters alone fifteen thousand male corpses are alleged to have been counted. Many of the women and children were taken into slavery. The Ghuzz stayed for several days searching out any hidden treasure. Those who told where their valuables were hidden were killed; those who refused to tell were tortured until they told and then killed. Only the inner city was able to defend itself behind its walls.

When the Ghuzz had sated their desire for plunder, they departed. But the respite was only temporary. After attacking Juvain and Isfarāʾin, they returned. This time the inner city was overrun and pillaged mercilessly. Again the Ghuzz departed, but still the city's ordeal continued; for the *ʿayyārūn*, the ubiquitous bandits who play an enigmatic role in Islamic history, now took their turn at plunder and destruction.

Then apparently all was over. One of Sanjar's officers named al-Muʾayyad Ay Abah took command of the situation and set about putting together the principality that he was destined to rule with comparative success for the next twenty years.

The city's losses both in property and human life had been immense, and the patriciate had suffered as much as the common people. The most illustrious casualty was Muḥammad b. Yaḥyā the director of the Niẓāmiya.[2] Dirt had been forced down his throat until he died. Other noted Shāfiʿīs who perished included Abū Manṣūr ʿAbd al-Khāliq ash-Shaḥḥāmī, who succumbed sometime after the attack of injuries inflicted by torture, and Abū al-Barakāt ʿAbd Allāh al-Furāwī,[3] who died the next year in the famine that followed the Ghuzz depredations. Lost also were a grandson of Abū al-Qāsim al-Qushairī named Aḥmad b. al-Ḥusain, and a disciple of the Qushairīs named ʿAbd ar-

2. ʿIbar, IV, 133–134; Old Subkī, IV, 197.

3. See chapter 11 and Qushairī genealogical key #66; and chapter 11 and Qushairī genealogical key #77.

Raḥmān b. ᶜAbd aṣ-Ṣamad al-Akkāf.[4] The latter had been taken and held for ransom and, after having been freed at the intercession of the captive Sanjar, had died of an illness contracted in his captivity. The Ḥanafīs suffered as well losing the qāḍī Ṣāᶜid b. ᶜAbd al-Malik aṣ-Ṣāᶜidī.[5]

Details of living conditions are lacking, but the political turmoil of the next few years which involved al-Muᵓayyad Ay Abah, the Ghuzz, and several other contenders for power could not have facilitated rapid recovery from the Ghuzz depredations. A famine immediately followed the sack of 1153/548, and in 1157/552 extraordinarily high prices are reported in the city indicating that agricultural production was still depressed.[6] How severe this continuing hardship was is hard to say, but it must certainly have contributed to the violent events of the next few years.

The leader of the Shāfiᶜī faction at that time was al-Muᵓayyad b. al-Ḥusain al-Muwaffaqī, the current head of the Basṭāmī family which had held the position of Shāfiᶜī leadership for close to two centuries.[7] The opposing factional chieftain was the naqīb of the ᶜAlids, Abū al-Qāsim Zaid b. al-Ḥasan al-Ḥasanī.[8] The party he headed was unquestionably the Ḥanafīs although no explicit statement of the fact is made. Toward the end of 1158/553 some of al-Muwaffaqī's Shāfiᶜī followers killed by mistake a man attached to Abū al-Qāsim Zaid.[9] Abū al-Qāsim Zaid demanded that al-Muwaffaqī turn the killers over to him for punishment, but al-Muwaffaqī refused on the grounds that Abū al-Qāsim's jurisdiction did not extend beyond the ᶜAlid family. Abū al-Qāsim gathered together his followers and attacked the Shāfiᶜīs, killing a number of them. Then he went on and set fire to the druggists' market, Muᶜādh Street, Ẓāhir Garden Street, and the home of the deceased Shāfiᶜī leader Imām al-Ḥaramain al-Juwainī in which al-Muwaffaqī, his great-grandson, was living.

The affair grew in the months that followed and soon the entire city was embroiled Al-Muᵓayyad al-Muwaffaqī called in Shāfiᶜī reinforcements from Ṭūs, Isfarāᵓin, and Juvain, and every night parties from the different quarters sallied forth to set fires in

4. See chapter 11 and Qushairī genealogical key #25. For latter individual see I. Athīr, XI, 200; I. Jauzī, X, 159; Old Subkī, IV, 246. For his father and more on the family's connections with the Qushairīs see Fārisī I, f56b–57a; II, f106a.

5. See chapter 13 and Ṣāᶜidī genealogical key #40.

6. I. Athīr, XI, 228.

7. See chapter 9 and Basṭāmī genealogical key #32.

8. See chapter 15 and Ḥasanī genealogical key #24.

9. I. Athīr, XI, 234–236; ᶜIbar, IV, 154; Rāwandī, *Rāḥat*, p. 182.

other quarters. To make matters still worse, sometime in the midst of the fighting the Ghuzz attacked and plundered the city for a third time.[10] Over a year passed in this way after the initial incident. Then an important figure on the side of Abū al-Qāsim Zaid was killed. This touched off full-scale warfare. The Shāfiᶜīs lost madrasas, mosques, and markets; but especially they lost men. The killing took such a toll among their party that al-Muwaffaqī was forced to flee the city. All Shāfiᶜī scholarly activities in Nishapur came to a halt, and the Ḥanafīs apparently had their victory.

However, the old pattern of state neutrality in patrician feuds had passed away with the disintegration of the Seljuq imperial apparatus. Before the year's end al-Muᵓayyad al-Muwaffaqī was back again and in the company of the other al-Muᵓayyad, the amir Ay Abah. The naqīb Abū al-Qāsim retreated behind the walls of the inner city while the reinforced Shāfiᶜīs took revenge in the rest of the city for the destruction earlier of their madrasas and mosques. Among the buildings destroyed was the Ḥanafī Ṣandalī madrasa, named for the man who a century earlier had fired the mobs with his own fanatic hatred of the Ashᶜarīs.[11] The citadel was besieged, and eventually the situation was brought under control. A truce of a kind seems even to have been put together.

The sack of the city at the hands of the Ghuzz and the subsequent devastation caused by factional fighting would have left permanent scars, but an effective truce and a recementing of the bond of patrician class interest at this time could still have saved something of patrician Nishapur. This was not to be. Fighting and looting continued even after Ay Abah had restored a semblance of order. In 1161/556 he tried one last time to end the turmoil by attacking the unruly elements and arresting the naqīb Abū al-Qāsim, whom he held responsible for the disorders.[12] In the fighting that ensued, the ᶜAqīl mosque, another Shāfiᶜī bastion, was destroyed along with its library. Eight Ḥanafī and seventeen Shāfiᶜī madrasas that had survived the previous troubles were destroyed, and twelve library collections were burned or sold off cheaply. Both parties suffered equally, a situation that may not have been unwelcome to Ay Abah who could not have wanted too strong a patrician element in his new principality.

The suburb of Shādyākh to the west of the city, which had been built up by the Ṭāhirids and restored by Alp Arslān only to fall once again into decay, was now

10. ᶜIbar, IV, 153; I. Jauzī, X, 189.
11. See Chapter 15 and Ḥasanī genealogical key #11.
12. I. Athīr, XI, 271–273.

selected by Ay Abah as the site for a new city of Nishapur.[13] He ordered the walls surrounding the suburb repaired. Being very much smaller than the city of Nishapur as a whole, Shādyākh was also much more defensible. Then Ay Abah and those people who trusted in him to restore peace took up their residence behind the new walls. The main city was almost completely in ruins after the latest fighting and was abandoned to those who still resisted Ay Abah's authority.

Since Ay Abah had come into the fray on the side of the Shāfiᶜīs, those remnants who stayed in the old city were mostly followers of the naqīb Abū al-Qāsim. They took refuge primarily in the defensible inner city and erected on the walls mangonels and other war machines by means of which they could bombard any other part of the city. There they waited fearfully for the attack that Ay Abah would have to make if his new Nishapur in Shādyākh was ever to be secure. The attack finally came in the middle of 1161/556. It took the form of a siege and lasted for at least two months.[14] Early in the operations a stone from a mangonel struck and killed the Shāfiᶜī leader al-Muʾayyad al-Muwaffaqī and a shaikh from Baihaq, but the death of their leader served only to increase the fury of the Shāfiᶜī patricians siding with Ay Abah. The inner city surrendered, but still the citadel held out only to capitulate the next year in 1162/557.[15]

With the fall of the citadel, the history of the old Nishapur comes to a close. The new Nishapur, huddling behind the walls of Shādyākh, was a much smaller town, dependent totally in the dangerous and unsettled political environment of the time upon the protection of Ay Abah. Members of some known Shāfiᶜī patrician families and of the Ṣāᶜidī family among the Ḥanafīs continued to live there, but the patriciate as a body was dead. No more would they dominate the life of the community and force rulers to treat them with kid gloves. The mysterious divisions within the patriciate had finally prevailed over their collective interest. As for the old Nishapur, patrician Nishapur, "where had been the assembly places of friendliness, the classes of knowledge, and the circles of patricians were now the grazing grounds of sheep and the lurking places of wild beasts and serpents."[16]

More than the paucity of sources, it is the elusiveness of the essential nature of the patrician factional struggle that blocks a full understanding of Nishapur's pitiful fall.

13. I. Athīr, XI, 273–274; Rāwandī, *Rāḥat*, p. 182.
14. I. Athīr, XI, 277–278; Rāwandī, *Rāḥat*, p. 182.
15. I. Athīr, XI, 282–283.
16. Rāwandī, *Rāḥat*, p. 182.

Patrician power had not reached some kind of historical dead end. The history of other cities suggests that had it not committed suicide the patriciate of Nishapur might have achieved still greater independence and autonomy. Only with the coming of the Mongols did the patrician era end in Khurasan and Transoxania. Perhaps it is through the study of the patriciates of those other cities that the clues necessary for a clearer understanding of the patrician factions of Nishapur will be found.

Part II | *Patrician Families*

Introduction

The patriciate of Nishapur has now been defined and described. Its various functions and powers in the society of the city have been set forth with greater or less precision as the sources have permitted. Yet, in a sense, the concrete reality of the patriciate has not been demonstrated. There is no word, no "*patricius*" or "burgher" or "citizen," to signal its existence. There are no charters or constitutions affirming its rights and obligations. Vague and general terms connoting social prestige crop up in the sources along with equally imprecise terms relating to the common people, but no orderly set of social strata can be deduced from them, much less any special recognition of the patrician class. Is the historian, then, playing false with his subject matter and forcing it into a mold of his own devising, or can the reality of the patriciate be demonstrated without reference to charters and formulae that probably never existed?

Self-indictment, naturally, is not the intent of this question. It is meant simply to indicate that there is a moot point here and one that can probably not be resolved to the complete satisfaction of anyone who wishes to debate it. The strongest argument for the real existence of the patriciate, however, is found in the material on which Part II is based. It is an argument from immersion in a vast quantity of biographical information. The fact, for example, that, with only the scantiest data on marriage and descent in female lines and without deleting the numerous biographies of transient scholars, almost half of the seventeen hundred odd people included in al-Fārisī's biographical dictionary can be fit onto two hundred or so family trees affords the most persuasive evidence of there being in the mind of the compiler a conscious recognition of certain, select families as having intrinsic worth. Further information would unquestionably show many more of these families to be bound together by marriage alliances, and a fuller text of al-Ḥākim's great biographical dictionary would serve to extend the family trees back farther toward their roots. But even within the existing limitations long and thorough acquaintance with the biographies leads the historian inescapably to the conclusion that just as dozens of reminiscences are evoked of the subject's uncles and cousins, the jobs they held and the things they did when he reads an individual biography, so the medieval Nishapuri would make way for a young shaikh hurrying to the mosque because in the back of his mind he knew who the shaikh's father and uncles were and what power they wielded, whose daughter his mother was, what lands he and his brothers had inherited, and how many camel loads of fine white cloth had just been dispatched to Baghdad by his businessman cousin.

The reality of the patriciate consisted in individuals and families who knew each other and recognized each other as being above the ordinary run of people. There was no formal membership in the patriciate. Being made a legal witness or approved to transmit ḥadīth did not confer status so much as certify that it had been obtained in rather more subtle ways. There is nothing extraordinary in all of this; upper classes frequently lack formal definition. But being informal and even intuitive, the concrete reality of patrician status can be sensed only to the degree that a thousand years later the surviving biographical dictionaries permit the historian to immerse himself in the milieu of the patriciate.

This will explain why the remainder of this book is devoted to the histories of nine separate families. When one chooses nine from many, criteria of representativeness and singularity conflict. Each patrician family has its own unique history, and none can truly represent the class as a whole. Still, deviation of too great a degree from the imaginary norm would only serve to distort the overall impression. These nine are therefore a compromise between the desire to include the most important and interesting and the desire to show what the average patrician family was like. In the balance, the latter desire probably gets short shrift.

One ancillary benefit that might be expected from this mode of approach is insight into the population characteristics of medieval Nishapur. Unfortunately, this insight is not great. Because of the very specific character of the population sample available, only a few general observations about population characteristics can be made. The average life span of those patricians whose length of life is known is seventy-five years, and there is some evidence that full maturity was considered to begin at age fifty. Of course, infant and child mortality are not indicated, and the patriciate undoubtedly enjoyed the highest standard of living combined with the least hazardous occupations. References to plural marriages occur but not too frequently. References to children born to very old men might be taken as indirect evidence of plural marriage; but old mothers are mentioned as well, and it is quite clear that a long childbearing period was the norm as it is in Persian society to this day. On the subject of inheritance, there are several cases of official positions being transferred at death to a brother rather than to a son, although examples of the contrary practice abound also.

Since families connected through marriage are treated as one in order to show the ramifications of marriage alliances, several last names will appear in the same family history. On the accompanying family tree it should always be clear which last name goes with which family members even though the last names are not normally written in for each individual. It must be borne in mind, however, that last names—technically, *nisbas* relating to town, tribe, trade, or forefather—were not regular and immutable. The name used by the grandson may not be that used by the grandfather. Family identification is better achieved by the part of the name known as the *nasab* which gives the individual's genealogy, "so-and-so the son of so-and-so the son of so-and-so." Genealogical reconstruction made from *nasabs* is the core of each family history; and despite truncated and transposed sections in many genealogies, the repetition of the same genealogy or parts of it in many biographies makes the resultant family trees quite reliable except where specifically noted.

On the family trees and genealogical key to sources two names have been given, when available, for each individual. The *ism* is what corresponds to the person's first name, for example, Muḥammad, Aḥmad, ᶜAlī, and is always given second; the *kunya* is an *ism* preceded by the word Abū meaning "father." Literally, Abū Muḥammad means "father of Muḥammad," and the full ism plus kunya Abū Muḥammad Aḥmad means "Aḥmad the father of Muḥammad." In actuality, however, there is no necessary relation between a man's kunya and the ism of any of his sons. Both ism and kunya were bestowed upon infants, and there was no compulsion for a man to name his child Muḥammad simply because his father had chosen to name him "father of Muḥammad." More often than not euphony, such as between Aḥmad and Muḥammad, or historical connection, such as between ᶜAlī and al-Ḥusain, governed which kunya was chosen to go with which ism; and there are a number of almost invariable combinations, such as Abū Ḥafṣ ᶜUmar. On other occasions, however, the ism and kunya of a grandfather or other relative were selected. The use of ism and kunya for identification on family trees does not necessarily reflect the everyday usage of the individual and his friends, however. A person might actually be known by any part of his name or be known by one part in one circle of acquaintances and another part in another. Any observations concerning nicknames or honorific titles, which became increasingly common throughout the period under examination, will be found in the text of the family history and not on the family tree. Frequently, mention of them is deleted altogether since their meaning and interpretation are very often unclear.

To minimize confusion of often similar or even identical names and to force some sort of order upon the sometimes too copious material, the following system of organization has been adopted: Within each family history, organization is by generation as signified by Roman numerals in the text and on the family tree. When the synchronization of generations goes awry, as occasionally happens between collateral branches of a family, it is indicated in the text. Each individual is identified by a numeral in parentheses which corresponds to his numeral on the family tree and genealogical key. The genealogical key supplies all biographical references, and footnotes are reserved for other types of information.

Finally, a word must be said about readability. Though in some ways the real meat of this study is in the family histories, one must unfortunately chew through quantities of breading to get to it. If the object were to give information on important men who came from Nishapur, only two or three figures from each family might be talked about in detail. But that is not the object. The reach, influence, and connections of a family cannot be shown if only the highlights are hit, nor can it be demonstrated that insignificant figures merited inclusion in biographical dictionaries solely because of their family background. The family is the subject of each history, and all of its known members must be treated. This can only be done at some cost in terms of readability.

7 / *Maḥmī–Ḥarashī–Bālawī*

The linking together through marriage of the Maḥmī, Ḥarashī, and Bālawī families affords an outstanding example of the merging in the patriciate of several discrete sources of social eminence: commercial wealth, landed aristocracy, and religious scholarship.

I–VI. All three families can be traced back to early origins. For a brief time in the year 676/56, the caliph ᶜUthmān's son Saᶜīd held the post of governor of Khurasan. The tradition of the Maḥmī family relates that travelling from Isfahan apparently to Herat by way of Nishapur, Saᶜīd b. ᶜUthmān reached the town of Bīshak in the district of Rukhkh around the modern town of Turbat-i Haidariya south of Nishapur.[1] There he fell ill and, one thing leading to another, eventually left behind a son. This son was named Maḥmi, and he had in turn a daughter named ᶜAin who married a local dignitary named Muḥammad b. an-Naḍir al-Bīshakī.

There follow three generations about which no details are known before the Maḥmī family emerges early in the tenth/fourth century as one of the great aristocratic houses of the Nishapur area. The great-grandson of an-Naḍir b. Muḥammad, Abū al-Ḥasan Aḥmad al-Maḥmī (1), is mentioned as one of the city's leading figures and in his children's biographies is called "The Grand" (*al-Akbar*) and raᵓīs,[2] but extensive information becomes available only for the generation of his children. By that time, three points are of interest for their indication of the family's status. First, great pride was taken in the family's descent from the caliph ᶜUthmān even though the descent was not lineal in the male line. Second, the family's wealth was still centered in the district of Rukhkh and hence was undoubtedly founded upon land ownership. If the story of the family's origin is true, Maḥmi, the illegitimate or possibly legitimate offspring of the caliph's son, probably married his daughter to the most important Muslim Persian landowner in the vicinity in an effective trade of prestigious name and complete legitimation in the eyes of the Arab conquerors for landed wealth and standing in the indigenous society. Third, the combination of dihqān status and caliphal descent had produced in the course of the intervening generations an elevation of the family to the highest ranks of the patriciate. The title raᵓīs is mentioned for several members of the family and is indicative of this status although it may apply to Rukhkh rather than to Nishapur.

1. I. Funduq, p. 126; Ḥākim, f18a.
2. See numbers 7 and 9 on Genealogical Key.

Before going further with the Maḥmī family, however, the origins of the Ḥarashīs and the Bālawīs require examination. The name al-Ḥarashī is usually found coupled with the name al-Ḥīrī. Al-Ḥarashī refers to an Arab tribe and al-Ḥīrī to the quarter al-Ḥīra, one of the wealthiest parts of Nishapur. The geographer Yāqūt reports the latest known member of the family as saying that the quarter al-Ḥīra was named after the city of al-Ḥīra in Iraq because his ancestors had come to Khurasan from that city and had named their settlement just outside the citadel of pre-Islamic Nishapur after their original home.[3] Be that as it may, the story clearly indicates that the family believed itself to date from the earliest period of Arab settlement in Nishapur. Exact corroboration of this belief is barred by insufficient information, but the family tree can be traced back far enough to make this claim of early settlement credible.

The earliest member of the family is said to have been Saᶜīd b. ᶜAbd ar-Raḥmān al-Ḥarashī, the lieutenant or successor (*khalīfa*) of the conqueror of Khurasan, ᶜAbd Allāh b. ᶜĀmir.[4] Nothing further is known of him, but he apparently did settle in Nishapur, because his grandson Aḥmad b. ᶜAmr b. Saᶜīd al-Ḥarashī (2) died there in 841/226. He was a religious scholar and had among his pupils another man named al-Ḥarashī, Abū ᶜAbd Allāh Muḥammad b. Aḥmad b. Ḥafṣ al-Ḥarashī (3). Abū ᶜAbd Allāh Muḥammad seems to have come from a less distinguished Ḥarashī family, but he was an outstanding legal scholar and held the post of examiner of legal witnesses (*muzakkī*). Thus, he merely added another feather to his cap by marrying the daughter of his teacher and great-granddaughter of the first important Ḥarashī.[5] Although he travelled much in search of legal knowledge, Abū ᶜAbd Allāh Muḥammad never met personally ash-Shāfiᶜī, who died in 820/204. Nevertheless, he became an authority on Shāfiᶜī law and was the first to introduce the new legal doctrine into Khurasan. This, naturally, assured his family a prominent position in the Shāfiᶜī party which they retained for another two centuries. Having firmly established his line, Abū ᶜAbd Allāh Muḥammad died in 877/263.

Three members of the family are known in the next generation. Two are nephews about whom nothing is preserved but their names, Ismāᶜīl b. ᶜAbdūs b. Aḥmad al-Ḥarashī (4), and ᶜAbd Allāh b. ᶜAbdūs b. Aḥmad al-Ḥarashī. The other is a son, Abū

3. Yāqūt, *Muᶜjam al-Buldān*, II, 331.

4. Samᶜānī, IV, 122.

5. Information on this marriage is contained in Dhahabī's biography of Abū ᶜAbd Allāh's son Abū ᶜAmr Aḥmad.

ᶜAmr Aḥmad al-Ḥarashī (5). These three were of the same generation as the aforementioned Abū al-Ḥasan Aḥmad al-Maḥmī. Abū ᶜAmr Aḥmad followed directly in his father's footsteps. He inherited wealth and leadership in the Shāfiᶜī party, and he too became a muzakkī. With him, for the first time, the family's attachment to the quarter of al-Ḥīra is marked by the additional surname al-Ḥīrī; and at his death in 929/317, his body was prayed over in the prayer ground of al-Ḥīra, a prayer ground that is not mentioned in later years and that was presumably encroached upon as the city grew and al-Ḥīra became an increasingly wealthy area in which to live.

At a parallel chronological stage in the Bālawī family, only one family member, Abū al-ᶜAbbās Muḥammad b. Aḥmad b. Bālūya (6), is specifically identifiable; and all that is known of him is that he was a prominent shaikh in the city and bore the nickname ᶜAḍīda. However, when the Bālawīs do emerge as an important family, it is clear that they come from a merchant background; thus it may safely be assumed that while the Maḥmīs were enjoying their rents and preening themselves on their caliphal connection and the Ḥarashīs were working to spread Shāfiᶜī legal ideas, the Persian Bālūya and his descendants were earning in commerce the fortune that would later project them into the patriciate.

VII. In this generation the Maḥmī and Ḥarashī families unite. Abū al-Ḥasan Aḥmad al-Maḥmī had four children. Abū Manṣūr ᶜUbaid Allāh (7) was probably the eldest son and was, like his father, a raᵓīs, probably of Nishapur but possibly of Rukhkh or some town in that locality. He was much more a secular than a religious figure. Only rarely did he relate ḥadīth; he was primarily respected for his attentiveness to the duties of public office and his lack of peculation. At his funeral in 968/357, prayers were led by his nephew, the grandson of one of his teachers, Abū Bakr Aḥmad b. al-Ḥasan al-Ḥarashī al-Ḥīrī, who will be discussed later.

The other two brothers, Abū ᶜAlī al-Ḥasan (8) and Abū al-ᶜAbbās Muḥammad are scarcely known beyond their names. The former did study and teach in Baghdad and was alive in 999/389. Since this puts him on a par with his brothers' sons in age, it is most likely that he was the cadet member of the family and Abū al-ᶜAbbās Muḥammad the middle son.

This leaves one daughter, Umm al-Ḥusain Jumᶜa (9), called besides al-Maḥmiya (feminine ending) al-ᶜUthmāniya because of the family's descent from the caliph ᶜUthmān. Like most other women whose biographies are preserved, Umm al-Ḥusain

Jumᶜa studied ḥadīth, not only in Nishapur but elsewhere as well when she made the Pilgrimage. Furthermore, she, or perhaps an unknown sister, married one of the sons of the Shāfiᶜī legist Abū ᶜAmr Aḥmad al-Ḥarashī al-Ḥīrī. This was Abū ᶜAlī al-Ḥasan (10). He seems to have been a somewhat colorless individual wedged between an important father and an important son, but his politic marriage did cement relations between these two prestigious Shāfiᶜī families as is clearly indicated by the fact that it was his son, Abū Bakr Aḥmad, who at the age of thirty-two or thirty-three pronounced the funeral prayer over the head of the Maḥmī family, Abū Manṣūr ᶜUbaid Allāh, just as he was to do thirty-one years later in 998/388 over the body of his own father.

Also to be mentioned in this generation is Abū Naṣr Muḥammad al-Ḥarashī al-Ḥīrī (11), like the foregoing Abū ᶜAlī al-Ḥasan, a son of Abū ᶜAmr Aḥmad; but no details are known about him.

In the other branch of the Ḥarashī family there is a son of ᶜAbd Allāh b. ᶜAbdūs named Abū Isḥāq Ibrāhīm al-Ḥarashī (12). He was a legal witness and lived in al-Ḥīra.

As for the Bālawīs, there are brief references to Abū Ḥāmid Aḥmad b. Muḥammad (13) and somewhat more information about Abū al-Ḥusain ᶜAbd al-Wāḥid who is also named al-Ḥīrī (14) and who died in 988/378.

VIII. In the Maḥmī family, three of the children of Abū al-Ḥasan Aḥmad al-Mahmī had offspring, including those produced by the union of Maḥmī and Ḥarashī.

Abū Manṣur ᶜUbaid Allāh al-Maḥmī, the senior member of the family, had a son named Abū al-Faḍl Muḥammad (15) who followed in his footsteps as he had in those of his father. Abū al-Faḍl Muḥammad al-Maḥmī was a raʾīs[6] and was lauded as "the crowning jewel of the Maḥmī family." He studied some in Nishapur and Iraq but taught little. His main concern was with being a leader in civic affairs, and at that he excelled. He died in 1009/399 before reaching old age.

Abū al-ᶜAbbās Muḥammad, the middle brother, had two sons. Abū Muḥammad ᶜAbd Allāḥ (16), unlike most of his relatives, devoted his youth to study. As time went on, however, he became increasingly occupied with the family estates and fortune. He had a palace in Mūlqābād, the choice quarter adjoining al-Ḥīra on the north side; and there he was buried in 991/381. The other son, Abū al-Qāsim an-Naḍir (17), must have been his grandfather's favorite, for he alone is styled "the grandson" (*al-ḥafīd*). But

6. See biography of his son Abū ᶜAmr ᶜUthmān.

beyond an ordinary amount of learning and teaching, his accomplishments are unknown. He died in 1005/395.

Last but not least are two sons born of the marriage between Abū ᶜAlī al-Ḥasan al-Ḥarashī al-Ḥīrī and Umm al-Ḥusain Jumᶜa al-Maḥmī. Abū Naṣr ᶜAlī al-Ḥarashi al-Ḥīrī (18) is only a cipher, but his brother was one of the most noted men of his generation.

Abū Bakr Aḥmad al-Ḥarashī al-Ḥīrī (19), also known as al-ᶜUthmānī because of his mother's caliphal descent, was born in 936/324 or 937/325. He had two distinct careers during his exceptionally long lifetime. His early training was in Shāfiᶜī law as befitted a member of his family. At this he was outstanding, and by his early twenties he was already participating in formal legal disputations.[7] He also studied theology according to the Ashᶜarī doctrine during the period when the wedding of Shāfiᶜī law and Ashᶜarī doctrine was being accomplished in the city. Naturally, he travelled during his studies, primarily to the centers of learning along the Pilgrimage route to Mecca.

There is nothing surprising about the fact that sometime in his early years Abū Bakr Aḥmad moved into the post of examiner of witnesses (muzakkī); this post had been held by previous members of his family. What is surprising is that from there he moved on to the post of chief qāḍī. He was virtually the last Shāfiᶜī qāḍī in Nishapur until at least the middle of the twelfth/sixth century. This is specifically remarked by his biographers. Furthermore, it is apparent from the chronological list of qāḍīs in appendix II that he was preceded as well as followed by a long string of Ḥanafīs. The reason for his seemingly anomalous elevation to the office cannot be determined with absolute certitude because nowhere are the years of his tenure of office given. Yet a very strong case can be made that he was appointed by Abū al-Ḥasan Muḥammad as-Sīmjūrī who was governor of Nishapur from 961/350 to 981/371. The Ḥanafī qāḍī known as Qāḍī al-Ḥaramain died in 962/351 leaving the office vacant, and the Sīmjūrid family of governors can be shown to have patronized on other occasions the Shāfiᶜī-Ashᶜarī faction.[8] What could have been more natural as a move to cement relations with the Shāfiᶜī-Ashᶜarī group than to appoint Abū Bakr Aḥmad, the leading Shāfiᶜī legist and descendant of the man who introduced the rite to Nishapur, to the traditionally Ḥanafī post? And again what could be more natural than to find him apparently

7. He engaged in disputation sessions during the lifetime of his teacher Abū al-Walīd Ḥassān al-Qurashī who died in 960/349.

8. See chapter 5 and Bulliet, "A Muᶜtazilite Coin," pp. 119–129.

out of a job and entering his second career as a ḥadīth scholar in 982/372, the year after his presumed Sīmjūrid patron lost the governorship?

Whether he served as chief qāḍī for all or only for part of the period 962/351–981/371, it was an experience that marked him for life. Whenever he is mentioned in later years, which he frequently is because of his teaching of ḥadīth, he is referred to as al-Qāḍī al-Ḥīrī or simply as al-Qāḍī.[9] Among the Ḥanafīs, a reference to al-Qāḍī, pure and simple, could only have produced confusion since there were many Ḥanafī qāḍīs. But among the Shāfiᶜīs, Abū Bakr Aḥmad al-Ḥarashī al-Ḥīrī was the one and only qāḍī;[10] no further description was needed. He was living proof, at least until his death in 1030/421, that the Ḥanafīs need not have a monopoly on judicial power.

Once he had lost the office, however, he needed employment, and in 982/372 he turned to the formal study of ḥadīth which he had studied routinely as a young man. Thus began his second career. Ten years later he himself began to teach ḥadīth, and he continued to do so up until his death at the age of ninety-six or ninety-seven. As the other members of his generation died, one after another, the value of his chain of transmission became increasingly magnified. Moreover, he took exceptional care in reciting ḥadīth so that despite his advancing age, he remained a reliable authority to within a few years of his death.

The Bālawī family comes onto the scene with a great rush. Aḥmad b. ᶜAbd Allāh b. Aḥmad b. Bālūya al-Bālawī had five sons, all named Muḥammad.[11] Not a great deal of information is available on any of them, but the overall picture of the family is clear. Abū Naṣr Muḥammad (20) is called "the broker's son." His brothers Abū Muḥammad Muḥammad (21) and Abū Bakr Muḥammad (22) are themselves called brokers (*jallāb*). A fourth brother, Abū Manṣūr Muḥammad (23), is called a clothesdealer (*kisāʾī*).[12] There is no indication of the profession of the fifth brother, Abū ᶜAlī Muḥammad (24). Thus, there is every reason to believe that the family was essentially commercial, although by this time it had been important in the city long enough to be described in

9. Bosworth's identification of "al-Qāḍī" with the Ḥanafī Abū al-ᶜAlāʾ Ṣāᶜid (*The Ghaznavids*, p. 175) is mistaken.

10. Abū ᶜAmr Muḥammad al-Basṭāmī was also a Shāfiᶜī qāḍī, but his tenure was the result of a transient political situation and was too brief to be significant (chapter 5).

11. The pertinent biographies are frequently guilty of deleting two rungs in the genealogical ladder.

12. The word is confusingly misspelled in the often defective manuscript of al-Ḥākim, but this is its most probable reading.

the biography of Abū Bakr Muḥammad as being one of the great houses with old wealth.

That the wealth of the family was impressive there can be no doubt. Abū Naṣr Muḥammad, in particular, after studying in Baghdad with his brother Abū Bakr from 898/285 to 903/290, was a regular attendant at the court of the newly risen Sāmānid dynasty until he finally tired of court life and retreated to Abū Bakr Muḥammad's mosque to end his days, leaving the job of currying favor with the mighty to his children. Besides this, there was sufficient leisure available to the brothers for them to engage in the affairs of the learned community and thus become truly a part of the patriciate. In addition to the two brothers already mentioned, Abū ᶜAlī Muḥammad also studied in Baghdad. He was a legal witness as well. Abū Muḥammad and Abū Naṣr were students of ḥadīth.

As for the sequence of the brothers Bālawī, nothing can be affirmed about Abū Manṣūr and Abū Muḥammad. Abū Naṣr was probably the oldest, dying in his eighties in 950/339. Then comes Abū Bakr, who died the next year but was only seventy-four at the time. And last comes Abū ᶜAlī, who died much later in 984/374 but at the age of ninety-four.

This is not all of the Bālawī family, however. From a collateral line in this generation come Abū Muḥammad ᶜAbd Allāh b. Aḥmad b. Muḥammad b. ᶜAbd Allāh b. Bālūya al-Bālawī (25) and his brother Abū al-Ḥusain (26).

Nothing is known about Abū al-Ḥusain, but Abū Muḥammad ᶜAbd Allāh was an active and influential person in the city as well as being, curiously enough, a devotee of Sufis who catered to the common people. He died in 988/378.

IX. The pre-eminent member of the Maḥmī house in the previous generation was the raᵓīs Abū al-Faḍl Muḥammad. He had two sons, ᶜAbd ar-Raḥmān, the elder, who is known only through his own sons, and Abūᶜ Amr ᶜUthmān (27), who became raᵓīs like his father. Beyond generalities about his aristocratic upbringing and details about whom he transmitted ḥadīth from, little is known about Abū ᶜAmr ᶜUthmān except that he served as a muzakkī and ardently supported Sufism. He was born in 1002/392 and died in 1088/481.

The only other Maḥmī in this generation is Abū Aḥmad ᶜUbaid Allāh (28) the son of Abū al-Qāsim an-Naḍir. Once again little information is given beyond his family's prominence and wealth and his teachers' names. He died in 1029/420.

The Ḥarashi side of the family, too, appears to decline in this generation. Abū Bakr Aḥmad al-Ḥīrī al-Ḥarashī did not produce a successor to the family position of leading Shāfiᶜī jurist. No biography of his one son, ᶜAbd ar-Raḥmān, is preserved; nor is there one of the man his daughter married, Muḥammad al-Bālawī, scion of the collateral line of Bālawī's represented in the previous generation by Abū Muḥammad ᶜAbd Allāh al-Bālawī and his brother Abū al-Ḥusain who may also have had a son named Muḥammad (29).

If the Maḥmī and Ḥarashī blood was running thin, however, the Bālawīs were still on the ascendant. Some ambiguity exists as to who was the son of whom, unfortunately, so one line of filiation must remain indefinite. But this does not apply to the youngest son of Abū Naṣr Muḥammad al-Bālawī, whose name, Abū Saᶜīd (30), has been preserved and nothing more, or to Abū Muḥammad ᶜAbd ar-Raḥmān (31), the son of Abū ᶜAlī Muḥammad al-Bālawī. Abū Muḥammad ᶜAbd ar-Raḥmān was a student of law and was a muzakkī as were others of his family and, indeed, as the early members of the Ḥarashī family had been. But more important, he was very well educated in ḥadīth. This education, combined with the prominence already obtained by the Bālawī family through commerce, led Abū ᶜAmr al-Baḥīrī[13] and another noted scholar to become interested in him and, in effect, to sponsor him for admission to the restricted company of ḥadīth teachers. Essentially, the convening of a ḥadīth class for him by the shaikhs of the city marks the final acceptance of the Bālawī clan to full membership in the patriciate. Unfortunately, less than a year after he had begun teaching in his house he died suddenly in 1019/410. Whether the marriage between his cousin and the daughter of Abū Bakr Aḥmad al-Ḥīrī al-Ḥarashī, also a sign of the Bālawīs' heightened status, took place before or after this date cannot be ascertained.

The final member of the Bālawī family in this generation is the one who is difficult to fix genealogically. His father was named Muḥammad, but in the previous generation there was a plethora of Muḥammads. His own name was Abū Naṣr Aḥmad (32), and he was alive in the year 1006/396, which effectively rules out Abū Naṣr Muḥammad and Abū Bakr Muḥammad, both of whom died more than fifty years before. Among the remaining three Muḥammad's, the only basis for choice is the rather flimsy one that Abū Manṣūr Muḥammad may have enjoyed the euphony of having a son named Abū

13. See chapter 12 and Baḥīrī genealogical key #5.

Naṣr Aḥmad, and it is on this basis that the filiation shown on the family tree is put forward. This being said, there is little to add about Abū Naṣr Aḥmad except that he was a legal witness in the family tradition.

X. The title raʾīs is held in this generation of the Maḥmī family by Abū al-Qāsim ʿAlī (33) who is described as the son of a raʾīs. Since he predeceased in 1080/472 his uncle, the raʾīs Abū ʿAmr ʿUthmān, it seems likely he inherited the title from his father as the eldest son of an eldest son and then died without having a son himself, thus passing it on to his uncle. As several other people bearing the title are known from this same period, the exact significance and locus of the title are in doubt in any case.

Aside from whatever function his title implies, Abū al-Qāsim ʿAlī went to Iraq and served there as a governor and courtier. When he returned to Nishapur, he enjoyed such status as to be able to hold ḥadīth classes on his own authority which were attended by all of the leading patricians. At this death he freed his slaves and bequeathed a portion of his estate to the poor and the needy with Abū Saʿd ʿAbd Allāh al-Qushairī, the eldest son of the great Ashʿarī Sufi, as trustee.

His brother Abū al-Ḥasan Aḥmad (34) does not have the title raʾīs. He lived most of the time in the area of Rukhkh and entered Nishapur only occasionally. He was born in 1008/398 and died in 1092/485. With him the Maḥmī family comes to an end. No further members can be traced in later generations.

There are still two names to be mentioned, however, belonging to members of the family who cannot be fitted onto the family tree for want of adequate genealogical information. Abū al-Maḥāsin Muḥammad b. ʿAbd Allāh b. Aḥmad al-Maḥmī (35) is particularly noteworthy because unlike every other member of his family, he was a Ḥanafī instead of a Shāfiʿī. Clearly this is an extraordinary case of a change of madhhab within a family, and it must have given rise to great awkwardness during the factional disturbances that plagued Nishapur during his lifetime, 1021/412–1098/491. The reason given for the change is that Abū al-Maḥāsin's maternal grandfather was a Ḥanafī and an important personage. Unfortunately, the details of this unusual marriage across factional lines are not given.

Abū Bakr ʿUbaid Allāh b. Muḥammad al-Maḥmī (36) is only slightly less noteworthy because of the second surname he bears, as-Sarrāj, "the saddler." Although he himself surely was not a saddler, he obviously had ancestors on the non-Maḥmī side of his lineage who were engaged in the saddlery business. There were several prominent families of this name in Nishapur, and the specific one involved here cannot be determined; but this link between a family of merchant background and one of landed aristocratic background is indicative of the equality of status enjoyed by the various components of the patriciate.

In the Ḥarashī line Abū Bakr Aḥmad al-Ḥīrī al-Ḥarashī had two grandsons after whom the family becomes untraceable. Abū al-Barakāt Masᶜūd b. ᶜAbd ar-Raḥmān al-Ḥarashī (37) is noted as a member of a wealthy and important family but does not himself seem to have amounted to much. He was born in 1014/404, and he died in 1082/475. Abū ᶜAbd Allāh Manṣūr b. Muḥammad b. ᶜAbd Allāh al-Bālawī al-Ḥīrī (38) was the son of Abū Bakr Aḥmad's daughter. He, too, seems to have left little mark.

In the other branch of the Bālawī family, Abū Naṣr Aḥmad had a son named Abū Bakr ᶜAlī (39) who carried on family tradition by being a muzakkī and also achieved prominence in the transmission of ḥadīth. Abū Muḥammad ᶜAbd ar-Raḥmān[14] had a son named Saᶜīd about whom nothing is known at all save that he married the daughter of Abū al-Ḥusain Aḥmad b. ᶜAbd ar-Raḥmān al-Kayyālī (40). The name Kayyālī means grain measurer and in terms of origin the family was probably much on a par with the Bālawīs, who were originally brokers. Abū al-Ḥusain Aḥmad al-Kayyālī was himself a wealthy estate owner, however. Evidently, like the Bālawīs, the Kayyālīs had risen to the level of the patriciate. Abū al-Ḥusain Aḥmad's brother, Abū Saᶜd Ismāᶜīl (41) was a Sufi who lived in the convent of Abū ᶜAbd ar-Raḥmān as-Sulamī and was known for the meticulously embroidered caps he made for as-Sulamī. Abū al-Ḥusain Aḥmad himself was a ḥadīth scholar. He was born in 994/384 and died in 1085/478. Besides the daughter who married al-Bālawī, he had a son named Masᶜūd.

XI. Only one name remains to be mentioned. The marriage between the Bālawī and Kayyālī families produced a son, Abū Saᶜīd ᶜAbd ar-Raḥmān al-Bālawī (42), who died in early adulthood.

14. His grandson's biography, which is the source for information about the link between the Bālawīs and Kayyālīs, gives his kunya as Abū Saᶜīd instead of Abū Muḥammad, but this could either be an error or evidence that ᶜAbd ar-Raḥmān al-Bālawī was known by two kunyas, a not unheard of practice.

Genealogical Key

Maḥmī–Ḥarashī–Bālawī

1.	Abū al-Ḥasan Aḥmad al-Maḥmī	Samᶜānī, II, 379.
2.	Aḥmad b. ᶜAmr al-Ḥarashī	ᶜIbar, I, 390; Ḥākim, f9a.
3.	Abū ᶜAbd Allāh Muḥammad al-Ḥarashī	Samᶜānī, IV, 125.
4.	Ismāᶜīl b. ᶜAbdūs al-Ḥarashī	Ḥākim, f19b.
5.	Abū ᶜAmr Aḥmad al-Ḥarashī	Ḥuffāẓ, III, 798–799; Ḥākim, f20b; I. Jauzī, VI, 225.
6.	Abū al-ᶜAbbās Muḥammad al-Bālawī	Ḥākim, f25a.
7.	Abū Manṣūr ᶜUbaid Allāh al-Maḥmī	Samᶜānī, f513a; Ḥākim, f44b.
8.	Abū ᶜAlī al-Ḥasan al-Maḥmī	Samᶜānī, f512b; T. Baghdād, VII, 277.
9.	Umm al-Ḥusain Jumᶜa al-Maḥmī	Ḥākim, f40b; Fārisī II, f50b.
10.	Abū ᶜAlī al-Ḥasan al-Ḥarashī	Samᶜānī, IV, 124; Ḥākim, f40b.
11.	Abū Naṣr Muḥammad al-Ḥarashī	Ḥākim, f48a.
12.	Abū Isḥāq Ibrāhīm b. ᶜAbd Allāh b. ᶜAbdūs al-Ḥarashī	Ḥākim, f30b.
13.	Abū Ḥāmid Aḥmad al-Bālawī	Subkī, III, 108, 110.
14.	Abū al-Ḥusain ᶜAbd al-Wāḥid al-Bālawī	Samᶜānī, II, 61; Ḥākim, f33a; Lubāb, I, 92.
15.	Abū al-Faḍl Muḥammad al-Maḥmī	Fārisī II, f2b; Ḥākim, f55b.
16.	Abū Muḥammad ᶜAbd Allāh al-Maḥmī	Samᶜānī, f513a.
17.	Abū al-Qāsim an-Naḍir al-Maḥmī	Samᶜānī, f513a; Fārisī I, f93b; II, f138b.
18.	Abū Naṣr ᶜAlī al-Ḥarashī	Fārisī II, f110b.
19.	Abū Bakr Aḥmad al-Ḥarashī "al-Qāḍī al-Ḥīrī"	Ḥākim, f36b; Fārisī II, f22a–b; Subkī, IV, 6–7; Samᶜānī IV, 122–124, 327–328; ᶜIbar, III, 141; Shadharāt, III, 217.
20.	Abū Naṣr Muḥammad al-Bālawī	Samᶜānī, II, 63; Ḥākim, f47b.
21.	Abū Muḥammad Muḥammad al-Bālawī	Ḥākim, f47a.

Maḥmī

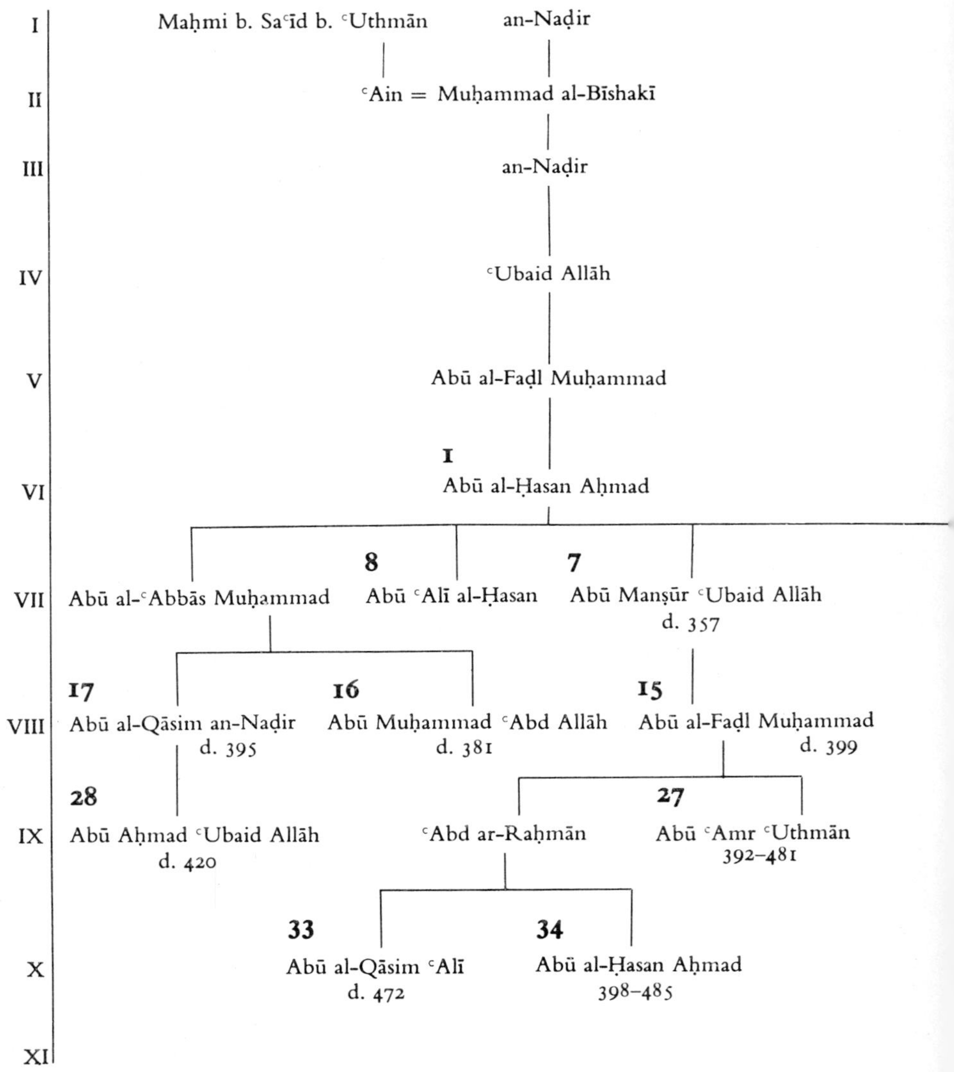

I	Maḥmi b. Saʿīd b. ʿUthmān an-Naḍir
II	ʿAin = Muḥammad al-Bīshakī
III	an-Naḍir
IV	ʿUbaid Allāh
V	Abū al-Faḍl Muḥammad
VI	**1** Abū al-Ḥasan Aḥmad
VII	Abū al-ʿAbbās Muḥammad **8** Abū ʿAlī al-Ḥasan **7** Abū Manṣūr ʿUbaid Allāh d. 357
VIII	**17** Abū al-Qāsim an-Naḍir d. 395 **16** Abū Muḥammad ʿAbd Allāh d. 381 **15** Abū al-Faḍl Muḥammad d. 399
IX	**28** Abū Aḥmad ʿUbaid Allāh d. 420 ʿAbd ar-Raḥmān **27** Abū ʿAmr ʿUthmān 392–481
X	**33** Abū al-Qāsim ʿAlī d. 472 **34** Abū al-Ḥasan Aḥmad 398–485
XI	

Ḥarashī

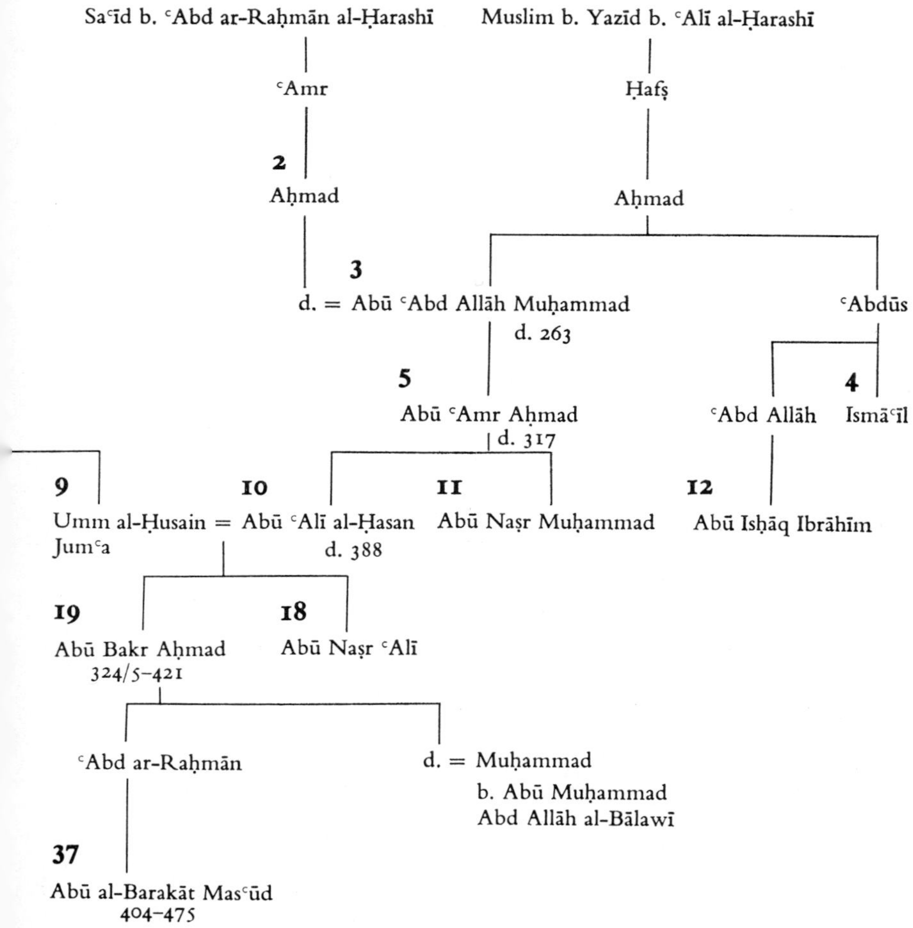

Saʿīd b. ʿAbd ar-Raḥmān al-Ḥarashī

ʿAmr

2 Aḥmad

3 d. = Abū ʿAbd Allāh Muḥammad
d. 263

Muslim b. Yazīd b. ʿAlī al-Ḥarashī

Ḥafṣ

Aḥmad

ʿAbdūs

5 Abū ʿAmr Aḥmad
d. 317

ʿAbd Allāh   **4** Ismāʿīl

9 Umm al-Ḥusain = Abū ʿAlī al-Ḥasan   **11** Abū Naṣr Muḥammad
Jumʿa   **10**   d. 388

12 Abū Isḥāq Ibrāhīm

19 Abū Bakr Aḥmad
324/5–421

18 Abū Naṣr ʿAlī

ʿAbd ar-Raḥmān

d. = Muḥammad
b. Abū Muḥammad
Abd Allāh al-Bālawī

37 Abū al-Barakāt Masʿūd
404–475

Bālawī

I

II

III

IV Bālūya

V ᶜAbd Allāh

VI Muḥammad

VII **13** Abū Ḥāmid Aḥmad

VIII **25** Abū Muḥammad ᶜAbd Allāh d. 378 — **26** Abū al-Ḥusain — **20** Abū Naṣr Muḥammad d. 339

IX daughter of Abū Bakr Aḥmad al-Ḥarashī = Muḥammad — **29** Muḥammad — **30** Abū Saᶜīd

X **38** Abu ᶜAbd Allāh Manṣūr al-Bālawī

XI

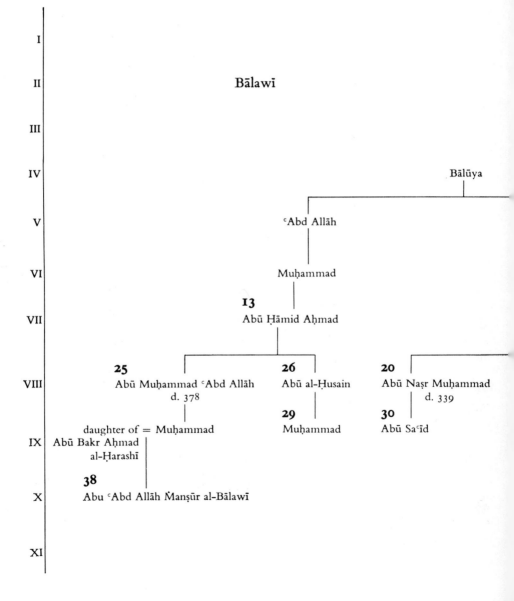

Bālawī (continued)

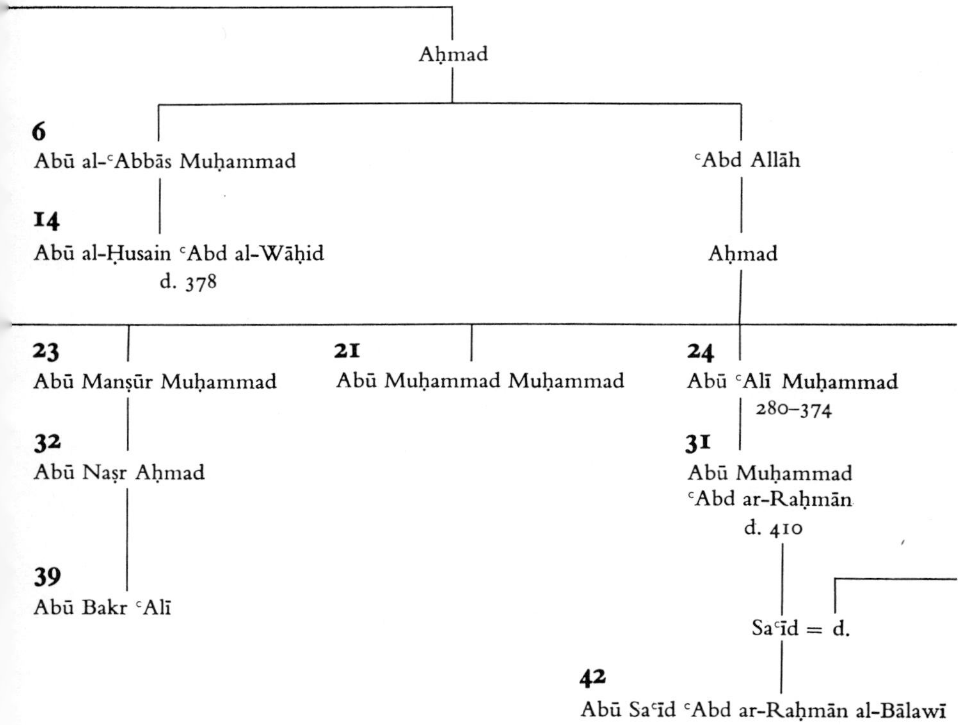
Aḥmad
6
Abū al-ᶜAbbās Muḥammad
ᶜAbd Allāh
14
Abū al-Ḥusain ᶜAbd al-Wāḥid
d. 378
Aḥmad
23
Abū Manṣūr Muḥammad
21
Abū Muḥammad Muḥammad
24
Abū ᶜAlī Muḥammad
280–374
32
Abū Naṣr Aḥmad
31
Abū Muḥammad
ᶜAbd ar-Raḥmān
d. 410
39
Abū Bakr ᶜAlī
Saᶜīd = d.
42
Abū Saᶜīd ᶜAbd ar-Raḥmān al-Bālawī

Bālawī (continued)

I

II

III

IV

V

VI

VII

22
Abū Bakr Muḥammad
266–340

ᶜAbd ar-Raḥmān al-Kayyālī VIII

40
Abū al-Ḥusain Aḥmad
384–478

41
Abū Saᶜd Ismāᶜīl IX

Masᶜūd X

XI

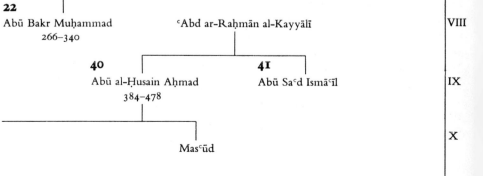

22.	Abū Bakr Muḥammad al-Bālawī	Sam^{c}ānī, II, 62.
23.	Abū Manṣūr Muḥammad al-Bālawī	Ḥākim, f48b.
24.	Abū ^{c}Alī Muḥammad al-Bālawī	Ḥākim, f47b; T. Baghdād, I, 282; I. Jauzī, VII, 124.
25.	Abū Muḥammad ^{c}Abd Allāh al-Bālawī	Sam^{c}ānī, II, 61–62; Ḥākim, f44a; Lubāb, I, 92.
26.	Abū al-Ḥusain b. Aḥmad al-Bālawī	Sam^{c}ānī, II, 62.
27.	Abū ^{c}Amr ^{c}Uthmān al-Maḥmī	^{c}Ibar, III, 298; Fārisī I, f59b; II, f109b.
28.	Abū Aḥmad ^{c}Ubaid Allāh al-Maḥmī	Fārisī I, f36a; II, f85a–b.
29.	Muḥammad b. Abū al-Ḥusain al-Bālawī	Subkī, IV, 256.
30.	Abū Sa^{c}īd b. Muḥammad al-Bālawī	Sam^{c}ānī, II, 63.
31.	Abū Muḥammad ^{c}Abd ar-Raḥmān al-Bālawī	Sam^{c}ānī, II, 62; ^{c}Ibar, III, 102; Fārisī I, f40a–b; II, f87b–88a; Shadharāt, III, 190–191.
32.	Abū Naṣr Aḥmad al-Bālawī	Ḥākim, f55b; Fārisī II, f24a.
33.	Abū al-Qāsim ^{c}Alī al-Maḥmī	Fārisī I, f65b; II, f113b.
34.	Abū al-Ḥasan Aḥmad al-Maḥmī	Fārisī II, f32a.
35.	Abū al-Maḥāsin Muḥammad al-Maḥmī (not on family tree)	Fārisī II, f17a; IAW, II, 63.
36.	Abū Bakr ^{c}Ubaid Allāh al-Maḥmī as-Sarrāj (not on family tree)	Fārisī II, f86b.
37.	Abū al-Barakāt Mas^{c}ūd al-Ḥarashī	Fārisī I, f77b; II, f126b.
38.	Abū ^{c}Abd Allāh Manṣūr al-Bālawī	Fārisī I, f88b; II, f129b.
39.	Abū Bakr ^{c}Alī al-Bālawī	Fārisī I, f61b; II, f111a–b.
40.	Abū al-Ḥusain Aḥmad al-Kayyālī	Fārisī II, f32a.
41.	Abū Sa^{c}d Ismā^{c}īl al-Kayyālī	Fārisī II, f42b–43a.
42.	Abū Sa^{c}īd ^{c}Abd ar-Raḥmān al-Bālawī	Fārisī II, f92b.

8 / *Māsarjisī*

Although in many ways and particularly in its latter days a rather commonplace patrician family, the Māsarjisī family does afford a striking example of conversion to Islam combined with maintenance of high social and religious status.[1] Māsarjis himself, grandfather of the first Muslim member of the family, was a leader of the Christian community in Nishapur, very probably a bishop. His name appears to be a compound of Mār Sergius, Mār being an Aramaic word for lord and occurring commonly as a high ecclesiastical title in the Nestorian church.[2] His son bore the very Christian name of ᶜĪsā, but nothing is known about him. It is only with his grandson that the family begins to appear in Muslim sources.

I. Abū ᶜAlī al-Ḥasan b. ᶜIsā b. Māsarjis al-Māsarjisī (1) died in either 853/239 or 854/240. His conversion to Islam had come at the hands of ᶜAbd Allāh b. al-Mubārak who died in 797/181.[3] Hence the greatest part of his life, more than seventy years, was lived as a Muslim. It is reported that ᶜAbd Allāh b. al-Mubārak, one of the most famous Khurasanian scholars of his time and himself a non-Arab of Khwarizmian and Turkish parentage, came to Nishapur and stayed for a while on ᶜĪsā Street, probably named for Abū ᶜAlī al-Ḥasan's father. Abū ᶜAlī al-Ḥasan used to ride by, and Ibn al-Mubārak singled him out because of his striking appearance and inquired who he was. Finding out that he was a Christian, Ibn al-Mubārak called upon Allah to bring him to Islam, and his prayer was answered. What is noteworthy in this tale is that Abū ᶜAlī al-Ḥasan's conversion came about not as part of an anonymous mass conversion but in response to a specific invitation, involving, one suspects, more than simply prayer, by an important, non-Arab, Muslim scholar. That he was specifically selected for proselytization by ᶜAbd Allāh b. al-Mubārak because he would be a key figure in the conversion of the Christian community in Nishapur as a whole seems more than likely.

II. Abū ᶜAlī al-Ḥasan had two daughters and one son. Abū al-Wafāʾ al-Muʾammal (2) is given the title raʾīs only in a late source, but even if he was not raʾīs of Nishapur,

1. The Barmakid family offers an instructive comparison, EI², I, 1033–36.

2. See *The Jewish Encyclopedia* (New York, 1901–1906), VIII, 317–318, and *Encyclopaedia of Religion and Ethics*, ed. J. Hastings (New York, 1908–1927), XII, 167–181. The place-name Mārsarjas mentioned by Ṭabarī in the year 747/129 apparently as being outside of Marv may be related to the family but is definitely not the source of their name (aṭ-Ṭabarī, *Taʾrīkh*, VII, 358).

3. IAW, I, 281–282; EI², III, 879; Ḥākim, f8a.

he was unquestionably one of its most eminent citizens. His learning and perfection of mind are noted in the biographies of him, but these are overshadowed by the statement that he loaned one million dirhams to ᶜAbd Allāh b. Ṭāhir, the semiautonomous ᶜAbbāsid governor of Khurasan whose seat of government was in Nishapur. Since Abū al-Wafāᵓ died in 931/319 and ᶜAbd Allāh b. Ṭāhir in 845/230, the loan may either be apocryphal or have been made to some other Ṭāhirid; whatever its basis in fact, it points to great wealth in the Māsarjisī family and active, although not necessarily voluntary, involvement with the Ṭāhirid dynasty.

The name of neither daughter has been preserved, nor are there biographies of their husbands although their names are known from the genealogies of their sons. But as interesting as it would be to know their ethnic and religious background, it is apparent that neither man enjoyed particularly high status, for their descendants all take their name Māsarjisī from their female ancestor.

III. Abū al-Wafāᵓ al-Muᵓammal had two sons. The elder was Abū Bakr Muḥammad (3), who was born in 875/261 and died in 961/350. A bit of poetry he composed for presentation to some vizier suggests continued relations with government, if, perhaps, less exalted ones than his father maintained. He was particularly noted for his faultless command of Arabic. When in 952/341 the entire family made the Pilgrimage together, the historian al-Ḥākim, then twenty years old, accompanied them and observed that Abū Bakr Muḥammad refused to speak Persian to anyone unless he knew that that person knew no Arabic and acquitted himself in Arabic so perfectly that many people did not believe that he spoke Persian at all.

His brother Abū al-Qāsim ᶜAlī (4) did not concern himself with courts and rulers. His only interest was religion, and he was well known for his piety. Although younger, he died before Abū Bakr Muḥammad in 960/349.

The establishment of the Māsarjisī family as pillars in the Shāfiᶜī madhhab was accomplished by the offspring of al-Ḥasan b. ᶜIsā's daughters. Abū al-Ḥasan Muḥammad b. ᶜAlī b. Sahl b. Muṣliḥ al-Māsarjisī (5) was born in 920/308. He took up the study of law and pursued it in Khurasan, Iraq, and the Hijaz. Eventually he settled down in Baghdad and became a disciple of Abū Isḥāq al-Marwazī[4] who was then the greatest living exponent of the Shāfiᶜī interpretation of law. When al-Marwazī moved to

4. I. Khallikān, I, 48–49.

Egypt late in life, al-Māsarjisī moved with him and remained in attendance until al-Marwazī's death in 951/340. Then he went back to Baghdad where he taught for a few years before returning to Nishapur in 955/344. Being singularly well grounded in Shāfiᶜī law, he immediately became a preeminent law teacher, and he taught ḥadīth as well, a class being convened for him in the Dār as-Sunna madrasa[5] by the family friend al-Ḥākim who was director of that institution. He died in 994/384.

The other daughter of Abū ᶜAlī al-Ḥasan b. ᶜĪsā had a son named Abū al-ᶜAbbās Aḥmad b. Muḥammad b. al-Ḥusain al-Māsarjisī (6). Nothing is known about him, however, except his date of death 925/313.

IV. Returning to the descendants of Māsarjis in the male line, Abū Bakr Muḥammad transmitted his fluent command of classical Arabic to his son Abū Muḥammad al-Ḥasan (7) whose accomplishments were in the area of polite manners and belles lettres (adab) rather than religion. However, during the family Pilgrimage of 952/341 Abū Muḥammad al-Ḥasan filled in for his father when the scholars of Baghdad invited the elder Māsarjisī to recite ḥadīth. His father, it seems, had forgotten to bring his notes along. Abū Muḥammad al-Ḥasan also had a ḥadīth class convened for him in Nishapur. He died in 964/353. The other son, Abū Ḥāmid Aḥmad (8), was a jurist and certifier of witnesses.

The more religious son of Abū al-Wafāʾ al-Muʾammal had two sons. Abū ᶜAbd Allāh Muḥammad (9) died in 990/380 at the age of seventy-one. Nothing more is known of him. Abū Muḥammad al-Ḥasan (10), surnamed al-Muʾammalī from his grandfather as well as al-Māsarjisī, was a ḥadīth scholar like his father and a legal witness. When he died in 1019/407, his body was prayed over in ᶜĪsā Street, where his great-grandfather had met conversion, and buried in the family tomb.

In the female lines, Abū al-Ḥasan Muḥammad b. ᶜAlī b. Sahl, the outstanding member of the family in the previous generation, had one son named Abū Bakr Muḥammad (11) who is only a cipher and after whom the line disappears. Abū al-ᶜAbbās Aḥmad b. Muḥammad b. al-Ḥusain in the other line had two sons who are equally unknown, Abū Muḥammad ᶜAbd Allāh (12) and Abū Aḥmad Muḥammad (13) who died in 927/315. Chronologically, this line is now a generation behind the others.

5. See Appendix I, #6.

V. The lineage of Abū Bakr Muḥammad cannot be traced in this generation. However, Abū ᶜAbd Allāh Muḥammad b. ᶜAlī b. al-Muᵓammal had a son for whom there is no separate biography named Abū Muḥammad ᶜUbaid Allāh al-Muᵓammalī. His brother Abū Muḥammad al-Ḥasan had a son known as Abū Bakr Shāh al-Muᵓammalī whose real given name was Abū Bakr Muḥammad (14). There are two biographies of him in al-Fārisī, one of which simply identifies him as coming from a house of wealth and leadership. The other tells of the family's retreat to an estate in the Baihaq area, from which Abū Bakr Shāh returned briefly in 1053/445 to recite ḥadīth in Nishapur. The Māsarjisī name, it should be noted, has by this time been entirely supplanted in this branch of the family.

As already mentioned, one of the female lines is extinct in this generation. In the other, Abū Muḥammad ᶜAbd Allāh had a son named Abū Naṣr Aḥmad (or possibly Muḥammad) (15), and Abū Aḥmad Muḥammad had two sons, one unnamed in the biographies and the other named Abū ᶜAlī al-Ḥusain (16). With this last named individual the Māsarjisī family once again attained scholarly and religious prominence to match its ongoing social prominence in Nishapur. Abū ᶜAlī al-Ḥusain was born in 911/298. At the age of twenty-three he began to travel in search of learning. He went to Iraq and then Syria, finally settling down for a long time in Egypt. His writings on ḥadīth were almost endless. Al-Ḥākim, the outstanding ḥadīth scholar of the next generation, knew of no ḥadīth collection longer than that made by Abū ᶜAlī al-Ḥusain, and he wrote many works in addition to his ḥadīth collection. There is no mention of when he returned to Nishapur, but at some time a class was convened for him to read from his works, and he died there in 976/365.

VI. The Māsarjisīs, or rather Muᵓammalīs, of the male line disappear completely after this generation, and the nature of their disappearance implies the fall of the entire clan. The remaining female line goes on for one more generation; but since chronologically it has dropped a generation behind the male line, it in fact comes to an end at the same time.

The tale of the family's decline is told in the biography of Abū Bakr Shāh al-Muᵓammalī, already mentioned, and in that of Abū al-Faḍl Aḥmad al-Muᵓammalī (17), the grandson of Abū al-Qāsim ᶜAlī al-Māsarjisī by way of his otherwise unknown son Abū Muḥammad ᶜUbaid Allāh. The latter biography records that Abū al-Faḍl Aḥmad was born into a family of ḥadīth scholars and legal witnesses which was one of the best known families in the city. But a change came over their affairs. Famine and the depredations of the Turkmen tribes brought about the destruction of their homes and the ruin of their quarter in the city. So the entire family left Nishapur and sought refuge on an estate they had in the region of Baihaq. The only return to Nishapur was that made by his uncle for teaching purposes in 1053/445. As for which Turkmen depredations are intended, they were surely those that preceded the coming of the Seljuqs; for Abū al-Faḍl Aḥmad was born in 950/339, and he would have been ninety years old at the time of the Seljuq takeover. The mention of famine suggests the year 1011/401 as the beginning of their ruin, for that was a terrible famine year.[6] Regardless of the exact timing, however, the entire incident underlines the close relation that existed between urban patrician status and rural landowning. Turkmen raids were confined to the countryside, and it is there that the family must have taken its primary losses. Likewise, it is there that the family retreated to try to salvage what remained of their once immense wealth.

All of this transpires in the next generation for the female line, however. An unknown brother of the great ḥadīth scholar Abū ᶜAlī al-Ḥusain had a son named Abū al-Ḥasan (18), who is known only for having led the funeral prayers for his famous uncle. Abū Naṣr Aḥmad, the cousin of Abū ᶜAlī al-Ḥusain, had a son as well. He was named Abū al-ᶜAbbās Aḥmad (19) after his great-grandfather. Like everyone else in his family, he studied ḥadīth. In 988/378 he died.

VII. Abū al-ᶜAbbās Aḥmad had a son named Abū Muḥammad ᶜAbd Allāh (20). Nothing is known of this last member of the Māsarjisī family, but presumably he was among those who retreated to the estate in Baihaq when the family's fortunes changed.

6. I. Funduq, pp. 175–176; Barthold, *Turkestan*, pp. 287–288.

Genealogical Key

Māsarjisī

1.	Abū ʿAlī al-Ḥasan	Samʿānī, f501a; Ḥākim, f10a; Lubāb, III, 83.
2.	Abū al-Wafāʾ al-Muʾammal	Samʿānī, f501a; Ḥākim, f28a; ʿIbar, II, 177.
3.	Abū Bakr Muḥammad	Samʿānī, f501b; Ḥākim, f53a.
4.	Abū al-Qāsim ʿAlī	Samʿānī, f501b; Ḥākim, f46b; I. Jauzī, VI, 397.
5.	Abū al-Ḥasan Muḥammad	Samʿānī, f501b; ʿIbar, III, 26; Ḥākim, f51b; Lubāb, III, 83; I. Khallikān, III, 340 (tr. IV, 175–176).
6.	Abū al-ʿAbbās Aḥmad	Ḥākim, f20b–21a; ʿIbar, II, 155.
7.	Abū Muḥammad al-Ḥasan	Samʿānī, f501b–502a; Ḥākim, f41a.
8.	Abū Ḥāmid Aḥmad	Ḥākim, f38b.
9.	Abū ʿAbd Allāh Muḥammad	Samʿānī, f501b.
10.	Abū Muḥammad al-Ḥasan	Fārisī I, f3a, II, f52a.
11.	Abū Bakr Muḥammad	Ḥākim, f54b.
12.	Abū Muḥammad ʿAbd Allāh	Ḥākim, f32b.
13.	Abū Aḥmad Muḥammad	Samʿānī, f502a; Ḥākim, f33b.
14.	Abū Bakr Shāh (Muḥammad)	Fārisī I, f30b; II, f72b, 8b–9a.
15.	Abū Naṣr Aḥmad	Ḥākim, f37a.
16.	Abū ʿAlī al-Ḥusain	Samʿānī, f502a; Ḥākim, f41b; ʿIbar, II, 336; I. Jauzī, VII, 81; Ḥuffāẓ, pp. 955–956; Shadharāt, III, 50.
17.	Abū al-Faḍl Aḥmad	Fārisī II, f28b.
18.	Abū al-Ḥasan	Samʿānī, f501b; Ḥuffāẓ, p. 956.
19.	Abū al-ʿAbbās Aḥmad	Samʿānī, f501b; Ḥākim, f39a.
20.	Abū Muḥammad ʿAbd Allāh	Ḥākim, f54b.

Māsarjisī

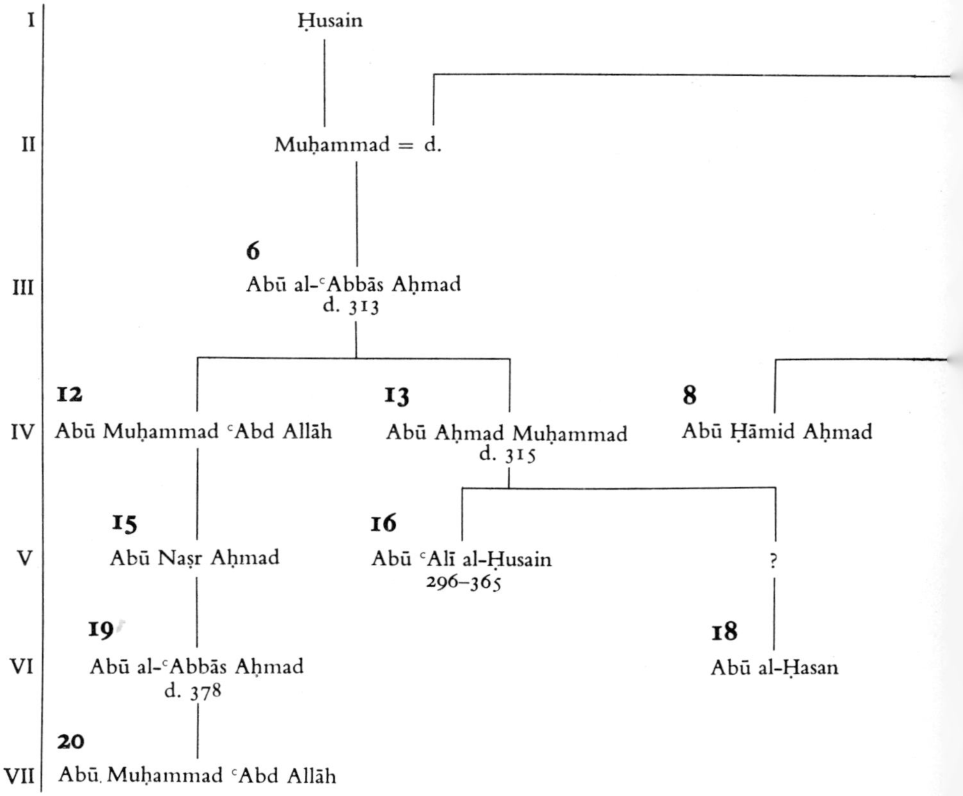

I	Ḥusain
II	Muḥammad = d.
III	**6** Abū al-ᶜAbbās Aḥmad d. 313
IV	**12** Abū Muḥammad ᶜAbd Allāh — **13** Abū Aḥmad Muḥammad d. 315 — **8** Abū Ḥāmid Aḥmad
V	**15** Abū Naṣr Aḥmad — **16** Abū ᶜAlī al-Ḥusain 296–365 — ?
VI	**19** Abū al-ᶜAbbās Aḥmad d. 378 — **18** Abū al-Ḥasan
VII	**20** Abū Muḥammad ᶜAbd Allāh

Māsarjisī (continued)

- Māsarjis
  - ᶜĪsā
    - **1** Abū ᶜAlī al-Ḥasan, d. 239 or 240
      - **2** Abū al-Wafāʾ al-Muʾammal, d. 319
        - **3** Abū Bakr Muḥammad, 261–350
          - **7** Abū Muḥammad al-Ḥasan, d. 353
        - **4** Abū al-Qāsim ᶜAlī, d. 349
          - **9** Abū ᶜAbd Allāh Muḥammad, 309–380
            - Abū Muḥammad ᶜUbaid Allāh
              - **17** Abū al-Faḍl Aḥmad, b. 339
          - **10** Abū Muḥammad al-Ḥasan, d. 407
            - **14** Abū Bakr Shāh (Muḥammad)

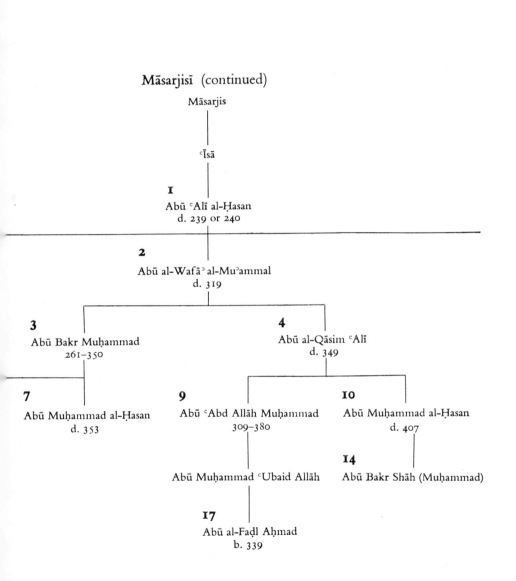

Māsarjisī (continued)

Muṣliḥ

Sahl — I

d. = ᶜAlī — II

5
Abū al-Ḥasan Muḥammad
308–384 — III

11
Abū Bakr Muḥammad — IV

V

VI

VII

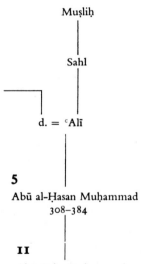

9 / *Basṭāmī–Ṣuᶜlūkī–Juwainī*

I–II. It was said of Abū Sahl Muḥammad aṣ-Ṣuᶜlūkī (1) that "the people of his age concurred that he was a sea of knowledge which was never emptied however many buckets were taken from it, a mountain of learning that no adversary could overcome except as the wind did." It was also said of him, this time by the famous Būyid vizier Ṣāḥib ibn al-ᶜAbbād: "I have never seen the like of him—and he has never seen the like of himself." From what is recorded about him, both statements seem to apply equally well to this poet, jurist, philologist, Sufi pillar of the Shāfiᶜī-Ashᶜarī faction in tenth/fourth century Nishapur.

He was named al-Ḥanafī because of his descent from the tribe of Banū Ḥanīfa, al-ᶜIjlī because of his descent from the tribe of Banū ᶜIjl, and al-Iṣbahānī because of his being born in or living for a number of years in Isfahan; but he was primarily known as aṣ-Ṣuᶜlūkī, a name that denotes a poor vagabond or desert wanderer.[1] There is no clue as to the origin of this name, which is sometimes associated with brigandage, and indeed the origin of Abū Sahl Muḥammad himself is not altogether certain. Ibn Khallikān reports that he was born in Isfahan, but there is very strong evidence that he was actually born in Nishapur. The year of his birth was 909/296, and he began to attend classes in ḥadīth when he was nine years old. Among his early teachers were Ibn Khuzaima[2] and Abū al-ᶜAbbās Aḥmad al-Māsarjisī,[3] who died in 923/311 and 925/313 respectively. While it is not actually unbelievable that a fifteen year old boy might have found his way from Isfahan to Nishapur to study under these scholars, it is altogether more probable that he was born in or near the latter city.

He excelled in his initial studies of ḥadīth and law, and at the tender age of twenty-one he engaged in scholarly debate before the Sāmānid vizier Abū al-Faḍl al-Balᶜamī. Then, in 934/322, he left Khurasan for Iraq, leaving behind an infant son. He did not return for fifteen years. Those were years filled with learning and steady growth in prestige. It was in Iraq that he became an expert in Ashᶜarī theology and a devotee of Sufi mysticism. Then he was invited to Isfahan, then one of the Būyid capitals, where he soon came to occupy a position of considerable importance.

The story is related that one cold winter's day in Isfahan Abū Sahl gave the cloak that he was wearing to a poor man and was obliged as a result to go off to teach his law class in a woman's cloak since in true ascetic tradition he did not himself own another cloak.

1. For observations on the social significance of the word, see Cahen, *Mouvements populaires*, p. 49.
2. Subkī, III, 109–119.
3. See chapter 8 and Māsarjisī genealogical key #6.

It so happened that that very day a delegation of local scholars including jurists, theologians, and grammarians came to summon him to appear before the ruler, who was apparently the great Būyid amir ᶜImād ad-Dawla. Obedient to the princely summons, Abū Sahl threw an outer garment over his woman's cloak and road off with the delegation. When the amir caught sight of him, he said in indignation, "Does he make light of me? The *imām* of the city riding dressed in a woman's robe!" But he was soon placated by Abū Sahl's ability to best in debate all of the assembled scholars on all subjects. This was not the last time that Abū Sahl demonstrated the commanding superiority of his erudition.

In 949/337 Abū Sahl's paternal uncle Abū aṭ-Ṭayyib Aḥmad aṣ-Ṣuᶜlūkī (2), himself known for his scholarship in law, philology, and ḥadīth, died, a blind but still productive old man, in Nishapur. Wanting to be in attendance at his uncle's funeral but knowing that the people of Isfahan would bend every effort to persuade him not to leave, Abū Sahl left the city in secret and returned to Nishapur bringing to an end his fifteen year absence. He sat for three days at his uncle's bier before the body was interred in the Bāghak cemetery, and out of respect all of the prominent jurists of both the Shāfiᶜī and Ḥanafī madhhabs sat with him.

His funeral vigil concluded, Abū Sahl did not return to Isfahan but settled down to teach in Nishapur. He had no more thought of wandering. Every day at noontime he held a class for dictating legal texts, and on every Wednesday evening he held a formal disputation. His position as the city's preeminent scholar of Shāfiᶜī law was soon recognized and respected by Ḥanafīs and Shāfiᶜīs alike. It was a position he was to retain until his death thirty-two years later. As time went on his teaching schedule changed so that Tuesday evenings were reserved for legal disputations and Saturday evenings for theological disputations, but not until 975/365, only four years before his death, did he finally give in to the repeated requests that were made of him to teach ḥadīth. He held his class in ḥadīth on Friday evenings.

There is little doubt but that it was Abū Sahl aṣ-Ṣuᶜlūkī who first supplied a strong backbone for the Shāfiᶜī-Ashᶜarī faction. His erudition was deep, his scholarship impeccable, and his educational standards rigorous and uncompromising. Abū ᶜAbd ar-Raḥmān as-Sulamī, the great Sufi of the following generation, was one of his students and is reported to have said that after a certain discourse that had gone on between him and Abū Sahl, he asked the master "Why?" In reply Abū Sahl said, "Do you not know that whoever says to his master 'Why?' shall never meet with success?" And in further testimony to Abū Sahl's rigorous authoritarianism, as-Sulamī quotes him as saying: "Disobedience toward parents can be erased by forgiveness; disobedience toward teachers can be erased in no way." It seems fitting that at his death in 980/369 Abū Sahl was buried beneath the spot where he had taught.

III. Abū Sahl's son Abū aṭ-Ṭayyib Sahl aṣ-Ṣuᶜlūkī (3) was not as imposing a man as his father, but he did not fall far short of his measure. He was not a Sufi, and he certainly owned more than one cloak. He was, in fact, a rich man with a reputation for open-handedness and largesse. At his father's death he was away visiting some of his estates, which caused his father sorer pain than did his illness; but if, as seems most probable, Abū Sahl had himself been absent from Nishapur during fifteen years of his son's youth, some deficiency in filial piety is perhaps understandable.

The date of Abū aṭ-Ṭayyib's birth is unknown and the date of his death in question. His career was spent primarily in the teaching of Shāfiᶜī law, and al-Ḥākim reports that on a certain Friday evening in 997/387 no less than five hundred inkpots were set out for his class. He followed in his father's footsteps in the field of Ashᶜarī theology as well. His services to the Shāfiᶜī-Ashᶜarī faction did not stop there, however. As important as was his teaching, even more important was the care and attention he paid to the education and upbringing of his twin Basṭāmī grandsons and his adopted protégé, the son of a man who was converted from the Ḥanafī to the Shāfiᶜī faction by his father Abū Sahl aṣ-Ṣuᶜlūkī's prestige and later murdered as a result, Abū ᶜUthmān Ismāᶜīl aṣ-Ṣābūnī.[4] These were the men who were to carry the Shāfiᶜī-Ashᶜarī faction to great heights in the early years of Seljuq rule.

As for the dates suggested for Abū aṭ-Ṭayyib's death, 997/387 is definitely too early considering his adoption of aṣ-Ṣābūnī. This leaves 1012/402 and 1014/404 between which there are no grounds for choice.

IV. One of the daughters of Abū aṭ-Ṭayyib Sahl aṣ-Ṣuᶜlūkī married Abū al-Futūḥ ar-Riḍā al-Ḥasanī (4), and a discussion of the match is contained in the history of the Ḥasanī family. The other daughter married Abū ᶜAmr Muḥammad al-Basṭāmī (5), and it was in the Basṭāmī family that the scholarship and authority of the Ṣuᶜlūkīs found its continuation. The antecedents of Abū ᶜAmr al-Basṭāmī cannot be traced; but since his

4. See chapter 10 and Ṣābūnī genealogical key #1.

family originated in the town of Bistam, their lack of roots in Nishapur need not imply lack of prominence in preceding generations. Abū ᶜAmr was a jurist and theologian and is described as being the equal of Abū aṭ-Ṭayyib aṣ-Ṣuᶜlūkī in family status and worldly accomplishment. At some time in his life he made an extremely successful journey to Baghdad where he was greatly honored and his brilliance recognized. It is hard to tell whether it was before or after his success in Baghdad that he came to be considered the leader of the Shāfiᶜī party in Nishapur, but the position was to continue in the family until the destruction of the city. Al-Fārisī, writing around 1029/420, says that the post had been in the Basṭāmī family for about 150 years, which would date Abū ᶜAmr's assumption of the post around 981/370.[5] He also held the post of chief qāḍī, apparently the last Shāfiᶜī ever to do so. The date of his appointment was 998/388, presumably during the brief return to power in the city of the pro-Shāfiᶜī Sīmjūrid family, and his tenure in office seems to have been very brief since Abū al-ᶜAlāʾ Ṣāᶜid's career in the same office is described as being uninterrupted from 987/377 to 1002/392. Thus, there seems to be ample justification for the remark that Abū ᶜAmr and Abū aṭ-Ṭayyib were equals and hence that the marriage alliance between the Ṣuᶜlūkīs and the Basṭāmīs was a perfectly natural one. Abū ᶜAmr died in 1016/407 or 1017/408.

Abū Ibrāhīm Ismāᶜīl al-Basṭāmī (6) did not share his brother Abū ᶜAmr's prominence. He was knowledgeable in law, poetry, and adab, but nothing more is known about him.

V. The two sons of Abū Ibrāhīm Ismāᶜīl al-Basṭāmī may be mentioned and forgotten, for nothing is known either of them or of their possible descendants. They were Abū ᶜAbd Allāh Muḥammad (7) and Abū aṭ-Ṭayyib Sahl (8), the latter obviously named for Abū aṭ-Ṭayyib Sahl aṣ-Ṣuᶜlūkī. The important members of this generation are the children of Abū ᶜAmr Muḥammad al-Basṭāmī, his two daughters and two sons.

Abū Muḥammad Hibat Allāh (9) and Abū al-Maᶜālī ᶜUmar (10) were twins. They were reared and educated by Abū aṭ-Ṭayyib Sahl aṣ-Ṣuᶜlūkī, their grandfather, possibly because of their father's sojourn in Baghdad, and it was aṣ-Ṣuᶜlūkī who gave them the nicknames by which they were invariably known, al-Muwaffaq for Abū Muḥammad, usually given as Imām al-Muwaffaq, and al-Muʾayyad for Abū al-Maᶜālī. Despite their

5. Fārisī II, f108b.

identical upbringing, however, al-Muwaffaq became a much more important personage than did his brother.

It was al-Muwaffaq who, while still only a youth, succeeded his father in the position of chief of the Shāfiᶜī madhhab. All teaching of Shāfiᶜī law throughout the city came under his jurisdiction, and even the most venerable Shāfiᶜī scholars, such as Abū Isḥāq al-Isfarāʾinī,[6] and Abū Ṭāhir az-Ziyādī,[7] recognized his authority. He had held this position of undisputed Shāfiᶜī leadership for some twenty years when the Seljuqs arose to challenge Ghaznavid supremacy in Khurasan, and it was Imām al-Muwaffaq who took the lead in arranging the city's change in allegiance to the new Turkish dynasty.[8] This, in turn, secured for him special favor in the eyes of the new rulers. It is possible that for a while he was actually the vizier of Ṭughril Beg,[9] but more probably he contented himself with the informal post of adviser and left the vizierate for someone of a less patrician and more bureaucratic mentality. Nāṣir-i Khusraw, who travelled through Nishapur in 1046/437, accords him the ambiguous title of *khwāja* of Ṭughril Beg,[10] and al-Fārisī says only that his word was listened to by the Seljuqs and the deference paid him was so great that whatsoever he wished to do he did.

Imām al-Muwaffaq's twin brother al-Muʾayyad benefited from the change to Seljuq government as well. Very little is known about al-Muʾayyad, but it is certain that he married the daughter of an ᶜAlid named Abū al-Ḥasan Muḥammad b. ᶜAlī al-Hamadhānī[11] and that he sat on the maẓālim court which was normally the exclusive province of the state bureaucracy. It was undoubtedly his brother's influence that secured for him the appointment, but it was more than simply a sinecure since it gave the Shāfiᶜīs a voice in the judicial arena from which they were usually excluded by Ḥanafī domination of the post of qāḍī. Considering that Abū ᶜUthmān Ismāᶜīl aṣ-Ṣābūnī, the protégé

6. Subkī, IV, 256–262; Ḥākim, f39b; Fārisī II, f35a–36a.

7. Fārisī II, f2a; Samᶜānī, VI, 360.

8. Bosworth's contention (*The Ghaznavids*, pp. 261–262) that Imām al-Muwaffaq bore the title Ṣāḥib-i Ḥadīthān signifying leadership of some sort of paramilitary organization analogous to that of the *aḥdāth* in Syria cannot be maintained. The title occurs in but a single reference, and the existence of such a group is unsupported by even indirect evidence. Most likely the epithet is a corruption of a phrase pertaining to Imām al-Muwaffaq's ḥadīth scholarship.

9. Harold Bowen, "Notes on Some Early Seljuqid Viziers," *Bulletin of the School of Oriental and African Studies*, 20 (1957), 105–110.

10. Nāṣir-i Khusraw, *Safarnāmeh*, ed. Muḥammad Dabīr Siyāqī (Tehran, 1956), p. 3.

11. Samᶜānī, f321b.

of Abū aṭ-Ṭayyib Sahl aṣ-Ṣuᶜlūkī, was at the same time serving as khaṭīb of the Congregational Mosque, the power of the Shāfiᶜī party was great indeed in the early years of Seljuq rule.

The palmy days were not to last for the Shāfiᶜīs, however, and the indirect cause of their coming to an end in the persecution of the Ashᶜarīs was Imām al-Muwaffaq himself. Abū Naṣr Manṣūr al-Kundurī came from a family of no great distinction in the town of Kundur on the southern edge of the Nishapur region.[12] He came to Nishapur to seek his fortune, and he sought it at the door of Imām al-Muwaffaq who was in a perfect position to advance the careers of talented young men. Imām al-Muwaffaq recognized his native talents and took him on as a protégé, introducing him in the course of time to the court of Ṭughril Beg. From there on al-Kundurī made his own way. He rose meteorically. Well before he was thirty years old he was vizier of Ṭughril's empire. Then he turned on the Shāfiᶜīs who had given him his start and launched the persecution that was to come close to destroying them in Nishapur. The timetable of these events cannot be ascertained in great detail, but al-Kundurī was born in 1019/410 and was still on cordial terms with the Shāfiᶜī community in 1043/434 when the poet Bākharzī first met him at an assembly in the house of Imām al-Muwaffaq.[13] The persecution seems to have started in 1048/440, presumably after the death of Imām al-Muwaffaq in that year which threw the leadership of the Shāfiᶜīs into the relatively inexperienced hands of his young son. Al-Muʾayyad lived on until 1073/465, but he is not known to have played any significant role in the persecution or in the restoration of the Shāfiᶜīs under Niẓām al-Mulk.

As for the two daughters of Abū ᶜAmr Muḥammad al-Basṭāmī, Ḥurra (11) was well educated and herself a teacher. She died after 1078/470. The two biographies of the other daughter ᶜĀʾisha (12) are so like the one of Ḥurra that there is a definite possibility that the two daughters are actually one and that Ḥurra (Noble, Wellborn) is meant as an epithet rather than as a name. Duplicated biographies under different names for the same person do occur in al-Fārisī, and this may be such a case. Unfortunately, a death date, which might settle the question, is not given for ᶜĀʾisha. Whatever the case may be, a daughter of Abū ᶜAmr married a man named Abū ᶜAlī al-Ḥusain al-Qārī (13) who was the raʾīs of Isfarāʾin. Little is known about him personally, save that he was wealthy

12. Fārisī I, f88a–b; II, f129b; I. Khallikān, IV, 222–227.

13. Abū al-Ḥasan ᶜAlī Bākharzī, *Dumya al-Qaṣr wa ᶜAṣra Ahl al-ᶜAṣr*, ed. Muḥammad Rāghib aṭ-Ṭabbākh (Aleppo, 1930), p.140.

and skilled in military affairs, but the match was an important one since Isfarāʾin was the point of origin of several of Nishapur's patrician families. Abū ᶜAlī died in 1036/427.

The Juwainī family, which eventually became linked with the Basṭāmīs, also flourished in Nishapur during this generation in the persons of the brothers Abū al-Ḥasan ᶜAlī al-Juwainī (14) and Abū Muḥammad ᶜAbd Allāh al-Juwainī (15). The former was a Sufi who spent long years in scholarly travelling, particularly in the holy cities of Arabia whence his nickname Shaikh of the Hijaz, and eventually settled in Nishapur where he taught ḥadīth in the Muṭarriz Mosque. He died in 1071/463. His brother, Abū Muḥammad, was a man of much greater importance and stature in the Shāfiᶜī community both in his own right and as the father of one of the greatest of Nishapur's Shāfiᶜī's, Imām al-Ḥaramain al-Juwainī.

Abū Muḥammad was born in Juvain, the district at the western extremity of the Nishapur region. He was educated there in adab by his father and in law as well, but he moved on for further legal training first to Nishapur, where he studied under Abū aṭ-Ṭayyib Sahl aṣ-Ṣuᶜlūkī, and then to Marv. He finally returned to Nishapur and settled down there in 1016/407. His career in Nishapur was tremendously successful, and he quickly became one of the foremost members of the Shāfiᶜī-Ashᶜarī faction. He was a prolific author, and his scholarly reputation even survived an attack made upon his integrity as a transmitter of ḥadīth by the no less prominent Shāfiᶜī Abū Bakr al-Baihaqī.[14] He died in 1047/438 before reaching old age and before the onset of the Ashᶜarī persecution. It was his son Imām al-Ḥaramain along with Imām al-Muwaffaq's son who had to bear the brunt of al-Kundurī's attack after their fathers' deaths.

VI. Imām al-Muwaffaq's successor as chief of the Shāfiᶜī madhhab and as their leader through the dark days of persecution was his son Abū Sahl Muḥammad (16). Abū Sahl was born in 1032/423 and was in Iraq studying at the time of his father's death. Returning to Nishapur, he was installed at the age of seventeen as head of the Shāfiᶜī madhhab, primarily through the influence of the Ashᶜarī Sufi Abū al-Qāsim al-Qushairī. Official recognition of his elevation to the post was sought from the sultan's government and was granted. But Abū Sahl's premature accession to so powerful a post did not go uncontested as had that of his father under similar circumstances to the same position. Subkī does not say who opposed the appointment; he only says that

14. Fārisī II, f29b–30b; Subkī, IV, 8–16.

it stirred up envy and opposition among important people. This opposition eventually reached a point of crisis, and Abū Sahl used the authority of his office to put it down, but the struggle, which was almost certainly within the Shāfiᶜī party, paved the way for the all-out attack of al-Kundurī and his Ḥanafī allies upon the Shāfiᶜīs in general and the Ashᶜarīs in particular. One possible point from which the opposition might have come is the Baḥīrī family, which appears neither to have been Ashᶜarī nor to have suffered much during the persecution, but the evidence for opposition by the Baḥīrīs is purely circumstantial.

When efforts to have the persecution lifted by means of direct petition to the sultan came to nothing, the struggle between the Shāfiᶜīs and their persecutors assumed a more militant form. An order went out for the arrest of Abū al-Qāsim al-Qushairī, the raᵓīs Abū al-Faḍl Aḥmad al-Furātī, Abū al-Maᶜālī ᶜAbd al-Malik al-Juwainī (who was to receive in exile his honorific title Imām al-Ḥaramain), and Abū Sahl Muḥammad. The first two were captured and imprisoned in the citadel. Al-Juwainī escaped the city in secret and made his way to exile in Arabia by way of Kirman. Abū Sahl Muḥammad chose to stay and fight. He withdrew to the area of Bākharz southeast of Nishapur and gathered together an armed force of his personal retainers. Then he returned to the city with the intention of freeing his imprisoned colleagues. He occupied a village he owned next to the city, and the commander of the militia within the city, whose name is unfortunately not given, prepared for a fight despite the fact that Abū Sahl's warlike preparations had convinced some of his enemies that it would be best simply to release the prisoners. The battle was met in the market area and waxed so fierce that the combatants began to run out of arrows. Abū Sahl's men were well on their way to winning a total victory when intermediaries intervened to seek a truce. It was at this point, presumably, that Abū Sahl was offered a bribe of one thousand dinars by his ᶜAlid brother-in-law Abū Muḥammad al-Ḥasan al-Ḥasanī to call off the fighting. The prisoners were freed, but on consultation with Abū Sahl all agreed that their victory was only temporary and that there was little choice for them but to trade the walls of a prison for the road of exile. So they left the city and set out northward for Ustuvā where the raᵓīs al-Furātī wielded considerable influence.

From Ustuvā, Abū Sahl headed for Rayy to try once again to appeal personally to the sultan to call off the persecution his vizier had begun, but his enemies were more successful in gaining the ear of the sultan and turned him against Abū Sahl and the Shāfiᶜīs. Instead of finding redress for his grievances, Abū Sahl was arrested and thrown into a fortress prison. His wealth was confiscated and his estates sold, a matter of no little importance since Abū Sahl is said to have been a very wealthy man. After he had been thus chastised, he was released from prison and allowed to join the other Ashᶜarīs in exile in Arabia. Altogether, some four hundred Ashᶜarīs found their way into exile.

Eventually, of course, the persecution came to an end with the accession to power in Nishapur of Alp Arslān and Niẓām al-Mulk. Al-Furātī had died in exile, but Abū Sahl, al-Qushairī and al-Juwainī returned. Like the others, Abū Sahl enjoyed particular favor under the new regime, and it was even suggested that he might become Alp Arslān's vizier. But he still had enemies who were bent upon destroying him. Either by the machinations of these enemies or from natural causes Abū Sahl Muḥammad died in 1064/456 the year after Alp Arslān succeeded his uncle Ṭughril Beg as sultan. He was only thirty-three years old.

Abū Sahl's brother Abū ᶜUmar Saᶜīd (17) played no part in the events just described. He seems to have been much younger than Abū Sahl, for he was reared in his household and outlived him by almost fifty years, dying in 1109/502. As for the two sisters of Abū Sahl, neither is known by name. One of them married Abū Muḥammad al-Ḥasan al-Ḥasanī (18) who has already been mentioned, and their descendants are mentioned in the history of the Ḥasanīs. The other, the older of the two, married her first cousin, a son of al-Muʾayyad named Abū ᶜUmar Sahl (19). He died in 1079/471, only six years after his father, before attaining full maturity, and very little is related concerning him. Al-Muʾayyad's other son Abū Bakr ᶜAbd Allāh (20) is equally obscure in the sources. He is referred to as qāḍī, but it seems quite certain that he never held the post in Nishapur.

Of the collateral branches of the Basṭāmī family, the raʾīs of Isfarāʾin, Abū ᶜAlī al-Ḥusain al-Qārī, had either two or three sons. The doubtful son is one Abū ᶜAlī al-Muẓaffar al-Isfarāʾinī aṭ-Ṭalḥī (21). His father's name was al-Ḥusain, but not enough of his genealogy is given to confirm the identification, and neither of the definitely known sons bears the nisba aṭ-Ṭalḥī. Nevertheless, Abū ᶜAlī's putative great-grandfather was named Ṭalḥa, so the nisba is not at all illogical. Abū ᶜAlī was a jurist and served as *ṣāḥib al-qubūl* or certifier of teachers in Isfarāʾin.

As for the definitely known sons of Abū ᶜAlī al-Ḥusain, Abū al-Ḥasan Muḥammad al-Isfarāʾinī (22) was raʾīs of Isfarāʾin and a poet and fatā besides. He did not, however, go along with the ceremonies and asceticism of the organized futūwa. He spent his life in Isfarāʾin but visited Nishapur frequently, and on one of those occasions he was received by Niẓām al-Mulk whom he eulogized in an ode. He died in 1094/487. His brother Abū al-Qāsim ᶜAlī al-Isfarāʾinī (23) is favored with a long biography by al-Fārisī, but large portions of it are so washed out as to be virtually unreadable. He was born in either 1017/408 or 1027/418 and held as his brother did the post of raʾīs. Which brother held the position first is not known. Despite a speech impediment, he taught law in a madrasa built by an ᶜAlid apparently in Isfarāʾin. The year of his death was probably 1088/480, but the reading of the text is uncertain.

Finally in this generation there is the towering figure of Imām al-Ḥaramain Abū al-Maᶜālī ᶜAbd al-Malik al-Juwainī (24), one of the greatest of all Ashᶜarī scholars and teacher of the even more famous al-Ghazzālī. Nothing like a full account of Imām al-Ḥaramain's life and works can be attempted within the scope of this family history, but a brief chronological outline of his life is essential for understanding the history of Nishapur after the accession of Alp Arslān.

Abū al-Maᶜālī ᶜAbd al-Malik al-Juwainī was born in Nishapur in 1028/419. His father's eminence guaranteed him a comfortable patrician life, but his own intellectual brilliance soon marked him as a person of extraordinary promise. He studied law under his father, and at his father's death in 1047/438 he took over his father's position teaching law, despite the fact that he was only nineteen years old. At the same time he continued his own studies of Ashᶜarī theology and legal theory at the Baihaqī madrasa under Abū al-Qāsim ᶜAbd al-Jabbār al-Iskāf al-Isfarāʾinī.[15] By the time of the Ashᶜarī persecution he was already one of the foremost Ashᶜarīs in the city as is indicated by his being among those marked for arrest. However, as has already been mentioned, he escaped arrest and went into exile in Arabia where he stayed for four years and earned the title Imām al-Ḥaramain or Imām of the two Holy Cities.

With the lifting of the persecution al-Juwainī returned to Nishapur almost as a conquering hero. While Abū Sahl Muḥammad al-Basṭāmī was never able to make good on the position of favor he enjoyed in the eyes of the new regime, Imām al-Ḥaramain was. When the Niẓāmiya madrasa was built in 1058/450, he was installed as its first director and teacher of law; and when the Manīᶜī Congregational Mosque was founded six years later the position of khaṭīb was awarded to him. That was also the year of the death of Abū Sahl Muḥammad al-Basṭāmī, and with his passing the position of chief of the Shāfiᶜī madhhab along with control of Shāfiᶜī endowments passed to al-Juwainī. Thus, for the last thirty years or so of his life until his death in 1085/478 Imām al-

15. See chapter 14 and Ḥaskānī genealogical key #7.

Ḥaramain al-Juwainī was the unchallenged leader of the Shāfiʿī faction both in official position and in scholarly accomplishment. When he died in the village of Bushtaniqān where he had been taken to recover from an illness, the mourning was overwhelming. The pulpit from which he had preached in the mosque was broken up, and his hundreds of students did the same to their pens and inkstands out of respect for his memory. His son led the prayers over his body which was then buried in his house only to be reburied a few years later in the cemetery of al-Ḥusain b. Muʿādh.

VII. Abū Sahl Muḥammad al-Basṭāmī had one son by the name of Abū al-Muqaddam al-Muwaffaq (25) whose birth had been a cause of great rejoicing among the Shāfiʿīs since it seemed to ensure the continuation of Basṭāmī leadership of the faction, but his promise was cut short by an early death in 1086/479. This left only one other descendant of Imām al-Muwaffaq, the son of his daughter and his nephew Abū ʿUmar Sahl b. al-Muʾayyad. This grandson of Imām al-Muwaffaq was named Abū Muḥammad Hibat Allāh al-Basṭāmī as-Sayyidī (26), and he was born in either 1051/443 or 1053/445. His second nisba as-Sayyidī was derived from his ʿAlid great-grandfather on his father's side. A grave and learned man, his position in the Shāfiʿī party was no doubt greatly enhanced by his marriage to the daughter of Imām al-Ḥaramain al-Juwainī; but there is no explicit confirmation of his succession to the official Shāfiʿī leadership position. Yet the fact that his grandson was later to hold the position makes it extremely probable that such a succession did take place after the death of the son of Imām al-Ḥaramain. Abū Muḥammad Hibat Allāh died in 1139/533.

Imām al-Ḥaramain's son Abū al-Qāsim al-Muẓaffar al-Juwainī (27) lived a turbulent life. He was born in Rayy and came to Nishapur as a child, which probably means that he was born around 1053/445 at the beginning of his father's exile and came to Nishapur only with the lifting of the persecution. He studied hard all of the many disciplines at which his father excelled, but he showed a special inclination toward those which his father had never taken up, namely, the use of the javelin, the bow, and the sword. However, despite his military leanings, he attempted to secure his father's position when Imām al-Ḥaramain died in 1085/478. At this he was thwarted, and he had to hold his law classes in the Muṭarriz Mosque instead of the Niẓāmiya madrasa. Whoever it was that prevented his succession to his father's post did not win a clear-cut victory, however, for Abū al-Qāsim still had his clique of followers who upheld his claim. Eventually, Abū al-Qāsim went to Iraq to lay the matter before Niẓām al-Mulk in person for adjudication and returned with his right to his father's position confirmed. Exactly what position he moved into upon his return is uncertain, but it seems most probable that he took over both as head of the Niẓāmiya and as chief of the Shāfiᶜīs. All of this must have taken place before Niẓām al-Mulk's death in 1092/485 which makes it very likely that the man who opposed Abū al-Qāsim's claims was Muḥammad b. Manṣūr an-Nasawī, an official in the state bureaucracy who held the title ᶜ*amīd* of Khurasan.[16] This is evident from the biography of a little known militant Shāfiᶜī which speaks of but does not go into detail about a violent set-to between Abū al-Qāsim al-Juwainī and the ᶜamīd of Khurasan in the year 1091/484.[17]

Once installed in what he had always believed was his rightful position, Abū al-Qāsim's life still remained turbulent. In 1095/488–1096/489 Nishapur became a pawn in a contest between contenders for the sultanate and suffered first a siege and then dismantlement of its fortifications.[18] Then immediately afterward an enormous uprising of the Karrāmiya broke out in the city, which was only put down by the combined efforts of the Shāfiᶜīs and the Ḥanafīs. Abū al-Qāsim was the leader of the Shāfiᶜī forces in the battle.[19]

Finally there came the last violent incident in Abū al-Qāsim's life which is unfortunately almost illegible in the text. During one of the chaotic interregnal periods of the sultanate, some unnamed person described as a *khārijī*, which presumably means an outsider rather than a member of the Kharijite sect, came to Nishapur and took over command of the city. Somehow in the ensuing course of events Abū al-Qāsim came to be opposed to the usurper. Then one day while speaking unfavorably of the rights of one of the contenders for the sultanate, presumably the same person as the usurper, he was tricked into taking poison by an assassin. His body was carried into the city, and his supporters staged some sort of demonstration, but nothing further developed. His affair, as al-Fārisī says, was at an end. The year was 1100/493.

The only other members of the Basṭāmī-Juwainī family complex in this generation are all relatively insignificant. Al-Muʾayyad's son Abū Bakr ᶜAbd Allāh had two sons, but they lived in Baihaq, or more properly the part of Baihaq known as Khusrawjird, rather than in Nishapur. Abū al-Ḥasan Muḥammad as-Sayyidī (28), named like his cousin for his paternal great-grandfather, studied under Imām al-Ḥaramain and held

16. Al-Ḥusainī, *Akhbār ʾud-Dawlat ʾis-Saljūqiyya*, ed. M. Iqbal (Lahore, 1933), pp. 32–34.
17. Subkī, IV, 113.
18. I. Athīr, X, 87; Claude Cahen, "Arslān Arghūn," *Encyclopaedia of Islam*, new ed., I, 662.
19. I. Athīr, X, 87; I. Funduq, pp. 268–269.

for a while the position of qāḍī in Baihaq. At another time he was the deputy raᵓīs, but in that post he exerted little influence. He married a woman from a prominent family of *ruᵓasāᵓ* in Baihaq, but the only children he had were three unnamed daughters born to him late in life by a Turkish concubine. He died in 1139/533. His brother Abū Naṣr al-Muᵓayyad (29) died in Khusrawjird in 1133/527.

In the Isfarāᵓinī branch of the family, the raᵓīs Abū al-Qāsim ᶜAlī seems to have had a son named Muḥammad; but his existence is only inferred from that of his son whose relation to the Isfarāᵓinī's is not definite.

VIII. The son of the putative Muḥammad al-Isfarāᵓinī mentioned at the end of the last generation was a certain ᶜAbd ar-Raḥmān b. Muḥammad b. ᶜAlī (30) who is mentioned by Ibn al-Athīr in the year 1162/557 as being raᵓīs of Isfarāᵓin when sultan Sanjar's lieutenant and successor in Nishapur, Ay Abah, took over Isfarāᵓin in the process of expanding his nascent principality. His father is described as having been a noblehearted man, but ᶜAbd ar-Raḥmān was a man of base nature. When he tried to defend the town from Ay Abah's army, he was defeated and led off a captive to Nishapur in its new incarnation in Shādyākh. He was killed while in prison there in 1163/558. The connection of this man with the Isfarāᵓinī branch of the Basṭāmī family is made on the basis that the office of raᵓīs of Isfarāᵓin was hereditary in that branch of the family and that ᶜAbd ar-Raḥmān's grandfather ᶜAlī would have been of the correct generation to be identical with the Abū al-Qāsim ᶜAlī al-Isfarāᵓinī who died around 1087/480.

The only other members of the family in this generation are two sons of Abū Muḥammad Hibat Allāh al-Basṭāmī as-Sayyidī and Imām al-Ḥaramain's daughter. Their names were Muḥammad and al-Ḥusain, but neither of them is known except through his son.

IX. The son of the otherwise unknown Muḥammad b. Hibat Allāh al-Basṭāmī was one ᶜAbd al-Malik (31) who became for a while the leader of the Shāfiᶜīs. Nothing more of significance is reported concerning him, however. As for his first cousin al-Muᵓayyad b. al-Ḥusain b. Hibat Allāh al-Muwaffaqī (32), whose nisba was obviously derived from his great-grandfather Imām al-Muwaffaq, the story of his leadership of the Shāfiᶜī party in the final wild devastation of Nishapur by factional warfare has been told in full in chapter six. He died in the very last stages of the struggle in 1161/556 when his side was on the verge of its final Pyrrhic victory. With his death the illustrious lineage of the Ṣuᶜlūkīs, Basṭāmīs, and Juwainīs passes from the historical record.

Juwainī

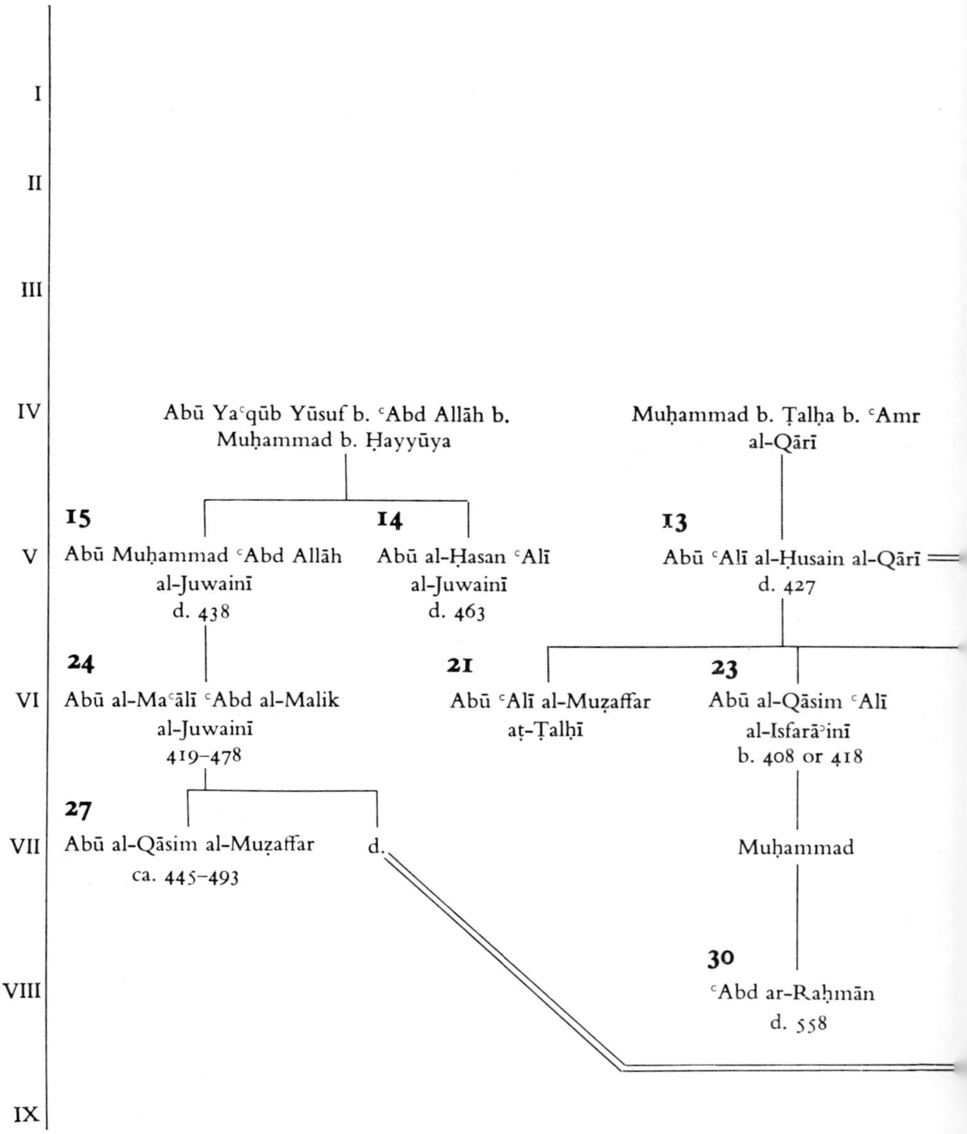

I

II

III

IV — Abū Ya'qūb Yūsuf b. 'Abd Allāh b.
Muḥammad b. Ḥayyūya

Muḥammad b. Ṭalḥa b. 'Amr
al-Qārī

V — **15** Abū Muḥammad 'Abd Allāh
al-Juwainī
d. 438

14 Abū al-Ḥasan 'Alī
al-Juwainī
d. 463

13 Abū 'Alī al-Ḥusain al-Qārī ═
d. 427

VI — **24** Abū al-Ma'ālī 'Abd al-Malik
al-Juwainī
419-478

21 Abū 'Alī al-Muẓaffar
aṭ-Ṭalḥī

23 Abū al-Qāsim 'Alī
al-Isfarā'inī
b. 408 or 418

VII — **27** Abū al-Qāsim al-Muẓaffar
ca. 445-493

d.

Muḥammad

VIII — **30** 'Abd ar-Raḥmān
d. 558

IX

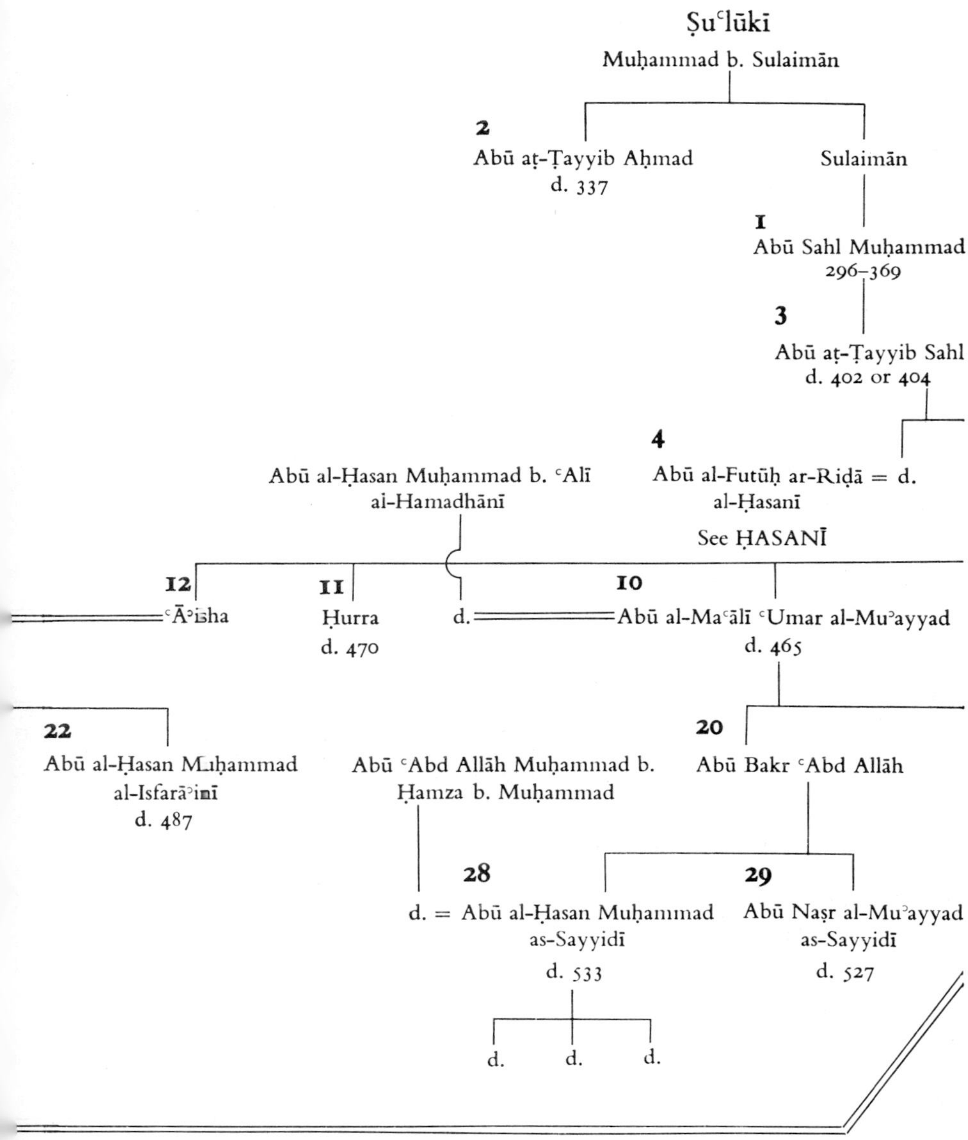
Ṣuᶜlūkī
Muḥammad b. Sulaimān
2
Abū aṭ-Ṭayyib Aḥmad
d. 337
Sulaimān
1
Abū Sahl Muḥammad
296–369
3
Abū aṭ-Ṭayyib Sahl
d. 402 or 404
4
Abū al-Ḥasan Muḥammad b. ᶜAlī
al-Hamadhānī
Abū al-Futūḥ ar-Riḍā = d.
al-Ḥasanī
See ḤASANĪ
12
ᶜĀᵓisha
11
Ḥurra
d. 470
d. = Abū al-Maᶜālī ᶜUmar al-Muᵓayyad
10
d. 465
22
Abū al-Ḥasan Muḥammad
al-Isfarāᵓinī
d. 487
Abū ᶜAbd Allāh Muḥammad b.
Ḥamza b. Muḥammad
20
Abū Bakr ᶜAbd Allāh
28
d. = Abū al-Ḥasan Muḥammad
as-Sayyidī
d. 533
29
Abū Naṣr al-Muᵓayyad
as-Sayyidī
d. 527
d.
d.
d.

Basṭāmī

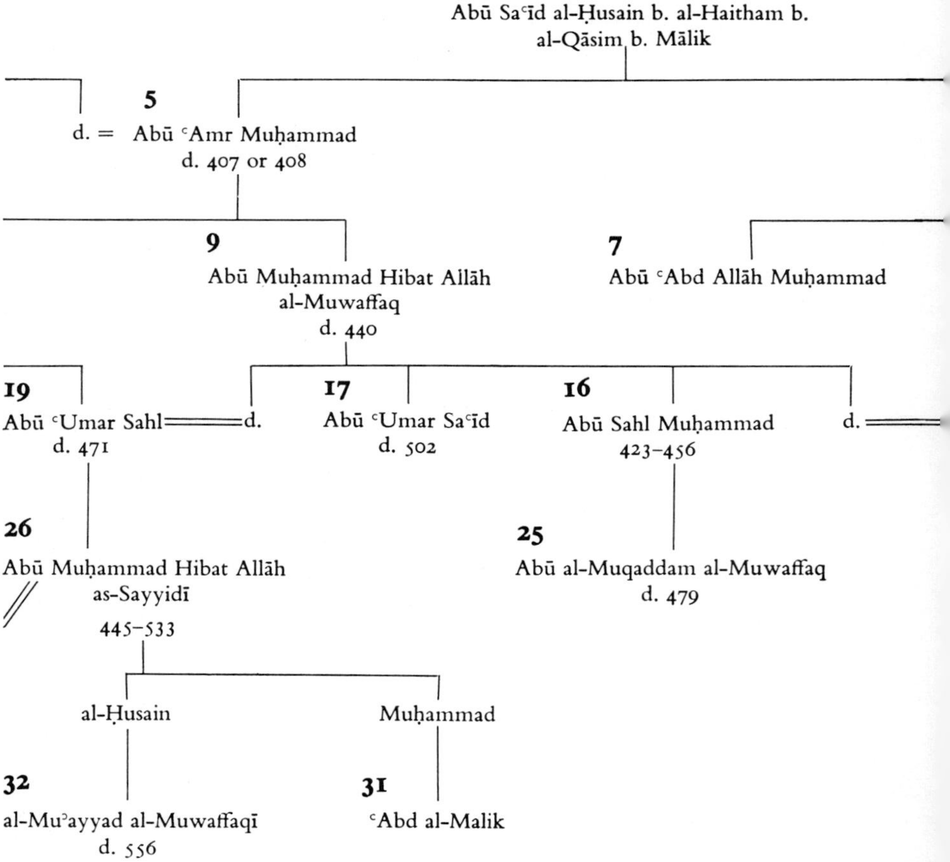
Abū Saʿīd al-Ḥusain b. al-Haitham b. al-Qāsim b. Mālik
5
d. = Abū ʿAmr Muḥammad
d. 407 or 408
9
Abū Muḥammad Hibat Allāh
al-Muwaffaq
d. 440
7
Abū ʿAbd Allāh Muḥammad
19
Abū ʿUmar Sahl = d.
d. 471
17
Abū ʿUmar Saʿīd
d. 502
16
Abū Sahl Muḥammad
423–456
d. =
26
Abū Muḥammad Hibat Allāh
as-Sayyidī
445–533
25
Abū al-Muqaddam al-Muwaffaq
d. 479
al-Ḥusain
Muḥammad
32
al-Muʾayyad al-Muwaffaqī
d. 556
31
ʿAbd al-Malik

I

II

III

6
Abū Ibrāhīm Ismāᶜīl

IV

8
Abū aṭ-Ṭayyib Sahl

V

18
Abū Muḥammad al-Ḥasan al-Ḥasanī
See ḤASANĪ

VI

VII

VIII

IX

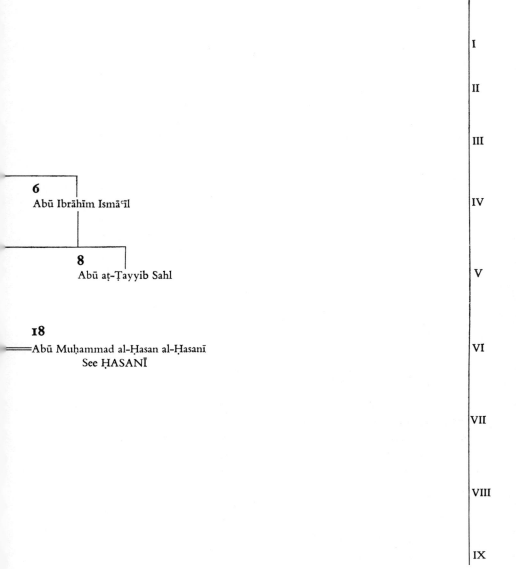

Genealogical Key

Basṭāmī–Ṣuᶜlūkī–Juwainī

1. Abū Sahl Muḥammad aṣ-Ṣuᶜlūkī	Ḥākim, f50b; Subkī, III, 167–73; Shadharāt, III, 69; Samᶜānī, f352a; I. Khallikān, III, 342–343.
2. Abū aṭ-Ṭayyib Aḥmad aṣ-Ṣuᶜlūkī	Ḥākim, f37b; Subkī, III, 43–44; Samᶜānī, f352b.
3. Abū aṭ-Ṭayyib Sahl aṣ-Ṣuᶜlūkī	Ḥākim, f42b; Subkī, IV, 393–404; IAW, I, 253–254; I. Khallikān, II, 153–154; Samᶜānī, f352a–b.
4. Abū al-Futūḥ ar-Riḍā al-Ḥasanī	See Ḥasanī genealogical key #12.
5. Abū ᶜAmr Muḥammad al-Basṭāmī	Ḥākim, f50a; Subkī, IV, 140–143; Fārisī II, f2a; ᶜIbar, III, 99; Samᶜānī, II, 232–233; Shadharāt, III, 187; I. Jauzī, VII, 285; T. Baghdād, II, 247–248.
6. Abū Ibrāhīm Ismāᶜīl al-Basṭāmī	Fārisī II, f37a.
7. Abū ᶜAbd Allāh Muḥammad al-Basṭāmī	Fārisī II, f13b.
8. Abū aṭ-Ṭayyib Sahl al-Basṭāmī	Fārisī II, f71a.
9. Abū Muḥammad Hibat Allāh al-Basṭāmī "Imām al-Muwaffaq"	Fārisī I, f94a–b; II, f139b; Subkī, V, 354–355.
10. Abū al-Maᶜālī ᶜUmar al-Basṭāmī "al-Muᵓayyad"	Fārisī I, f58a–b; II, f108a–b (see fig. 1, this volume); Subkī, V, 303.
11. Ḥurra al-Basṭāmī	Fārisī I, f18a.
12. ᶜĀᵓisha al-Basṭāmī	Fārisī I, f73b; II, f118b.
13. Abū ᶜAlī al-Ḥusain al-Qārī	Fārisī II, f57a.
14. Abū al-Ḥasan ᶜAlī al-Juwainī	Fārisī I, f64a–b; II, f112b–113a; Subkī, V, 298–299; Samᶜānī, III, 430.
15. Abū Muḥammad ᶜAbd Allāh al-Juwainī	Fārisī I, f31a; II, f79b–80a; ᶜIbar, III, 188; I. Khallikān, II, 250–251; Subkī, V, 73–94; Shadharāt, III, 261–262;

	Samᶜānī, III, 429–430; GAL, I, 386, Supp. I, 667; EI^2, II, 605.
16. Abū Sahl Muḥammad al-Basṭāmī	Fārisī II, f19a; Subkī, III, 390–393; IV, 208–211.
17. Abū ᶜUmar Saᶜīd al-Basṭāmī	Fārisī II, f69b.
18. Abū Muḥammad al-Ḥasan al-Ḥasanī	See Ḥasanī genealogical key #21.
19. Abū ᶜUmar Sahl al-Basṭāmī	Fārisī II, f71a.
20. Abū Bakr ᶜAbd Allāh al-Basṭāmī	Fārisī II, f83a.
21. Abū ᶜAlī al-Muẓaffar aṭ-Ṭalḥī	Fārisī II, f132b.
22. Abū al-Ḥasan Muḥammad al-Isfarāᵓinī	Fārisī II, f15a.
23. Abū al-Qāsim ᶜAlī al-Isfarāᶜinī	Fārisī I, f68a; II, f114b.
24. Abū al-Maᶜālī ᶜAbd al-Malik al-Juwainī "Imām al-Ḥaramain"	Fārisī I, f48a–49a; II, f95b–96a; Subkī, V, 165–222; Samᶜānī, III, 430–431; ᶜIbar, III, 291; Shadharāt, III, 358–362; I. Khallikān, II, 341–343; GAL I, 388, Supp. I, 671; EI^2, II, 605–606.
25. Abū al-Muqaddam al-Muwaffaq al-Basṭāmī	Fārisī II, f135a.
26. Abū Muḥammad Hibat Allāh al-Basṭāmī as-Sayyidī	Fārisī II, f140b; Old Subkī, IV, 321; ᶜIbar, IV, 93; Samᶜānī, f321b.
27. Abū al-Qāsim al-Muẓaffar al-Juwainī	Fārisī I, f89b–90a; II, f132b; Subkī, V, 330.
28. Abū al-Ḥasan Muḥammad as-Sayyidī	Samᶜānī, f321b; I. Funduq, p. 219.
29. Abū Naṣr al-Muᵓayyad as-Sayyidī	I. Funduq, p. 219.
30. ᶜAbd ar-Raḥmān b. Muḥammad b. ᶜAlī	I. Athīr, XI, 282.
31. ᶜAbd al-Malik b. Muḥammad al-Basṭāmī	Old Subkī, IV, 262–263.
32. Al-Muᵓayyad b. al-Ḥusain al-Muwaffaqī	I. Athīr, XI, 234–236, 277–278.

10 / Ṣābūnī–Furātī

I–III. The one truly outstanding figure in the Ṣābūnī family was the Shaikh al-Islām Abū ᶜUthmān Ismāᶜīl (1). It is regrettable that Abū ᶜUthmān's lineage is not better known, because it is quite clear that his great eminence in Nishapur was based as much upon his ancestry as upon his own personal gifts. Even what is known about his family background is confusing. Subkī remarks that he was well connected on both his father's and his mother's side, but the information that he gives pertains primarily to the latter. His mother, who was named Zain al-Bait, was the daugher of an ascetic known as Abū Saᶜd az-Zāhid, who was himself the great-grandson on his paternal grandmother's side of Abū Saᶜd Yaḥyā b. Manṣūr b. Ḥasanūya as-Sulamī, known as Abū Saᶜd az-Zāhid the Elder.

No more is known about the figures in this genealogy, but somehow through them Abū ᶜUthmān was related to many of the leading patrician families of the tenth/fourth century: the Ḥanafīs(?), the Faḍlīs, the Shaibānīs, the Qurashīs (descendants of Nishapur's conqueror ᶜAbd Allāh b. ᶜĀmir), the Tamīmīs, the Muzanīs, and the Ḍabbīs (of whom the historian al-Ḥākim was a member). Unfortunately, this information does not tally exactly with that given in the biography of Abū al-Faḍl ᶜUmar al-Harawī (2), a broadly educated Ḥanbalī scholar from Herat who died in 1034/425 and who is described as the maternal uncle of Abū ᶜUthmān Ismāᶜīl aṣ-Ṣābūnī. His father who died in 1000/390 was named Abū Saᶜd (Ibrāhīm) as he should have been if al-Harawī was in fact the brother of aṣ-Ṣābūnī's mother; but his grandfather's name is given as Ismāᶜīl while hers is given as Aḥmad. Where the error lies in this welter of names cannot be ascertained, and it must be accepted at face value that Abū ᶜUthmān aṣ-Ṣābūnī was connected through his mother both with a Ḥanbalī from Herat and several of Nishapur's old established families.

On his father's side, Subkī gives no details to back up his assertion of illustrious descent, and the surname Ṣābūnī, "Soapmaker," suggests that although his father was himself a prominent preacher, he was not more than a generation or two removed from the soap vats. Presumably, he was a person whose patrician status was based in the first instance upon commercial success and subsequently confirmed by an advantageous marriage to a well-connected woman.

But of far greater interest than his genealogy is Abū Naṣr ᶜAbd ar-Raḥmān aṣ-Ṣābūnī's factional affiliation. He is normally referred to as Abū Naṣr al-Wāᶜiẓ (The Preacher), and there is every reason to believe that he is identical with the man of the same name spoken of in Subkī's biography of the Shāfiᶜī-Ashᶜarī great, Abū Sahl

Muḥammad aṣ-Ṣuᶜlūkī.[1] Subkī relates that Abū Naṣr the Preacher was a Ḥanafī who converted to the Shāfiᶜī faction in the time of Abū Sahl. His conversion came about through a dream, as did so many religious experiences of that age. In the dream, Abū Naṣr saw the Prophet Muḥammad during what was presumably the last illness of Abū Sahl. What the Prophet said to him convinced him that the followers of Abū Sahl enjoyed special divine favor, and as a result he became one of their number.

Abū Sahl died in 980/369. Twelve years later in 992/382 Abū Naṣr aṣ-Ṣābūnī was murdered "on account of fanaticism (taᶜaṣṣub) and factionalism (madhhab)."[2] Abū ᶜUthmān was nine years old at the time of his father's murder. Abū aṭ-Ṭayyib Sahl aṣ-Ṣuᶜlūkī, the son of Abū Sahl, adopted him in effect and took charge of his education and his affairs.[3] When Abū ᶜUthmān was sixteen and had already been preaching for six years, he was formally installed in his father's old preaching post. All of the leading figures in the Shāfiᶜī faction, including Ibn Fūrak[4] and Abū Isḥāq al-Isfarāʾinī,[5] attended his sessions of preaching and marvelled at his abilities, in particular at his verbal facility in both Arabic and Persian. Unquestionably, his abilities were worthy of the eulogies made to them, but it is equally certain that they would never have been displayed in such a fashion had he not been the son of a highly respected convert and martyr to the Shāfiᶜī cause.

Abū ᶜUthmān's life after the inception of his preaching career was marked by one success after another, although the dates of each success are hard to pin down. His educational travels took him beyond the usual boundaries for such journeys. Besides visiting the educational centers strung out along the Khurasan Highway between Herat and Mecca, he travelled in Syria and Palestine where he met the famous blind poet Abū al-ᶜAlāʾ al-Maᶜarrī, along the coast of the Caspian Sea, and into northern India. When he had settled once again in Nishapur, he was appointed to the office of khaṭīb in the Old Congregational Mosque and recognized as Shaikh al-Islām. The former position, which he held until the beginning of the persecution of the Ashᶜarīs, had been held before him by Abū al-Ḥasan ᶜAlī al-Qaṭṭān, a Ḥanafī-Muᶜtazilī who died in 1015/405.[6]

1. Subkī, III, 170.
2. Subkī, IV, 274.
3. See chapter 9 and Basṭāmī genealogical key #3.
4. See chapter 11 and Qushairī genealogical key #28.
5. Subkī, IV, 256–262; Ḥākim, f39b; Fārisī II, f35a–36a.
6. Fārisī I, f63b; II, f112b; IAW, I, 374.

When and how he came to be recognized as Shaikh al-Islām is nowhere indicated, nor is it definite that he had any predecessor in the position.[7]

With Abū ᶜUthmān holding the posts of khaṭīb and Shaikh al-Islām, the position of the Shāfiᶜī-Ashᶜarī faction was almost overwhelming in Nishapur by the fourth decade of the eleventh/fifth century. Abū aṭ-Ṭayyib Sahl aṣ-Ṣuᶜlūkī, who had looked after the upbringing and education of Abū ᶜUthmān, had paid equal attention to the upbringing of his own twin grandsons, Abū Muḥammad Hibat Allāh al-Basṭāmī known as Imām al-Muwaffaq,[8] and Abū al-Maᶜālī ᶜUmar al-Basṭāmī known as al-Muʾayyad;[9] unfortunately he did not live to see his Ṣābūnī protégé elevated to two of the most important positions in the city, his grandson Imām al-Muwaffaq become formal head of the Shāfiᶜī madhhab and top advisor to the sultan Ṭughril Beg, and his other grandson al-Muʾayyad move into a position on the sultan's maẓālim court.

The only position that remained in Ḥanafī hands was that of chief qāḍī in which the Ṣāᶜidī family was unshakeable. The fourth position of importance in the patrician political arena, that of raʾīs, was held by Abū al-Faḍl Aḥmad al-Furātī (3) who was not only a Shāfiᶜī but was married to one of Abū ᶜUthmān's daughters thus completing the family nexus of Shāfiᶜī power. Not a great deal is known about Abū al-Faḍl Aḥmad. He travelled and he taught, but it was the dignity of his position as raʾīs rather than the value of his chain of authorities for transmitting the oral tradition that prompted people to study under him. After marrying the daughter of aṣ-Ṣabūnī, who must have been a great deal younger than he, he married a woman from the Ṣāᶜidī family. Whether he intended by this alliance to bring about some kind of reconciliation between the Shāfiᶜīs and the Ḥanafīs or whether his intentions were less ambitious, the match did not save him from persecution along with the other Ashᶜarīs at the hands of ᶜAmīd al-Mulk al-Kundurī and Abū Naṣr Aḥmad aṣ-Ṣāᶜidī. He was one of the four Shāfiᶜī leaders imprisoned in the persecution, and after being freed, he died on the way into exile in 1054/446.

The little that is known about Abū al-Faḍl's life is augmented by information concerning his family background. He was not from a Nishapuri family. His father Abū al-Muẓaffar Muḥammad al-Furātī (4) was raʾīs of the district of Ustuvā and died sometime after 1029/420; his uncle Abū Naṣr Naṣr al-Furātī al-Khubushānī (5) lived as a

7. See chapter 13, footnote 2.
8. See chapter 9 and Basṭāmī genealogical key #9.
9. See chapter 9 and Basṭāmī genealogical key #10.

scholar patrician in Khubushān, also known as Khūjān (modern Qūchān), the main town in Ustuvā. His grandfather Abū ᶜAmr Aḥmad b. Ubiy al-Furātī al-Ustuvāʾī (6) was well known as a scholar and ascetic. In short, Abū al-Faḍl Aḥmad came from a prominent provincial family but one that had not previously been of importance in Nishapur. His rise to the office of raʾīs seems definitely to have been a product of the coming to power of the Seljuqs and of his position in the Shāfiᶜī-Ashᶜarī clique that benefited most directly from the Seljuq takeover. Therefore, his marriage with Abū ᶜUthmān aṣ-Ṣābūnī's daughter must be seen as a crucial step in his rise to prominence, since it was what confirmed his position among the Shāfiᶜīs.

Curiously, the fate that overcame Abū al-Faḍl al-Furātī and the three other Ashᶜarī leaders during the persecution passed over Abū ᶜUthmān aṣ-Ṣābūnī even though he was a central figure in the edifice of Shāfiᶜī-Ashᶜarī power. Judging from the fact that his predecessor died in 1015/405 and Abū ᶜUthmān is reported to have held the office for twenty some years, he must have left the post of khaṭīb at the very start of the persecution. But there is no indication that he was replaced as Shaikh al-Islām. Nor are any other acts of persecution reported concerning him or his children. Considering his unswerving belief in the doctrines of the Ashᶜarī school, which is testified to by his last testament preserved by Subkī,[10] this immunity from harm is peculiar indeed. What it may indicate, however, is that as Shaikh al-Islām Abū ᶜUthmān had become so much the symbolic leader of the patriciate as a whole that he was considered to be personally above factional politics. Confirmation of this possibility might be seen in the fact that despite the continuing ban on his party, Abū ᶜUthmān's funeral following his death in an epidemic in 1057/449 was attended by a countless multitude who heard his brother and his son pray for him in the great plaza in front of the governor's palace named for al-Ḥusain b. Muᶜādh. He was laid to rest beside his father in the family shrine on Ḥarb Street.

Mention of Abū ᶜUthmān's brother introduces a somewhat anomalous figure in the history of the Sābūnī family. Abū Yaᶜlā Isḥāq aṣ-Ṣābūnī as-Sajazī (7) is as shadowy and unknown a person as his brother is famous. He was a Sufi, and he substituted for his brother in convening preaching sessions whenever illness or travel prevented him from performing his functions as Shaikh al-Islām. Yet he seems to have held no positions in his own right. It is likely that he spent some major portion of his life in the province of Sistan given the additional nisba as-Sajazī that is included in his name, but he was

10. Subkī, IV, 285–292.

certainly in Nishapur at the time of his brother's death and six years later when he himself died in 1063/455 at the age of eighty. He, too, was prayed over in al-Ḥusain b. Muᶜādh Square and interred in the tomb on Ḥarb Street.

As a Sufi, Abū Yaᶜlā fills in one element of the Shāfiᶜī-Ashᶜarī-Sufi syndrome seemingly lacking in his brother, but perhaps the spirit of Sufism was not really lacking in Abū ᶜUthmān. There is an anecdote in the biography of the ecstatic Sufi Abū Saᶜīd b. Abī al-Khair which puts Abū ᶜUthmān in attendance at one of Abū Saᶜīd's discourses in which the Sufi's finger became miraculously visible through his coat.[11] Upon seeing this Abū ᶜUthmān, along with his fellow Ashᶜarīs Abū al-Qāsim al-Qushairī, himself a Sufi, and Abū Muḥammad al-Juwainī, the father of Imām al-Ḥaramain al-Juwainī, became carried away in the mystic transport of the moment and threw off his own cloak. If there is a kernel of truth in this story, it would indicate, taken in conjunction with his brother's Sufism and the fact that one of his own disciples is referred to as a *murīd*, a term normally used exclusively for Sufi discipleship,[12] that Abū ᶜUthmān may have been as much at home in mystic contemplation as he was in the other religious sciences.

IV. Abū ᶜUthmān had seven children about whom information has been preserved, and Abū Yaᶜlā had one. Only three of the eight were males, all sons of Abū ᶜUthmān. The eldest child of Abū ᶜUthmān was a son named Abū Naṣr ᶜAbd Allāh (8). He exhibited all the fine qualities expected of his good birth and in time began to stand in for his father declaiming the khuṭba in the congregational mosque. Doubtless he would have succeeded his father as khaṭīb had not political turmoil and early death intervened. Even if he never became khaṭīb, however, his good breeding and refined manners recommended him to the Sultan as a diplomatic emissary. Presumably, he performed this service for Ṭughril Beg. It was during one of his travels, possibly the one that took him to the land of the Byzantines, that he died in the prime of life in 1049/441. His body was returned to Nishapur for burial.

The primary biography of Abū ᶜUthmān's second son, Abū Bakr ᶜAbd ar-Raḥmān (9) is unfortunately badly defaced in the manuscript. Like his older brother he was an attractive and gracious young man of worldly tastes. Although the reading is doubtful, it seems that after starting out as an apprentice to his father in his duties as Shaikh

11. Nicholson, *Studies in Islamic Mysticism*, p. 73.
12. Fārisī II, f128a.

al-Islām, his tastes changed to such things as hunting and possibly the futūwa. Eventually, after his father's death, he left Nishapur for Isfahan where he met the vizier Niẓām al-Mulk. He had his brother's skill at ingratiating himself with the mighty besides which he was a member of the Shāfiᶜī-Ashᶜarī faction which Niẓām al-Mulk had re-established in Nishapur. As a result, he became a member of the vizier's entourage and a sufficiently trusted member to be appointed in the course of time chief qāḍī of Azerbaijan. After some time in Azerbaijan, Abū Bakr returned once again to Nishapur. He convened for himself a session for reciting ḥadīth, probably in the family madrasa,[13] and perhaps claimed and was refused some kind of recognition. The truth of the matter may have been lost forever to a few drops of water sprinkled on the page, but whatever happened, Abū Bakr left Nishapur once again for Isfahan where he lived until his death before 1107/500.

The third and youngest son of Abū ᶜUthmān was Abū Saᶜd Saᶜīd (10). Less worldly and more religious than his two brothers, he became the repository of the hopes of the ᶜulamāʾ for someone to fill Abū ᶜUthmān's position after his death. Originally his brother Abū Bakr had been viewed as their father's successor, but Abū Bakr's eschewal of convening classes and ordering scholarly affairs had forced the patriciate to look to Abū Saᶜd or face the burden of shifting the post of Shaikh al-Islām to another family, a task that would certainly have entailed prolonged debate and jeopardized the political equilibrium between the parties. What actually happened, of course, was that the external and unforeseen influence of ᶜAmīd al-Mulk al-Kundurī and then Niẓām al-Mulk upset the equilibrium and produced the next Shaikh al-Islām, in the person of Niẓām al-Mulk's lieutenant Abū ᶜAlī Ḥassān al-Manīᶜī, but in the waning years of the Ghaznavid period hopeful eyes fastened on Abū Saᶜd Saᶜīd. For his part, Abū Saᶜd tried to live up to these hopes, and he became an exceedingly popular religious figure among the general populace. All of his promise was cut off, however, when he died before reaching full adulthood.

Turning now to the Ṣābūnī daughters, Abū ᶜUthmān had three whose names are known and his brother Abū Yaᶜlā one. To go with these four there are five husbands, so there must be an additional daughter whose name has not been recorded. Sorting out which husband goes with which daughter is far from easy, but it seems more than likely that the unknown daughter was the one who married Abū al-Faḍl Aḥmad al-Furātī since a spouse of such importance would probably have been named in his wife's

13. For references to the Ṣābūnī madrasa see Appendix I, #14.

biography if it had been written. There is no specific indication, however, whether the son of Abū al-Faḍl, Abū Saᶜīd Muḥammad (11), was the offspring of his Ṣābūnī wife, his Ṣāᶜidī wife, or another wife entirely. No details at all are known about Abū Saᶜīd Muḥammad, but his name is the same as that of Abū al-ᶜAlāᵓ Ṣāᶜid's father, which would tend to favor the Ṣāᶜidī wife, while his children seem to belong in the Shāfiᶜī camp. As for the daughters whose names are known, an effort has been made to assign them husbands in the most logical fashion, but the possibility of a *post hoc* adulterous connection must be admitted.

Zahrāᵓ or Fāṭima (12) was the eldest. She is graciously styled "the pearl in the Ṣābūnī oyster, the apple of the Ṣābūnī eye." In her service and companionship she was like a sister to her father, from which it might be surmised that he was an early widower. She was well educated, as were her sisters, and was herself a teacher. Her husband by a process of elimination seems to have been Abū al-Ḥasan ᶜAlī az-Zuhrī (13), a preacher about whom nothing is known except his date of death 1072/464. It seems fitting that a woman whose main devotion was to her father should have had an insignificant husband.

The second daughter, born in 1012/404, was Khadīja (14). Learned and exceptionally pious, she bore twin sons to her husband, whose name is quite certain, Abū Bakr Muḥammad at-Tamīmī (15). He was a jurist from a wealthy if not too prominent family. When he died in 1084/477, eleven years before his wife, the funeral prayers were recited by his brother-in-law Abū Bakr ᶜAbd ar-Raḥmān aṣ-Ṣābūnī, who must have returned to Nishapur from Azerbaijan by that time; but his body was buried in al-Ḥusain cemetery rather than in the Ṣābūnī mausoleum.

Mubāraka (16), also known as Sittiyak, was born in 1024/415. Following the example of her uncle rather than her father, she became a Sufi and lavished all of her wealth upon her fellow Sufis. Her husband seems to have been one Abū Isḥāq Ibrāhīm al-Jīlī (17), judging from the fact that both of them were buried in al-Ḥīra cemetery; but if that was the case, then Mubāraka must have enjoyed a long widowhood. Abū Isḥāq Ibrāhīm died in 1059/451 when she was only thirty-six, and she did not die until 1097/490. This might explain where she got the money to spend on her Sufi brethren, if not her Sufism itself.

Abū Isḥāq aṣ-Ṣābūnī's daughter Karīma (18) was as educated as her cousins, but nothing more is known about her. Her husband was probably Abū al-Faḍl Shāfiᶜ aṭ-Ṭuraithīthī (19). This match seems likely because the phrasing associates Abū al-Faḍl Shāfiᶜ by marriage to "the Ṣābūnī family" rather than to the Shaikh al-Islām himself as is the case with the other sons-in-law. Abū al-Faḍl was born in 1008/400 in the town of Ṭuraithīth or Ṭurshīz southwest of Nishapur, later famous as an Assassin stronghold. His marriage to Karīma was doubtless connected with the fact that like her father he was a Sufi, and an important Sufi at that, one of the residents of the convent of Abū ᶜAbd ar-Raḥmān as-Sulamī. In 1095/488 he died and was buried in Ganjarūd cemetery on the south side of town.

V. This is the last generation in which the Ṣābūnī family can be traced, but the vigor of at least one of its branches suggests that this is the result of the petering out of sources rather than of the family. The twin sons born to Khadīja and her husband Abū Bakr Muḥammad at-Tamīmī constitute the active branch. The elder of them was Abū Saᶜd al-Ḥasan (20). He was also the less aggressive of the two although he did convene a class "after the manner of his family and relations." He died of a fall in 1121/515.

The younger twin Abū Saᶜīd al-Ḥusain (21) was more outgoing and charming. He was thoroughly educated, primarily by his grandfather, in ḥadīth and Qurᵓan interpretation and taught these subjects in a light manner interspersed with witticisms and anecdotes. His classes, which he convened on his own authority, were held in the ᶜAqīl mosque, a Shāfiᶜī stronghold. He predeceased his twin in 1113/506 and was buried like his father and later his brother in al-Ḥusain cemetery.

These twin grandsons represent the solid, scholarly heritage of Shaikh al-Islām Abū ᶜUthmān, but the more worldly line of Abū ᶜUthmān's second son Abū Bakr ᶜAbd ar-Raḥmān continued in this generation as well. Abū Bakr had two sons. Abū ᶜUthmān Ismāᶜīl (22), obviously named for his grandfather, died in Rayy in 1123/517 and, given his father's long residence in Isfahan and Azerbaijan, may never have lived much in Nishapur. The other son Abū al-Maḥāsin Isḥāq (23) was born in Nishapur but accompanied his father to Isfahan where he studied and began to teach. Then at some point he returned to Nishapur where he held a class in the Manīᶜī Congregational Mosque. Beyond this, nothing is known about him.

Finally, there is a very brief entry for Abū al-Ḥasan ᶜAlī b. Shāfiᶜ aṭ-Ṭuraithīthī aṣ-Ṣābūnī (24), the grandson, if husband has been correctly matched with wife, of Abū ᶜUthmān's brother Abū Yaᶜlā Isḥāq. Unfortunately, nothing of interest is said about him except that he was a Sufi as his father and grandfather had been.

This still leaves, however, the Furātī family which continues into this generation but which may not actually be related by blood to the Ṣābūnīs. Abū Saᶜīd Muḥammad had two sons. Abū al-Faḍl Aḥmad al-Furātī al-Khūjānī (25) was a qāḍī in the town of Khūjān (Khubushān) and died in 1149/544. His brother Abū ʿAbd Allāh Saʿīd al-Furātī al-Khūjānī (26) was qāḍī and raʾīs as well, and furthermore he was a noted poet. Unfortunately, the comparatively lengthy biography devoted to him by al-Fārisī waxes more poetic than informative in describing him, and little more can be gleaned from it than that his family was illustrious, apparently related through some unknown marriage connection to a family of vizieral rank, and that he himself experienced various ups and downs in life before becoming an object of veneration. He died in the decade beginning in 1136/530.

Genealogical Key

Ṣābūnī–Furātī

1. Abū ʿUthmān Ismāʿīl aṣ-Ṣābūnī	Fārisī II, f38a–39a; Subkī, IV, 281–292; ʿIbar, III, 219; Shadharāt, III, 182–183; Yāqūt, *Irshād*, II, 118; Lubāb, II, 44; T. Islām, pp. 472–475; GAL, I, 362, Supp. I, 618.
2. Abū al-Faḍl ʿUmar al-Harawī	Fārisī I, f58a; II, f108a (see fig. 1, this volume); T. Islām, p. 252.
3. Abū al-Faḍl Aḥmad al-Furātī	Fārisī II, f28b; T. Islām, pp. 429–430.
4. Abū al-Muẓaffar Muḥammad al-Furātī	Fārisī II, f5a.
5. Abū Naṣr Naṣr al-Furātī al-Khubushānī	Fārisī I, f92b; II, f137a.
6. Abū ʿAmr Aḥmad al-Furātī al-Ustuwāʾī	Ḥākim, f55b.
7. Abū Yaʿlā Isḥāq aṣ-Ṣābūnī as-Sajazī	Fārisī II, f46b; ʿIbar, III, 235; Shadharāt, III, 296.
8. Abū Naṣr ʿAbd Allāh aṣ-Ṣābūnī	Fārisī I, f34a; II, f82b–83a; T. Islām, p. 390.
9. Abū Bakr ʿAbd ar-Raḥmān aṣ-Ṣābūnī	Fārisī I, f44b; II, f92a; Old Subkī, IV, 244.
10. Abū Saʿd Saʿīd aṣ-Ṣābūnī	Fārisī I, f25a; II, f69a.
11. Abū Saʿīd Muḥammad al-Furātī	Samʿānī, f420b.
12. Zahrāʾ (Fāṭima) aṣ-Ṣābūnī	Fārisī I, f21b; II, f66b.
13. Abū al-Ḥasan ʿAlī az-Zuhrī	Fārisī II, f112b.
14. Khadīja aṣ-Ṣābūnī	Fārisī I, f18b–19a; II, f63a.
15. Abū Bakr Muḥammad at-Tamīmī	Fārisī II, f16a.
16. Mubāraka (Sittiyak) aṣ-Ṣābūnī	Fārisī I, f30a; II, f72b.
17. Abū Isḥāq Ibrāhīm al-Jīlī	Fārisī II, f36a.
18. Karīma aṣ-Ṣābūnī	Fārisī II, f126a.
19. Abū al-Faḍl Shāfiʿ aṭ-Ṭuraithīthī	Fārisī I, f82a; II, f73a–b; Samʿānī, f370b.

Furātī

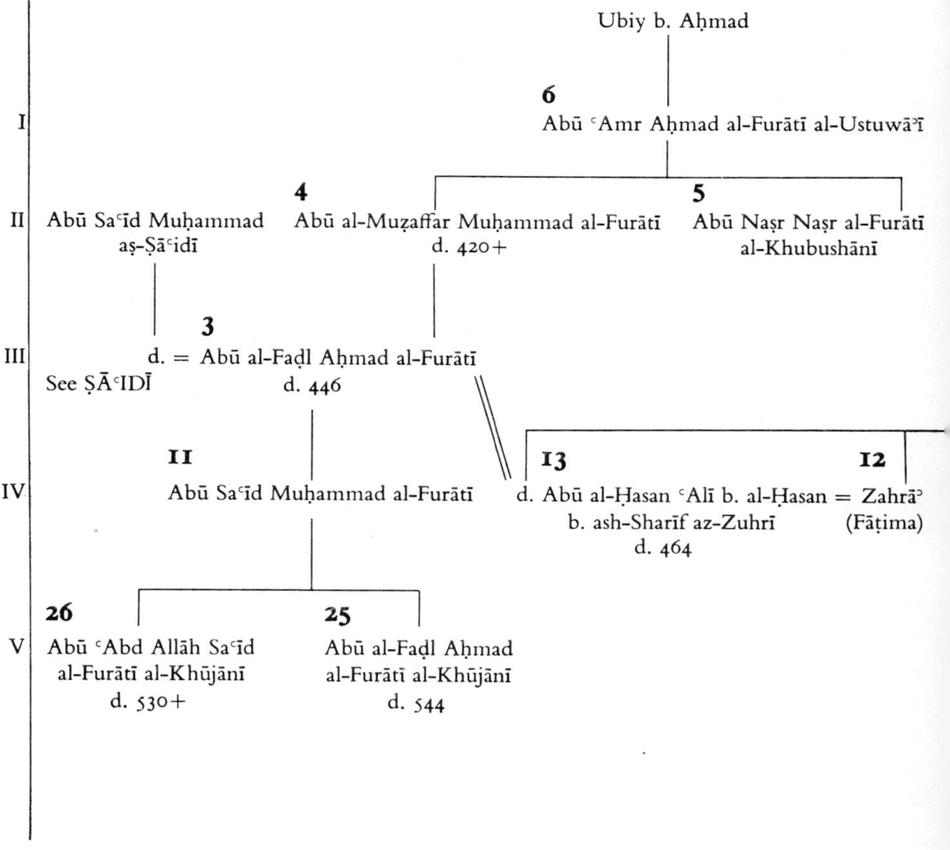
Ubiy b. Aḥmad
6
Abū ᶜAmr Aḥmad al-Furātī al-Ustuwāʾī
4
Abū al-Muẓaffar Muḥammad al-Furātī
d. 420+
5
Abū Naṣr Naṣr al-Furātī
al-Khubushānī
Abū Saᶜīd Muḥammad
aṣ-Ṣāᶜidī
3
d. = Abū al-Faḍl Aḥmad al-Furātī
d. 446
See ṢĀᶜIDĪ
11
Abū Saᶜīd Muḥammad al-Furātī
13
d. Abū al-Ḥasan ᶜAlī b. al-Ḥasan
b. ash-Sharīf az-Zuhrī
d. 464
12
= Zahrāʾ
(Fāṭima)
26
Abū ᶜAbd Allāh Saᶜīd
al-Furātī al-Khūjānī
d. 530+
25
Abū al-Faḍl Aḥmad
al-Furātī al-Khūjānī
d. 544
I
II
III
IV
V

Ṣābūnī

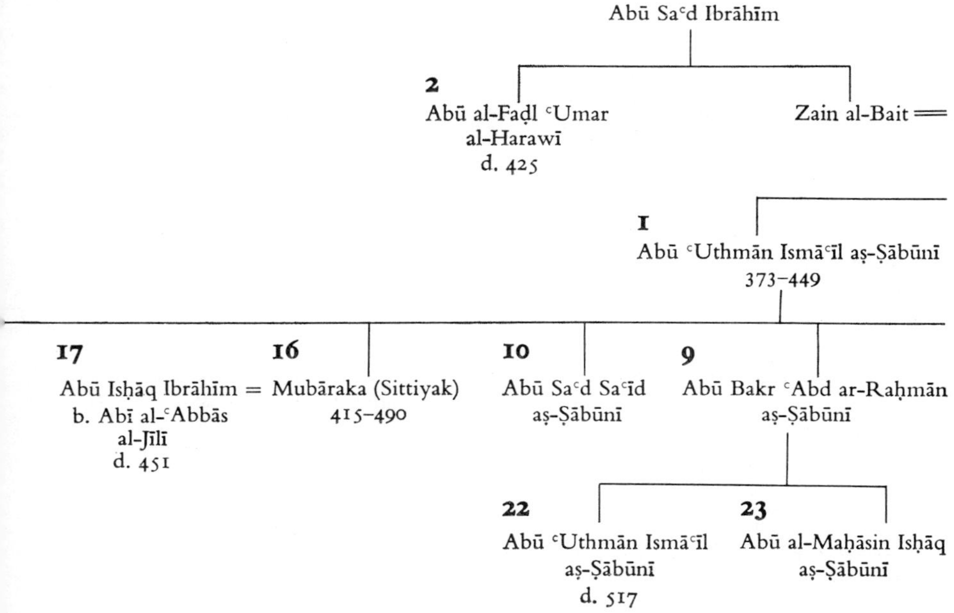
Abū Sa^{c}d Ibrāhīm
2
Abū al-Faḍl ^{c}Umar al-Harawī d. 425
Zain al-Bait =
1
Abū ^{c}Uthmān Ismā^{c}īl aṣ-Ṣābūnī 373–449
17
Abū Isḥāq Ibrāhīm = b. Abī al-^{c}Abbās al-Jīlī d. 451
16
Mubāraka (Sittiyak) 415–490
10
Abū Sa^{c}d Sa^{c}īd aṣ-Ṣābūnī
9
Abū Bakr ^{c}Abd ar-Raḥmān aṣ-Ṣābūnī
22
Abū ^{c}Uthmān Ismā^{c}īl aṣ-Ṣābūnī d. 517
23
Abū al-Maḥāsin Isḥāq aṣ-Ṣābūnī

Ṣābūnī (continued)

= Abū Naṣr ᶜAbd ar-Raḥmān b. Aḥmad b. Ismāᶜīl b. Ibrāhīm b. ᶜĀmir b. ᶜĀʾid aṣ-Ṣābūnī

7
Abū Yaᶜlā Isḥāq aṣ-Ṣābūnī
as-Sajazī
d. 455

8
Abū Naṣr ᶜAbd Allāh
aṣ-Ṣābūnī
d. 441

14
Khadīja
404–488

= **15**
Abū Bakr Muḥammad b. Maḥmūd
b. Sūrah at-Tamīmī
d. 477

18
Karīma =

21
Abū Saᶜīd al-Ḥusain
at-Tamīmī
d. 506

20
Abū Saᶜd al-Ḥasan
at-Tamīmī
d. 515

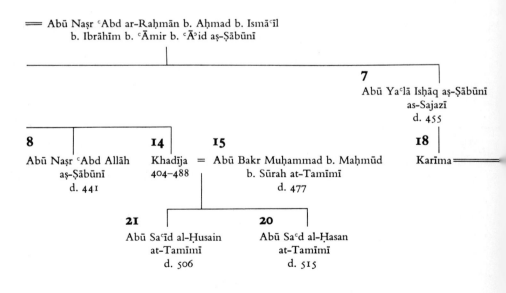

ᶜAlī b. Abī al-Faḍl

19
Abū al-Faḍl Shāfiᶜ aṭ-Ṭuraithīthī
400–488

24
Abū al-Ḥasan ᶜAlī aṭ-Ṭuraithīthī
aṣ-Ṣābūnī

I

II

III

IV

V

20.	Abū Sa^{c}d al-Ḥasan at-Tamīmī	Fārisī I, f8a; II, f55a.
21.	Abū Sa^{c}īd al-Ḥusain at-Tamīmī	Fārisī I, f11b–12a; II, f59a.
22.	Abū ^{c}Uthmān Ismā^{c}īl aṣ-Ṣābūnī	Fārisī II, f44b.
23.	Abū al-Maḥāsin Isḥāq aṣ-Ṣābūnī	Fārisī II, f47a–b.
24.	Abū al-Ḥasan ^{c}Alī aṣ-Ṣābūnī aṭ-Ṭuraithīthī	Fārisī II, f116b.
25.	Abū al-Faḍl Aḥmad al-Furātī al-Khūjānī	Sam^{c}ānī, V, 224; Sam^{c}ānī, f420b.
26.	Abū ^{c}Abd Allāh Sa^{c}īd al-Furātī al-Khūjānī	Fārisī I, f25b–27a; II, f69b; Sam^{c}ānī, V, 223–224.

11 / *Qushairī–Fūrakī–Ṣaffār–Fārisī–Shaḥḥāmī–Furāwī*

The extensiveness and interrelatedness of Nishapur's patrician families comes through most forcefully in this complex of families. Six major and several minor families numbering seventy-nine individuals spread over seven generations do not fit easily into the format that has been adopted for the other family histories; nor is the situation improved by the relatively large number of important personages involved. It would be possible to split this chapter into several separate chapters for the sake of convenience as has been done elsewhere, but there is an important reason for not doing this. The closeness of the connection between these six families goes beyond their multiple marriage links. All are Shāfiʿīs; all are Ashʿarīs; but beyond these important bonds there is evidence in biography after biography of a family consciousness that crosses marital linkages in a way not so apparent in other families. This feeling of kinship is too important to be sacrificed to expediency.

Whence derives this greater than usual family identity is perhaps an idle question. Possibly it is a mechanical function of the greater volume of information available. Then again it may be traceable to the membership in this family of the historian al-Fārisī from whom much of the primary source information comes. But there is also the possibility of something more substantial being at the root of it. Looking at the family tree in comparison with those of the other families discussed in this section, one cannot help noticing that every ancestral line becomes untraceable at a comparatively advanced date. Is this coincidence, or is there possibly a parvenu flavor about the family which inspired in it a greater feeling of identity? Biography by biography there are no obvious arrivistes; nor, indeed, would evidence of such be expected in so closed a social class. The distinction within the patriciate between old family and parvenu, if it existed, would have made itself felt in ways too subtle to be mentioned in brief biographies, particularly ones written or edited by one of the parvenus. Nevertheless, besides the lack of depth in the several family lineages, there is the fact that no marriage link has been uncovered between this family network and the two other important Shāfiʿī-Ashʿarī houses of the Ṣābūnīs and the Basṭāmī-Juwainīs. Furthermore, of the six major segments of the family, at least four of them originated outside of Nishapur and came to the city rather late, while the other two stem from the unsophisticated trades of coppersmith (Ṣaffār) and fat renderer (Shaḥḥām).

Speculation about subtleties of social standing aside, however, the fact remains that this unwieldy congeries of families calls for treatment as a single extensive clan and must be accommodated to the format already established. The way this will be done is to divide the chapter loosely into six sections, one devoted to each major portion of the clan. The divisions, which are indicated on the family tree, will be overstepped for reasons of continuity and synchrony; but the main discussion of each individual will be contained in the appropriate division.

Qushairī

I. In both genealogy and importance the Qushairīs deserve to be treated first. The central drama of this family and of the entire clan is the following: Abū al-Qāsim ᶜAbd al-Karīm al-Qushairī (3) came to Nishapur with little to recommend him. He acquired a thorough grounding in Shāfiᶜī law, Ashᶜarī theology, and a moderate brand of Sufism; and he married Fāṭima, the daughter of his Sufi master. Then, while he proceeded to make a great name for himself as a scholar, she bore eleven children, six sons who became important in their own right and five daughters whose marriages drew various other families into the Qushairī orbit.

The story does not begin here, however; it begins with Fāṭima's father, Abū al-Qāsim al-Qushairī's father-in-law, Abū ᶜAlī al-Ḥasan b. ᶜAlī ad-Daqqāq (1). Although his name indicates that he was a miller by trade or from a family of millers, everything that is known about Abū ᶜAlī ad-Daqqāq concerns his activities as a Sufi and religious scholar. His date of birth is not given, but his Sufi mentor Abū al-Qāsim an-Naṣrābādī[1] resided in Nishapur only between the years 951/340 and 976/365, so he must have been intellectually aware during some fairly substantial portion of that period.

The Sufism that he imbibed from an-Naṣrābādī and subsequently passed on to his son-in-law was of the "sober" variety and had been received by an-Naṣrābādī with only one intermediary from al-Junaid himself.[2] It conflicted in no way with the legal studies that Abū ᶜAlī was also pursuing under various Shāfiᶜī scholars in Marv. In due time his excellence as a Sufi was recognized, and he became an object of admiration and patronage, which latter he encouraged the more by being reluctant to accept. His personal life was austere and his respect for temporal power negligible. Even after he had begun to preach in the Muṭarriz Mosque, an important Shāfiᶜī-Ashᶜarī institution,[3] he continued to preach as well in the commercial warehouses as had been customary in

1. Ḥākim, f39b; Shadharāt, III, 58–59; as-Sulamī, *Ṭabaqāt*, 484–488. References to numerous other biographies will be found in Sulamī.

2. The full chain of Sufi descent is given in Subkī, V, 157. For al-Junaid see EI², II, 600.

3. Abū ᶜAlī's predecessor there was Abū Masᶜūd Aḥmad ar-Rāzī, Fārisī II, f26b–27a.

an earlier day when, presumably, religion and business activity had gone more closely hand in hand.

The year 1001/391 was a big year for Abū ᶜAlī. In that year his daughter Fāṭima was born and his madrasa, later to be the Qushairī madrasa, was built. Upon Fāṭima, long his only child, he lavished much attention, educating her as he would a son. And he paid equally close attention to the building of his madrasa, eschewing any tainted money and accepting only the most honestly come by donations from upright men and his own disciples. The last fourteen years of his life until his death in 1015/405 he spent guiding his Sufi flock in this madrasa where he was in due course succeeded by his son-in-law Abū al-Qāsim al-Qushairī.

Abū al-Qāsim al-Qushairī's parents are virtually unknown. His father was Hawāzin b. ᶜAbd al-Malik b. Ṭalḥa b. Muḥammad, a descendant of Arabs of the tribe of Qushair who had settled in the area of Ustuvā, north of Nishapur. His mother was descended from Arabs of the tribe of Sulaim who had settled in the same area. The father died when Abū al-Qāsim was only a child, and the inclusion of his maternal uncle's biography in the biographical dictionary of Nishapur suggests that he and his mother were taken in by this man, Abū ᶜAqīl ᶜAbd ar-Raḥmān b. Muḥammad b. Sulaimān as-Sulamī al-Māyiqī (for the village of Māyiq ad-Dasht in Ustuvā) (2), who was one of the important dihqāns in the area. But whether that was the case or not, Abū al-Qāsim had little in his favor in Nishapur proper when he came there as a young man. Though there were then and had been illustrious Nishapuris with his tribal background, such as the great traditionist Muslim b. al-Ḥajjāj al-Qushairī and the contemporary Sufi Abū ᶜAbd ar-Raḥman as-Sulamī, a shared Arab descent counted for little in the Persianized society of the eleventh/fifth century.

II. Abū al-Qāsim ᶜAbd al-Karīm b. Hawāzin al-Qushairī (3) first saw the light of day in the year 986/376 in Ustuvā. His initial education in Ustuvā was in Arabic and polite letters (adab), and he later became known for his Arabic and poetry. He also acquired somewhere along the way an unscholarly command of horsemanship and weaponry. But after coming to Nishapur at an indeterminable date with the intent of getting the taxes reduced on a village he owned, he developed a taste for religious studies.[4] Not only did he become the premier Sufi disciple of Abū ᶜAlī ad-Daqqāq, but

4. Abū al-Qāsim had other estates as well which he held in partnership with another Nishapuri (Fārisī I, f28a).

he also studied Shāfiʿī law under Abū Bakr Muḥammad b. Bakr aṭ-Ṭūsī an-Nauqānī[5] and Ashʿarī theology first under Ibn Fūrak, whose grandson his daughter would later marry, and then under Abū Isḥāq al-Isfarāʾinī.[6]

The determination of when Abū al-Qāsim began to teach is complicated by the fact that shortly after he had joined the Sufi retinue of Abū ʿAlī ad-Daqqāq, his mentor convened a session for him in the Muṭarriz Mosque. This appears to have been a session for preaching rather than teaching, however, and to have been only temporary during the period when Abū ʿAlī was in the town of Nasā where he had founded, or was then founding, a Sufi convent.[7] In his own right, al-Qushairī seems to have done no teaching, or at any rate no teaching of ḥadīth, until 1046/437 when he convened a class for himself in, presumably, his father-in-law's old madrasa.

By that time he was a recognized pillar in the Shāfiʿī party. The events intervening between Abū ʿAlī's death and his disciple's emergence as an important figure are rather difficult to sort out, however. It is not even entirely clear that he inherited the headship of Abū ʿAlī's madrasa. That may have come to him only with his marriage to Fāṭima bint Abī ʿAlī ad-Daqqāq. Having been born in the year the *madrasa* was built, 1001/391, Fāṭima was only fourteen at the time of her father's death. Although this does not rule out a marriage to Abū al-Qāsim during her father's lifetime, the fact that her eldest surviving son was not born until 1023/414, some nine years after her father's death, combined with Abū al-Qāsim's joining the Sufi company of Abū ʿAbd ar-Raḥmān as-Sulamī after Abū ʿAlī's death suggests that in actuality Abū al-Qāsim waited a number of years before marrying her and taking over the madrasa.

Abū al-Qāsim developed friendships with the other Shāfiʿī leaders, and he made the Pilgrimage with two of the most important of them, Abū Muḥammad al-Juwainī, the father of Imām al-Ḥaramain al-Juwainī, and Abū Bakr Aḥmad al-Baihaqī.[8] On the journey the three of them attended ḥadīth classes in various cities.

As a result of this great advance from early obscurity to eminence as a Sufi and association in the leadership of the Shāfiʿī party in Nishapur, Abū al-Qāsim became so prominent as to be an obvious target of attack during al-Kundurī's persecution of the

5. Subkī, IV, 121; Fārisī II, f3a.
6. Subkī, IV, 256–262; Ḥākim, f39b; Fārisī II, f35a–36a.
7. Subkī, IV, 330; Nicholson, *Studies in Islamic Mysticism*, p. 19.
8. Subkī, IV, 8–16.

Ashᶜarīs. When the order came to arrest the top Ashᶜarī leaders, his was one of the four names on it, and he spent some time prisoned in the citadel at Nishapur before being released by force of arms. After that he sojourned in Baghdad, arriving there in 1056/448, and was honored by the caliph al-Qāᵓim bi-amriᵓllāh. When he returned, it was to the city of Ṭūs where he had kinsfolk and where he and his family stayed until 1063/455 when the new regime of Alp Arslān and his vizier Niẓām al-Mulk made it safe to return to Nishapur. He was then seventy-nine years old, and he lived out his remaining ten years quietly, as the leadership of the Ashᶜarīs was taken over by his younger fellow-exile Imām al-Ḥaramain.

Abū ᶜAlī ad-Daqqāq's daughter Fāṭima (4) has already been mentioned as her father's pride and joy and as Abū al-Qāsim's fertile wife, but her own prestige as a scholar was far from negligible. She was officially certified to teach ḥadīth, and, as she died in her ninetieth year in 1087/480, traditions from the masters she had learned from early in life were deemed particularly valuable.

Abū ᶜAlī also had a son, Ismāᶜīl (5), who is rarely mentioned but who seems to have grown to adulthood. He was born to a different wife than Fāṭima, apparently a later one of humble background judging from his obscurity and from Abū ᶜAlī's madrasa being inherited by or through Fāṭima.

III. Abū al-Qāsim was the father of six sons and at least five daughters. Since Fāṭima was the mother of all of the sons and at least four of the daughters, she was most probably his only wife. Evidently, Fāṭima bore at least two children after the age of fifty.

The oldest son was Abū Saᶜd ᶜAbd Allāh (6), born in 1023/414. He was a proper son of his father, for he not only stood out as a scholar and Sufi but was also proficient in Arabic and composed poetry in that language. Al-Fārisī makes the interesting remark that "if he had lived, he would have become unquestionably the Shaikh al-Islām wa al-Mashāyikh (Shaikh of Islam and of the Shaikhs) in Khurasan and Iraq because of his prominence, his lineage, and his learning." Considering that Abū Saᶜd died in 1084/477 at the age of sixty-three, this can hardly be interpreted as a graceful way of lamenting someone prematurely deceased; it must mean that he was in fact in line for the office of Shaikh al-Islām in Nishapur, and by exaggeration all of Khurasan and Iraq, when next it fell vacant. It was then held by the Ḥanafī leader Abū Naṣr Aḥmad aṣ-Ṣāᶜidī, however, who did not die until 1089/482. It is illustrative of the essentially neutral character of the office that it was contemplated that it would shift back to a Shāfiʿī after aṣ-Ṣāʿidī's death, a virtual impossibility in the parallel office of chief qāḍī.

The second son whose birthdate is known is Abū Saʿīd ʿAbd al-Wāḥid (7), born in 1027/418. He was a man of letters and learning like his brother but seems to have been of a more pietistic nature. After Abū Saʿd's death in 1084/477, Abū Saʿīd took over as head of the family, and on the death the next next year of Imām al-Ḥaramain al-Juwainī, who was one year younger than he, he took over the important post of khaṭīb in the Manīʿī Congregational Mosque. He served in this post with unexampled eloquence for fifteen years until his own death in 1101/494.

His succession to one post held by Imām al-Ḥaramain raises an interesting question concerning the latter's other important post, that of directorship of the Niẓāmiya madrasa. The directorship of the madrasa appears to have gone first to al-Juwainī's son and then to ʿAlī Ilkiyā al-Harrāsī.[9] Yet Abū Saʿīd convened a ḥadīth class there for himself, something he could not have done if he had not been in charge of that activity. Probably what happened was that upon the death of Imām al-Ḥaramain, Abū Saʿīd succeeded him as khaṭīb but, lacking the legal training to take over the teaching of law in the Niẓāmiya, succeeded him there, possibly on an interim basis, only in his capacity as arbiter of who would be allowed to teach ḥadīth. Unfortunately, there is a further note that his convening of the class took place during the lifetime of his father Abū al-Qāsim, during which time Imām al-Ḥaramain was unquestionably running the Niẓāmiya. If this is so, Abū Saʿīd would seem to have been holding a more exalted post as director of ḥadīth in the Niẓāmiya than his father, which is highly unlikely. All in all, the most convenient solution is to regard the last note as referring to a different class, perhaps one convened under his father's supervision in the family madrasa.

When he was past sixty, Abū Saʿīd's piety took him for the second time on the long trip to Mecca. When he died, he was buried beside his older brother, his father, and his grandfather Abū ʿAlī ad-Daqqāq in the Qushairī madrasa.

Pietism was still more a characteristic of Abū al-Qāsim's third son, Abū Manṣūr ʿAbd ar-Raḥmān (8), born in 1029/420. Despite Abū al-Qāsim's fame, life in his household remained austere and devotional, and the effect upon Abū Manṣūr was to make him into something of a recluse. He was educated, like his brothers, both in Nishapur and

9. Fārisī I, f72a; II, f116a; Old Subkī, IV, 281–282.

elsewhere, and he taught ḥadīth himself, but he held no posts and did not live much of a public life. He first went to Baghdad in his twenties when his father went into exile there. He returned again on Pilgrimage in 1079/471. After returning to Nishapur, he stayed there until his mother's death in 1087/480 after which he went once again to Mecca and sojourned there until his death two years later.

Abū al-Qāsim's fourth son, Abū Naṣr ᶜAbd ar-Raḥīm (9) became the most famous and was probably the most able. He died in his eighties in 1120/514, so his birth must have taken place before 1043/434. His father, under whom he received his early education, had died by the time Abū Naṣr reached his thirtieth birthday, and the culmination of his learning and his mastery of Shāfiᶜī law and Ashᶜarī theology came at the feet of Imām al-Ḥaramain al-Juwainī.

He had only been studying under Imām al-Ḥaramain for four years, however, when the event transpired that made him famous, or notorious depending upon one's doctrinal position.[10] While making the Pilgrimage in 1077/469, Abū Naṣr had a class convened for him in Baghdad. Deliberately or inadvertently, he expounded his Ashᶜarī beliefs in such a way that the feelings of the Ḥanbalī faction became enflamed. A great riot broke out, and lives were lost on both sides. News of the riot was carried to Niẓām al-Mulk at Isfahan. The illustrious vizier correctly saw in the incident a serious threat to his overall religious policy which consisted of attempting to control the Shāfiᶜī-Ashᶜarī party throughout the empire by means of patronage while withholding support from them whenever they threatened to upset the balance between the factions in any particular place. Now the relative peace in Baghdad between the dominant Ḥanbalīs and the intruding Ashᶜarīs was threatened. Accordingly, he summoned Abū Naṣr to Isfahan where he honored him but also admonished him. The admonishment had more telling effect than the honors, for after Abū Naṣr returned to Nishapur, he spent the remainder of his life rather quietly in study and teaching.

Abū al-Fatḥ ᶜUbaid Allāh (10), the fourth son of Fāṭima and Abū al-Qāsim, was born in 1052/444 when his father was sixty-eight and his mother fifty-three. He alone of the six sons became a full-time Sufi. Pious dispositions and Sufi leanings are ascribed to some of the others, but only Abū al-Fatḥ is actually called a Sufi. However, he did not practice his Sufism in Nishapur. After going on the Pilgrimage he moved to Isfarāʾin and settled down there where he eventually died in 1127/521.

10. For a detailed description of the incident see Makdisi, *Ibn ᶜAqīl*, pp. 350–366.

This leaves, finally, Abū al-Muẓaffar ᶜAbd al-Munᶜim (11), born one year after Abū al-Fatḥ. Still a young man when his father died, Abū al-Muẓaffar was taken in by his older brother Abū Naṣr and accompanied him to Baghdad on his ill-fated Pilgrimage. The incident of 1077/469 left no taint upon him, however, as it did upon his brother, and he returned to Baghdad while making the Pilgrimage at least two more times. After returning to Nishapur from his third Pilgrimage, he departed again to go to Kirman where he was received with honor. At last, he returned for good to Nishapur and adopted a more sedentary life. As the last of the sons of Abū al-Qāsim, traditions from his mouth took on a special value. In 1138/532 he died at the age of eighty-seven, bringing to a close a generation of brothers spanning 118 years from the birth of the first to the death of the last.

But there still remain the daughters to be accounted for. Only one of the five daughters, Umm ar-Rahīm Karīma (12), is given a separate biography, but she is probably typical of her sisters. Her inclusion in the biographical dictionary is certainly attributable to her being the mother of the compiler, Abū al-Ḥasan ᶜAbd al-Ghāfir al-Fārisī, rather than to any extraordinary distinction she achieved in her own right. Thus, when her biography relates that she was brought up in a tradition of learning and piety, received a good education, and shunned silken clothing and display, a similar upbringing may be assumed for her sisters. She was born in 1031/422 and died in 1093/486, but an account of her husband's and children's lives will be reserved for the section devoted to the Fārisī family.

The husbands of her sisters, with the exception of the one who married into the Fūrakī family which will be treated separately, can best be mentioned here, however. One sister, an older one bearing also the name Karīma, married her first cousin once removed, that is, the son of Abū al-Qāsim's maternal uncle Abū ᶜAqīl ᶜAbd ar-Raḥman as-Sulamī who has been spoken of earlier. His name was Abū ᶜAmr ᶜAbd al-Wahhāb as-Sulamī al-Māyiqī (13), and he was a companion of Abū al-Qāsim in the early days when he was a disciple of Abū ᶜAlī ad-Daqqāq. In all likelihood, he had come to Nishapur with his cousin and become a Sufi at the same time. He made the Pilgrimage with Abū al-Qāsim and studied at various points along the way, but he was always primarily a Sufi and did not acquire the extensive erudition his cousin did. Like Abū al-Qāsim and various other members of the family, however, he did try his hand at poetry, but in the Persian language rather than the Arabic, which seems a bit strange considering the stress on Arab background and expertise in Arabic found in other family biographies but which really exemplifies the relative insignificance by the eleventh/fifth century of the distinction between Arab and Persian. Abū ᶜAmr did not stay for the rest of his life in Nishapur but returned to Ustuvā and built there in Māyiq ad-Dasht, his native village, a Sufi convent upon which he spent much of his own money and to which he assigned the revenues of an estate in perpetuity. He died in the decade beginning in 1077/470.

Very little is known about another of Abū al-Qāsim's sons-in-law, Abū Bakr Ismāᶜīl b. ᶜUmar b. Abī Naṣr aṣ-Ṣairafī aṣ-Ṣūrī (14). He was evidently a money changer (*ṣairaf*) by profession and a Syrian from the town of Ṣūr by descent,[11] but nothing more is recorded save the year of his death 1097/490.

The last of Abū al-Qāsim's sons-in-law that will be treated here affords a rare example of a bureaucrat in the service of the central government marrying into an important patrician family. Abū Aḥmad al-Ḥasan b. Aḥmad b. Amīrak b. Yaḥyā (15) claimed descent from a noted patrician of earlier times, but the line of descent is not traceable and his father and paternal uncle were secretaries. His status was derived not from his lineage but from his position as secretary for Abū Saᶜd Muḥammad b. Manṣūr, known as the ᶜAmīd of Khurasan, who held high office under Ṭughril Beg and Alp Arslān.[12] As his master was illiterate, Abū Aḥmad al-Ḥasan's position was an important and powerful one, and the title raʾīs which he bears is surely connected with it. Nevertheless, it was his connection with the Qushairīs that confirmed his status in society. He applied himself assiduously to religious studies and good works although his capacity to undertake the latter suffered at some point from a deterioration in his affairs, attributable, no doubt, to a change in his or his patron's political fortune. He died in 1126/520.

Abū Aḥmad al-Ḥasan had a brother named Abū Manṣūr Dilārām (16) who was not a secretary. He was a saddler and a Sufi and lived in Sarakhs where he had a Sufi convent.

IV. Thirteen grandchildren of Abū al-Qāsim and Fāṭima are known, but here only the children of their sons and of the three daughters whose husbands have already been discussed will be treated.

The eldest son, Abū Saᶜd ᶜAbd Allāh, had two sons, but neither of them achieved

11. As the vocalization of the name is not given, there are several possible alternatives given by adh-Dhahabī (Mushtabah, II, 413). Ṣūr is only the most probable.

12. The ᶜAmīd of Khurasan was Muḥammad b. Manṣūr an-Nasawī (al-Ḥusainī, *Akhbār*, pp. 32–34).

much note, being overshadowed within the family as they were by their uncles. Their names were Abū al-Makārim ᶜAbd ar-Razzāq (17) and Abū al-Barakāt ᶜAbd al-Ḥamīd (18), and both received excellent educations, the former being inclined toward Sufism and studying as far away as Khwarizm and the latter studying law under Imām al-Ḥaramain.

Of the two sons of the second son, Abū Saᶜīd ᶜAbd al-Wāḥid, one, Abū al-Maḥāsin ᶜAbd al-Mamājid (19), amounted to no more than his two cousins just mentioned. The other, Abū al-Asᶜad Hibat ar-Raḥmān (20), inherited the leadership of the family and the office of khaṭīb of the Manīᶜī Congregational Mosque from his father on the latter's death in 1101/494. Abū al-Asᶜad was thirty-four years old at that time, and he lived for another fifty-four years, dying in 1153/548 one of the most revered religious scholars in Khurasan. There is nothing to indicate that his death was connected with the devastation of Nishapur by the Ghuzz which took place in the same year.

Abū al-Qāsim's third son, Abū Manṣūr ᶜAbd ar-Raḥmān, had one son by the name of Abū al-Futūḥ ᶜAbd aṣ-Ṣamad (21). He does not appear to have lived too much of his life in Nishapur, for one sojourn in Isfahan is mentioned and another in Samarqand, while in Nasaf he held the office of khaṭīb for a time. Nothing more is known of him.

The last son for whom offspring are recorded is the fourth son, Abū Naṣr ᶜAbd ar-Raḥīm. He had a daughter, who married into the Ṣaffār family, the history of which will be recounted later, and a son named Abū al-Qāsim Faḍl Allāh (22). Abū Naṣr afforded his son whatever education he had a taste for with the exception that he forbade him to join the futūwa and live the life of a celibate. As a result, Abū al-Qāsim shunned scholarship and the life laid open to him by his high birth. He died in 1124/518, four years after his father.

All three daughters whose husbands have already been mentioned had children. The putative Syrian money changer Abū Bakr Ismāᶜīl aṣ-Ṣairafī aṣ-Ṣūrī had a son named Abū al-Fatḥ ᶜAbd al-Wahhāb (23) who dabbled in a variety of things but gained renown in none, and Abū al-Maᶜālī ᶜAbd al-ᶜAzīz as-Sulamī (24), the offspring of al-Qushairī's cousin, achieved no more. He died in 1084/477. The apparent son of the third daughter was a secretary named Aḥmad (25) who was killed by the Ghuzz in 1153/548.

V. Very little remains of the direct Qushairī lineage in this generation although, as will be seen later, two of the related families survived the destruction of the city fairly well. Aside from a great-granddaughter in the Fārisī family and a great-grandson in the Ṣaffār family, there are two great-grandsons in the lines already traced. Abū al-Maᶜālī ᶜAbd al-ᶜAzīz as-Sulamī had a son named Abū Muḥammad ᶜAbd Allāh (26). He died sometime after 1165/560. Of more importance, however, is Abū Khalaf ᶜAbd ar-Raḥmān (27), the blind son of the head of the family in the previous generation, Abū al-Asᶜad Hibat ar-Raḥmān. Abū Khalaf was born in 1101/494 and inherited the position of khaṭīb in the Manīᶜī Congregational Mosque from his father. He must have held the post for only a short time or have shifted to a different mosque, however, for the Manīᶜī mosque was destroyed along with the rest of the city between 1153/548 and 1161/556. He died in 1164/559.

Fūrakī

I. One of the men Abū al-Qāsim al-Qushairī studied under in Nishapur was Abū Bakr Muḥammad b. al-Ḥasan b. Fūrak (28), one of the greatest of the Ashᶜarī theologians. Like al-Qushairī, Ibn Fūrak was not a native of Nishapur; but he came to the city as an established scholar rather than as a young man seeking tax relief. Ibn Fūrak was probably born in Isfahan, and he studied the doctrines of al-Ashᶜarī in Iraq under al-Ashᶜarī's pupil al-Bāhilī. Then he went to Rayy where his new teachings aroused substantial opposition. Hearing of the trouble Ibn Fūrak was having in Būyid Rayy and seeing an opportunity of attracting to Nishapur someone who could furnish them a strong ideological base, the leading Shāfiᶜīs, including the historian al-Ḥākim, went to their patron Abū al-Ḥasan Muḥammad b. Ibrāhīm as-Sīmjūrī and persuaded him to send a messenger to invite Ibn Fūrak to Nishapur. This must have occurred before 983/372 since after that date as-Sīmjūrī was no longer governor.

Responding to the invitation, Ibn Fūrak arrived and took up his residence in a house and madrasa made from a converted convent provided by the governor. And with that began the golden age of Ashᶜarī theology in Nishapur which finally culminated in al-Ghazzālī. But it was not just as a teacher that Ibn Fūrak made his mark in the city; he also played an active role in the leadership of the Shāfiᶜī party. This made him, as it made the chief qāḍī Abū al-ᶜAlāʾ Ṣāᶜid among the Ḥanafīs, a prime target for the Karrāmīs in their attempt to break the power of the patrician parties. This attempt began around 1010/400 with the appointment of the Karrāmī leader to the post of raʾīs of the city by Sultan Maḥmūd. Once the Karrāmī persecution of alleged heretics was under way, Ibn Fūrak was summoned to Ghazna to defend himself against a charge of heresy brought by the Karrāmī leader. His defence was successful, just as the qāḍī Abū al-ᶜAlāʾ Ṣāᶜid's was to be, but on the way home in 1015/406 he was poisoned, presumably by Karrāmī agents. His body was buried in al-Ḥīra Cemetery.

II. All of Ibn Fūrak's children were daughters. One married into the Ṣaffār family whose history will be told later, and another married a man named Sahl b. Abī Sahl for whom no biography is preserved. The husbands of the other two are known and should be discussed here.

Ṭāhir b. al-Ḥusain b. Muḥammad ar-Rawaqī aṭ-Ṭūsī (29) came from a family of wealth and status in the city of Ṭūs, more specifically from the village of Rawah near Ṭūs whence derives the nisba ar-Rawaqī. He studied Ashᶜarī theology under Ibn Fūrak and was a close friend and associate of Abū al-Qāsim al-Qushairī, with whom he corresponded when in Ṭūs and lived when in Nishapur.

The other husband, Abū Manṣur Muḥammad b. al-Ḥusain b. Abī Ayyūb (30), was also a student of Ibn Fūrak, but nothing more is told of him except that he died in 1030/421.

III. Ibn Fūrak had five known grandsons from his four daughters. Two of them will be mentioned with the Ṣaffār family. Of the others, the unknown Sahl b. Abī Sahl had an almost equally obscure son named Abū ᶜUthmān Ismāᶜīl (31).

The son of Ṭāhir ar-Rawaqī, on the other hand, was a man of prominence in the half of Ṭūs known as Ṭābarān. His name was Abū al-Ḥasan ᶜUbaid Allāh ar-Rawaqī (32). He was primarily a student of Shāfiᶜī law, having studied under Imām al-Ḥaramain's father, Abū Muḥammad al-Juwainī. It is noteworthy that he taught law in Ṭūs in both the Arabic and Persian languages. He also authored legal opinions although he did little in the field of ḥadīth. When his father's friend al-Qushairī was staying in Ṭūs waiting for the anti-Ashᶜarī persecution in Nishapur to abate, Abū al-Ḥasan arranged for him to preach, and he was similarly well received when he visited Nishapur.

As for Abū Manṣūr Muḥammad b. al-Ḥusain b. Abī Ayyūb, he had one son by a slave concubine and another by Ibn Fūrak's daughter. The former was named Abū al-Ḥasan ᶜAlī al-Ayyūbī (33) and is said to have been more pious and gifted than his half brother. He was reared in Nishapur but left and settled in Abīvard where he distinguished himself as a disseminator of Ashᶜarī notions. He was also a Sufi.

His better born but less estimable half brother was Abū Bakr Aḥmad al-Fūrakī (34).

The criticism levied against him is that he concerned himself more with temporal than religious honors, and there seems to be justice in the accusation. His credentials as a member of the Shāfiᶜī-Ashᶜarī group in Nishapur were impeccable. Born in 1017/408, he married one of the daughters of Abū al-Qāsim al-Qushairī, his grandfather's student, and he is described in his son's biography as one of the most contentious, ostentatious, and noisy of the Ashᶜarī fityān. When the Ashᶜarī time of trial came, however, he did not stand unequivocally with his fellow Ashᶜarīs. While they were in exile, Abū Bakr Aḥmad was currying favor with the Seljuq court, and he appears in the year 1059/451 as an official envoy of Ṭughril Beg. After that his name crops up from time to time in Baghdad where he made his residence. In 1068/460 he appears placating the Ḥanbalīs. The next year he is involved once in some trouble with the Caliph's court because of his Ashᶜarī views, and another time he commits a *faux pas* while attempting to honor Abū Ḥanīfa. A few years later in 1077/469 Abū Bakr Aḥmad's brother-in-law Abū Naṣr al-Qushairī touched off a riot in Baghdad by his Ashᶜarī preaching, and Abū Bakr Aḥmad apparently did likewise at some unspecified time. Thus, al-Fūraki's dedication to the beliefs of his grandfather and father-in-law, while consistent, does indeed seem to have taken second place, at least in certain instances, to his desire to preserve his favored position in the eyes of the government. He died in Baghdad in 1085/478.

IV. Not much is recorded about Abū ᶜAlī Muḥammad al-Fūraki (35) the son of Abū Bakr Aḥmad. He lived in Nishapur and was brought up by his grandfather Abū al-Qāsim al-Qushairī. Presumably, his mother had continued living in Nishapur when his father took up residence in Baghdad. He died in 1120/514.

Ibn Fūrak had one other great-grandson in the lines being traced here. This was Abū Bakr Muḥammad aṭ-Ṭūsī ar-Rawaqī (36). He lived in Ṭūs like his father and grandfather and studied under Abū al-Qāsim al-Qushairī when he was living in that city waiting for the situation in Nishapur to improve. This places his date of birth at least as early as 1053/445 since he would have had to be at least four or five to have attended the classes. He was proficient in adab, law, and theology. When he died in 1121/515, funeral prayers were said for him *in absentia* in the Manīᶜī Congregational Mosque in Nishapur which is indicative of the regard in which he was held by the Shāfiᶜī community there. The leader of the prayers was the historian al-Fārisī, who was distantly related to him, being the son of the sister-in-law of his first cousin once removed.

V. Abū Bakr Muḥammad ar-Rawaqī had a son named Asᶜad about whom nothing is known.

VI. The last known descendant of Ibn Fūrak in the lines here being traced is Abū al-Barakāt Saᶜīd ar-Rawaqī (37), the son of the Asᶜad in the previous generation. All that is said of him is that he came from an illustrious family.

Ṣaffār

The family name of Coppersmith notwithstanding, by the time the Ṣaffār family appears in history, it had attained great wealth and through land purchases had come to be classed as a dihqān family. How recently this transformation had taken place is indeterminable, but information does exist on where the Ṣaffār landholdings were. The earliest member of the family bears the nisba al-Faryābādī or something resembling it. This presumably represents the name of the village they owned. The family as a whole is given the nisba az-Zunjī by Yāqūt,[13] who identifies Zunj as an area near Nishapur. This is controverted, however, by adh-Dhahabī who calls them ar-Rīkhī,[14] which in Arabic looks exactly like az-Zunjī with the dots that differentiate between letters rearranged. He identifies Rīkh as an area near Nishapur. Samᶜānī,[15] finally, acknowledges the existence of neither of these nisbas but remarks that ar-Rukhkhī as a nisba, which does not look the same as the other two, refers to a district near Nishapur properly called Rukhkh but popularly known as Rīkh. He does not attach the Ṣaffārs to this area, but the biography of one of them does.[16] Thus, the Ṣaffārs' village of Faryābād was located in the district of Rukhkh, south of Nishapur, and Yāqūt's information is based upon a misreading of some text. This makes them neighbors, more or less, of the Maḥmī family whose estates were in the same district.

I. Abū ᶜAlī al-Qāsim b. Ḥabīb b. ᶜAbdūs aṣ-Ṣaffār al-Faryābādī (38) was a legal witness and a wealthy man. He is also described as "the *khaṭīb* of the assemblies (*maḥāfil*) and tongue of the people of the city (*balad*)." This is an intriguing remark since the title

13. Yāqūt, *Muᶜjam al-Buldān*, III, 153.
14. Mushtabah, I, 328.
15. Samᶜānī, VI, 101.
16. Fārisī I, f89a.

khaṭīb is almost invariably reserved for the man charged with delivering the khuṭba in a congregational mosque at the noon prayer on Friday. Abū ᶜAlī al-Qāsim certainly did not hold this position, for it was held by his contemporary Abū ᶜUthmān Ismāᶜīl aṣ-Ṣābūnī. It is tempting to see in this phrase evidence of some kind of municipal office, such as official city spokesman or moderator of city assemblies, particularly since his grandson's biography refers to Abū ᶜAlī al-Qāsim as having been "khaṭīb of the assemblies in Nishapur" thus implying that this hypothetical office was known in other cities as well. Temptation will not substitute for proof, however, and this must remain a conjecture.

II. Abū Bakr Muḥammad aṣ-Ṣaffār (39) seems to have begun the succession of Ṣaffār jurisconsults. His father was a witness and a man of affairs, but Abū Bakr Muḥammad was a distinguished Shāfiᶜī jurist. He was a student of Abū Muḥammad al-Juwainī and taught in his place when he went on the Pilgrimage with Abū al-Qāsim al-Qushairī and Abū Bakr Aḥmad al-Baihaqī. Since the Pilgrimage often took more than a year to complete, this substitution is evidence that he enjoyed the complete trust of al-Juwainī. In addition, he taught ḥadīth in the Muṭarriz Mosque, the stronghold of the Shāfiᶜī-Ashᶜarī faction.

One strange note in his biography is a reference to his lack of wealth alongside the remark that he came from a family of great wealth. Presumably, this signifies a loss of income consequent upon the family's move from the world of money to the world of scholarship, but no explanation is offered.

Abū Bakr Muḥammad died in 1076/468. It is indicative of the close relations among all parts of this clan that members of the Shaḥḥāmī and Furāwī families, the only segments of the clan with which Abū Bakr Muḥammad's descendants are not known to have intermarried, are listed as his students.

III. Abū Bakr Muḥammad had two sons. Abū Ibrāhīm Ismāᶜīl (40) studied Shāfiᶜī law under Imām al-Ḥaramain al-Juwainī, only five years his senior, and served as his father's assistant in his ḥadīth classes. Beyond that nothing is known except his date of birth, 1033/424, and his date of death, 1098/491.

His brother, Abū Saᶜd Manṣūr (41), was also a jurist. Moreover, he was a student of Abū al-Qāsim al-Qushairī and a son-in-law of Ibn Fūrak. He passed most of his life in

Rukhkh, however, living in his village and taking care of his estate. He died there in 1112/506.

IV. Abū Saᶜd Manṣūr had two children, a daughter ᶜĀʾisha (42), who is merely a name, and a son Abū Naṣr Aḥmad (43). He lived on the family estates as his father had, but was nevertheless well educated. He married Umm al-Ghāfir Durdāna, sister of the historian al-Fārisī. Since he is also a grandson of Ibn Fūrak, the Fūrakī, Ṣaffār, and Fārisī segments of the clan are thus united. He was born in 1057/449 and died in 1139/533 in the village of Zīrwān in Rukhkh.

V. Both of the sons of Abū Naṣr Aḥmad distinguished themselves as jurists. Abū Bakr al-Qāsim (44), all of whose complicated relations with Ibn Fūrak, Abū al-Qāsim al-Qushairī, Abū ᶜAlī ad-Daqqāq, and Abū al-Ḥusain ᶜAbd al-Ghāfir al-Fārisī are spelled out in detail, was a student of his mother's maternal uncle, Abū Naṣr al-Qushairī, in both law and theology. He was supported in his education by his maternal grandfather, Abū ᶜAbd Allāh Ismāᶜīl al-Fārisī. His promising career was cut short, however, by his murder at noon on a Friday in 1122/516. No details are given, but the singular timing of the deed suggests that factional rivalry was the cause.[17]

Abū Ḥafṣ ᶜUmar (45) was born in 1084/477 and was granted the time to fulfill his promise since he died in 1158/553 during the period of Nishapur's devastation, although no connection between the two events is indicated. He was active as a jurist and a ḥadīth scholar. Although he counted among his teachers ᶜAbd al-Wāḥid al-Qushairī, it was the daughter of his brother's Qushairī mentor, Abū Naṣr, that he married, thus completing the web of marital relations involving the Ṣaffār family.

VI. With Abū Saᶜd (Saᶜīd) ᶜAbd Allāh (46) the blood of the Ṣaffārs, Fūrakīs, Qushairīs, and Fārisīs is carried on into the new but pitifully reduced city of Nishapur that rose beside the ruins of the great metropolis. He was born in 1114/508, so that he was able to hear ḥadīth from his grandfather Abū Naṣr al-Qushairī before his death in 1120/514. Like his forebears, he specialized in law and studied under the same members of the

17. One large riot between Ḥanafīs and Shāfiᶜīs is known to have taken place sometime during the reign of Sanjar, and it may be the one involved here. Al-Ḥusainī, *Akhbār*, 125–126.

Furāwī and Shaḥḥāmī families who had studied in their childhood under his great-great-grandfather. He died in the year 1204/600.

VII. The last of the Ṣaffārs and the latest member that has been found of any of the great Nishapuri families is the son of Abū Saᶜd ᶜAbd Allāh, Abū Bakr al-Qāsim (47). A Shāfiᶜī jurist like all the others, he was born in 1139/533, studied under Wajīh ash-Shaḥḥāmī and Abū al-Asᶜad al-Qushairī, Abū al-Qāsim's grandson, and died at the hands of the Mongols when they entered Nishapur and slaughtered the populace in 1221/618.[18]

Fārisī

I. This being the family of the historian of Nishapur Abū al-Ḥasan ᶜAbd al-Ghāfir al-Fārisī, substantial information is given about its various members. The first member of the Fārisī family in Nishapur was Abū ᶜAbd Allāh Muḥammad b. ᶜAbd al-Ghāfir al-Fārisī al-Fasawī (48) who came originally from the town of Fasā in the province of Fārs. Although it is not explicitly stated, it is clear that he was a merchant and an associate in the Khān al-Furs, the caravanserai that served as commercial and social center for the merchants from Fārs in Nishapur. The only bit of religious lore which seems to have passed the lips of Abū ᶜAbd Allāh Muḥammad is a story, quoted in full, of how the caliph ᶜAlī determined the sex of a hermaphrodite.[19] He died in 1010/400.

II. The elder of Abū ᶜAbd Allāh Muḥammad's two sons was Abū Bakr Aḥmad (49), who was born in 961/350 and died before his father. He was one of the merchants belonging to the Khān al-Furs. The younger son, Abū al-Ḥusain ᶜAbd al-Ghāfir (50), was born in 964/353 and died in his ninety-sixth year in 1056/448. Like his father and brother he was a merchant and served also as trustee in all family affairs on account of his upright character.

In time, however, his fame as a transmitter of ḥadīth overshadowed his success as a trader. In his childhood he had attended along with his brother the classes of Abū

18. For the destruction of Nishapur by the Mongols see ᶜAta-Malik Juvainī, *The History of the World Conqueror*, tr. J. A. Boyle (Cambridge, Mass., 1958), I, 169–278.
19. He counted the ribs.

Aḥmad Muḥammad al-Julūdī[20] to hear recited the famous *Ṣaḥīḥ* of Muslim b. al-Ḥajjāj, recognized along with that of al-Bukhārī as the two most authoritative collections of prophetic traditions. Since al-Julūdī died in 979/368, not too many students could have followed the Fārisī brothers at his feet, and none of those that did attained the prodigious age of ninety-five. Thus, Abū al-Ḥusain ᶜAbd al-Ghāfir by sheer longevity became the sole possessor of this important line of transmission. When he was around fifty years old a class was convened for him to teach the *Ṣaḥīḥ*, and he taught it until the end of his life. After the death in 1015/405 of the historian al-Ḥākim, who also transmitted from al-Julūdī, Abū al-Ḥusain emerged as one of the most important scholars in the city.[21] It is in this way that a not particularly distinguished family of merchants from the Khān al-Furs took its place among the elite of the patriciate. At this death, his body was prayed over by the Shaikh al-Islām Abū ᶜUthmān aṣ-Ṣābūnī before being interred in Bāb al-Muᶜammir Cemetery.

There are many people named al-Fārisī who are generally described as being related to this particular family of Fārisīs but whose connections are not spelled out. Endogamy was probably the general practice among the merchant families of the Khān al-Furs. One relative is concretely pinned down in this generation, however. This is Abū al-Ḥusain Muḥammad b. ᶜAbd al-Malik al-Fārisī (51), the brother of one of Abū al-Ḥusain ᶜAbd al-Ghāfir's wives. He was a merchant and an associate in the Khān al-Furs, and he also served as muezzin and prayer leader in the mosque in the Khān al-Furs. He was not only a brother-in-law but also a very close associate of Abū al-Huṣain ᶜAbd al-Ghāfir through thick and thin, and he died in the same year 1056/448.

III. Although at least two wives are indicated for Abū al-Ḥusain ᶜAbd al-Ghāfir, only one child is known, Abū ᶜAbd Allāh Ismāᶜīl (52), and that one was born when his father was seventy years old in 1032/423. There is no suggestion of a commercial background in Abū ᶜAbd Allāh's biography. The Khān al-Furs is not mentioned for him or his descendants. Instead, the quantity and quality of his learning is stressed. The change in status that overtook the family with his father's emergence as an important teacher is thus quite evident. Foremost among his teachers was Abū al-Qāsim al-

20. This man was one of the rare members of the Thawrī madhhab in Nishapur, Samᶜānī, III, 307–309.

21. That Abū al-Ḥusain became an important teacher only after the death of al-Ḥākim is indicated by the fact that of his 111 known students, none is recorded as being born before 1014/404.

Qushairī whose daughter Umm ar-Raḥīm Karīma he married. After leaving his family and going on the Pilgrimage from 1063/455 to 1071/463,[22] Abū ᶜAbd Allāh was certified to teach and had a class in ḥadīth convened for him in the ᶜAqīl mosque, a Shāfiᶜī institution where the famous Ashᶜarī theologians Abū Isḥāq al-Isfarāʾinī[23] and ᶜAbd al-Qāhir al-Baghdādī[24] had taught before him. He was also a certifier of legal witnesses (muzakkī). He died in 1111/504.[25]

IV. Abū ᶜAbd Allāh had four children, a son who died in childhood,[26] a daughter who married into the Ṣaffār family, another daughter who married into the Rashīdī family, and a second son, the historian Abū al-Ḥasan ᶜAbd al-Ghāfir al-Fārisī (53). He was born in 1059/451 but must have been brought up primarily by his mother in the household of her father Abū al-Qāsim al-Qushairī since his own father was gone from the city for some ten years during his early childhood. By the age of five he knew the Muslim creed in Persian, and in addition to his regular elementary schooling he began to attend ḥadīth sessions at the age of seven. He became exceedingly well grounded in the teachings of his grandfather al-Qushairī, but other teachers occupied his time as well, including his grandmother Fāṭima bint Abī ᶜAlī ad-Daqqāq, his two Qushairī uncles Abū Saᶜd ᶜAbd Allāh and Abū Saᶜīd ᶜAbd al-Wāḥid, and Imām al-Ḥaramain al-Juwainī with whom he studied law for four years.

Eventually, he began to travel outside Nishapur to further his learning and make his own career as a teacher. First he went to places nearby, such as Nasā, and then farther afield to Khwarizm. After that he went to Ghazna and on to Lahore and India. At last he returned from his travels and settled down to teach ḥadīth in the ᶜAqīl Mosque where his father had taught. Since there seems to have been only one ḥadīth teacher at a time in the ᶜAqīl Mosque, Abū al-Ḥasan ᶜAbd al-Ghāfir probably began teaching there after his father's death in 1111/504. He also began then a career of writing in which he turned out a number of books including the *Siyāq li-Taʾrīkh Naisābūr* which was

22. The date of his Pilgrimage is given in his biography and the fact of his being absent from Nishapur for some ten years terminating in 1071/634 is given in his son's.

23. See footnote 6 to this chapter.

24. Fārisī I, f55a–b; II, f105a; Subkī, V, 51–52.

25. Al-Fārisī has 1113/507.

26. The fact that the only son of Abū ᶜAbd Allāh Ismāᶜīl other than ᶜAbd al-Ghāfir died in childhood is disclosed in the biography of a pretended son of his, Fārisī I, f25a–b; II, f69a–b.

completed in 1124/518.[27] According to later sources, he also served as khaṭīb, but this seems unlikely as his first cousin Abū al-Asᶜad Hibat ar-Raḥmān al-Qushairī, who is known to have held the post, did not die until nineteen years after ᶜAbd al-Ghāfir's death in 1135/529.

His sister, Umm al-Ghāfir Durdāna (54), is described as a learned and very pious girl, like ᶜAbd al-Ghāfir a student of all her Qushairī relations. She married Abū Naṣr Aḥmad aṣ-Ṣaffār and saw her son marry her first cousin, the daughter of Abū Naṣr al-Qushairī. Her grandson Abū Saᶜd ᶜAbd Allāh aṣ-Ṣaffār transmitted ḥadīth from her brother ᶜAbd al-Ghāfir.

The other daughter, whose name is unknown and who may conceivably have been an aunt instead,[28] married a merchant and jurist named Abū ᶜAbd Allāh Muḥammad b. Maḥmūd ar-Rashīdī (55). The last name, which means rightly guided, was given to his father because of his uncanny good luck in business. He was born in 1020/411 and died in 1105/498. His body was buried in the cemetery in Ziyād Square.

V. The son of Umm al-Ghāfir Durdāna has already been mentioned with the Ṣaffār family, and the daughter of Abū al-Ḥasan ᶜAbd al-Ghāfir, Umm Salma Sittiyak (Little Lady), is known only as the wife of her husband who will be mentioned with the Shaḥḥāmī family. This leaves only the children of Abū ᶜAbd Allāh Muḥammad ar-Rashīdī. One of them, Abū al-Maᶜālī Maḥdūd ar-Rashīdī (56), fell into error through the study of philosophy. He bequeathed his books to the Manīᶜī Congregational Mosque where they were destroyed along with the other books in the mosque library (except one)[29] during the sack of the city by the Ghuzz tribesmen.

Another son, Abū al-Qāsim Ismāᶜīl ar-Rashīdī (57), lived his life outside of Nishapur as part of the retinue of the sultan Muḥammad b. Malikshāh. He died in 1109/502, the same year as an otherwise unknown third brother Abū al-Futūḥ.

27. The manuscript text of the *Siyāq* (Fārisī II) gives 1116/510 as the year of completion. However, fifty-six biographies contain death dates after that date as opposed to only eleven with death dates after 1124/518. If al-Fārisī added occasional notes to his text after its completion, it is easier to believe that he did it on eleven than on fifty-six occasions.

28. The word *ṣahr* which describes her husband can mean either brother-in-law or son-in-law. In the latter case it would surely mean son-in-law of ᶜAbd al-Ghāfir's father.

29. One of the books from the Manīᶜī Congregational Mosque was saved from destruction and is still extant, ᶜAlī Muᵓayyad Thābatī, *Taᵓrīkh-i Nīshābūr* (Tehran, 1956), p. 33.

Shaḥḥāmī

II. The association of the Shaḥḥāmīs and Furāwīs with the four families already discussed is late in coming but is eventually quite close. For the generation of Abū ᶜAlī ad-Daqqāq and Ibn Fūrak no member of the Shaḥḥāmī house is traceable. For the generation of Abū al-Qāsim al-Qushairī, however, there is a biography of Abū Bakr Muḥammad ash-Shaḥḥām ash-Shurūṭī (58). If it is not simply a copyist's error, the name ash-Shaḥḥām in place of the ash-Shaḥḥāmī born by all later members of the family would seem to indicate that this Abū Bakr Muḥammad was himself in the fat-rendering business and not just the descendant of someone in that trade. His other name, ash-Shurūṭī, on the other hand, points to expertise in the drafting of contracts (*sharṭ* pl. *shurūṭ* = condition of a contract, the contract document),[30] an activity which some of his descendants also engaged in. Unfortunately, the remainder of his biography is unilluminating. It remarks upon his piety and learning and gives al-Ḥusain Cemetery as his place of burial in 1050/442, but there is nothing to confirm the suggestion that Abū Bakr Muḥammad was a prosperous merchant who made the leap into the patriciate by way of specialization in contract law.

III. Of the three sons of Abū Bakr Muḥammad, the eldest, Abū Saᶜīd Ḥamza (59), and the youngest, Abū ᶜAlī al-Ḥusain (60), were of little note. The former, who is specifically described as not having the quality of his brothers, died in the decade beginning in 1068/460; and the latter, a jurist, died in the preceding decade. Both were buried in the family tomb in al-Ḥusain Cemetery.

It was the middle son, Abū ᶜAbd ar-Raḥmān Ṭāhir (61), who achieved real prominence and established the Shaḥḥāmīs as a leading Shāfiᶜī family. Ṭāhir specialized in law and contracts following his father, and he wrote shurūṭ officially for the court.[31] At this he was outstanding. He composed books on shurūṭ and also a book in Persian on laws and ordinances. Yet the great prominence that he attained was not attained in this way.

The end of the persecution of the Ashᶜarīs came in 1058/450 when Alp Arslān succeeded his father as governor of Nishapur with Niẓām al-Mulk as his vizier. The

30. Another man is reported to have made his living drawing up contracts in the Great Crossroads Market, Fārisī II, f30b.

31. EI^{1}, IV, 335.

Niẓāmiya madrasa was founded in that year and put under the direction of the returned exile Imām al-Ḥaramain al-Juwainī. Five years later, after Alp Arslān had become sultan following Ṭughril Beg, Niẓām al-Mulk's lieutenant Abū ʿAlī Ḥassān al-Manīʿī,[32] who had been installed as raʾīs and Shaikh al-Islām to safeguard Niẓām al-Mulk's control of the situation, built out of his own funds a congregational mosque to counterbalance the old Congregational Mosque which was still under Ḥanafī control. The khaṭīb of the new Manīʿī Congregational Mosque was Imām al-Ḥaramain al-Juwainī, and the office later passed to the Qushairī family.

Exactly how Abū ʿAbd ar-Raḥmān Ṭāhir fit himself into this picture is unclear. Somehow he was chosen by Niẓām al-Mulk to be the *mustamliʾ* in his ḥadīth classes, that is, to repeat the traditions as they were dictated in a loud enough voice to be heard by the entire assembly. Then, when the new mosque was built, a special enclosure for the study of ḥadīth was built into it called the Shaḥḥāmī Garth (Ḥaẓīra ash-Shaḥḥāmī).[33] Since al-Manīʿī built the mosque out of his own funds, this naming may signify only that Ṭāhir ash-Shaḥḥāmī was the first person to teach ḥadīth in the Shaḥḥāmī Garth, but whether he paid for its construction or was simply its first director, such intimate connection with this buttress of Niẓām al-Mulk's new religious policy is further proof of the special favor he enjoyed in the eyes of the vizier. It was also in the Manīʿī Congregational Mosque that the historian al-Fārisī joined in the prayers over Ṭāhir's body in 1086/479. He had been born in 1009/399.

IV. Abū ʿAbd ar-Raḥmān Ṭāhir had one daughter and three sons. Ẓarīfa (62), the daughter, is given a separate biography in which her teachers are listed; but it is under the name Zumra that she appears as the wife of Abū ʿAbd Allāh Muḥammad al-Furāwī. The eldest son, Abū Naṣr Khalaf (63), seems to be distinguished primarily for his friendship with al-Fārisī, who wrote his biography. He was born in 1051/443 and died in 1092/485. Al-Fārisī led the prayers for him in the Manīʿī Congregational Mosque. With the other two sons, however, the prominence of the family can be seen to continue.

Abū al-Qāsim Zāhir (64), the second son, followed closely in his father's footsteps. He was a mustamliʾ and writer of shurūṭ for the qāḍī's court. He was unsurpassed in the

32. Fārisī I, f15a–17b; II, f61b.

33. There is one reference to a Shaḥḥāmī madrasa which is presumably the same thing as the Shaḥḥāmī Garth, Fārisī II, f128a.

art of composing documents of all sorts, and great reliance was placed on him in such matters. Beyond that he turned his hand to nursing and even more to the recitation of ḥadīth. The latter activity he engaged in every Friday before the noon prayer for some twenty years in the Shaḥḥāmī Garth, being the fifth person after his father to teach there.[34] Yet despite these manifold good works, his reputation was marred by irregular attendance at prayers. The excuse he gave was that he combined several prayer sessions in one, but this did not keep some people from shunning him. Ibn al-Jauzī, who reports this information which al-Fārisī is silent on, remarks that such negligence is reproved but not totally forbidden for those who tend the sick, but the later biographers have preserved the charge only, without this mitigation. Zāhir was born in 1054/446 and died in 1139/533. He was buried with the rest of the family in al-Ḥusain Cemetery.

The third brother, Abū Bakr Wajīh (65), was born in 1063/455. Neither a composer of legal documents nor a loud voiced repeater of traditions, he was a simple pious student of ḥadīth who studied in Herat, Baghdad, and the Hijaz. He served as khaṭīb and preacher for the smaller towns in the Nishapur district, including Qaṣr ar-Rīḥ which may have been in the neighborhood of the Ṣaffār estates. To later biographers, however, his main achievement was regular attendance at prayers in which he surpassed his brother's poor performance. He died in 1146/541.

Also in this generation is one ᶜAlī who is presumably the son of Abū ᶜAlī al-Ḥusain the brother of Ṭāhir. His existence is only inferred from that of his son to be mentioned in the next generation, however.

V. Abū Manṣūr ᶜAbd al-Khāliq (66), one of the sons of Abū al-Qāsim Zāhir, married Umm Salma Sittiyak, daughter of ᶜAbd al-Ghāfir al-Fārisī, great-granddaughter of Abū al-Qāsim al-Qushairī and Fāṭima bint Abī ᶜAlī ad-Daqqāq, and niece of Abū Naṣr Aḥmad aṣ-Ṣaffār.[35] Clearly, she was a most eligible young lady in Shāfiᶜī circles. Being, like the others of this generation, still a young man when al-Fārisī stopped writing, less is known about him than might be wished. It is certain, however, that he followed the family tradition in shurūṭ and *istimlāᵓ*. He was born in 1082/475 and died in 1153/549 of tortures inflicted by the Ghuzz in their sack of the city. Nothing of substance is known about his sister Saᶜīda (67) or his brother Abū Saᶜd Ṭāhir (68).

34. The intervening teachers died in 1087/480 (Fārisī II, f41b), 1090/483 (Fārisī II, f13b–14a), 1097/490 (Fārisī II, f34a), and 1101/494 (Fārisī II, f47b–48a).

35. Evidence of this marriage is found in Samᶜānī, VI, 45.

Equally negligible is the information given for Abū Naṣr Khalaf's two children, Fāṭima (69) and Abū al-Muẓaffar ᶜAbd al-Karīm (70). The latter died after 1145/540. Only slightly better is the luck with Abū Bakr Wajīh's children. One son, Bakr (71), is a cipher, but the other one, Khalīl (72), is known to have followed the family trade of writing shurūṭ and was called ash-Shurūṭī because of it as were several of his forebears.

Finally, there is one last Shaḥḥāmī to be mentioned. This is Abū ᶜAlī al-Ḥusain b. ᶜAlī (73). He died in 1150/545 in Marv and is entitled raᵓīs. He is specifically said to be of the Shaḥḥāmī family of Nishapur, but since his grandfather's name is not given, absolute certainty is wanting as to his precise connection with the family. The descent shown on the family tree from Abū ᶜAbd ar-Raḥmān Ṭāhir's brother Abū ᶜAlī al-Ḥusain is based solely upon the likelihood of a grandson being given the same name as his grandfather. Whether this identification is precisely correct or not, however, the possibility that this man was raᵓīs of the major city of Marv suggests that the Shaḥḥāmī family had important branches outside of Nishapur.

Furāwī

III. There is universal agreement that Furāwa was a small town on the way to Khwarizm where ᶜAbd Allāh b. Ṭāhir built a *ribāṭ*, or fortified caravanserai, in the days of the caliph Maᵓmūn. There is not agreement on the spelling of the name, however. Most sources spell it Furāwa, but Yāqūt and adh-Dhahabī do not. The latter spells it Farāwa in his book devoted to the proper spelling of place-names.[36] The majority opinion in this case is buttressed by the mot "al-Furāwī alfu rāwī," or, loosely, "al-Furāwī is worth a thousand other reciters." Good grammar does not permit the substitution of an "a" for the "u"; therefore the spelling followed here will be al-Furāwī and not al-Farāwī.

This little dispute is not at all germane to the history of the Furāwī family. The biography of the first family member in Nishapur, Abū Muḥammad al-Faḍl (74), betrays no sign of the family's place of origin. Nor is the second nisba of Abū Muḥammad al-Faḍl, aṣ-Ṣāᶜidī, explicated any better. The later Ḥanafī historian Ibn Abī al-Wafāᵓ was deceived by this second name into thinking that the Furāwīs were

36. Mushtabah, II, 500; Yāqūt, *Muᶜjam al-Buldān*, IV, 245.

Ḥanafīs related to the Ṣāᶜidī family of Nishapur and accordingly includes two of them in his Ḥanafī biographical dictionary. This identification is quite clearly wrong, but the true meaning of aṣ-Ṣāᶜidī is lost.

Back to Abū Muḥammad al-Faḍl, he was a Sufi of the generation of Abū al-Qāsim al-Qushairī's sons and an ardent disciple of Abū al-Qāsim. No more is related concerning him except that he studied in Bukhara and lived from 1023/414 to 1094/487.

IV. One son of Abū Muḥammad al-Faḍl, Abū al-Ḥasan, is known only from a brief reference in his father's biography; the other is the most important member of the family, Abū ᶜAbd Allāh Muḥammad al-Furāwī aṣ-Ṣāᶜidī (75). The biography of Abū ᶜAbd Allāh that at one time existed in al-Fārisī's *Siyāq* has disappeared from the extant manuscripts, but it is quoted at length by Subkī. Born around 1049/441 and reared in the Sufi ways of his father, Abū ᶜAbd Allāh began at the age of six to study ḥadīth. His studies were extensive both in Nishapur and elsewhere, and they situate him in the heart of the Qushairī nexus. Abū al-Qāsim al-Qushairī, his father's mentor; ᶜAbd al-Ghāfir al-Fārisī, whose daughter his Shaḥḥāmī nephew married; and Abū Bakr Muḥammad aṣ-Ṣaffār are all numbered among his teachers; but his main studies were under Imām al-Ḥaramain al-Juwainī in Shāfiᶜī law.

After Imām al-Ḥaramain's death in 1085/478, al-Furāwī made a long Pilgrimage in the course of which he preached in Baghdad and studied in Mecca and Medina. Then he returned to his wife Zumra or Ẓarīfa ash-Shaḥḥāmī and settled down as imām of the Muṭarriz Mosque and professor of law in the Nāṣiḥiya madrasa, a Shāfiᶜī institution founded by a lieutenant of Niẓām al-Mulk named Abū Muḥammad al-Fandurjī and titled Nāṣiḥ ad-Dawla. He was unrelated to the Ḥanafī Nāṣiḥī family.[37]

Much more is related about Abū ᶜAbd Allāh dealing with the excellence of his teaching and the propriety of his life style, including the tidbit that he once wore a coarse black shirt and a small turban; but the sum of these remarks is simply that he became one of the paramount figures in the Shāfiᶜī camp and an important transmitter of learning from the great Shāfiᶜīs of earlier generations. Among his students was Abū Saᶜd ᶜAbd Allāh aṣ-Ṣaffār from the other long-lived branch of the clan.

He died in 1136/530.

37. Another teacher in the same madrasa may be found in Fārisī I, f52b–53a. On Nāṣiḥ ad-Dawla see Fārisī I, f70a; Samᶜānī, f432a.

V. A son and a daughter were born to Abū ᶜAbd Allāh Muḥammad and Zumra ash-Shaḥḥāmī. Sharīᶜa (76) was the name of the daughter, but nothing more is recorded. The son was Abū al-Barakāt ᶜAbd Allāh (77). He was a specialist in shurūṭ like his maternal grandfather Ṭāhir ash-Shaḥḥāmī and may well have been brought up largely under Shaḥḥāmī influence since he was born in 1081/474, and his father began his long Pilgrimage when he was still a young child. He died in 1154/549, a victim not of Ghuzz torture, like his cousin ᶜAbd al-Khāliq ash-Shaḥḥāmī, but of the famine that came on the heels of the Ghuzz devastation.

VI. Abū al-Maᶜālī ᶜAbd al-Munᶜim (78), the son of Abū al-Barakāt ᶜAbd Allāh, died in 1191/587.

VII. Finally, sharing with his distant cousin Abū Bakr al-Qāsim aṣ-Ṣaffār the distinction of carrying the Qushairī clan into its seventh generation, Abū al-Fatḥ (or Abū al-Qāsim) Manṣūr al-Furāwī (79), son of Abū al-Maᶜālī ᶜAbd al-Munᶜim, brings this history of the Qushairīs and related families to a close. A certifier of legal witnesses, he was born in 1128/522, and he died in 1211/608, one of the last scholars whom people travelled to Nishapur to study under. In another ten years Nishapur would be made a wasteland and his Ṣaffār cousin part of a pyramid of skulls by the invading armies of Genghis Khan.

Genealogical Key

Qushairī

1. Abū ᶜAlī al-Ḥasan ad-Daqqāq	Fārisī I, f1b–2b; II, f52a; Subkī, IV, 329–331; ᶜIbar, III, 93.
2. Abū ᶜAqīl ᶜAbd ar-Raḥmān as-Sulamī	Fārisī I, f39b–40a; II, f87b; Subkī, V, 155.
3. Abū al-Qāsim ᶜAbd al-Karīm al-Qushairī	Fārisī I, f49a–51a; II, f97a; ᶜIbar, III, 259; Subkī, V, 153–162; Shadharāt, III, 319–322; I. Khallikān, II, 375–377; EI^1, II, 1160.
4. Fāṭima bint Abī ᶜAlī ad-Daqqāq	Fārisī I, f76a–b; II, f123a–b; ᶜIbar, III, 296.
5. Ismāᶜīl b. Abī ᶜAlī ad-Daqqāq	Fārisī I, f2b, f33a.
6. Abū Saᶜd ᶜAbd Allāh al-Qushairī	Subkī, V, 68–69; Fārisī I, f32b–33a; II, f82a; ᶜIbar, III, 287; Shadharāt, III, 354.
7. Abū Saᶜīd ᶜAbd al-Wāḥid al-Qushairī	Fārisī I, f52a–b; II, f98a–b; ᶜIbar, III, 339; Subkī, V, 225–228; Shadharāt, III, 401.
8. Abū Manṣūr ᶜAbd ar-Raḥmān al-Qushairī	Fārisī I, f43b–44a; II, f91b–92a; Subkī, V, 105–106.
9. Abū Naṣr ᶜAbd ar-Raḥīm al-Qushairī	Fārisī I, f45b–46a; II, f93b–94a; ᶜIbar, IV, 33; Shadharāt, III, 321–322; IV, 45; I. Khallikān, II, 377–378; Old Subkī, IV, 249–253.
10. Abū al-Fatḥ ᶜUbaid Allāh al-Qushairī	Fārisī I, f39a; II, f86b–87a; Old Subkī, IV, 269–270.
11. Abū al-Muẓaffar ᶜAbd al-Munᶜim al-Qushairī	Fārisī I, f57b; II, f108a (see fig. 1, this volume); ᶜIbar, IV, 88; Old Subkī, IV, 264; I. Jauzī, X, 75; Shadharāt, IV, 99.
12. Umm ar-Raḥīm Karīma al-Qushairī	Fārisī II, f125b–126a.

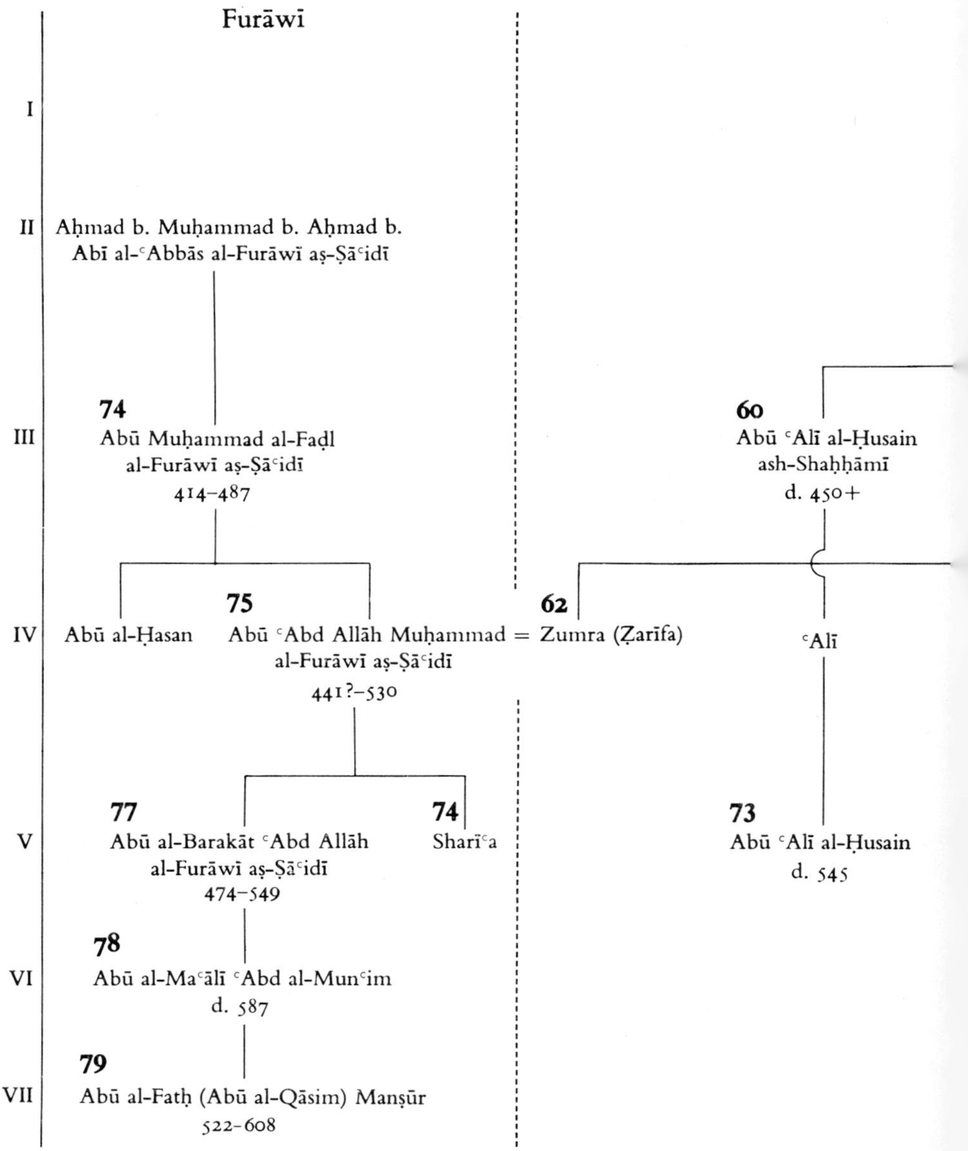
Furāwī
I
II
Aḥmad b. Muḥammad b. Aḥmad b. Abī al-ᶜAbbās al-Furāwī aṣ-Ṣāᶜidī
III
74
Abū Muḥammad al-Faḍl al-Furāwī aṣ-Ṣāᶜidī 414–487
60
Abū ᶜAlī al-Ḥusain ash-Shaḥḥāmī d. 450+
IV
Abū al-Ḥasan
75
Abū ᶜAbd Allāh Muḥammad al-Furāwī aṣ-Ṣāᶜidī 441?–530
=
62
Zumra (Ẓarīfa)
ᶜAlī
V
77
Abū al-Barakāt ᶜAbd Allāh al-Furāwī aṣ-Ṣāᶜidī 474–549
74
Sharīᶜa
73
Abū ᶜAlī al-Ḥusain d. 545
VI
78
Abū al-Maᶜālī ᶜAbd al-Munᶜim d. 587
VII
79
Abū al-Fatḥ (Abū al-Qāsim) Manṣūr 522–608

Shaḥḥāmī

Abū Naṣr Muḥammad b. Aḥmad b.
Muḥammad b. Yūsuf

58
Abū Bakr Muḥammad
ash-Shaḥḥāmī ash-Shurūṭī
d. 442

61
Abū ᶜAbd ar-Raḥmān Ṭāhir
ash-Shaḥḥāmī ash-Shurūṭī
399–479

59
Abū Saᶜīd Ḥamza ash-Shaḥḥāmī
d. 460+

65
Abū Bakr Wajīh ash-Shaḥḥāmī
455–541

63
Abū Naṣr Khalaf ash-Shaḥḥāmī
443–485

72
Khalīl ash-Shaḥḥāmī
ash-Shurūṭī

71
Bakr

69
Fāṭima

70
Abū al-Muẓaffar ᶜAbd al-Karīm
d. 540+

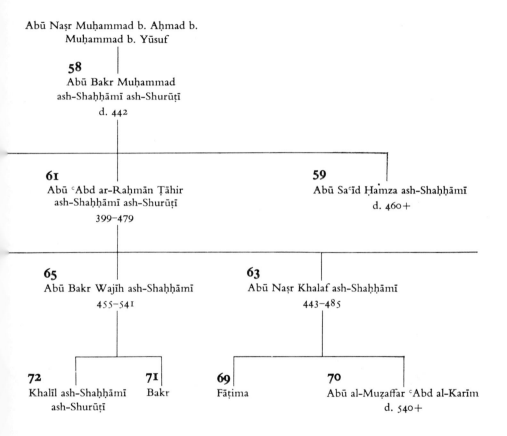

Shaḥḥāmī (continued)

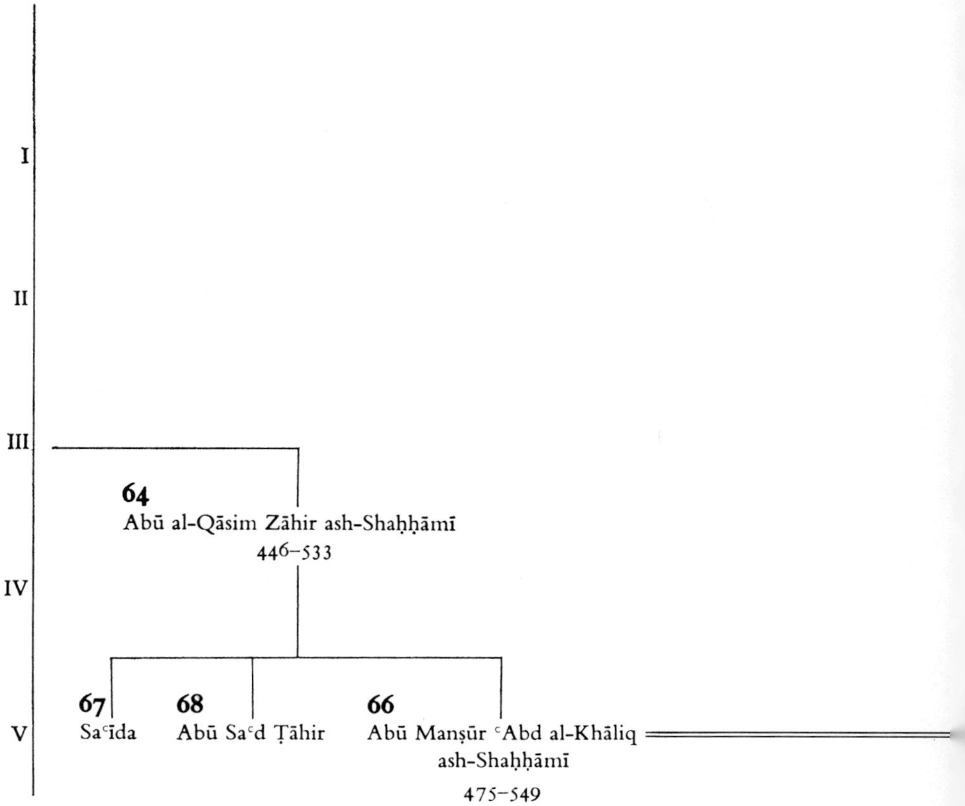

Fārisī

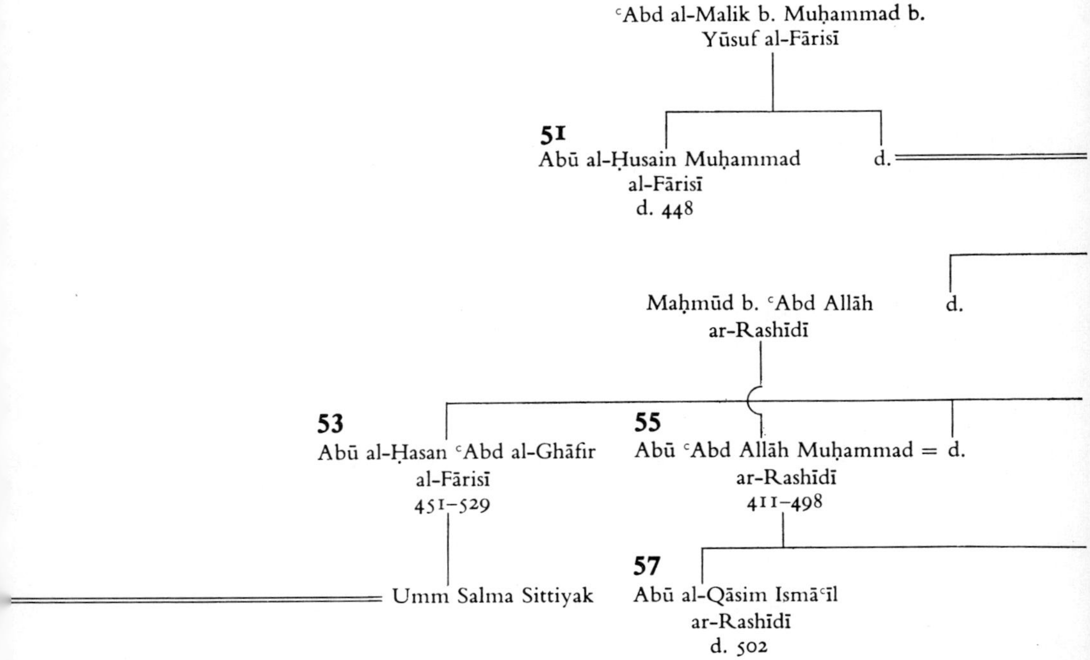
ᶜAbd al-Malik b. Muḥammad b. Yūsuf al-Fārisī
51 Abū al-Ḥusain Muḥammad al-Fārisī d. 448
d.
Maḥmūd b. ᶜAbd Allāh ar-Rashīdī
d.
53 Abū al-Ḥasan ᶜAbd al-Ghāfir al-Fārisī 451–529
55 Abū ᶜAbd Allāh Muḥammad ar-Rashīdī 411–498
= d.
57 Abū al-Qāsim Ismāᶜīl ar-Rashīdī d. 502
Umm Salma Sittiyak

Fārisī (continued)   Qushairī

ᶜAbd al-Ghāfir b. Muḥammad b. Aḥmad
b. Muḥammad b. Saᶜīd

I

48
Abū ᶜAbd Allāh Muḥammad
al-Fārisī al-Fasawī
d. 400

II

50
Abū al-Ḥusain ᶜAbd al-Ghāfir
al-Fārisī
353–448

49
Abū Bakr Aḥmad
al-Fārisī
b. 350

III

52
Abū ᶜAbd Allāh Ismāᶜīl = Umm ar-Raḥīm Karīma
al-Fārisī   al-Qushairī
423–486   422–486

10
Abū al-Fatḥ ᶜUbaid Allāh
al-Qushairī
444–521

IV

s.   **54**
Umm al-Ghāfir Durdāna = Abū Naṣr Aḥmad
al-Fārisī   aṣ-Ṣaffār ar-Rīkhī

43

23
Abū al-F
ᶜAbd al-Wahh
aṣ-Ṣairaf

V

56
Abū al-Maᶜālī
Maḥdūd
ar-Rashīdī

Abū al-Futūḥ
ar-Rashīdī
d. 502

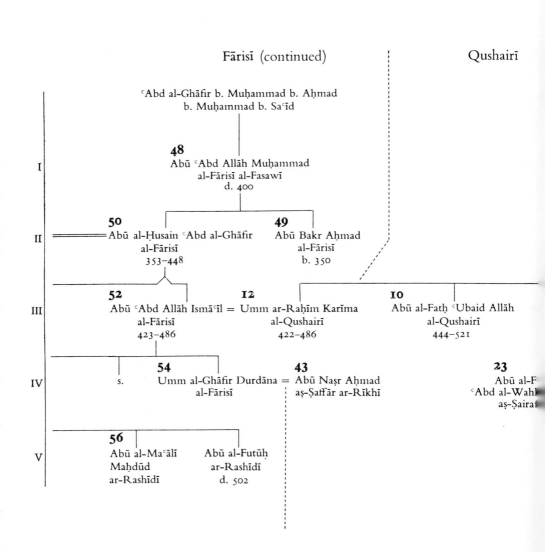

Qushairī (continued)

ʿUmar b. Abī Naṣr

14
=Abū Bakr Ismāʿīl
aṣ-Ṣūrī aṣ-Ṣairafī
d. 490

7
Abū Saʿīd ʿAbd al-Wāḥid
al-Qushairī
418–494

19
Abū al-Maḥāsin
ʿAbd al-Mamājid
al-Qushairī

20
Abū al-Asʿad
Hibat ar-Raḥmān
al-Qushairī
460–548

27
Abū Khalaf ʿAbd ar-Raḥmān al-Qushairī
494–559

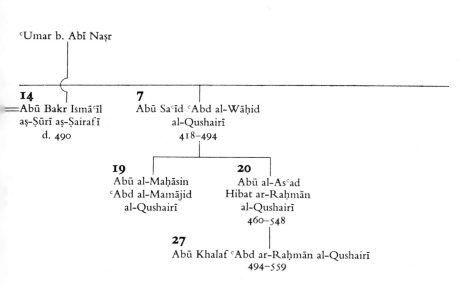

Qushairī (continued)

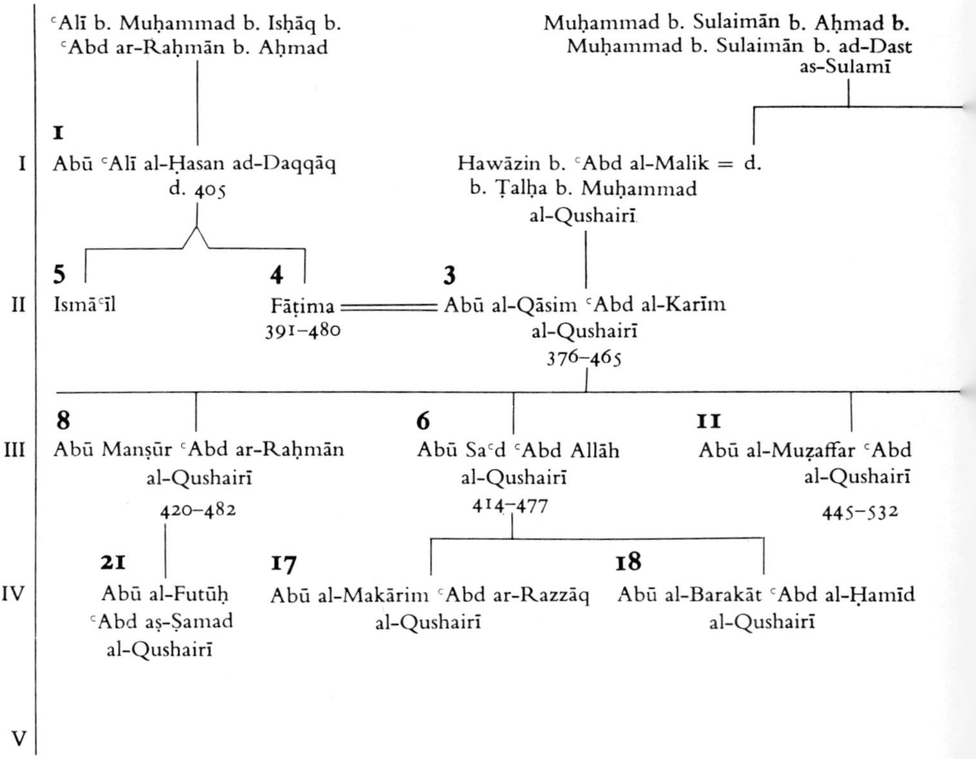
ʿAlī b. Muḥammad b. Isḥāq b. ʿAbd ar-Raḥmān b. Aḥmad
Muḥammad b. Sulaimān b. Aḥmad b. Muḥammad b. Sulaimān b. ad-Dast as-Sulamī
I
1
Abū ʿAlī al-Ḥasan ad-Daqqāq d. 405
Hawāzin b. ʿAbd al-Malik = d.
b. Ṭalḥa b. Muḥammad al-Qushairī
II
5
Ismāʿīl
4
Fāṭima 391–480
3
Abū al-Qāsim ʿAbd al-Karīm al-Qushairī 376–465
III
8
Abū Manṣūr ʿAbd ar-Raḥmān al-Qushairī 420–482
6
Abū Saʿd ʿAbd Allāh al-Qushairī 414–477
11
Abū al-Muẓaffar ʿAbd al-Qushairī 445–532
IV
21
Abū al-Futūḥ ʿAbd aṣ-Ṣamad al-Qushairī
17
Abū al-Makārim ʿAbd ar-Razzāq al-Qushairī
18
Abū al-Barakāt ʿAbd al-Ḥamīd al-Qushairī
V

Qushairī (continued)

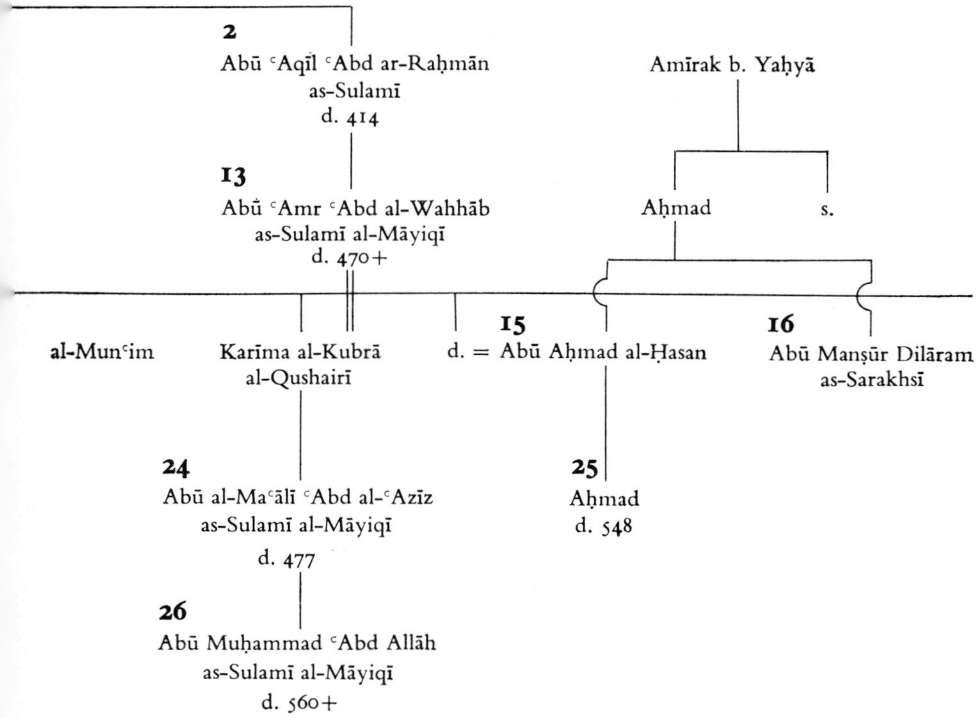
2
Abū ᶜAqīl ᶜAbd ar-Raḥmān
as-Sulamī
d. 414
13
Abū ᶜAmr ᶜAbd al-Wahhāb
as-Sulamī al-Māyiqī
d. 470+
Amīrak b. Yaḥyā
Aḥmad
s.
al-Munᶜim
Karīma al-Kubrā
al-Qushairī
15
d. = Abū Aḥmad al-Ḥasan
16
Abū Manṣūr Dilāram
as-Sarakhsī
24
Abū al-Maᶜālī ᶜAbd al-ᶜAzīz
as-Sulamī al-Māyiqī
d. 477
25
Aḥmad
d. 548
26
Abū Muḥammad ᶜAbd Allāh
as-Sulamī al-Māyiqī
d. 560+

Qushairī (continued)

I

II

III

9
Abū Naṣr ᶜAbd ar-Raḥīm
al-Qushairī
d. 514

d. =

IV

22
Abū al-Qāsim Faḍl Allāh
al-Qushairī
d. 518

d. = **45**
Abū Ḥafṣ ᶜUmar
aṣ-Ṣaffār ar-Rīkhī

V

VI

VII

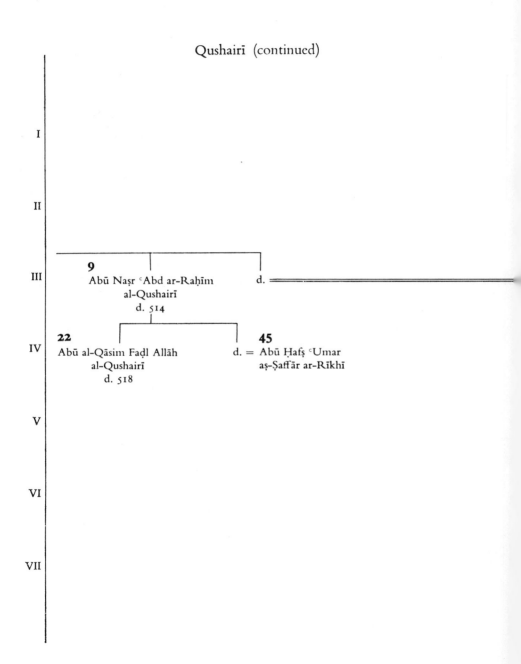

Fūrakī

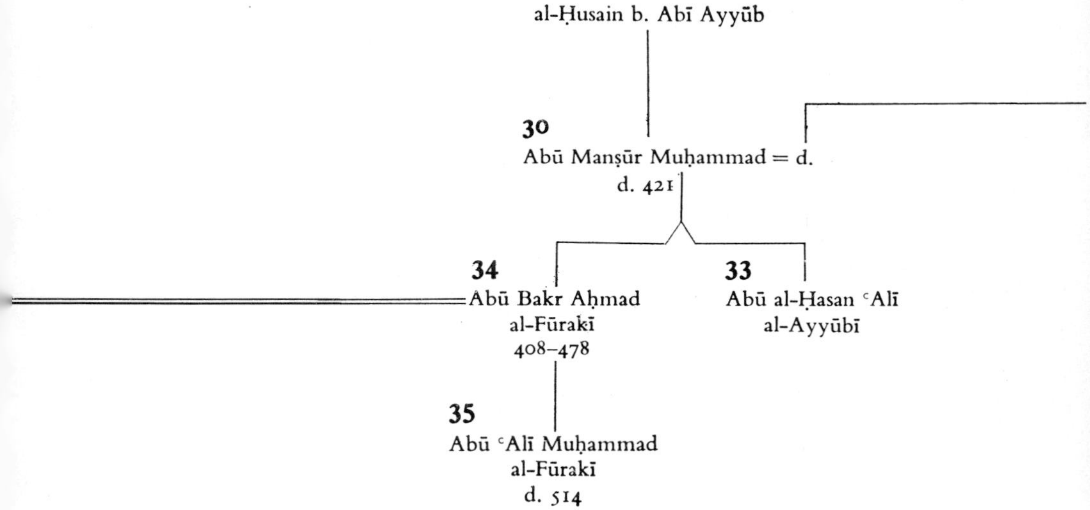
al-Ḥusain b. Abī Ayyūb
30
Abū Manṣūr Muḥammad = d.
d. 421
34
Abū Bakr Aḥmad
al-Fūrakī
408–478
33
Abū al-Ḥasan ᶜAlī
al-Ayyūbī
35
Abū ᶜAlī Muḥammad
al-Fūrakī
d. 514

Fūrakī (continued)

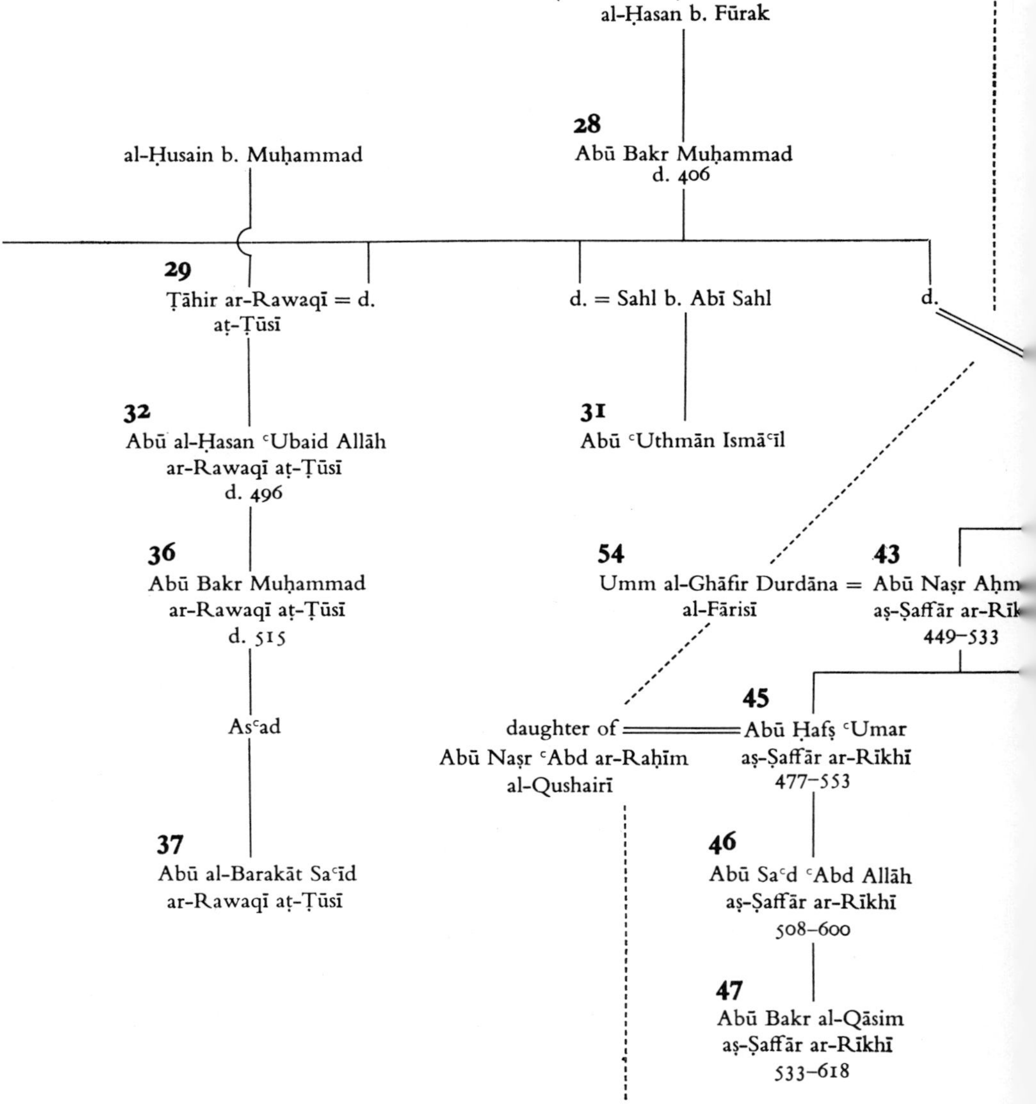

Ṣaffār

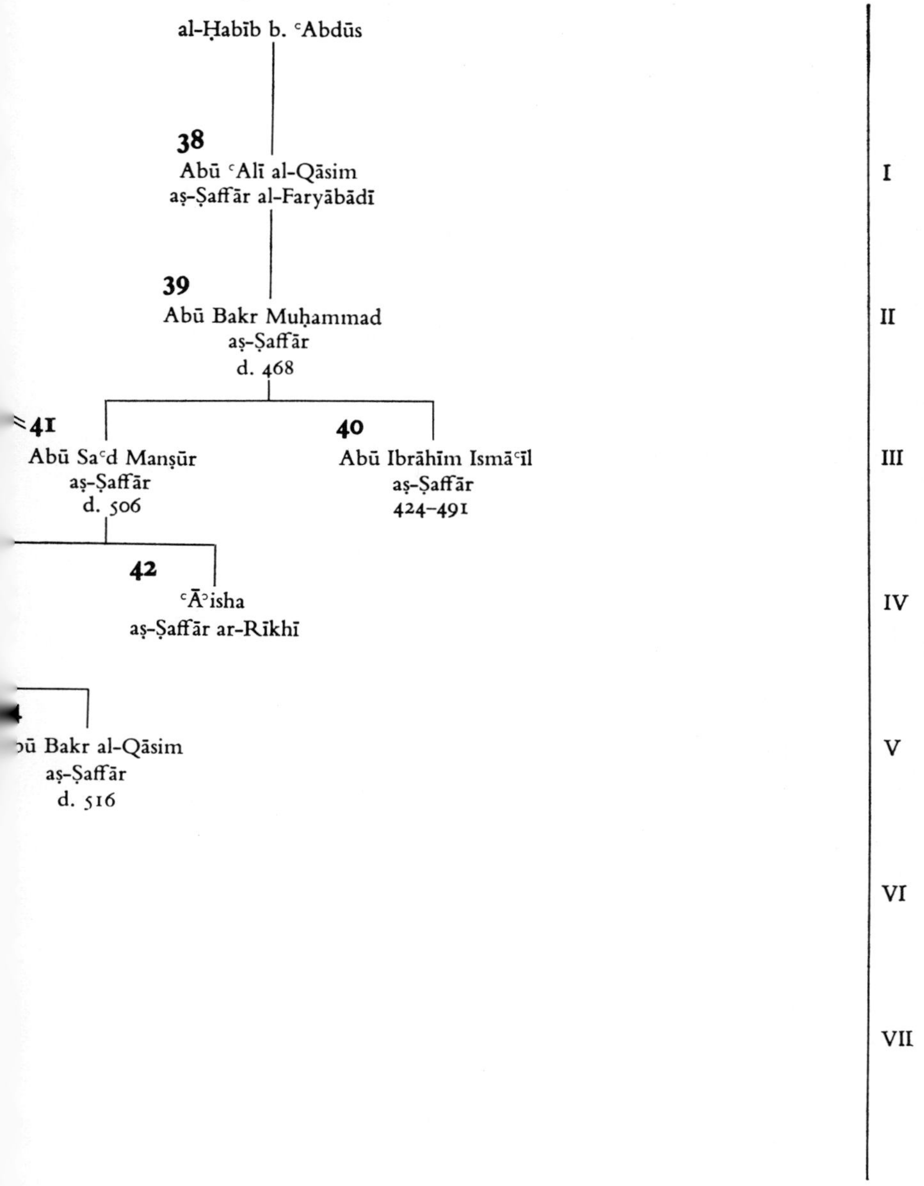
al-Ḥabīb b. ᶜAbdūs
38
Abū ᶜAlī al-Qāsim
aṣ-Ṣaffār al-Faryābādī
39
Abū Bakr Muḥammad
aṣ-Ṣaffār
d. 468
41
Abū Saᶜd Manṣūr
aṣ-Ṣaffār
d. 506
40
Abū Ibrāhīm Ismāᶜīl
aṣ-Ṣaffār
424–491
42
ᶜĀᵓisha
aṣ-Ṣaffār ar-Rīkhī
ū Bakr al-Qāsim
aṣ-Ṣaffār
d. 516
I
II
III
IV
V
VI
VII

13. Abū ʿAmr ʿAbd al-Wahhāb as-Sulamī al-Māyiqī	Fārisī I, f54a; II, f103a; Samʿānī, f504b; Lubāb, III, 92.
14. Abū Bakr Ismāʿīl aṣ-Ṣūrī aṣ-Ṣairafī	Fārisī II, f44b.
15. Abū Aḥmad al-Ḥasan b. Aḥmad b. Amīrak	Fārisī I, f7b–8a; II, f54b.
16. Abū Manṣūr Dilārām b. Aḥmad b. Amīrak	Fārisī I, f59b; II, f63b.
17. Abū al-Makārim ʿAbd ar-Razzāq al-Qushairī	Fārisī II, f104b.
18. Abū al-Barakāt ʿAbd al-Ḥamīd al-Qushairī	Fārisī II, f100a–b.
19. Abū al-Maḥāsin ʿAbd al-Mamājid al-Qushairī	Fārisī II, f108a (see fig. 1, this volume).
20. Abū al-Asʿad Hibat ar-Raḥmān al-Qushairī	Fārisī II, f141a; ʿIbar, IV, 125; Shadharāt, IV, 140–141; Old Subkī, IV, 322.
21. Abū al-Futūḥ ʿAbd aṣ-Ṣamad al-Qushairī	Fārisī II, f102a; *Taʾrīkh Samarqand*, f29a.
22. Abū al-Qāsim Faḍl Allāh al-Qushairī	Fārisī I, f76a; II, f166b.
23. Abū al-Fatḥ ʿAbd al-Wahhāb aṣ-Ṣairafī	Fārisī II, f103b.
24. Abū al-Maʿālī ʿAbd al-ʿAzīz as-Sulamī	Fārisī II, f101b.
25. Aḥmad b. al-Ḥasan	I. Athīr, XI, 181–182.
26. Abū Muḥammad ʿAbd Allāh as-Sulamī al-Māyiqī	Samʿānī, f505a.
27. Abū Khalaf ʿAbd ar-Raḥmān al-Qushairī	Old Subkī, IV, 249.

Fūrakī

28. Abū Bakr Muḥammad b. al-Ḥasan b. Fūrak	Fārisī II, f2a; Subkī, IV, 127–135; ʿIbar, III, 94; Shadharāt, III, 181–182; I. Khallikān, III, 402; EI^2 III, 766.

29. Ṭāhir b. al-Ḥusain aṭ-Ṭūsī ar-Rawaqī	Fārisī I, f84b, 80a; II, f76b–77a.
30. Abū Manṣūr Muḥammad b. al-Ḥusain b. Abī Ayyūb	Subkī, IV, 47; III, 370.
31. Abū ʿUthmān Ismāʿīl b. Sahl b. Abī Sahl	Fārisī II, f44b.
32. Abū al-Ḥasan ʿUbaid Allāh ar-Rawaqī	Fārisī I, f39a; II, f86b.
33. Abū al-Ḥasan ʿAlī al-Ayyūbī	Fārisī I, f65a.
34. Abū Bakr Aḥmad al-Fūrakī	Fārisī II, f33a; Subkī, IV, 79; I. Jauzī, VIII, 204, 248–249, IX, 17; Makdisi, "Autograph Diary," XVIII, 249, XIX, 302.
35. Abū ʿAlī Muḥammad al-Fūrakī	Fārisī II, f21a–b.
36. Abū Bakr Muḥammad aṭ-Ṭūsī ar-Rawaqī	Fārisī II, f21a.
37. Abū al-Barakāt Saʿīd ar-Rawaqī	Ibn Mākūlā, *Al-Ikmāl*, IV, 217 fn. 3 (ultimately from Samʿānī but not in text).

Ṣaffār

38. Abū ʿAlī al-Qāsim aṣ-Ṣaffār al-Faryābādī	Fārisī II, f123b.
39. Abū Bakr Muḥammad aṣ-Ṣaffār ar-Rīkhī	Fārisī II, f13b; Subkī, IV, 194–195; ʿIbar, III, 268; Mushtabah, I, 328; I. Jauzī, VIII, 299–300; Shadharāt, III, 331.
40. Abū Ibrāhīm Ismāʿīl aṣ-Ṣaffār	Fārisī II, f44b.
41. Abū Saʿd Manṣūr aṣ-Ṣaffār	Fārisī I, f89a; II, f130b.
42. ʿĀʾisha aṣ-Ṣaffār ar-Rīkhī	Mushtabah I, 329.
43. Abū Naṣr Aḥmad aṣ-Ṣaffār ar-Rīkhī	Yāqūt, *Muʿjam al-Buldān*, III, 153; Mushtabah, I, 328.
44. Abū Bakr al-Qāsim aṣ-Ṣaffār	Fārisī II, f124a.
45. Abū Ḥafṣ ʿUmar aṣ-Ṣaffār ar-Rīkhī	Fārisī II, f109b; Mushtabah, I, 328; ʿIbar, IV, 153; Old Subkī, IV, 285.

46. Abū Saʿd ʿAbd Allāh aṣ-Ṣaffār ar-Rīkhī	Old Subkī, V, 58–59; Mushtabah, I, 328–329; ʿIbar, IV, 312.
47. Abū Bakr al-Qāsim aṣ-Ṣaffār ar-Rīkhī	ʿIbar, V, 74; Mushtabah, I, 329.

Fārisī

48. Abū ʿAbd Allāh Muḥammad al-Fārisī al-Fasawī	Fārisī II, f5a–b.
49. Abū Bakr Aḥmad al-Fārisī	Fārisī II, f29b.
50. Abū al-Ḥusain ʿAbd al-Ghāfir al-Fārisī	Fārisī I, f56b; II, f105b–106a; Shadharāt, III, 277–278.
51. Abū al-Ḥusain Muḥammad al-Fārisī	Fārisī II, f8b.
52. Abū ʿAbd Allāh Ismāʿīl al-Fārisī	Fārisī II, f44a; ʿIbar, IV, 7–8; Shadharāt, IV, 7–8.
53. Abū al-Ḥasan ʿAbd al-Ghāfir al-Fārisī	Fārisī II, f145a–b; Ḥuffāẓ, pp. 1275–76; Old Subkī, IV, 255; Shadharāt, IV, 93; I. Khallikān, II, 391–392.
54. Umm al-Ghāfir Durdāna	Fārisī I, f19b; II, f63b–64a.
55. Abū ʿAbd Allāh Muḥammad ar-Rashīdī	Fārisī II, f17a; Samʿānī, VI, 131–132; Lubāb, I, 468.
56. Abū al-Maʿālī Maḥdūd ar-Rashīdī	Samʿānī, VI, 132–133; Lubāb, I, 468–469.
57. Abū al-Qāsim Ismāʿīl ar-Rashīdī	Fārisī II, f45a.

Shaḥḥāmī

58. Abū Bakr Muḥammad ash-Shaḥḥām ash-Shurūṭī	Fārisī II, f10b.
59. Abū Saʿīd Ḥamza ash-Shaḥḥāmī	Fārisī I, f14a; II, f60b.
60. Abū ʿAlī al-Ḥusain ash-Shaḥḥāmī	Fārisī II, 58a.
61. Abū ʿAbd ar-Raḥmān Ṭāhir ash-Shaḥḥāmī ash-Shurūṭī	Fārisī I, f80a–b; II, f77a; ʿIbar, III, 294; Shadharāt, III, 363.
62. Ẓarīfa ash-Shaḥḥāmī	Fārisī II, f78a; Samʿānī f370b; Subkī, VI, 168.

63. Abū Naṣr Khalaf ash-Shaḥḥāmī	Fārisī I, f18b; II, f62b–63a.
64. Abū al-Qāsim Zāhir ash-Shaḥḥāmī	Fārisī I, f21a–b; II, f66b; I. Jauzī, X, 79–80; ᶜIbar, IV, 91; Shadharāt, IV, 102.
65. Abū Bakr Wajīh ash-Shaḥḥāmī	Fārisī II, f139a; I. Jauzī, X, 124; Yāqūt, *Muᶜjam al-Buldān*, IV, 357; ᶜIbar, IV, 113; Shadharāt, IV, 130.
66. Abū Manṣūr ᶜAbd al-Khāliq ash-Shaḥḥāmī	Fārisī II, f108a (see fig. 1, this volume); ᶜIbar, IV, 137; Shadharāt, IV, 153.
67. Saᶜīda ash-Shaḥḥāmī	Fārisī I, f30a; II, f72b.
68. Abū Saᶜd Ṭāhir ash-Shaḥḥāmī	Fārisī II, f77b.
69. Fāṭima ash-Shaḥḥāmī	Fārisī II, f123b.
70. Abū al-Muẓaffar ᶜAbd al-Karīm ash-Shaḥḥāmī	Fārisī II, f97b (in margin).
71. Bakr ash-Shaḥḥāmī	Fārisī II, f50a.
72. Khalīl ash-Shaḥḥāmī ash-Shurūṭī	Fārisī I, f18b; II, f63a.
73. Abū ᶜAlī al-Ḥusain ash-Shaḥḥāmī	ᶜIbar, IV, 123; Shadharāt, IV, 139–140.

Furāwī

74. Abū Muḥammad al-Faḍl al-Furāwī aṣ-Ṣāᶜidī	Fārisī I, f75a–b; II, f121b–122a.
75. Abū ᶜAbd Allāh Muḥammad al-Furāwī aṣ-Ṣāᶜidī	Subkī, III, 371; VI, 166–170; IAW, II, 107; ᶜIbar, IV, 83; I. Khallikān, III, 418–419; Yāqūt, *Muᶜjam al-Buldān*, IV, 245.
76. Sharīᶜa al-Furāwī	Fārisī II, f74a.
77. Abū al-Barakāt ᶜAbd Allāh al-Furāwī aṣ-Ṣāᶜidī	IAW, I, 288–289; Shadharāt, IV, 153.
78. Abū al-Maᶜālī ᶜAbd al-Munᶜim al-Furāwī	ᶜIbar, IV, 262.
79. Abū al-Fatḥ (Abū al-Qāsim) Manṣūr al-Furāwī	ᶜIbar, V, 29; Shadharāt, V, 34; Yāqūt, *Muᶜjam al-Buldān*, IV, 245.

12 / *Baḥīrī*

The grip of the Ḥanafīs and of the Ṣāᶜidī family in particular on the judicial organization in Nishapur was not really as complete as a look at the names of the known qāḍīs and *ḥākims* makes it appear. There was another part of the judicial system, as well, the certification of legal witnesses; and in that the Shāfiᶜīs played an important role. This is clearly seen in the Baḥīrī family.

I. As is so often the case, the early origins of the family are difficult to trace. Baḥīr b. Nūḥ b. Ḥayyān b. Mukhtār, the family's eponym, had a son named Muḥammad who may or may not be the Abū ᶜAbd Allāh Muḥammad al-Isfarāᵓinī (1) indicated on the family tree. The father's name is unpointed in the manuscript; and while Baḥīr is a likely reading, it is not certain. There is nothing else to connect the family with the town of Isfarāᵓin, but such an origin would explain why earlier family members do not appear in Nishapur. Abū ᶜAbd Allāh Muḥammad's biography belongs to the category of those who died between ca. 816/200 and ca. 882/270. He apparently had a brother named Saᶜīd.

II. Jaᶜfar the son of Muḥammad and Muḥammad the son of Saᶜīd are known only through their descendants' genealogies.

III. Abū al-ᶜAbbās Muḥammad b. Muḥammad b. Saᶜīd b. Baḥīr (2) died between ca. 926/314 and 947/335. His second cousins, Muḥammad b. Jaᶜfar and al-Ḥasan b. Jaᶜfar have left no trace.

IV. Finally, information about the family becomes more abundant. Muḥammad b. al-Ḥasan b. Jaᶜfar (3) sojourned in Baghdad where he taught traditions he had learned from his second cousin once removed of the previous generation, Abū al-ᶜAbbās Muḥammad. He died in 999/389. All later members of the Baḥīrī family are descended from his first cousin Abū al-Ḥusain Aḥmad b. Muḥammad b. Jaᶜfar (4). A legal witness and a ḥadīth scholar, he studied in both Nishapur and Iraq and taught in the Dār as-Sunna madrasa in Nishapur where al-Ḥākim convened a class for him in 985/375. He died three years later.

V. Abū al-Ḥusain Aḥmad's only son, Abū ᶜAmr Muḥammad (5), was born in 945/333. He is the first of the family to be called a muzakkī, or certifier of legal witnesses, but he is best known to his biographers as a teacher of traditions. Apparently he did not get off to a good start in his ḥadīth studies because the Prophet had to appear to him in a dream and advise him to waste no further time on the transmitters he was studying. But once set aright, he did very well. He studied in Iraq and the Hijaz sometime after the year 971/360 and is reported to have been teaching in Baghdad in 990/380. This could either represent one long period of study and travel outside of Nishapur beginning after the birth of one of his sons in 975/364 or two different journeys, but the former alternative is closer to the life pattern of other Nishapuri patricians. He died in 1006/396 and was buried in the cemetery of Mūlqābād, a wealthy quarter just north of al-Ḥīra quarter.

Also in this generation is a man who became the father-in-law of one of Abū ᶜAmr Muḥammad's sons. Abū Muḥammad ᶜAbd Allāh b. Abī Naṣr Aḥmad al-Maṣāḥifī al-Jāmiᶜī as-Simsār (6) has an exceptionally informative name. He was a broker (*simsār*) by profession and a copier of the Qur᾽an (*maṣāḥif* pl. of *maṣḥaf* = copy of the Qur᾽an) by pious avocation. He is said to have copied the holy text eight hundred and eighty times. Furthermore, he frequented the congregational mosque (*jāmi*ᶜ) so much that it, too, entered into his name. Of course, this was long before the Ashᶜarī persecution and the resultant construction of the Manīᶜī Congregational Mosque after which the Shāfiᶜīs completely abandoned the Old Congregational Mosque to the Ḥanafīs. In 1026/417 or 1028/419 he died.

VI. Abū Naṣr ᶜAbd ar-Raḥmān (7) appears to have been the firstborn of Abū ᶜAmr Muḥammad's four sons and to have been the one to inherit the post of muzakkī although all of the others were witnesses and are said to come from a family of muzakkīs. He died in 1009/399 only three years after his father, and the post passed on to his brother ᶜAmr.

Abū Ḥāmid Baḥīr (8) was in all probability the next son, judging from the fact that in subsequent generations his line appears chronologically to be substantially older than those descending from his brothers. His being a witness is about all that is recorded of him. His wife, the daughter of Abū Muḥammad ᶜAbd Allāh as-Simsār al-Maṣāḥifī al-Jāmiᶜī of the previous generation, is a complete unknown.

The third in line, Abū ᶜAbd ar-Raḥmān ᶜAmr (9), is called "chief of the muzakkīs of his generation." He also taught ḥadīth in the Old Congregational Mosque up until his death in 1054/446. Unlike the previous instance of a connection with the Old

Congregational Mosque in this family, Abū ᶜAbd ar-Raḥmān ᶜAmr's retention of his teaching post there in the midst of the persecution of the Ashᶜarīs may be very significant. Since all Ashᶜarīs were proscribed from teaching positions, he must have belonged to a non-Ashᶜarī faction of the Shāfiᶜī party. The statement in the biography of one of the leaders of the persecution that "the factional rivalry (taᶜaṣṣub) led to the splitting of the Shāfiᶜīs into factions (iftirāq) [and] the annihilation (īdāᵓ) of the Ashᶜarīs"[1] quite clearly alludes to the existence of non-Ashᶜarī Shāfiᶜīs in Nishapur, and the Baḥīrīs would appear to have been prominent among them. It is hard to say, however, whether this is connected in any way with their involvement in the Ḥanafī dominated judicial system. The matter is further complicated by the fact that one of Abū ᶜAbd ar-Raḥmān's sons was an Ashᶜarī and Abū ᶜUthmān Ismāᶜīl aṣ-Ṣābunī, an unswerving Ashᶜarī, did not lose his position as Shaikh al-Islām in the persecution although he was replaced as khaṭīb of the Old Congregational Mosque. Coincidentally, it was aṣ-Ṣābūnī who said the funeral prayers for Abū ᶜAbd ar-Raḥmān ᶜAmr in the middle of Mūlqābād quarter prior to his interment in the family tomb at the gate of the quarter.

The fourth son, Abū ᶜUthmān Saᶜīd al-Mūlqābādī (10), was a legal witness, but otherwise his life was quite unlike his brothers'. He served in the army of Maḥmūd of Ghazna during Maḥmūd's famous invasions of India, and he distinguished himself by his bravery. Which of Maḥmūd's many campaigns he participated in cannot be determined. The first campaign took place around the year 1000/390 when Abū ᶜUthmān, who was born in 975/364, was twenty-five. Maḥmūd died in 1030/421. Thus, there is a great range within which Abū ᶜUthmān could have performed his military feats.

But regardless of when he went on campaign, Abū ᶜUthmān found time not only to acquire a sound education in ḥadīth in Iraq, Sarakhs, Marv, and Nishapur but to take up the Sufi robe. He built in the quarter of Mūlqābād a Sufi convent, a library, and a mosque. Then late in life he was called upon to teach ḥadīth in the Old Congregational Mosque in the place of his brother who died in 1054/446. Once again the freedom of the Baḥīrīs from persecution as Ashᶜarīs is evident. He died five years later in 1059/451.

VII. The sons of Abū Naṣr ᶜAbd ar-Raḥmān were Abū al-Ḥasan ᶜAbd Allāh (11) and Abū Muḥammad ᶜAbd al-Ḥamīd (12). Both were muzakkīs, the latter a legal

1. Fārisī I, f68a.

scholar as well. Both were wealthy and honored men. Beyond that, however, the sources have little to say. Abū al-Ḥasan taught ḥadīth but whether in succession to his uncle in the Old Congregational Mosque is not reported. Abū Muḥammad lost his sight late in life and lived confined to his house until his death in the decade beginning in 1068/460.

Abū Ḥāmid Baḥīr had one son, Abū al-Qāsim Muṭahhar (13). His training was in law, and he served in some capacity in the qāḍī's court. Although he was certified to teach ḥadīth, no details about his teaching are given.

The older of Abū ᶜAbd ar-Raḥmān ᶜAmr's two sons was Abū ᶜAmr ᶜUbaid Allāh (14), born in 1007/397. He was in every way overshadowed, however, by his exceptional younger brother twenty-two years his junior. In fact, nothing much more is known of him except that he died in 1089/482.

His remarkable younger brother, born in 1028/419, was Abū Saᶜīd Ismāᶜīl (15). Muzakkī, jurist, head of the Baḥīrī family, married to his first cousin, meticulously observant of the rules of ritual purity, Abū Saᶜīd appears also to have been, unlike his father and uncle, an Ashᶜarī.[2] He was a very close associate of the Qushairī family and a long time student of Abū al-Ḥusain ᶜAbd al-Ghāfir al-Fārisī of that family. At some unspecified time, he experienced a deterioration in his financial affairs which caused him to sell his last remaining estate. From being a landowner, he became a merchant until he had recouped sufficient of his losses to purchase some estates once again. The comparative desirability of living by rents as opposed to trade is quite clear here. When his affairs were on a sound footing once again, he made the Pilgrimage to Mecca and on his return became one of the recognized pillars of the scholarly community. He taught traditions first in the ᶜImādiya madrasa and subsequently in the Manīᶜī Congregational Mosque. Towards the end of his life he became blind, and he died shortly after his son Muḥammad in the year 1108/501. Prayers were said for him at the gate known as Bāb aṭ-Ṭāq, and he was buried "with his kinsmen" in al-Ḥīra Cemetery. Since it is stated elsewhere that the family tomb was at the gate of Mulqābād quarter, Bāb aṭ-Ṭāq must be the name of that gate, and it must have been the connecting gate between Mūlqābād and al-Ḥīra.

2. In addition to the circumstantial evidence of closeness to the Qushairīs and a post in the Manīᶜī Congregational Mosque, al-Fārisī's statement that he was "excellent of faith" (*ḥasan al-iᶜtiqād*) employs a phrase that he seems to reserve for Ashᶜarīs. Possibly the breaking of the persecution had the effect of making all of the Shāfiᶜīs come round to siding with the victorious Ashᶜarīs.

As for the children of Abū ᶜUthmān Saᶜīd, Jumᶜa or ᶜĀʾisha (16), his daughter, became the wife of her just mentioned cousin Abū Saᶜīd Ismāᶜīl b. ᶜAmr al-Baḥīrī. Hers is a characteristically sparse woman's biography which only gives the names of some of her teachers. She outlived her husband and died in 1110/504.

One of her two brothers, Abū Ḥafṣ ᶜUmar (17), was stricken with deafness and could not enter into the scholarly way of life. The other, Abū Naṣr ᶜAbd al-Jabbār (18), dressed in Sufi garments of his own tailoring. He died in 1052/444.

VIII. With the eighth generation the Baḥīrī family passes from the historical record. A son of Abū Saᶜīd Ismāᶜīl has already been mentioned as dying in the same year as his father. Nothing else is known of him. The son of Abū al-Qāsim Muṭahhar, Abū Saᶜd Muḥammad (19), belongs chronologically to the previous generation, having been born in 1025/416 and dying in 1093/486. He is intriguingly described as being pure of heart but strange and savage of nature.

And finally comes the latest known member of the family, Abū Bakr ᶜAbd ar-Raḥmān (20), son of Abū al-Ḥasan ᶜAbd Allāh b. ᶜAbd ar-Raḥmān. He studied under Abū al-Qāsim al-Qushairī and died at the age of eighty-seven in 1145/540.

Genealogical Key

Baḥīrī

1.	Abū ʿAbd Allāh b. Baḥīr al-Isfarāʾinī	Ḥākim, f15a.
2.	Abū al-ʿAbbās Muḥammad b. Muḥammad b. Saʿīd	Ḥākim, f33b.
3.	Muḥammad b. al-Ḥasan b. Jaʿfar	I. Jauzī, VII, 205; T. Baghdād, II, 213–214; Samʿānī, II, 106.
4.	Abū al-Ḥusain Aḥmad b. Muḥammad b. Jaʿfar	Samʿānī, II, 105; ʿIbar, II, 368; Shadharāt, III, 84; Lubāb, I, 100; Ḥākim, f38b.
5.	Abū ʿAmr Muḥammad	Samʿānī, II, 105–106; Mushtabah, I, 49; ʿIbar, III, 61; Lubāb, I, 101; T. Baghdād, I, 350–351; I. Jauzī, VII, 232; Ḥuffāẓ, pp. 1082–83; Shadharāt, III, 148; Ḥākim, f48a.
6.	Abū Muḥammad ʿAbd Allāh al-Maṣāḥifī as-Simsār al-Jāmiʿī	Fārisī I, f81b, 85a; II, f78b.
7.	Abū Naṣr ʿAbd ar-Raḥmān	Fārisī I, f40b; II, f88a.
8.	Abū Ḥāmid Baḥīr	Fārisī II, f49b; Mushtabah, I, 49.
9.	Abū ʿAbd ar-Raḥmān ʿAmr	Fārisī I, f73a; II, f118a.
10.	Abū ʿUthmān Saʿīd al-Mūlqābādī	Fārisī I, f22b; II, f67a–b; ʿIbar, III, 226; Samʿānī, II, 106; Mushtabah, I, 49.
11.	Abū al-Ḥasan ʿAbd Allāh	Fārisī I, f32b; II, f81b.
12.	Abū Muḥammad ʿAbd al-Ḥamīd	Fārisī I, f53a–b; II, f100a.
13.	Abū al-Qāsim Muṭahhar	Fārisī I, f90b; II, f133a–b; Mushtabah, I, 50.
14.	Abū ʿAmr ʿUbaid Allāh	Fārisī I, f38b; II, f87a–b.
15.	Abū Saʿīd Ismāʿīl	Fārisī II, f43b–44a; Mushtabah, I, 50; Old Subkī, IV, 207; I. Jauzī, IX, 158.
16.	Jumʿa (or ʿĀʾisha)	Fārisī II, f51b, 118b–119a.

Baḥīrī

I — Saᶜīd

II — Muḥammad

III — **2** Abū al-ᶜAbbās Muḥammad
d. between 314–335

IV

V — **6** Abū Muḥammad ᶜAbd Allāh al-Maṣāḥifī
as-Simsār al-Jāmiᶜī
d. 417 or 419

VI — d. = **8** Abū Ḥāmid Baḥīr

10 Abū ᶜUthmān Saᶜīd al-Mūlqābādī
364–451

VII — **13** Abū al-Qāsim Muṭahhar

18 Abū Naṣr
ᶜAbd al-Jabbār
d. 444

17 Abū Ḥafṣ ᶜUmar

16 Jumᶜa =
(ᶜĀʾisha)
d. 504

VIII — **19** Abū Saᶜd Muḥammad
416–486

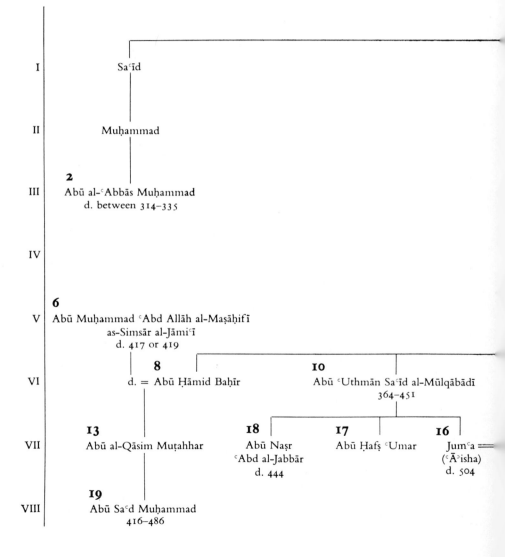

Baḥīrī (continued)

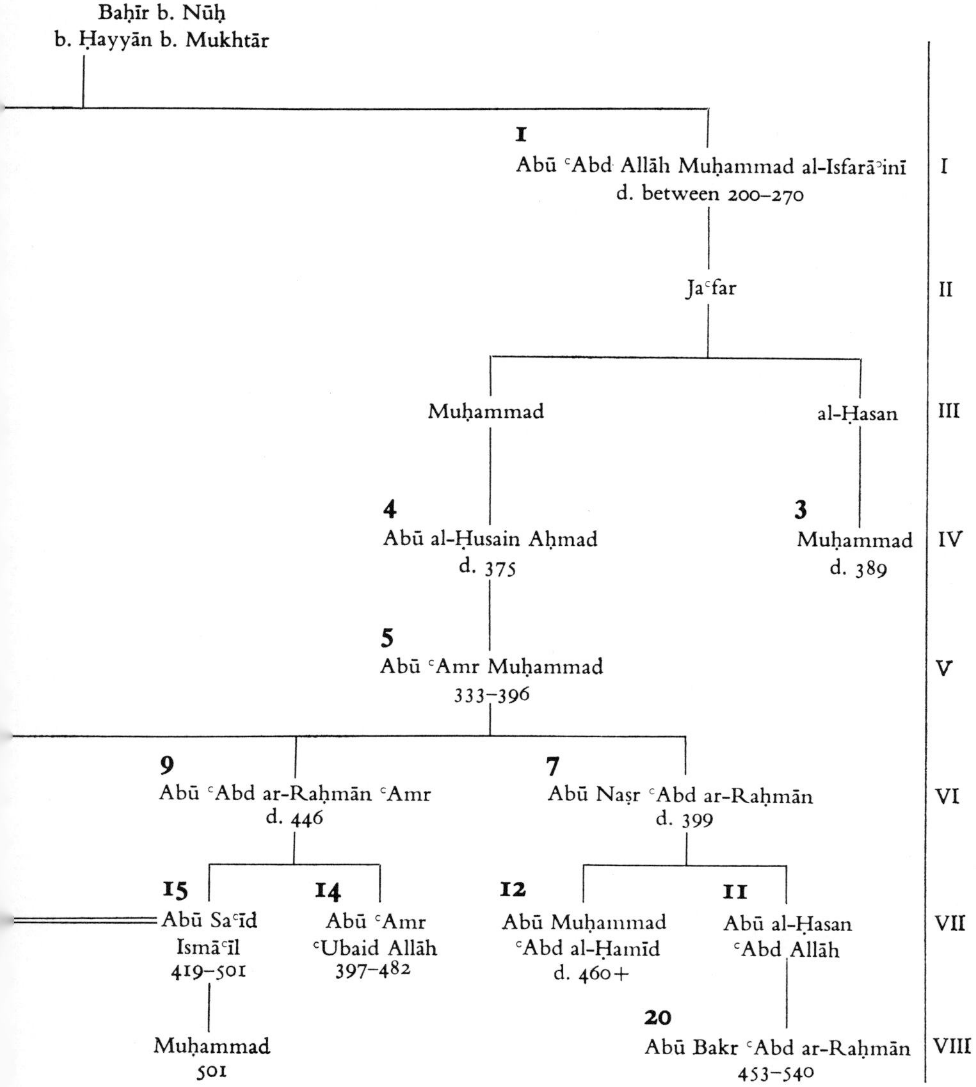
Baḥīr b. Nūḥ
b. Ḥayyān b. Mukhtār
1
Abū ᶜAbd Allāh Muḥammad al-Isfarāᵓinī
d. between 200–270
I
Jaᶜfar
II
Muḥammad
al-Ḥasan
III
4
Abū al-Ḥusain Aḥmad
d. 375
3
Muḥammad
d. 389
IV
5
Abū ᶜAmr Muḥammad
333–396
V
9
Abū ᶜAbd ar-Raḥmān ᶜAmr
d. 446
7
Abū Naṣr ᶜAbd ar-Raḥmān
d. 399
VI
15
Abū Saᶜīd
Ismāᶜīl
419–501
14
Abū ᶜAmr
ᶜUbaid Allāh
397–482
12
Abū Muḥammad
ᶜAbd al-Ḥamīd
d. 460+
11
Abū al-Ḥasan
ᶜAbd Allāh
VII
Muḥammad
501
20
Abū Bakr ᶜAbd ar-Raḥmān
453–540
VIII

17. Abū Ḥafṣ ^{c}Umar	Fārisī I, f59b; II, f109b.
18. Abū Naṣr ^{c}Abd al-Jabbār	Fārisī II, f99b.
19. Abū Sa^{c}d Muḥammad	Fārisī II, f16b.
20. Abū Bakr ^{c}Abd ar-Raḥmān	Fārisī II, f92b; ^{c}Ibar, IV, 110; Shadharāt, IV, 125–126.

13 / *Ṣāᶜidī–Nāṣiḥī–Ismāᶜīlī*

I–III. The Ṣāᶜidī family appears in Nishapur with great suddenness. The first member of the family in town was also one of its two most important members, although no member of the family was actually insignificant. That first member was the man from whom the family took its name, Abū al-ᶜAlāᵓ Ṣāᶜid b. Muḥammad b. Aḥmad b. ᶜAbd Allāh (1). He was born in 954/343 into what seems to have been a family of government officials in Ustuvā, northwest of Nishapur on the other side of the mountains. He studied adab, the belletristic discipline of the government secretarial profession, first under his father Abū Saᶜīd Muḥammad (2) and then under a man from Nishapur to which place his family had presumably moved.[1] Only after that did he take up the study of law, the field in which he was to become famous. He studied law under the leading Muᶜtazilī of Nishapur, the Ḥanafī qāḍī Abū Naṣr Muḥammad b. Muḥammad b. Sahl,[2] and another Ḥanafī qāḍī Abū al-Haitham ᶜUtba.[3] Having mastered Ḥanafī law, in 985/375, when he was thirty-one years old, he went on the Pilgrimage to Mecca. It was a protracted journey as was customary, and Abū al-ᶜAlāᵓ studied ḥadīth on the way under scholars from Kufa and Baghdad. But in Baghdad someone denounced him to the caliph's court for having prevented by means of a legal opinion he had delivered in Nishapur the refurbishing of the tomb of Hārūn ar-Rashīd at Ṭūs. This was not a light charge since the reigning caliph was a descendant of Hārūn ar-Rashīd and naturally concerned himself with the maintenance of family and caliphal dignity. Summoned to explain his opinion, Abū al-ᶜAlāᵓ ably acquitted himself by arguing that he had acted in the public interest and out of practicality since to have restored the tomb of Hārūn would have provoked the Shiᶜites who lived about the nearby tomb of the Shiᶜite Imam ᶜAlī ar-Riḍā to riot and hence have disrupted the caliph's realm. This defense earned him plaudits rather than condemnation, and he returned to Nishapur with more prestige than he had had when he left.

To his already established prestige as a capable legist he then proceeded to add the dignity of being attached to a dihqān family. His mother was from Baihaq, the sister of a poet named Abū Muḥammad Ismāᶜīl b. Muḥammad (3), and Abū al-ᶜAlāᵓ married into a Baihaqi family as well. His bride was the daughter of a wealthy, aristocratic landowner named Abū Muḥammad al-Muᶜallā al-Baihaqī (4). This man had occupied

1. This man was Abū Bakr Muḥammad b. al-ᶜAbbās al-Khwārizmī (Ḥākim, f51b).

2. IAW, II, 117; Ḥākim, f53a. Ibn Abī al-Wafāᵓ entitles him Shaikh al-Islām, but this is not confirmed elsewhere and, given the plethora of errors in Ibn Abī al-Wafāᵓ, may well be a mistake.

3. Ḥākim, f47a; IAW,I, 342–343; ᶜIbar, III, 94; Shadharāt, III, 181.

at one time the office of raʾīs of Nishapur, and his daughter was an excellent choice since she seems to have been his primary heir through whom all of his lands came into the possession of the Ṣāʿidī family where they remained for the next two centuries. During his lifetime he was an important figure in the family.

Abū al-ʿAlāʾ Ṣāʿid was well on his way to success. He was a recognized and now wealthy jurist, and in 987/377 the first of his three sons was born. In that same year he travelled to the Sāmānid capital of Bukhara in the entourage of Abū Naṣr Aḥmad al-Mīkālī, a member of the most powerful of the dihqān families of Nishapur, whose father had recently died and who was presumably going to Bukhara to ensure the regular transfer of his father's lands to himself.[4] In Bukhara Abū al-ʿAlāʾ attended a class held by a certain Abū Bakr Muḥammad b. Faḍl. This man was probably the distinguished scholar surnamed al-Faḍlī al-Kamārī who died in Bukhara in 991/381 at the age of eighty and left behind him a family which continued to be important for another 150 years.[5] Abū al-ʿAlāʾ impressed the old man and gained his favor, which was communicated before long to the Sāmānid court. The upshot was that the governor of Nishapur, Abū ʿAlī as-Sīmjūrī, received a letter from his Sāmānid suzerain saying: "We are amazed, considering the excellence of your upbringing and the abundance of your intelligence, that there exists in Nishapur a man the likes of Ṣāʿid whose status we have not raised." Abū ʿAlī as-Sīmjūrī was not slow to take this barely veiled command and immediately appointed Abū al-ʿAlāʾ qāḍī. He held the post until Nishapur was occupied for good by Maḥmūd b. Sabuktakīn. Maḥmūd first gained the city in 994/384 as a reward for fighting, together with his father Sabuktakīn, on the Sāmānid side against the rebelling Sīmjūrids. He was simply a Sāmānid governor at this time, however, and could not depose the qāḍī on his own authority. In 997/387 Sabuktakīn died and so did the Sāmānid amir. The resulting situation was quite confusing.[6] Maḥmūd quit the city to fight his brother for the right to succeed to Sabuktakīn's semi-independent appanage in Ghazna. The new Sāmānid amir was compelled by the intrigues of the Bukhara court to grant Nishapur to another Turkish general. Almost as soon as he got to town, this general was attacked by the Sīmjūrids, who at least held the city long enough to appoint the Shāfiʿī leader Abū ʿAmr Muḥammad al-Basṭāmī

4. Abū Naṣr's father Abū al-Qāsim ʿAlī al-Mīkālī died in 376/986; Baihaqī, *Tārīkh-i Baihaqī*, ed. Nafīsī, III, 1008. See also chapter 5.

5. IAW, II, 107–109.

6. Bulliet, "A Muʿtazilite Coin," pp. 119–129.

to a very brief term as qāḍī.[7] Hard on the heels of that fight, Maḥmūd returned in 998/388 and retook the town. By now he was openly defiant of Sāmānid authority; he traded recognition of the incumbent ᶜAbbāsid caliph in Baghdad, which the Sāmānids had withheld saying that he had been illegally installed, for recognition as an independent ruler. Naturally, this meant a fight with the Sāmānids. In the course of that fight Nishapur was briefly taken by the Sāmānids on two occasions, and it did not definitively fall to Maḥmūd until 1001/391. Abū al-ᶜAlāᵓ was definitively deposed as qāḍī and probably had some of his wealth confiscated in 1002/392.

The reason for this fall from power is not specified, but with such political turmoil it would hardly be surprising if Abū al-ᶜAlāᵓ made the mistake at some point of showing favor to Maḥmūd's opposition. His original acquisition of the post had come, after all, through the Sāmānid court, and he could easily have supported his old patrons during one of their late reoccupations of the city. Whatever mistake Abū al-ᶜAlāᵓ made, however, it must have been made towards the end of the unsettled period, because Maḥmūd's brother, Naṣr, built a madrasa for him while he was governing Nishapur for Maḥmūd, and he held the post of governor in 999/389–1000/390.[8]

Abū al-ᶜAlāᵓ's replacement was another Ḥanafī, his old teacher Abū al-Haitham ᶜUtba, who held the office until 1005/405, and Abū al-ᶜAlāᵓ himself retired to his new madrasa where he taught law and issued a multitude of legal opinions (*fatwas*). But his retirement was disturbed during the period of Karrāmī domination of Nishapur after 1010/400.[9] Having accused many prominent figures of being heretical Ismāᶜīlīs, the Karrāmī leader Abū Bakr Muḥammad b. Maḥmashād topped off his witch hunt by indicting Abū al-ᶜAlāᵓ on the charge of being a Muᶜtazilī. This charge, which was probably true, amounted to heresy in the fundamentalist eyes of Abū Bakr Muḥammad, but being a Muᶜtazilī was not generally regarded at that time with the same opprobrium as being an Ismāᶜīlī. Abū al-ᶜAlāᵓ countered the charge by accusing Abū Bakr Muḥammad of anthropomorphist beliefs, which charge was probably true also. Seeing a dangerous standoff developing, Abū Bakr Muḥammad tried to drop the entire affair, but Abū al-ᶜAlāᵓ persevered, seeing from his viewpoint a possible opportunity for

7. See chapter 9 and Basṭāmī genealogical key #5.

8. Edouard de Zambaur, *Manuel de généalogie et de chronologie pour l'histoire de l'Islam* (Hannover, 1927), p. 7.

9. ᶜUtbi, *Kitab-i-Yamini*, pp. 471–484; C. E. Bosworth, "The Rise of the Karāmiyyah in Khurasan," *Muslim World*, 50 (1960), 5–14.

breaking the power of the Karrāmī leader. The matter came to trial in Ghazna. The judge was Abū Muḥammad ᶜAbd Allāh an-Nāṣiḥi, a fellow Ḥanafī one of whose daughters was later to marry Abū al-ᶜAlāᵓ's youngest son. Moreover, to make matters even worse for the Karrāmī leader, Naṣr b. Sabuktakīn supported his protégé. Whatever it was that had brought about Abū al-ᶜAlā's removal from the post of qāḍī, it had not spoiled his relations with the sultan's brother, and he triumphed in court with no difficulty. Karrāmī power in Nishapur went into eclipse soon thereafter.

By the end of the Karrāmī ordeal, Abū al-ᶜAlāᵓ was over sixty, and his two older sons were entering upon their productive years. He remained, however, the elder statesman of the Ḥanafī faction and came into the limelight one last time when the Seljuq Turks occupied Nishapur in 1036/428.[10] He was an old man, and his faction had prospered under Ghaznavid rule. Moreover, he probably knew from personal history what were the consequences of backing the wrong horse. Consequently, when the leading patricians of the city, led by the leader of the Shāfiᶜīs, came to persuade him to concur in their decision to surrender the city to the Seljuqs, he gave only the most grudging support. Then when Ṭughril Beg came in person, he refused to go with the other patricians to receive him. Only on the second day did he deign to attend upon the new ruler. If the Ghaznavids had ever retaken the city and held it, they would have been unable to fault Abū al-ᶜAlāᵓ on his conduct. But that was not to happen. And even if it had, Abū al-ᶜAlāᵓ would not have been around to witness it. He died in 1040/431.

As already noted, Abū al-ᶜAlāᵓ had three sons. In order of age, they were Abū al-Ḥasan Ismāᶜīl born in 987/377, Abū Saᶜīd Muḥammad born in 990/380, and Abū Muḥammad ᶜUbaid Allāh born almost thirty years later in 1018/409. The first two sons were definitely the offspring of the Baihaqi wife mentioned earlier, but the probability is obviously quite great that the third son was by another wife. The eldest son, Abū al-Ḥasan Ismāᶜīl (5), began his studies at the not unusual age of six and studied in both Nishapur and Iraq. He was appointed qāḍī of Rayy sometime after 1028/420 when Maḥmūd captured the city from the Būyids. He rose there to the post of chief qāḍī, and then he was transferred to Nishapur where he was qāḍī for both the city and the surrounding area as far as and including Ṭūs and Nasā. The date of this transfer is not provided, but he definitely taught a class in Nishapur in 1041/432 which year also saw

10. The traditional date of the Seljuq occupation of Nishapur, 1037/429, is brought into question by a Seljuq dinar from the Nishapur mint with the date 1036/428 in the collection of the American Numismatic Society.

the transfer from Ghaznavid to Seljuq rule in Rayy. It appears probable, therefore, that he stayed at Rayy as long as it remained under Ghaznavid control and then returned to Nishapur, which had come under definitive Seljuq control in 1040/431, to take up a position that his aged father had doubtless secured for him from the new rulers. In Nishapur his father's prestige and his own financial scrupulousness as qāḍī gained him a position of eminence and trust. Eventually Ṭughril Beg picked him as his emissary on some mission to Fars province, and there he took sick and died near Ahwaz in 1051/443. His body was returned to Nishapur and buried beside that of his father in the family tomb.

Curiously little is known about the middle brother, Abū Saᶜīd Muḥammad (6), whose biography is not given by al-Fārisī. He held the post of qāḍī but not, apparently, at a high level, and is best known for being the father of Abū Naṣr Aḥmad aṣ-Ṣāᶜidī, who will be mentioned in the next generation. He died in 1042/433, but there is nothing to suggest that his death was connected with the appointment of his older brother to the post of qāḍī around the same time.

Abū al-ᶜAlāᵓ's youngest son, Abū Muḥammad ᶜUbaid Allāh (7), benefited like his older brother from Seljuq patronage. Having been born during the period of his father's greatest eminence, he enjoyed an excellent upbringing, marred only by a tendency to stutter which prevented him from preaching. Sometime after his father's death, Ṭughril Beg made him chief qāḍī of Hamadhān, in which post he conducted himself with the same probity that his brother was known for. Eventually he was deposed, however, most probably after the accession of Alp Arslān in 1063/455 which signalled the beginning of Ḥanafī decline and Shāfiᶜī ascendance in Nishapur. He returned to Nishapur and lived there, a much admired man, in ascetic and pious retirement until his death in 1093/486. Prayers over his body were conducted at Bāb aṭ-Ṭāq, and he was buried across from the Old Congregational Mosque which he had frequented during his retirement.

Before leaving these three sons of the Ḥanafī patriarch, a digression must be made upon the matter of the marriage of the youngest son, Abū Muḥammad ᶜUbaid Allāh. His wife was the daughter of the Ghaznavid chief qāḍī Abū Muḥammad Abd Allāh an-Nāṣiḥī (8), who had been instrumental in the acquittal of Abū al-ᶜAlāᵓ Ṣāᶜid and the disgracing of the Karrāmiya as mentioned earlier. He was a man of probity and importance who taught law and wrote a short work on abeyance of rights in Ḥanafī law. He also taught ḥadīth in Baghdad while making the Pilgrimage in 1021/412. In 1055/447 he died. His children, however, are what make him important for the Ṣāᶜidī family. By marrying his daughter, Abū Muḥammad ᶜUbaid Allāh aṣ-Ṣāᶜidī acquired at least three sisters-in-law and four brothers-in-law and in so doing tied his family to several other families.

The youngest of the new Nāṣiḥī brothers-in-law, Isḥāq (9), died while still quite young. Another, Abū Saᶜd ᶜAlī, is known only through his sons. Of the other two, Abū Ṣāliḥ Yaḥyā (10) was born in 1034/425 and was thus quite a bit younger than Abū Muḥammad ᶜUbaid Allāh aṣ-Ṣāᶜidī. A teacher of law and jurisconsult in the family tradition, he was a qāḍī for a time in the city of Marv. He died in 1102/495. The fourth brother was named Abū Bakr Muḥammad (11). He, too, specialized in law, but he was also accomplished in belles lettres, poetry, and Muᶜtazilī theology. He even debated his views with the great Ashᶜarī theologian Imām al-Ḥaramain al-Juwainī. Still, it was in law that he made his mark by becoming the qāḍī of Nishapur. How long he held the post and when is not known, but complaints about graft and corruption among his subordinates eventually brought about his transfer to the qāḍī-ship of Rayy. In 1090/483 he went on the Pilgrimage; on his way back to Rayy the next year he died near Isfahan.

As for the three daughters of an-Nāṣiḥī who became sisters-in-law of Abū Muḥammad ᶜUbaid Allāh aṣ-Ṣāᶜidī, one of them married an unknown person named Aḥmad b. ᶜUrwa and had a son who will be mentioned in the next generation. Another married one of the sons of Abū Saᶜd ᶜAbd ar-Raḥīm al-Ismāᶜīlī as-Sarrājī (12). The name Sarrājī indicates a family background in the saddlery business, but Abū Saᶜd ᶜAbd ar-Raḥīm was best known as a Ḥanafī jurist. Born in 917/305, he worked as the deputy for a qāḍī whose name is unfortunately obliterated in the manuscript and at some point was elected to the post of qāḍī by the patricians of the city. This outright election without any participation by the central government was obviously not customary, for Abū Saᶜd was dubbed thereby the Elected Qāḍī (al-Qāḍī al-Mukhtār); unfortunately, there is no notation of exactly when the election took place. Yet it must have occurred after 1005/405, the last year of Abū al-Haitham ᶜUtba's tenure in office, and sufficiently prior to Abū Saᶜd's death in 1036/427 for the nickname to come into common use. Politically this period is one of undisputed Ghaznavid rule in Nishapur; hence whatever circumstances gave rise to the extraordinary election of the qāḍī, they were not connected with any kind of anarchic interregnum.

The Elected Qāḍī had five sons. The one who married an-Nāṣiḥī's daughter was Abū al-Ḥasan Aḥmad al-Ismāᶜīlī as-Sarrājī (13). He was not a qāḍī like his father, but he was in the judicial system being both a ḥākim and a muzakkī. By virtue of these posts and the eminence of his father and father-in-law, he became an important member of the judicial council (*majlis al-qaḍāᵓ*) and one of the leaders of the Ḥanafī faction. Perhaps his most important function in connection with his leadership in the Ḥanafī faction was convening the sessions of public preaching that followed the Friday prayer in the Old Congregational Mosque. Public preaching played an important role in mustering popular support in factional disputes, and the Old Congregational Mosque was the major Ḥanafī stronghold in the days of al-Kundurī's persecution. In his later years Abū al-Ḥasan taught ḥadīth in his home, and he died in 1077/469.

Mentioning this man in connection with the Ṣāᶜidī family to which he was related only as the brother-in-law of a sister-in-law may seem a bit far-fetched, but that such relationships, which would be quite tenuous by today's standards, were regarded as significant and vital in the oligarchic society of Nishapur's patriciate was clearly demonstrated, in this instance, at the death of Abū al-Ḥasan Aḥmad. The man who prayed over his body was Abū al-Qāsim Manṣūr aṣ-Ṣāᶜidī, the nephew of the Ṣāᶜidī to whom he was distantly related; but more important is the fact that the prayer was performed in the Ṣāᶜidī madrasa where the body was interred with the other members of the Ṣāᶜidī family. This privilege would surely not have been accorded even a prominent Ḥanafī unless it was felt that he was a part of the family.

The other sons of the Elected Qāḍī were Ismāᶜīl (14); Abū Ḥanīfa Muḥammad (15), who was a Muᶜtazilī and died in 1064/456; Abū Naṣr Saᶜīd (16), who lived from 989/379 to 1037/429; and Abū al-Ḥasan Masᶜūd (17), who was born in 986/376 and died in the same year as his brother just mentioned 1037/429. None of the four was particularly distinguished, but they received the appropriate education and were part of the patrician class. Only Abū al-Ḥasan Aḥmad, the brother who married an-Nāṣiḥī's daughter, had sons whose biographies are known and will be mentioned in the next generation. This may indicate that the family was marginally patrician and that only an advantageous connection with the Nāṣiḥī and Ṣāᶜidī houses kept this one member from sinking out of the patriciate.

Finally, an-Nāṣiḥī's fourth daughter married a man named Abū al-Faḍl ᶜAbd Allāh al-Ḥīrī (18). This man taught Ḥanafī law and wrote legal opinions, being particularly knowledgeable about the practical ramifications of the law. He died in 1084/477. Although the matter is not entirely clear, his family qualification for marriage to the daughter of so important a man, besides that indicated by residence in the wealthy quarter of al-Ḥīra, may have been that he was the first cousin of the prominent blind scholar Abū ᶜAbd ar-Raḥmān Ismāᶜīl al-Ḥīrī (19). His presumed father, Abū Bakr Muḥammad al-Ḥīrī (20), was a legal witness and a dealer in cotton cloth and seems to have accompanied his blind nephew in his educational journeys to places as far away as Baghdad. Abū ᶜAbd ar-Raḥmān Ismāᶜīl was adept at Qurᵓan reading, exegesis, preaching, law, and ḥadīth and wrote on all of them. He was also a Shāfiᶜī, however, which casts doubt upon the entire putative relationship. If he was related to an-Nāṣiḥī's son-in-law, he was very much older, for he was born in 971/361, and was over seventy when he died. This makes him older than an-Nāṣiḥī himself.

IV. Only seven offspring of Ṣāᶜidī brothers-in-law and sisters-in-law appear in this generation after which the collateral lines drop out of sight. These seven will be considered later. The primary focus now falls on the Ṣāᶜidīs proper, the offspring of the three sons of the Ḥanafī patriarch Abū al-ᶜAlāᵓ Ṣāᶜid. The eldest son Abū al-Ḥasan Ismāᶜīl, who was qāḍī first of Rayy and then of Nishapur, had two sons. The career of Abū ᶜAlī al-Ḥasan (21) seems to have been strangely aborted. He started out as his father's deputy when he was qāḍī of Nishapur, and from there he was appointed qāḍī in his own right by Ṭughril Beg. As was customary with the Ṣāᶜidī family, he acted with great probity in this office. He also attended the maẓālim court regularly. At some point, however, he suffered a severe loss in status and lived under a cloud until his death in 1079/472. It may be surmised that since he probably succeeded his father as qāḍī after his father's death in 1051/443, he had been in the post only a short time when the governorship of Nishapur fell to Alp Arslān and his vizier Niẓām al-Mulk and that he fell afoul of the new regime in some way. However, other members of the family managed to survive the restoration of Shāfiᶜī strength under Alp Arslān without permanent diminution of status.

His brother Abū al-Qāsim Manṣūr (22) had a very similar but rather more distinguished career. He also began as a deputy qāḍī for his father and went on to become qāḍī in his own right, but he attained the rank of chief qāḍī, which his brother seems not to have reached. In addition to this he wrote legal opinions, was in charge of the maẓālim court, not normally under patrician control, and apparently served as khaṭīb in the Old Congregational Mosque.[11] It is noted that he was a fervid Ḥanafī partisan,

11. Abū al-Qāsim Manṣūr probably became khaṭīb after the deposition of the persecution leader aṣ-Ṣandalī (see next footnote) from that post at the time of Alp Arslān's accession to power. There

and the power to promote his factional interest accruing to him from these various offices was obviously quite great. Moreover, to his mundane political power he added intellectual prestige. He was an accomplished Arabist and studied in Baghdad, Hamadhān, Rayy, and Transoxania. He died in 1077/470.

The second son of Abū al-ᶜAlāᵓ Ṣāᶜid, Abū Saᶜīd Muḥammad, had two sons also, Abū Saᶜd Yaḥyā and Abū Naṣr Aḥmad, born in 1010/401 and 1019/410 respectively and hence, like their cousins just discussed, growing into manhood during the lifetime of the old patriarch. The elder of these two, Abū Saᶜd Yaḥyā (23), started out as a qāḍī in Nishapur but moved on to become qāḍī of Rayy, a post held earlier by his uncle. The bulk of his career being spent in that city, little more is noted concerning him except that he died there in 1068/460.

Abū Naṣr Aḥmad (24), the younger son, was, next to his grandfather, the most important member of the Ṣāᶜidī family. While the other sons and grandsons of Abū al-ᶜAlāᵓ followed careers more or less cut out for them by their grandfather, Abū Naṣr Aḥmad built upon this heritage to carve out for himself a position in Nishapur of still greater power and influence. Having been favored from birth with high social rank, he followed the customary educational regime and studied abroad in Bukhara and Baghdad as well as in Nishapur. But his own inclinations were entirely in another direction. He was an exceptionally handsome and muscular young man, and he devoted himself primarily to learning the arts of horsemanship and weaponry. As a result, when troubled times came, and, as ᶜAbd al-Ghāfir al-Fārisī puts it, the winds of the family of Seljuq began to blow, Abū Naṣr Aḥmad became raᵓīs of Nishapur around the year 1039/430. Although it is not clear whether he came by this office by local election or by Ghaznavid or Seljuq appointment, he was in any case acceptable enough to the Seljuqs to be holding the office ten years later.

This was also the decade of the rise of ᶜAmīd al-Mulk al-Kundurī to the office of vizier under Ṭughril Beg. Sometime after 1048/440 these two men got together. They had been born in the same year and were then little over thirty years old. They were both in positions of authority with that of Abū Naṣr Aḥmad being augmented by the fact that either his uncle or his cousin was chief qāḍī while his brother was chief qāḍī in Rayy where Ṭughril's court was then situated. How these two ambitious young men came together and what the exact nature of their bargain was can only be guessed at from the ensuing events.

---

had been a period of confusion in the office prior to aṣ-Ṣandalī, however, and Abū al-Qāsim may have held it for a brief time between Abū ᶜUthmān Ismāᶜīl aṣ-Ṣābūnī and aṣ-Ṣandalī.

ᶜAmīd al-Mulk al-Kundurī, who had begun his career as a protégé of the Shāfiᶜī leader Imām al-Muwaffaq al-Basṭāmī only to see his opportunity in the Shāfiᶜī party cut off by the rise of better connected younger men such as Imām al-Muwaffaq's son and Imām al-Ḥaramain al-Juwainī, promulgated a governmental decree forbidding any Ashᶜarī from teaching or holding any religious post in lands under Seljuq domination. There can be no question but that the target of this decree was the Shāfiᶜī/Ashᶜarī party in Nishapur. On the scene in Nishapur Abū Naṣr Aḥmad, from his position as raʾīs, took all manner of unspecified steps to persecute the Shāfiᶜīs. The third ally in this persecution was a learned but fanatical preacher named Abū al-Ḥasan ᶜAlī aṣ-Ṣandalī.[12] He added to the official acts of al-Kundurī and Abū Naṣr Aḥmad the power of mob action by the common people. Eventually, with the exile of the Shāfiᶜī leaders in 1053/445, "the persecution led to the splintering of the Shāfiᶜīs into smaller factions, the annihilation of the Ashᶜarīs, and the suppression of the Karrāmiya."[13]

The inclusion of the Karrāmiya in the persecution, which was officially directed only at Ashᶜarī theology, although later recognized to have encompassed other factions, indicates the true intent of its perpetrators.[14] Abū Naṣr Aḥmad, al-Kundurī, and aṣ-Ṣandalī were attempting to turn Nishapur over to total and unquestionable Ḥanafī domination. The offices of raʾīs and khaṭīb which had traditionally been Shāfiᶜī now were Ḥanafī. The Shāfiᶜī leaders were all in exile. As far as could be foreseen the persecution was a complete success.

But the edifice of Ḥanafī domination collapsed even faster than it had arisen. The reason for this collapse was the accession of Alp Arslān, the future sultan, to the governorship of Nishapur on the retirement of his father Chaghrī Beg in 1058/450. Chaghrī Beg seems never to have questioned his brother Ṭughril Beg's governance of Nishapur even though it was technically under his jurisdiction, but Alp Arslān and even more his vizier Niẓām al-Mulk took a very active interest in the city and within a year had broken the Ḥanafī political monopoly and had re-established the Shāfiᶜīs.

Abū Naṣr Aḥmad was stripped of his offices and sent on a mission to Transoxania where he remained safely removed from Nishapuri politics until Malikshāh replaced his father Alp Arslān as sultan in 1072/465. Then he was recalled to Nishapur and

12. See Chapter 15 and Ḥasanī genealogical key #11.

13. Fārisī I, f68a–b.

14. Recognition that the persecution encompassed more than just the Ashᶜarī faction is found in ᶜIbar, III, 299.

eventually installed as chief qāḍī and recognized as Shaikh al-Islām. He taught ḥadīth in the Old Congregational Mosque and in general reassumed the position of leadership his forbears had held. In 1089/482 he died and was buried in the family mausoleum on the Street of the Fullers (Sikka al-Qaṣṣārīn). At the height of his power he had come closer to making Nishapur into a Ḥanafī principality under his rule, analogous to that set up by the Āl-i Burhān in Bukhara around the same time, than any patrician was ever to come.[15]

Before we move on to the children of Abū al-ᶜAlāʾ's third son, notice must be taken of a daughter of one of the older brothers. For convenience sake, she is represented on the family tree as the daughter of Abū Saᶜīd Muḥammad, but her father could equally well have been Abū al-Ḥasan Ismāᶜīl. What makes her particularly interesting is that she married Abū al-Faḍl Aḥmad b. Muḥammad al-Furātī (25), who was not only raʾīs of Nishapur but was also one of the four Shāfiᶜī leaders singled out for arrest by al-Kundurī and Abū Naṣr Aḥmad. His first wife was the daughter of Abū ᶜUthmān Ismāᶜīl aṣ-Ṣābūnī, one of the most important figures in the Shāfiᶜī party. It is impossible to say what al-Furātī had in mind in seeking a second wife from the camp of the enemy, but if he thought thereby to conciliate the two parties, events proved his optimism unwarranted.

Since the third son of Abū al-ᶜAlāʾ Ṣāᶜid was markedly younger than his two brothers, his children were too young to play any role in the events of the Ashᶜarī persecution. The only known son is Abū al-Fatḥ ᶜAbd al-Malik (26) who appears, despite his two important grandfathers, Abū al-ᶜAlāʾ Ṣāᶜid and Abū Muḥammad ᶜAbd Allāh an-Nāṣiḥī, to have been nothing more than a law teacher and jurisconsult in the family madrasa. He died in 1108/501. There appears also to have been a daughter who married a man named Abū ᶜAlī al-Faḍl as-Sardādī (27) about whom it is recorded only that he was from a family of legal witnesses.

Finally, there are the various relations by marriage through this third son of Abū al-ᶜAlāʾ. In the Nāṣiḥī family Abū Saᶜd ᶜAlī had two sons named Abū al-Qāsim Sahl (28) and Abū al-Ḥasan Ismāᶜīl (29). Neither of them made any mark that has survived. The later is recorded as being born around 1009/400 and dying in 1093/486. He was thus the right age to have been active in the time of the Ashᶜarī persecution, but his name does not arise in that context. Another brother-in-law, Abū Bakr Muḥammad an-Nāṣiḥī, had a son who was slightly more important. This was Aḥmad an-Nāṣiḥī (30)

15. Omeljan Pritsak, "Āl-i Burhān," *Der Islam*, 30 (1952), 81–96.

who served as a judge and as a teacher of Ḥanafī law in the madrasa of the Sultan.[16] He died in 1121/515. Still a third brother-in-law, Abū Ṣāliḥ Yaḥyā an-Nāṣiḥī, had a son named Abū Saᶜīd ᶜAbd ar-Raḥmān (31) who served as a qāḍī and died after 1107/500. The exact year is too garbled to be deciphered.

As for the sisters-in-law, the one who married Aḥmad b. ᶜUrwa had a son named Abū al-Ḥusain ᶜAbd ar-Raḥīm (32) who lived a quiet life as a law teacher and jurisconsult and died in 1116/510. In the next generation his son became involved with his Ṣāᶜidī cousins. Her sister who married the son of the Elected Qāḍī had two sons. Abū Saᶜīd al-Ḥasan al-Ismāᶜīlī (33) studied under the Ṣāᶜidīs and died in 1112/506; his brother Abū ᶜAbd Allāh Nāṣir al-Ismāᶜīlī (34) deliberately shunned the public and official life he was born to and lived in seclusion, dying in 1115/509.

V. Abū ᶜAlī al-Ḥasan b. Ismāᶜīl b. Ṣāᶜid had two sons. Abū al-Faḍl al-Ḥusain (35) became qāḍī not of Nishapur but of Ṭuraithīth (Ṭurshīz) and then of Baihaq where the Ṣāᶜidīs had had property and family connections for three generations. There are two reports of his death. One puts it in Sabzavar, one of the towns that made up the Baihaq urban area, in 1114/508; the other gives the place as Nishapur and the year as 1117/511. The latter account gives a more precise date and adds that he was buried in the tomb on the Street of the Fullers, but this does not constitute a pressing reason for preferring it to the former. Abū Bakr ᶜAlī (36), the other son, did not live a public life and was not particularly well known. Until his father's marked loss of status, spoken of earlier, he had enjoyed the easy life of the well born; but reduced circumstances brought this to and end, and his later life was spent in penury. In his last years he went blind and died in 1114/508. Possibly the confusion in the death date of his brother is due to a confounding of their two biographies.

Abū al-Qāsim Manṣūr of the same branch of the family had only one son. Just as he himself appears to have escaped whatever catastrophe hit his brother Abū ᶜAlī al-Ḥasan, so his son, named Abū al-ᶜAlāᵓ Ṣāᶜid (37) after his great-grandfather, lived a more prominent life than did his two cousins. He was regarded as a promising scion of the Ṣāᶜidī house from youth and used to attend all kinds of classes and disputations in the company of his father and uncle. His father made him his deputy in the office of khaṭīb

16. This is presumably the madrasa reported by Nāṣir-i Khusraw in 1046/437 to have been built at the command of Ṭughril Beg next to the saddlers' market (Nāṣir-i Khusraw, *Safarnāmeh*, p. 3). Other men who taught there are mentioned in IAW, I, 135, and Yāqūt, *Muᶜjam al-Buldān*, I, 517.

and then set him up in the family madrasa to teach law. Naturally, Ḥanafī leaders felt obliged to attend his classes, but even the Shāfiᶜī Imām al-Ḥaramain al-Juwainī had praise for his elegant demeanor and sterling character. After his father's death in 1077/470 he became khaṭīb, law teacher, and preacher in his own right and applied himself assiduously to learning and to refurbishing the Ṣāᶜidī madrasa from its endowment.

By this time Malikshāh was sultan, and Abū al-ᶜAlāʾ Ṣāᶜid's first cousin once removed, Abū Naṣr Aḥmad, had been recalled to town and reinstated as qāḍī. It was probably this relative that brought the promising new member of the family to the attention of the government. Abū al-ᶜAlāʾ Ṣāᶜid was made a qāḍī in Khwarizm and then sent along with an unnamed amir and ᶜamīd on an embassy from Malikshāh to the Ghaznavid sultan in Ghazna. The mission was apparently successful, and he returned to Nishapur and thence once again to Khwarizm. Some time later he went on the Pilgrimage and presented himself at the caliph's court in Baghdad where he was honored with gifts and praise. On his return to Nishapur he convened a class for himself in the Old Congregational Mosque and engaged his own sons and youths from other top patrician families as his assistants. Then in 1113/506 he was stricken with fever and died.

Just as Abū al-ᶜAlāʾ Ṣāᶜid gained from the return to favor in the reign of Malikshāh of his older cousin Abū Naṣr Aḥmad, so to an even greater degree did Abū Naṣr's own son, the only member of the middle branch of the family in this generation, Abū Saᶜīd Muḥammad (38). Born during the peak period of Ḥanafī power in 1052/444, Abū Saᶜīd grew up while his father was in diplomatic exile in Transoxania. With his father's return to grace, however, he was in line to inherit the office of chief qāḍī which he did along with that of Shaikh al-Islām and raʾīs. His "temporal domain" (*dunyā*), as his biographers put it, was thus broad indeed. The balance between Ḥanafīs and Shāfiᶜīs that had been somewhat restored by his father's return seems to have begun to shift back to the Ḥanafī side with this great accumulation of power by Abū Saᶜīd Muḥammad. After the turn of the century in the reign of Sultan Sanjar, animosity between the two factions broke out again in open warfare as it had in the 1050's/440's,[17] and the Ḥanafī leader in the renewed warfare may well have been Abū Saʾīd. But as late as 1096/489 the two factions were still friendly enough to see their common interest and join forces in a bloody riot against the revived Karrāmī sect.[18] The Shāfiᶜīs, led by the

17. Al-Ḥusainī, *Akhbār*, pp. 125–126.
18. I. Athīr, X, 87; I. Funduq, p. 268.

son of Imām al-Ḥaramain al-Juwainī, and Ḥanafīs, led by Abū Saᶜīd Muḥammad, emerged victorious, but it took the aid of a contingent from Baihaq, where Abū Saᶜīd's cousin Abū al-Faḍl al-Ḥusain was qāḍī, to do the trick. Nevertheless, this was only a temporary alliance of the patricians against a common threat, and it could not be expected to outlast long the particular incident. By the time of Abū Saᶜīd's death in 1133/527, the two parties were at daggers' points with the sharper dagger, it seems, in the hands of the Ḥanafīs.

The cadet line of the family becomes inconsequential in this generation. Abū al-Fatḥ ᶜAbd al-Malik, who was himself an unimpressive figure, had two sons about whom virtually nothing is recorded. Abū Saᶜd Yaḥyā (39) studied law under his father, and the other son, Ṣāᶜid (40), became a qāḍī and was killed in the Ghuzz attack on the city in 1153/548.

From the collateral lines of the family there is little to be noted. Among all the inlaws of the Nāṣiḥī family there is only one name in this generation. Abū Jaᶜfar Muḥammad b. ᶜAbd ar-Raḥīm b. Aḥmad b. ᶜUrwa (41) was the grandson of a daughter of the old chief qāḍī an-Nāṣiḥī and hence of a sister-in-law of Abū Muḥammad ᶜUbaid Allāh aṣ-Ṣāᶜidī. Although it seems rather unlikely that a relationship of such remoteness would have counted for much, it is probably not mere coincidence that after studying law under his father and in Marv, Abū Jaᶜfar Muḥammad returned to Nishapur and became a teaching assistant for the Ṣāᶜidī chief qāḍī and Shaikh al-Islām of the same generation Abū Saᶜīd Muḥammad. He must have been appreciably younger than Abū Saᶜīd, but he predeceased him in 1125/519.

VI. By the sixth generation information on the Ṣāᶜidi family begins to peter out. ᶜAbd al-Ghāfir al-Fārisī died in 1134/529 and is generally less informative about his younger contemporaries than he is about the generation or two before them. In the previous generation he unaccountably left out any biography of Abū Saᶜīd Muḥammad, one of the most important members of the family, and it is entirely possible that important members of this generation were likewise slighted either by being skipped over entirely or being given only the briefest notice.

For example, Abū al-ᶜAlāʾ Ṣāᶜid, who was the foremost representative of the senior line of the family in the last generation, had two sons. Judging from what al-Fārisī has to say about these two, both of whose biographies are unfortunately included only in the more truncated of the two manuscripts of his work, neither was of any great stature. Abū al-Ḥasan Ismāʿīl (42) received a good education from his illustrious relatives and settled in Samarqand; Abū al-Maʿālī Asʿad (43) was likewise well educated and became noted as a debater. Only the title Glory of the Imāms (Sharaf al-Aʾimma) borne by the latter suggests that he followed in the family tradition of Ḥanafī leadership. However, in his case there are two other extant biographies in different sources which tell much more about him. In fact, Abū al-Maʿālī Asʿad followed his father as khaṭīb of the Old Congregational Mosque as well in teaching law and preaching and became renowned for his learning. He also followed in his father's footsteps by being in good repute at the court of the sultan. He died in 1133/527. Whether his brother in Samarqand carried with him the family prestige and established it in that city there is no way of telling, but clearly silence on al-Fārisī's part cannot be taken as proof that he was a nonentity.

Another line of the senior branch of the family that continues in this generation but is not mentioned by al-Fārisī is that descending from the first cousin of the father of the two men just discussed. Abū al-Faḍl al-Ḥusain b. al-Ḥasan, had settled in Baihaq as previously related; he had two sons, one with the traditional family name of Ṣāʿid (44) and the other named Abū ʿAlī al-Ḥasan (45) after his grandfather. Ṣāʿid became khaṭīb of the Baihaq area and then qāḍī of Nishapur, first as deputy for one of his judicial relatives and then in his own right. He died in Nishapur in 1138/532. Abū ʿAlī al-Ḥasan followed his brother as qāḍī of Nishapur for a period of four months. The brevity of his tenure in office is unexplained.

Switching now to the middle branch of the family, al-Fārisī fails to say anything about the sons of Abū Saʿīd Muḥammad just as he keeps silent about their important father. Actually, there were two sons. There is little besides dates, 1088/481–1156/551, recorded about one of them, Abū al-Mafākhir ʿAzīz (46) although he was at some time the qāḍī of Nishapur. His older brother, born in 1082/475, is of somewhat greater interest. His name was Abū al-Qāsim Manṣūr (47), but he was known as Burhān, short for Burhān ad-Dīn, the title borne by the contemporary patrician rulers of Bukhara. He, too, was qāḍī of Nishapur and was particularly noted for his religious devotion, being a great frequenter of the Old Congregational Mosque where his cousin was khaṭīb. He died in 1157/552.

In the cadet branch, the qāḍī Ṣāʿid who died in the Ghuzz attack upon the city had a son named Yaḥyā (48) who is known from an anecdote concerning the poet ʿAṭṭār. Yaḥyā was a qāḍī like his father and had a son whose name is unknown.

VII. Finally, information on the family comes to an end. Abū al-Qāsim Manṣūr had a son named ᶜAlī (49) who was qāḍī of Nishapur but died in Rayy in 1159/554. In addition, in the Baihaq line one Abū al-Ḥasan Ismāᶜīl (50), the son of either Ṣāᶜid or Abū ᶜAlī al-Ḥasan, was qāḍī of some of the areas around Baihaq. Beyond this nothing is known. Nishapur had been destroyed and with it the Ṣāᶜidī madrasa and the Old Congregational Mosque, the two bastions of family power and prestige.[19] In Baihaq, where there were family estates, the line continued, and perhaps in some of the cities to which members of the family had migrated, such as Rayy and Samarqand, it did so as well.[20] As a great patrician house, however, it seems to have reached an end.

19. See chapter 6.

20. No direct connection has been uncovered between the Ṣāᶜidīs of Nishapur and the no less illustrious Ṣāᶜidīs who led the Ḥanafī faction of Isfahan. The existence of such a link is assumed by Zabīh Allāh Ṣafā (*Taʾrīkh-i Adabiyāt dar Īrān* [Tehran, 1956–1957], II, p. 61), and it is entirely possible that it may someday be found.

Genealogical Key

Ṣāʿidī–Nāṣiḥī–Ismāʿīlī

1.	Abū al-ʿAlāʾ Ṣāʿid	Fārisī I, f86a–87a; II, f74a–b; IAW, I, 261–262; ʿIbar, III, 174; Shadharāt, III, 248; T. Baghdād, IX, 344–345.
2.	Abū Saʿīd Muḥammad b. Aḥmad b. ʿAbd Allāh	IAW, II, 16.
3.	Abū Muḥammad Ismāʿīl b. Muḥammad b. Jaʿfar	I. Funduq, pp. 181–182.
4.	Abū Muḥammad al-Muʿallā al-Baihaqī	I. Funduq, pp. 172–174.
5.	Abū al-Ḥasan Ismāʿīl aṣ-Ṣāʿidī	Fārisī II, f39a–b; IAW, I, 151–152.
6.	Abū Saʿīd Muḥammad aṣ-Ṣāʿidī	IAW, II, 61.
7.	Abū Muḥammad ʿUbaid Allāh aṣ-Ṣāʿidī	Fārisī I, f38b–39a; II, f87b; IAW, I, 277.
8.	Abū Muḥammad ʿAbd Allāh an-Nāṣiḥī	Fārisī I, f31a–b; II, f80a; IAW, I, 274–275; T. Baghdād, IX, 443; GAL, I, 373, Supp. I, 637.
9.	Isḥāq an-Nāṣiḥī	Fārisī II, f47b.
10.	Abū Ṣāliḥ Yaḥyā an-Nāṣiḥī	Fārisī I, f96b; II, f142b–143a; IAW, II, 214.
11.	Abū Bakr Muḥammad an-Nāṣiḥī	Fārisī II, f18a; IAW, II, 64–65; I. Jauzī, IX, 60; ʿIbar, III, 306; Shadharāt, III, 372.
12.	Abū Saʿd ʿAbd ar-Raḥīm al-Ismāʿīlī as-Sarrājī, al-Qāḍī al-Mukhtār	Fārisī I, f45a; II, f92b–93a; IAW, I, 311.
13.	Abū al-Ḥasan Aḥmad al-Ismāʿīlī	Fārisī II, f30b–31a.
14.	Ismāʿīl al-Ismāʿīlī	Fārisī II, f40a.
15.	Abū Ḥanīfa Muḥammad al-Ismāʿīlī	Fārisī II, f11b.
16.	Abū Naṣr Saʿīd al-Ismāʿīlī	Fārisī I, f23b; II, f68a.
17.	Abū al-Ḥasan Masʿūd al-Ismāʿīlī	Fārisī I, f77b; II, f126b.

Ismāʿīlī Sarrājī

I
Aḥmad b. Muḥammad b. ʿAbd Allāh
b. Muḥammad b. ʿAbd ar-Raḥmān

II
12
Abū Saʿd ʿAbd ar-Raḥīm al-Ismāʿīlī as-Sarrājī
d. 447

III
14
Ismāʿīl

15
Abū Ḥanīfa Muḥammad
d. 456

16
Abū Naṣr Saʿīd
379–429

17
Abū al-Ḥasan Masʿūd
376–429

IV
34
Abū ʿAbd Allāh Nāṣir
d. 509

V

VI

VII

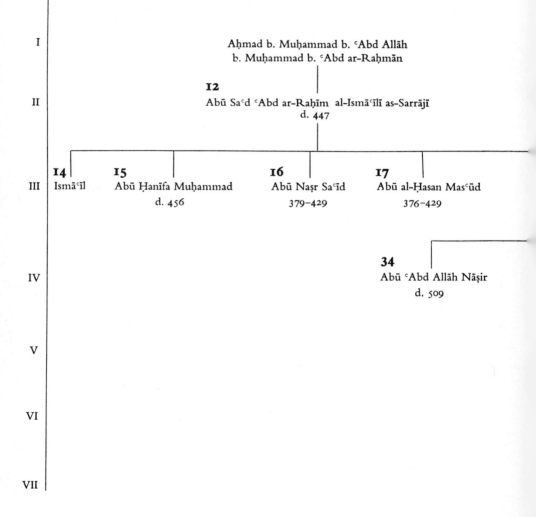

Ismāᶜīlī Sarrājī (continued)

13
Abū al-Ḥasan Aḥmad = daughter of Abū Muḥammad ᶜAbd Allāh an-Nāṣiḥī
d. 469

33
Abū Saᶜīd al-Ḥasan
d. 506

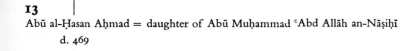

Nāṣiḥī

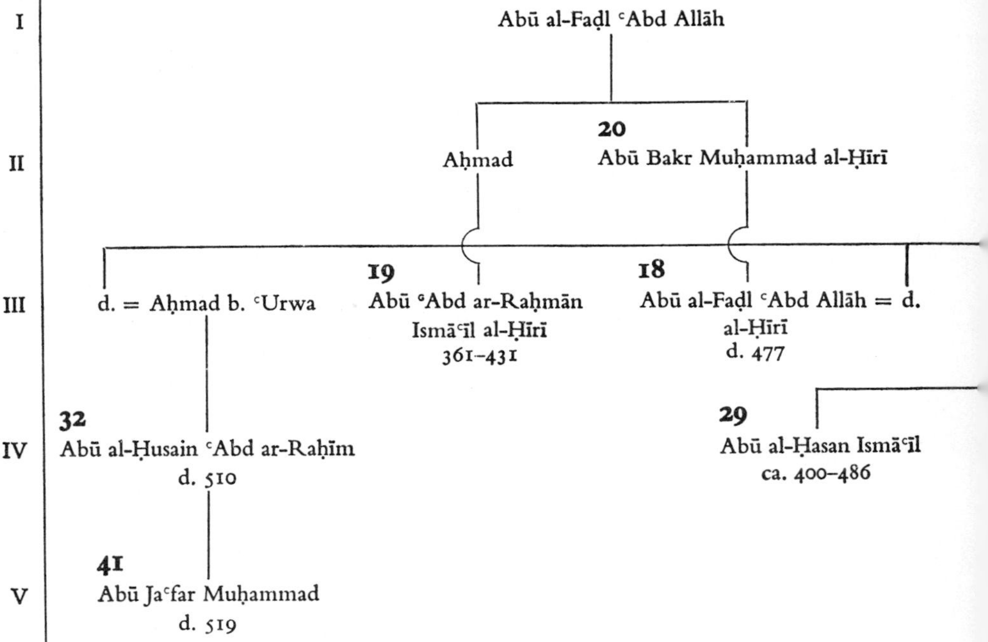

I   Abū al-Faḍl ᶜAbd Allāh

            20
II   Aḥmad   Abū Bakr Muḥammad al-Ḥīrī

          19   **18**
III   d. = Aḥmad b. ᶜUrwa   Abū ᶜAbd ar-Raḥmān   Abū al-Faḍl ᶜAbd Allāh = d.
                          Ismāᶜīl al-Ḥīrī   al-Ḥīrī
                          361–431   d. 477

      32   **29**
IV   Abū al-Ḥusain ᶜAbd ar-Raḥīm   Abū al-Ḥasan Ismāᶜīl
            d. 510   ca. 400–486

      41
V   Abū Jaᶜfar Muḥammad
            d. 519

Nāṣiḥī (continued)

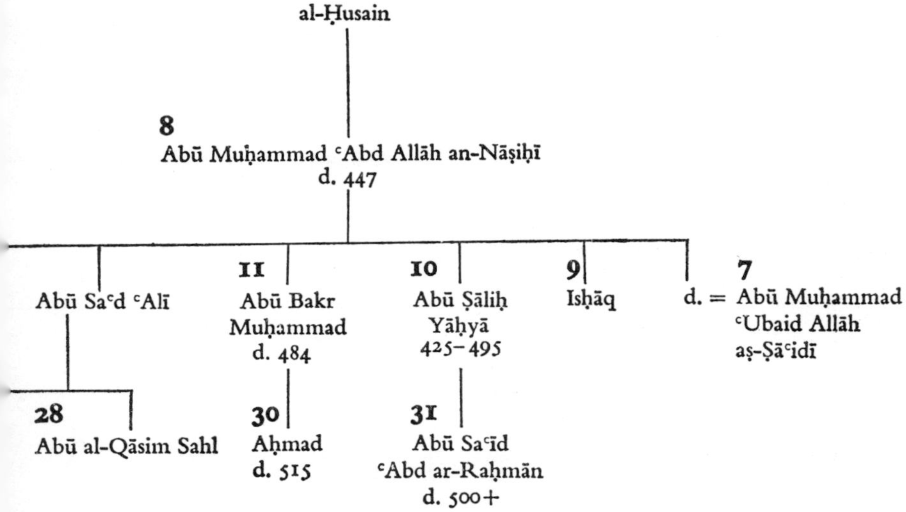

Ṣāʿidī

I   **4**
Abū Muḥammad al-Muʿallā
al-Baihaqī

II   d.

III   daughter of ======== **7**
Abū Muḥammad ʿAbd Allāh   Abū Muḥammad ʿUbaid Allāh
an-Nāṣiḥī   409–486

IV   **27**   **26**   **24**
Abū ʿAlī al-Faḍl = d.   Abū al-Fatḥ ʿAbd al-Malik   Abū Naṣr Aḥmad
as-Sardādī   d. 501   410–482

V   **40**   **39**   **38**
Ṣāʿid   Abū Saʿd Yaḥyā   Abū Saʿīd Muḥammad
d. 548   444–527

VI   **48**   **47**
Yaḥyā   Abū al-Qāsim Manṣūr
                   475–552

VII   s.   **49**
            ʿAlī
            d. 554

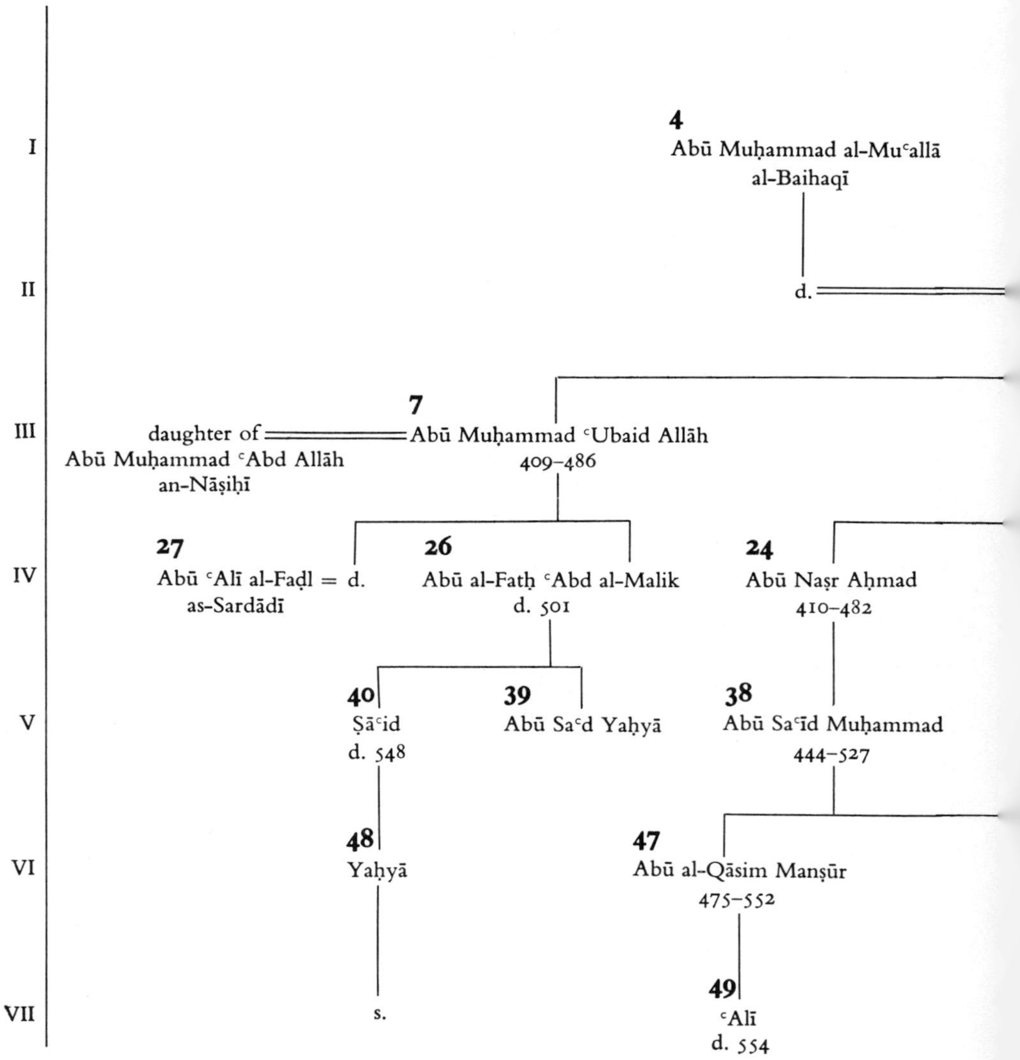

Ṣāᶜidī (continued)

Aḥmad b. ᶜAbd Allāh

Muḥammad b. Jaᶜfar

2
Abū Saᶜīd Muḥammad = d.

3
Abū Muḥammad Ismāᶜīl

1
= Abū al-ᶜAlā᾽ Ṣāᶜid
343–431

6
Abū Saᶜīd Muḥammad
380–433

23
Abū Saᶜd Yaḥyā
401–460

25
d. = Abū al-Faḍl Aḥmad
al-Furātī
See ṢĀBŪNĪ

22
Abū al-Qāsim Manṣūr
d. 470

37
Abū al-ᶜAlā᾽ Ṣāᶜid
d. 506

46
Abū al-Mafākhir ᶜAzīz
481–551

42
Abū al-Ḥasan Ismāᶜīl

43
Abū al-Maᶜālī Asᶜad
d. 527

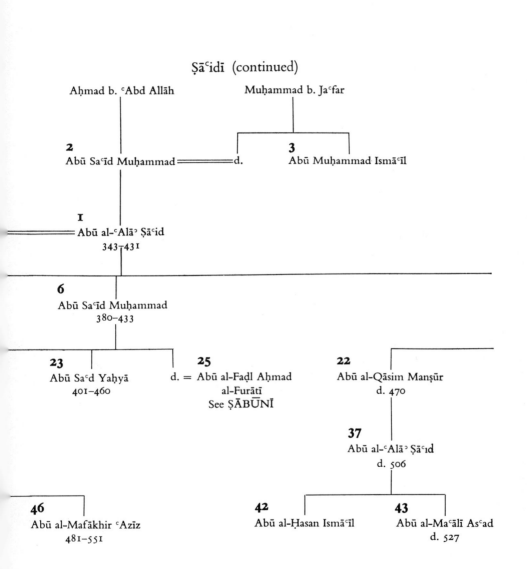

Ṣāᶜidī (continued)

I

II

5
Abū al-Ḥasan Ismāᶜīl
377–443 III

21
Abū ᶜAlī al-Ḥasan
d. 472 IV

36
Abū Bakr ᶜAlī
d. 508

35
Abū al-Faḍl al-Ḥusain
d. 508 or 511 V

44
Ṣāᶜid
d. 532

45
Abū ᶜAlī al-Ḥasan VI

50
Abū al-Ḥasan Ismāᶜīl VII

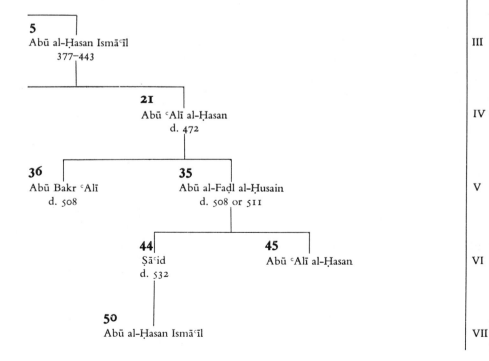

18. Abū al-Faḍl ʿAbd Allāh al-Ḥīrī	Fārisī I, f35b; II, f83b–84a.
19. Abū ʿAbd ar-Raḥmān Ismāʿīl al-Ḥīrī	Fārisī II, f37b; I. Jauzī, VIII, 105; Subkī, IV, 265–266; T. Baghdād, VI, 313–314; Shadharāt, III, 245; ʿIbar, III, 171.
20. Abū Bakr Muḥammad al-Ḥīrī	Fārisī II, f7b.
21. Abū ʿAlī al-Ḥasan aṣ-Ṣāʿidī	Fārisī I, f6a; II, f54a; IAW, I, 190.
22. Abū al-Qāsim Manṣūr aṣ-Ṣāʿidī	Fārisī I, f79b; II, f129a–b; IAW, II, 182.
23. Abū Saʿd Yaḥyā aṣ-Ṣāʿidī	Fārisī I, f96a; II, f142b; IAW, II, 215–216.
24. Abū Naṣr Aḥmad aṣ-Ṣāʿidī	Fārisī II, f33a–34a; IAW, I, 105–106; ʿIbar, III, 299; Shadharāt, III, 366; I. Jauzī, IX, 49–50.
25. Abū al-Faḍl Aḥmad b. Muḥammad al-Furātī	See Ṣābūnī genealogical key #3.
26. Abū al-Fatḥ ʿAbd al-Malik aṣ-Ṣāʿidī	Fārisī I, f49a; II, f96a; IAW, I, 331.
27. Abū ʿAlī al-Faḍl as-Sardādī	Fārisī II, f122a.
28. Abū al-Qāsim Sahl an-Nāṣiḥī	Fārisī I, f28a; II, f71a.
29. Abū al-Ḥasan Ismāʿīl an-Nāṣiḥī	Fārisī II, f42a.
30. Aḥmad an-Nāṣiḥī	IAW, I, 106.
31. Abū Saʿīd ʿAbd ar-Raḥmān an-Nāṣiḥī	IAW, I, 310.
32. Abū al-Ḥusain ʿAbd ar-Raḥīm b. Aḥmad b. ʿUrwa.	IAW, I, 311.
33. Abū Saʿīd al-Ḥasan al-Ismāʿīlī	Fārisī II, f54b.
34. Abū ʿAbd Allāh Nāṣir al-Ismāʿīlī	Fārisī II, f136a–b.
35. Abū al-Faḍl al-Ḥusain aṣ-Ṣāʿidī	Fārisī II, f59a; IAW, I, 208–209; I. Funduq, pp. 246–247.
36. Abū Bakr ʿAlī aṣ-Ṣāʿidī	Fārisī I, f70b; II, f116a.
37. Abū al-ʿAlāʾ Ṣāʿid aṣ-Ṣāʿidī	Fārisī I, f87b, 83a; II, f75a; IAW, I, 262–263; I. Jauzī, IX, 172.
38. Abū Saʿīd Muḥammad aṣ-Ṣāʿidī	IAW, II, 22; ʿIbar, IV, 72; I. Jauzī, X, 33.
39. Abū Saʿd Yaḥyā aṣ-Ṣāʿidī	Fārisī II, f143b.
40. Ṣāʿid aṣ-Ṣāʿidī	I. Athīr, XI, 182.

41. Abū Jaʿfar Muḥammad b. ʿAbd ar-Raḥīm	IAW, II, 80.
42. Abū al-Ḥasan Ismāʿīl aṣ-Ṣāʿidī	Fārisī II, f45b; IAW, I, 152.
43. Abū al-Maʿālī Asʿad aṣ-Ṣāʿidī	Fārisī II, f49a; IAW, I, 142–143; I. Jauzī, X, 31–32.
44. Ṣāʿid aṣ-Ṣāʿidī	I. Funduq, p. 246; IAW, I, 260.
45. Abū ʿAlī al-Ḥasan aṣ-Ṣāʿidī	I. Funduq, p. 246.
46. Abū al-Mafākhir ʿAzīz aṣ-Ṣāʿidī	IAW, I, 347.
47. Abū al-Qāsim Manṣūr aṣ-Ṣāʿidī	IAW, II, 183–184; I. Athīr, XI, 228.
48. Yaḥyā aṣ-Ṣāʿidī	Dawlatshāh, *Tadhkirat-i Shuʿarāʾ*, pp. 141–142.
49. ʿAlī aṣ-Ṣāʿidī	I. Athīr, XI, 253.
50. Abū al-Ḥasan Ismāʿīl aṣ-Ṣāʿidī	I. Funduq, p. 246.

14 / *Ḥaskānī*

What is so extraordinary about the Ḥaskānī[1] family is the utter lack of connection between its two branches. Nowhere in the biographies is there a trace of recognition of kinship between them. Yet the objective evidence for their being from the same family is too substantial to be ignored. Family genealogies on both sides go back to one Muḥammad b. Ḥaskān albeit the genealogy appears to be incomplete in the Iskāf branch. Ḥaskān, it must be noted, is a name of exceeding rarity. But beyond that, both family branches have a second name, and both names mean shoemaker. One is Ḥadhdhāʾ and the other Iskāf. Evidently, this represents a conscious effort to deny a relationship that in fact existed.

The reason for lack of kindred spirit among the Ḥaskānīs is not difficult to find. The Ḥadhdhāʾ branch is Ḥanafī and Muʿtazilī, the Iskāf branch Shāfiʿī and Ashʿarī. The surmise that at some point in the family history a deep and abiding political and philosophical split took place in the family cannot be far wrong. There may have been additional factors, of course. The Iskāf branch comes from Isfarāʾin, and this may signify a geographical as well as a political division, but that Ḥanafī-Shāfiʿī rivalry is at the heart of the matter appears certain.

I. Abū al-Ḥasan Muḥammad as-Suḥūrī (1) would appear to be the earliest traceable member of the Ḥadhdhāʾ Ḥaskānīs, but the matter is in doubt because of the erratic spelling of Ḥaskān in the manuscript. The significance and spelling of as-Suḥūrī are equally uncertain.

II. With Abū Naṣr Aḥmad al-Ḥadhdhāʾ (2) the family really becomes identifiable. Abū Naṣr was born not too long after 932/320 and remembered meeting his father when he returned from a military campaign in 942/330. Although a Ḥanafī himself, his associates were not all Ḥanafīs; it was on the Pilgrimage in the company of the Sufi Abū al-Qāsim an-Naṣrābādī[2] in 976/365 that he had all of his books stolen by the ʿayyārūn. Whether this happened near Nishapur or elsewhere is not mentioned. As a result of the incident, however, his irreplaceable notes from early classes were lost and he had to restrict his reciting of ḥadīth to later sources, not that it made much difference since his recitations were error ridden and unreliable anyway. In 993/383 he made the

1. The spelling Ḥaskānī follows Mushtabah, I, 265.
2. Ḥākim, f39b; Shadharāt, III, 58–59; as-Sulamī, *Ṭabaqāt*, 484–488.

Pilgrimage a second time with his son Abū Muḥammad ᶜAbd Allāh, and in 1032/423 he died.

Unfortunately, the one biography of Abū Naṣr does not tell of the marriage he apparently contracted with a daughter of the Qurashī family. This connection, which certainly existed but not necessarily in this generation, is of particular interest because it links the Ḥaskānī family with one of the oldest Arab families in Nishapur, the descendants of the Muslim conqueror of the city ᶜAbd Allāh b. ᶜĀmir b. Kuraiz. The Qurashī Kuraizī family remained prominent in the city from the time of the conquest until its destruction some five hundred years later, but it is hard to tell which of its branches the Ḥaskanīs became allied to.[3] Nevertheless, any connection at all with such a family is significant of social acceptability.

The husband of Abū Naṣr's sister, Abū al-Ḥusain Muḥammad b. ᶜAbd Allāh al-Qaṣṣār, is not given a separate biography. The name Qaṣṣār indicates that he or his forebears were fullers.

III. This is the generation in which the Iskāf branch of the family makes its appearance, but the story of the Ḥadhdhāᵓ Haskānīs will be continued first.

Abū Naṣr Aḥmad had two sons. Abū Saḥl ᶜAbd ar-Rahīm (3) was a pious and ascetic man who did not take part in the general competition to collect ḥadīth lessons from famous transmitters. However, this does not mean that he did not study ḥadīth. In fact, he studied as far away as Syria and the Hijaz. It means simply that he did not retain his notes and took no interest in passing on the traditions he heard. Only his well-known nephew Abū al-Qāsim gleaned from him any of his learning. He died in 1063/455.

The other son, Abū Muḥammad ᶜAbd Allāh (4), was surnamed al-Qurashī al-Kuraizī, but he was known by the name al-Ḥadhdhāᵓ. Since his brother does not bear the additional surnames, separate mothers may be indicated, but there is no concrete evidence for this. He was born in 974/363, two years before his father's first departure for Mecca and Medina. Spending the infancy or childhood of one's children on the long Pilgrimage journey seems to have been a common procedure in Nishapur. He did not study as a child but appears rather to have been brought up in the family trade of shoe-making. His studies began only when he accompanied his father on a second Pilgrimage

3. For contemporary lineal descendants of ᶜAbd Allāh b. ᶜĀmir in the male line see Fārisī I, f94a–b; II, f122b, 140a.

in 993/383. Although he became a preacher in the mosque of the Great Crossroads Market, his primary occupation in life was business. From apparent success in that arena he moved on to become ḥākim, or judge, for the rural areas around the city. He died in retirement in 1058/450.

Abū Muḥammad's personal involvement in the family occupation is further testified to by the occupation of his brother-in-law. Abū aṭ-Ṭayyib Sahl as-Sarrājī (5) was a saddler. He, too, went on to a more patrician calling, however, as an administrator of pious endowments in Rayy. He was born in 990/380 and died in Rayy at a comparatively young age in 1038/429.

A first cousin, the son of Abū Naṣr Aḥmad's sister, is also recorded for this generation. He was Abū al-Qāsim ᶜAbd al-Malik al-Qaṣṣār (6), a preacher and ascetic.

Over on the Shāfiᶜī side of the family things start off suddenly with the important figure of Abū al-Qāsim ᶜAbd al-Jabbār al-Isfarāᵓinī al-Iskāf (7). A student of the noted Ashᶜarī Abū Isḥāq al-Isfarāᵓinī,[4] Abū al-Qāsim instructed in theology the even more noted Imām al-Ḥaramain. Beyond generalities, unfortunately, little more is related concerning him save that he was deaf and served as imām in a place known as the Baihaqī *duwaira*.[5] He died in 1060/452 and was buried in Shāhanbar Cemetery.

IV. Keeping to the Shāfiᶜī side of the family, Abū al-Qāsim ᶜAbd al-Jabbār had two sons, Abū Ḥāmid Aḥmad (8) a jurist and Abū Bakr Muḥammad (9) a theologian. A death date of 1125/519 is all that is known of the former, but his brother is said to have been imām of the Manīᶜī Congregational Mosque for a while. The latter son was buried in Shāhanbar Cemetery, and the former probably was too.

Abū al-Qāsim ᶜUbaid Allāh al-Ḥadhdhāᵓ (10) was probably the most important member of any generation of the Ḥanafī branch of the Ḥaskānīs. Although noted in part for his Qurashī Kuraizī descent, his real distinction was in learning. He studied law with the qāḍī Abū al-ᶜAlāᵓ Ṣāᶜid and bore the title ḥākim indicating perhaps that he followed his father in a rural judgeship. He was also of a Muᶜtazilī bent in theology.

4. Subkī, IV, 256–262; Ḥākim, f39b; Fārisī II, f35a–36a.

5. This is probably the same as or related to the Baihaqī madrasa. The word *duwaira* is here a diminutive of the word *dār* (house, palace) and most certainly the same as the *dār* of Abū al-Ḥasan al-Baihaqī mentioned in Fārisī II, f94a–b. There are many references to the madrasa of Abū al-Ḥasan al-Baihaqī, a well-known Shāfiᶜī institution. See also Subkī, V, 99 n. 3. The word *duwaira* is applied to the Sufi *khāngāh* of Abū ᶜAbd ar-Raḥmān as-Sulamī. Fārisī II, f6b, 43a, 73b, 115a.

But ḥadīth was his specialty. He authored nearly one hundred works large and small, and according to al-Fārisī, who uses him as a source frequently, his knowledge of traditions and their transmitters was unequalled in his generation. He died sometime after the year 1178/470.

Abū al-Qāsim's brother Masᶜūd (11) is a mere cipher.

V. The Shāfiᶜī branch of the family ends quite abruptly with Saᶜd (12), the son of Abū Bakr Muḥammad. Saᶜd's training was in law and theology, which he studied both in Nishapur and Transoxania. After the death of his father, he returned from Transoxania and took up his residence in the Baihaqī madrasa, which was probably the same institution in which his grandfather had been prayer leader.[6] He taught law but not in the madrasa in which he lived. He taught, rather, in a mosque situated at the intersection of Ḥarb Street and the main east-west highway that bisected the city. The Baihaqī madrasa was on Sayyār Street.[7]

Over on the Ḥanafī side, Abū al-Qāsim ᶜUbaid Allāh had three sons and a daughter. Abū ᶜAlī Muḥammad (13) was probably the oldest son; the title ḥākim indicates that he succeeded to his father's and grandfather's judicial position. He died in 1111/504. The youngest son was Abū al-Faḍl Wahb Allāh (14). He spent his life in seclusion in various convents although he did do some teaching. This leaves the middle son, Abū Saᶜīd Ṣāᶜid (15), about whom nothing of substance is reported.

The sister of these three brothers married the son of another shoemaker, Abū Ḥāmid Aḥmad b. ᶜAlī b. Muḥammad b. ᶜAbdūs b. al-Ḥadhdhāʾ (16). He lived from 1027/418 to 1112/506.

Their first cousin, son of their uncle Masᶜūd, was named Saᶜīd (17) and was born in 1065/457. Nothing more is known of him.

VI. In this final generation the Ḥaskānī family is represented solely by the son of the brother-in-law Abū Ḥāmid Aḥmad. His name was Abū al-Muẓaffar Jāmiᶜ (18), and he is surnamed al-Ḥadhdhāʾ though not al-Ḥaskānī. No further details are known about him.

6. See preceding note.
7. Fārisī II, f25b; I. Funduq, p. 158.

Genealogical Key

Ḥaskānī

1. Abū al-Ḥasan Muḥammad as-Suḥūrī	Ḥākim, f50a.
2. Abū Naṣr Aḥmad al-Ḥadhdhāʾ	Fārisī II, f24a.
3. Abū Sahl ʿAbd ar-Raḥīm al-Ḥadhdhāʾ	Fārisī II, f93a.
4. Abū Muḥammad ʿAbd Allāh al-Ḥadhdhāʾ al-Qurashī	Fārisī I, f32a; II, f80b–81a; IAW, I, 270.
5. Abū aṭ-Ṭayyib Sahl as-Sarrājī	Fārisī I, f27b; II, f70b.
6. Abū al-Qāsim ʿAbd al-Malik al-Qaṣṣār	Fārisī II, f95a.
7. Abū al-Qāsim ʿAbd al-Jabbār al-Isfarāʾinī al-Iskāf	Fārisī I, f53a; II, f99a; Subkī, III, 370; V, 99–100.
8. Abū Ḥāmid Aḥmad al-Isfarāʾinī al-Iskāf	Fārisī II, f35a.
9. Abū Bakr Muḥammad al-Isfarāʾinī al-Iskāf	Fārisī II, f15b.
10. Abū al-Qāsim ʿUbaid Allāh al-Ḥadhdhāʾ al-Qurashī	Fārisī I, f38a–b; II, f86a; IAW, I, 338; Ḥuffāẓ, pp. 1200–01.
11. Masʿūd al-Ḥadhdhāʾ	Fārisī II, f127a.
12. Saʿd al-Isfarāʾinī al-Iskāf	Fārisī I, f27a–b; II, f70a.
13. Abū ʿAlī Muḥammad al-Ḥadhdhāʾ	Fārisī II, f20b; IAW, II, 88.
14. Abū al-Faḍl Wahb Allāh al-Ḥadhdhāʾ	Fārisī I, f94a; II, f139a.
15. Abū Saʿīd Ṣāʿid al-Ḥadhdhāʾ	Fārisī I, f83b; II, f75a–b.
16. Abū Ḥāmid Aḥmad b. ʿAlī b. al-Ḥadhdhāʾ	Fārisī II, f24b–25a.
17. Saʿīd al-Ḥadhdhāʾ	Fārisī II, f70a.
18. Abū al-Muẓaffar Jāmiʿ al-Ḥadhdhāʾ	Fārisī II, f51b.

Ḥaskānī

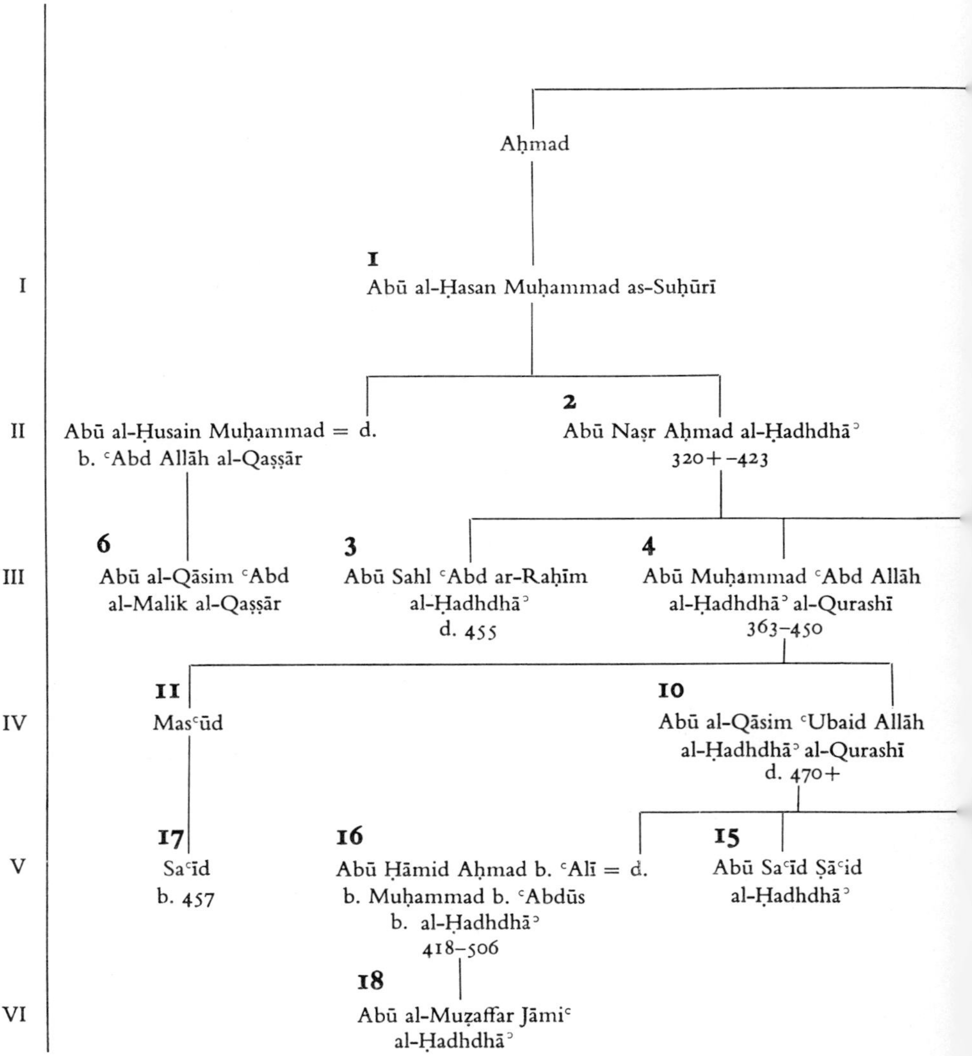
Aḥmad
I
1
Abū al-Ḥasan Muḥammad as-Suḥūrī
II
Abū al-Ḥusain Muḥammad = d.
b. ᶜAbd Allāh al-Qaṣṣār
2
Abū Naṣr Aḥmad al-Ḥadhdhāᵓ
320+-423
III
6
Abū al-Qāsim ᶜAbd
al-Malik al-Qaṣṣār
3
Abū Sahl ᶜAbd ar-Raḥīm
al-Ḥadhdhāᵓ
d. 455
4
Abū Muḥammad ᶜAbd Allāh
al-Ḥadhdhāᵓ al-Qurashī
363-450
IV
11
Masᶜūd
10
Abū al-Qāsim ᶜUbaid Allāh
al-Ḥadhdhāᵓ al-Qurashī
d. 470+
V
17
Saᶜīd
b. 457
16
Abū Ḥāmid Aḥmad b. ᶜAlī = d.
b. Muḥammad b. ᶜAbdūs
b. al-Ḥadhdhāᵓ
418-506
15
Abū Saᶜīd Ṣāᶜid
al-Ḥadhdhāᵓ
VI
18
Abū al-Muẓaffar Jāmiᶜ
al-Ḥadhdhāᵓ

Ḥaskānī (continued)

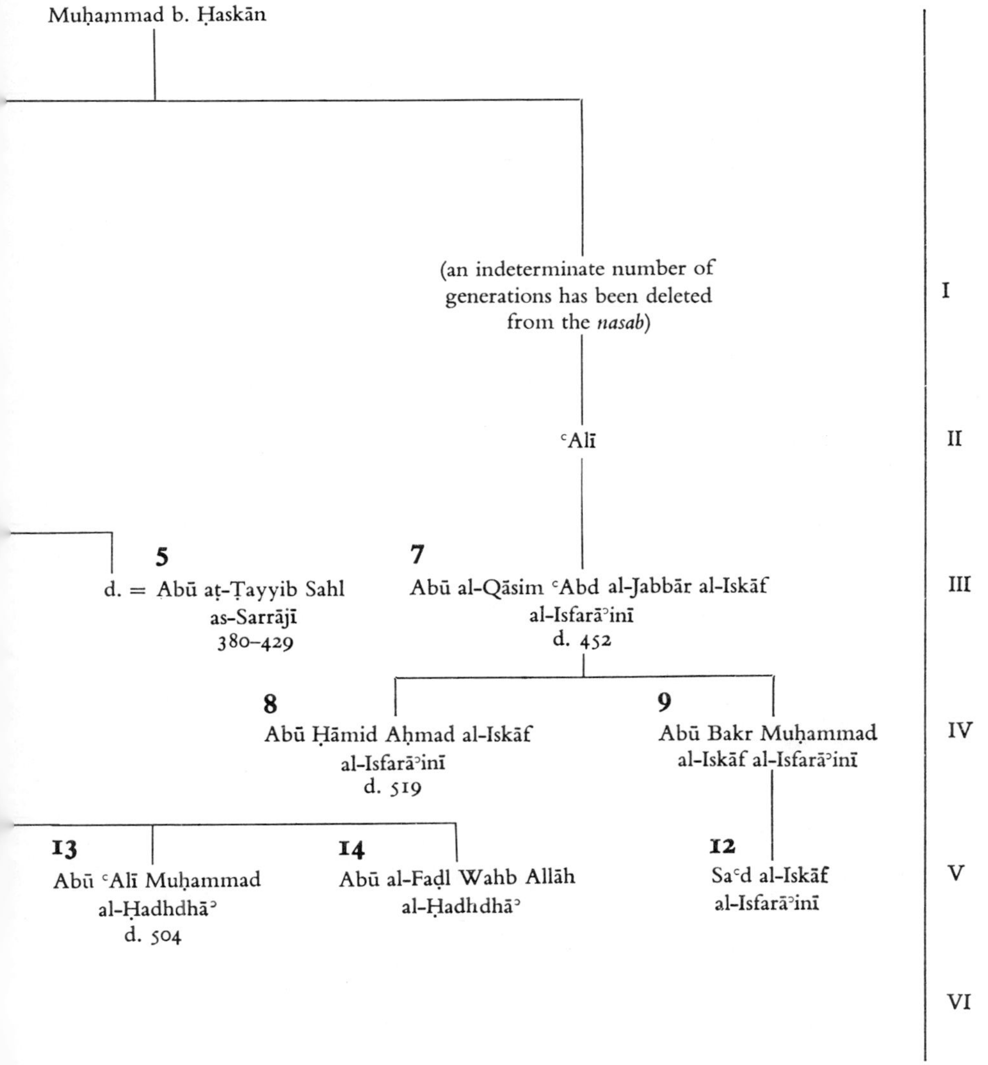

15 / Ḥasanī

Quite apart from any considerations of Shiᶜism or anti-Shiᶜism, the tremendous respect in which descendants of the Prophet Muḥammad have been held throughout Islamic history constitutes an important social fact. The ᶜAlids are a blood aristocracy without peer, a special category in Islamic society whose individual members may belong to any other social category as well. Marriage to an ᶜAlid with the concomitant acquisition of the Prophetic bloodline for one's progeny has a real value that may oftentimes prove greater than maintaining for some social or political purpose one's separateness from the particular ᶜAlid family involved. Thus, in a sense, an ᶜAlid family may be "above" social and political distinctions. In it warring parties might meet and mingle. In Nishapur, the Ḥasanī family provides a clear demonstration of this.

I. Abū ᶜAbd Allāh al-Ḥusain al-Ḥasanī aṭ-Ṭabarī (1) was nine generations removed from ᶜAlī, the cousin and son-in-law of Muḥammad, eight generations from al-Ḥasan the family's eponym. These progenitors played no part in the history of Nishapur, however, and their lives need not be recounted here. Abū ᶜAbd Allāh came originally from Ṭabaristān, one of the provinces along the Caspian Sea. Little is known about his life, but it seems certain that he was not a Shiᶜite. Al-Ḥākim says: "I never heard him mention ᶜUthmān without saying 'the martyred caliph, may God be pleased with him' and weeping, or ᶜĀᵓisha without saying 'the righteous one daughter of the righteous one, the beloved of the beloved of God' and weeping." In Shiᶜite circles of a militant sort, such praise for ᶜUthmān, who was believed to have unfairly secured the office of caliph when ᶜAlī should have had it, and ᶜĀᵓisha, who lent her influence as Muḥammad's favorite wife to a rebellion against ᶜAlī, could easily have sparked serious rioting. Abū ᶜAbd Allāh al-Ḥusain died in 966/355.

II. He had three sons. Zaid (2) and Abū ᶜAlī Muḥammad (3) are only names, but Abū al-Ḥasan Muḥammad (4) is a very significant figure. Subkī classes him as a Shāfiᶜī and gives him the title naqīb, which signifies that a person is the official chief of the ᶜAlids in a given locality. There is nothing to corroborate the former attribution, and the latter title was certainly not his, for his son is explicitly described by al-Fārisī, a more reliable source, as being the first of his house to hold the post of naqīb. Still, Abū al-Ḥasan Muḥammad is significant as the progenitor of a line of naqībs and as a traditionist in his own right. Al-Ḥākim convened a ḥadīth class for him, presumably in the Dār as-Sunna madrasa, and the inkwells of a thousand students were counted in the throng that came to study under him. He died quite suddenly, though not apparently at a young age, in 1011/401.

III. With one exception, the remaining known members of the Ḥasanī family in Nishapur are descendants of the traditionist Abū al-Ḥasan Muḥammad. The one exception is Abū al-Faḍl Aḥmad (5), the son of Abū al-Ḥasan Muḥammad's brother Abū ᶜAlī Muḥammad. Unlike his uncle, from whom he transmitted ḥadīth, he was a Ḥanafī, in fact, a teacher of Ḥanafī law. Something unspecified happened to cause his financial situation to deteriorate, but before that he had been the most outstanding ᶜAlid in the city. His line of the family drops from the historical record with his death in 1056/448.

Abū al-Ḥasan Muḥammad had four sons. Abū Jaᶜfar Dāʾūd (6) was the oldest son and the first member of the Ḥasanī family to hold the post of naqīb which had been held by the Ḥusainī branch of the ᶜAlids.[1] The transfer of the office came about as the result of some controversy between the Ḥusainīs and the Ḥasanīs that was decided when the Shāfiᶜīs took the part of the Ḥasanīs. The Ḥusainī family remained dominant in Baihaq, and a number of its members are given biographies in al-Fārisī's dictionary. The transfer took place during the lifetime of Abū Jaᶜfar's father Abū al-Ḥasan Muḥammad, but Abū al-Ḥasan was not the first of the family to hold the position. The title raʾīs was acquired along with that of naqīb, and the exact distinction between the two is unclear. That there was a distinction is certain, however, as the titles become separated in later generations.

Abū Jaᶜfar Dāʾūd died in 1012/402 only seven months after his father, and the position of naqīb passed on to his brother Abū Muḥammad al-Ḥasan (7). Unfortunately, the biography of Abū Muḥammad is one of the few truly important biographies that cannot be found in the extant manuscripts of al-Fārisī although it surely existed in the original. The only biographical source for him is a very inadequate one and serves only to confirm that he inherited the title raʾīs along with that of naqīb.

A third son, Abū ᶜAbd Allāh al-Ḥusain (8), died in 1014/404. In his son's biography it is stated that he was older than his brother Abū Jaᶜfar Dāʾūd. This does not appear probable, however, since Abū Jaᶜfar is himself described as his father's oldest son and since Abū ᶜAbd Allāh never held the post of naqīb which went to Abū Muḥammad

1. I. Funduq, p. 255; Bosworth, *The Ghaznavids*, pp. 196–197.

instead of him after Abū Jaᶜfar's death. Nothing is known about Abū ᶜAbd Allāh's political affiliations, but the fact that his son married the daughter of the Shāfiᶜī leader Abū aṭ-Ṭayyib Sahl aṣ-Ṣuᶜlūkī (9), whose life has been recounted elsewhere, and became thereby a close relation of the Shāfiᶜī Basṭāmī family indicates where his sympathies probably lay.

The youngest son of Abū al-Ḥasan Muḥammad by far was Abū al-Barakāt Hibat Allāh (10). He was born when his father had passed the age of ninety and given up the hope of siring any more sons. His name Hibat Allāh, meaning Gift of God, was given on this account. When he died in 1060/452, he had outlived not only his brothers and his cousin but all of his nephews as well. He was reared with his brothers' sons until he left home while still a youth to make the Pilgrimage. It was while studying in the various cities along the Pilgrimage route that he conceived his lifelong passion for the study of ḥadīth. He was already wealthy and prestigious and could easily afford to spend his life in teaching, which he pursued first in the Old Congregational Mosque and subsequently in his own home in Mūlqābād quarter.

Although he died after the ascendance of Alp Arslān and Niẓām al-Mulk and the subsequent rehabilitation of the Shāfiᶜīs, his later years were passed during the persecution of the Ashᶜarīs, a fact of no little interest since his son married the daughter of one of the three most important leaders of the persecution, Abū al-Ḥasan ᶜAlī b. al-Ḥasan aṣ-Ṣandali (11). Whether Abū al-Barakāt or his son can be considered on this account to have gone along with aṣ-Ṣandalī's militant Ḥanafī policy is difficult to say, but the possibility is certainly a real one.

As for aṣ-Ṣandalī, he affords a rare example of an individual of no particularly distinguished background who rose to a position of tremendous power within the patriciate. Significantly, that power was built in the first instance upon a popular following rather than upon any official position. He began as an ordinary student of Ḥanafī law and Muᶜtazilī theology with an extraordinary amount of hatred for anyone who was not a Ḥanafī and Muᶜtazilī. Through his fanatic preaching he acquired a following among the common people which little by little grew until it burst out in a full-scale persecution of Shāfiᶜīs, Ashᶜarīs, and Karrāmīs. Aṣ-Ṣandalī was the rabble-rouser; Abū Naṣr Aḥmad aṣ-Ṣāᶜidī, as leader of the Ḥanafīs, was the person who lent the persecution stature and respectability; and ᶜAmīd al-Mulk al-Kundurī was its protector and official promulgator in the Seljuq government. At first, aṣ-Ṣandalī seems to have been the prime mover. After a period of flux following the removal of Abū ᶜUthmān Ismāᶜīl aṣ-Ṣābūnī as khaṭīb of the Old Congregational Mosque, it was aṣ-Ṣandalī who acquired that post which for nine years gave him control over official pronouncements of eulogy or damnation. Abū Naṣr Aḥmad aṣ-Ṣāᶜidī took over at the same time the office of raʾīs, which had previously been a Shāfiᶜī position. But in the long run it was Ṣāᶜidīs, representing "old family" Ḥanafīs within the patriciate, who profited the most among the persecutors. Aṣ-Ṣandalī went off to Baghdad with Ṭughril Beg; when he came back, the hated Ashᶜarīs had returned to Nishapur in force. Aṣ-Ṣandalī cut his ties with the government and was forced to withdraw into retirement, but the Ṣāᶜidīs bounced back after a relatively brief period out of favor and emerged unscathed with their hold on the judicial system still secure and with the posts of khaṭīb in the Old Congregational Mosque and Shaikh al-Islām newly in their grasp. The remainder of aṣ-Ṣandalī's life was spent trading vindictive comments with his numerous enemies, but his power was broken. He died in 1091/484 and was buried in his madrasa.

IV. Abū al-Futūḥ ar-Riḍā (12), the son of Abū ᶜAbd Allāh al-Ḥusain, married the daughter of aṣ-Ṣuᶜlūkī; his first cousin, who married aṣ-Ṣandalī's daughter in the opposite camp, was Abū al-Ḥasan Muhammad (13). Unfortunately, too little is known about either of them to ascertain the effects of their marital ties. Indeed, because of the great age spread between their fathers, they were not really contemporaries. Abū al-Futūḥ died in 1054/446 in the middle of the Ashᶜarī persecution while Abū al-Ḥasan died over seventy years later in 1123/517.

Abū al-Ḥasan Muḥammad's brother, Abū al-Ghanāʾim Ḥamza (14), the other scion of the younger branch of the family, adds another sort of peculiarity to the family history. While his assorted relations seem all to have been tied in to some degree with one of the Sunni factions, Abū al-Ghanāʾim made the very most of his ᶜAlid descent. He grew up as a conscientious student of ḥadīth albeit something of a dandy, a trait that increased after his father's death. He married a cousin from the branch of the family in which the office of naqīb had become hereditary. Her father's name is not given, but she must have been of the next generation since there was such a difference in age between Abū al-Ghanāʾim's father and his uncle the naqīb.

His lineage and marriage meant little, however, until he chanced to move to the city of Marv. There suddenly he was a celebrity among the ᶜAlids both because of the relative importance of his line of descent and because of his kinship with the naqībs of

Nishapur. All of this was played up by a local leader of the ᶜAlids in Marv to such an extent that Abū al-Ghanāʾim became the object of tremendous veneration and financial support. In short, he began to lead an almost princely life in Marv. Nevertheless, he eventually tired of his sumptuous life and returned to Nishapur cutting his ties with Marv. In penance, perhaps, for his years of grand living, Abū al-Ghanāʾim spent the remainder of his days in pious retirement filling his hours with religious studies and devotions and leaving his house only for such things as attendance at funerals.

This leaves, finally, the line of descent from the naqīb Abū Muḥammad al-Ḥasan, his brother Abū Jaᶜfar Dāʾūd, the first naqīb, having died without known issue. The older of Abū Muḥammad's two sons and the one who succeeded him as naqīb was Abū al-Qāsim Zaid (15). He lived from 998/388 to 1048/440, through the period of transition from Ghaznavid to Seljuq rule, and he played an instrumental role in the surrender of the city to the invading Turks. In the report on the surrender sent to the Ghaznavid court and written by the chief of the postal service in Nishapur from concealment in the house of Abū al-Qāsim, the naqīb is portrayed in the same light as the Ḥanafī leader Abū al-ᶜAlāʾ Ṣāᶜid as being only reluctantly acquiescent in the surrender, which is shown as being engineered primarily by Imām al-Muwaffaq al-Basṭāmī, the Shāfiᶜī leader. It can hardly be doubted, given the provenance of the document, that this is exactly how Abū al-Qāsim wished the various faction leaders to appear to the Ghaznavid sultan who, he may well have imagined, might soon be reoccupying the city.[2] On the religious side, he is said not to have transmitted any ḥadīth because he died on the threshold of maturity. The age of fifty, it would seem, was equated with full attainment of wisdom and character by the patricians of Nishapur.

The successor of Abū al-Qāsim Zaid was his brother, Abū al-Maᶜālī Ismāᶜīl (16). He was younger by two years than Abū al-Qāsim and survived him by eight years, dying in 1056/448. He was a teacher of ḥadīth, well educated by the shaikhs of Nishapur and of the cities along the Pilgrimage road. He had also visited in Ghazna at one time in the company of his brother. But for all of that, he was a man who enjoyed the prestige of his position. His house was never empty of his retinue of boon companions, and he freely indulged in the pleasures of conviviality and listening to songs. There is no mention whether the long illness he died from was in any way connected with these pursuits.

2. This document is translated by Bosworth in *The Ghaznavids*, pp. 252–257.

V. Abū ᶜAbd Allāh al-Futūḥ (17), son of Abū al-Futūḥ ar-Riḍā and grandson of Abū aṭ-Ṭayyib Sahl aṣ-Ṣuᶜlūkī, is the only Ḥasanī of this or any subsequent generation outside the line of the naqībs. This realistically reflects, no doubt, the extraordinary prestige of that title. For the first and last time in the Ḥasanī family there is reference in his biography to the Shiᶜa, and that reference is of a negative sort. Abū ᶜAbd Allāh is said to have been inclined toward the Sunnis, whose company he preferred, and to have avoided connection with Shiᶜite extremists. There is the implication here that others of his family were in thick with the Shiᶜite extremists, but concrete evidence is lacking. Abū ᶜAbd Allāh was born in 1033/424 and died in 1093/486.

Both of the brother naqībs of the previous generation had offspring. Abū al-Maᶜālī Ismāᶜīl had four sons, of whom three are known, and perhaps one daughter. That is to say, his cousin Abū al-Ghanāʾim received such an extravagant reception in Marv because of his marriage connection with the line of naqībs, and through a daughter of Abū al-Maᶜālī is as reasonable a way as any for the connection to have been made. Although Abū al-Maᶜālī was naqīb at the time of his death and was survived by no brothers, the office passed not to his children but to the son of his brother, the previous holder of it. There is no explanation given of this peculiar line of succession, but his own sons did inherit the title raʾīs which had previously been linked with that of naqīb.

Abū Ṭālib al-Qāsim (18) was the youngest son and held the title raʾīs. He died in the district of Juvain in 1098/491. Abū ᶜAbd Allāh al-Ḥusain (19) did not bear the title raʾīs. He was a close friend from childhood of the historian al-Fārisī's father and accompanied him on travels. The Fārisī family, of course, is part of the complex of Shāfiᶜī-Ashᶜarī families centering on the figure of Abū al-Qāsim al-Qushairī. He died in 1095/488. The third son, Abū Jaᶜfar Dāʾūd (20), was not only entitled raʾīs but long outlived his younger brother who also bore the title, dying finally in 1122/516. How, then, the younger brother came by the title is a mystery unless he held it by virtue of his position in Juvain. Abū Jaᶜfar was a shrewd and stingy man primarily concerned with the management of his own estates and affairs. At his death, he was prayed over by an otherwise unknown son at Bāb aṭ-Ṭāq, the gate separating al-Ḥīra from Mūlqābād, and buried in his house.

While the sons of Abū al-Maᶜālī had to satisfy themselves with whatever perquisites went with the title of raʾīs, the title of naqīb was inherited by his nephew Abū Muḥammad al-Ḥasan (21), the son of Abū al-Qāsim Zaid. Little is known about Abū Muḥammad, who died in 1077/469, and this is regrettable because what is known is intriguing. He was married to the daughter of the Shāfiᶜī leader Imām al-Muwaffaq al-Basṭāmī (22), whose surrender of the city to the Seljuqs his father seems to have disapproved of, and was therefore the brother-in-law of one of the four Shāfiᶜīs who were marked for arrest at the height of the Ashᶜarī persecution, namely, Abū Sahl Muḥammad b. Imām al-Muwaffaq al-Basṭāmī. According to Subkī, Abū Muḥammad came to Abū Sahl at the height of the factional struggle to intercede with him for an end to the warfare. He laid at his feet a thousand dinars and apologized for coming upon him unannounced. Subkī's narration goes no further, but the import of this vignette is startling. It definitely implies that at least at the time when Abū Sahl Muḥammad was mustering forces to free his colleagues from prison, the momentum in the affair was felt to be with the Shāfiᶜīs. From the usual accounts of the persecution, preserved for the most part in works of Shāfiᶜī authorship, the distinct impression is gained that the Shāfiᶜīs were entirely abused and almost entirely helpless in the face of the tyranny of al-Kundurī. To bribe their leader a thousand dinars to stop the fighting in such a situation would seem almost ludicrous. Yet it happened, and with the naqīb of the ᶜAlids as an intermediary.

VI. There is no traceable line in the Ḥasanī family from henceforward except the line of the naqībs in which the names Abū Muḥammad al-Ḥasan and Abū al-Qāsim Zaid alternate. The Abū al-Qāsim Zaid (23) of this generation is little more than a name. He may not even have been a naqīb although the title was certainly held by his descendants. He died somewhere away from Nishapur in 1095/488.

VII. Abū Muḥammad al-Ḥasan b. Abī al-Qāsim Zaid is known only from his son's genealogy.

VIII. The central role that the naqīb Abū al-Qāsim Zaid b. Abī Muḥammad al-Ḥasan (24) played in the tragedy of Nishapur's destruction has already been recounted earlier in this book. All that remains to be done here is to question how it came about that the ᶜAlids, whose history in the city had always been an ambiguous or intermediary one with respect to the hostile factions, came in the end to have the power and the single-mindedness to fight their Shāfiᶜī opponents to the death, the death of their mutual city. But to this question the historical sources provide no answer.

Genealogical Key

Ḥasanī

1. Abū ʿAbd Allāh al-Ḥusain aṭ-Ṭabarī	Ḥākim, f41b; I. Jauzī, VII, 34–35; Al-Amīn, *Aʿyān ash-Shīʿa*, XXVI, 33.
2. Zaid	Ḥākim, f42b.
3. Abū ʿAlī Muḥammad	Ḥākim, f50a.
4. Abū al-Ḥasan Muḥammad	Ḥākim, f50a; Subkī, III, 148; ʿIbar, III, 76; Shadharāt, III, 162.
5. Abū al-Faḍl Aḥmad	Ḥākim, f55a (?, date of death seems wrong for this reference); IAW, I, 100.
6. Abū Jaʿfar Dāʾūd	Ḥākim, f42a; Fārisī I, f19a; II, f63a–b.
7. Abū Muḥammad al-Ḥasan	Al-Amīn, *Aʿyān ash-Shīʿa*, XXIII, 115–116.
8. Abū ʿAbd Allāh al-Ḥusain	Fārisī I, f8a; II, f55b.
9. Abū aṭ-Ṭayyib Sahl aṣ-Ṣuʿlūkī	See Basṭāmī Genealogical Key #3.
10. Abū al-Barakāt Hibat Allāh	Fārisī I, f94b; II, f139b.
11. Abū al-Ḥasan ʿAlī b. al-Ḥasan aṣ-Ṣandalī	Fārisī I, f68a–b; II, f114b–115a; IAW, I, 357–359.
12. Abū al-Futūḥ ar-Riḍā	Fārisī II, f64b.
13. Abū al-Ḥasan Muḥammad	Fārisī II, f20b.
14. Abū al-Ghanāʾim Ḥamza	Fārisī I, f13b–14a; II, f60a–b.
15. Abū al-Qāsim Zaid	Fārisī II, f65b.
16. Abū al-Maʿālī Ismāʿīl	Al-Amīn, *Aʿyān ash-Shīʿa*, XI, 202; Fārisī II, f39b.
17. Abū ʿAbd Allāh al-Futūḥ	Fārisī I, f76a; II, f122b–123a.
18. Abū Ṭālib al-Qāsim	Fārisī II, f124a.
19. Abū ʿAbd Allāh al-Ḥusain	Fārisī II, f58b.
20. Abū Jaʿfar Dāʾūd	Fārisī I, f19a; II, f63b.
21. Abū Muḥammad al-Ḥasan	Fārisī II, f54b; Subkī, IV, 211.

Ḥasanī

I

II
2
Zaid

III
9
Abū aṭ-Ṭayyib Sahl
aṣ-Ṣuᶜlūkī
See BASṬĀMĪ

8
Abū ᶜAbd Allāh al-Ḥusain
d. 404

IV
d. ══ **12** Abū al-Futūḥ ar-Riḍā
d. 446

22
Abū Muḥammad Hibat Allāh
al-Basṭāmī
See BASṬĀMĪ

V
17
Abū ᶜAbd Allāh al-Futūḥ
424–486

d. ══

VI

VII

VIII

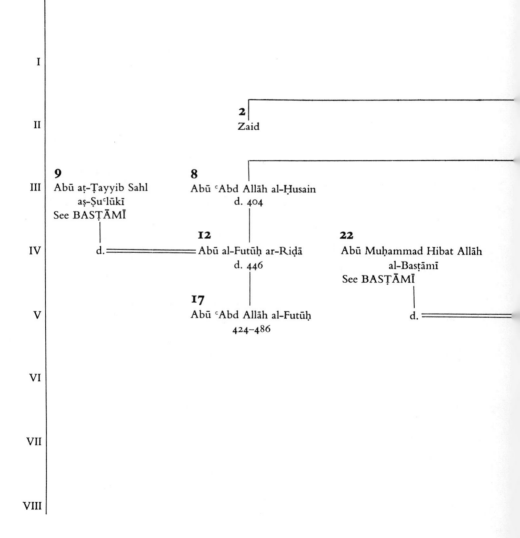

Ḥasanī (continued)

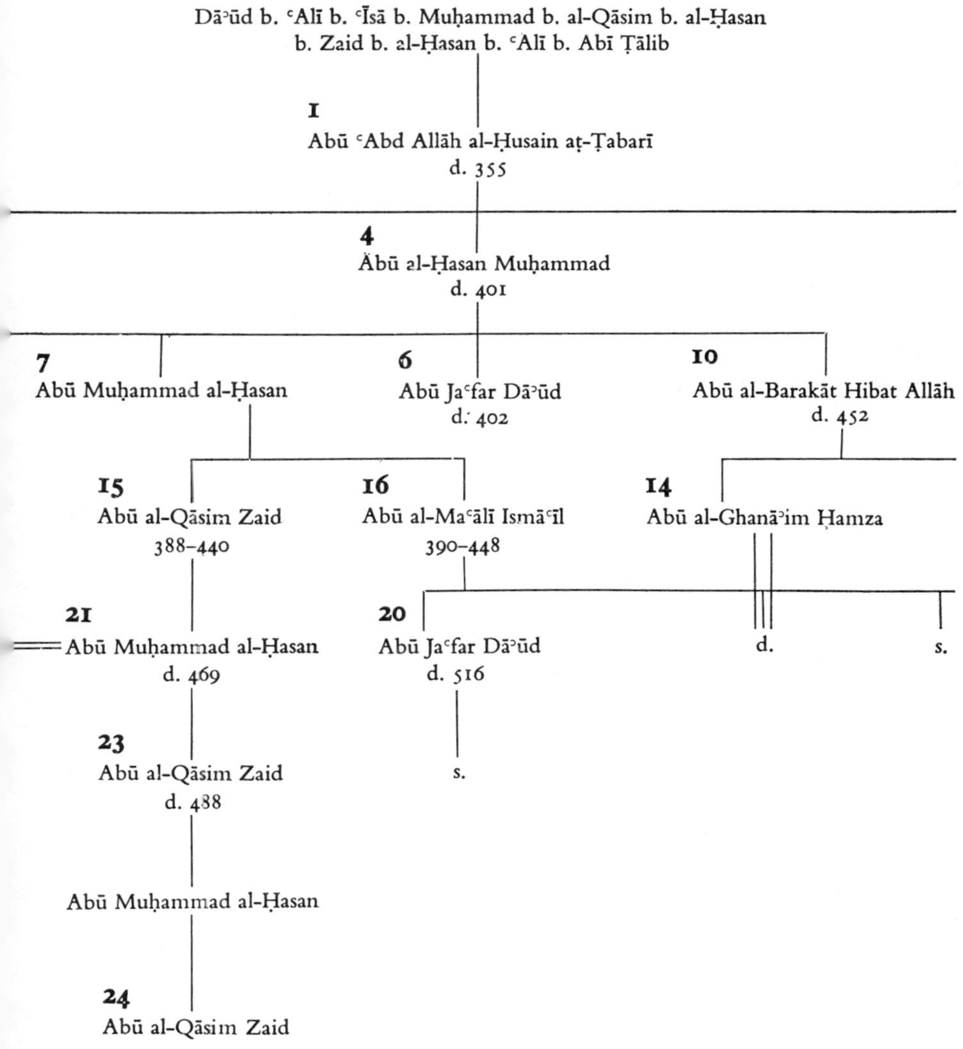
Dā᾽ūd b. ᶜAlī b. ᶜĪsā b. Muḥammad b. al-Qāsim b. al-Ḥasan b. Zaid b. al-Ḥasan b. ᶜAlī b. Abī Ṭālib
1
Abū ᶜAbd Allāh al-Ḥusain aṭ-Ṭabarī
d. 355
4
Abū al-Ḥasan Muḥammad
d. 401
7
Abū Muḥammad al-Ḥasan
6
Abū Jaᶜfar Dā᾽ūd
d. 402
10
Abū al-Barakāt Hibat Allāh
d. 452
15
Abū al-Qāsim Zaid
388–440
16
Abū al-Maᶜālī Ismāᶜīl
390–448
14
Abū al-Ghanā᾽im Ḥamza
21
Abū Muḥammad al-Ḥasan
d. 469
20
Abū Jaᶜfar Dā᾽ūd
d. 516
d.
s.
23
Abū al-Qāsim Zaid
d. 488
s.
Abū Muḥammad al-Ḥasan
24
Abū al-Qāsim Zaid

Ḥasanī (continued)

I

3
Abū ᶜAlī Muḥammad

II

5
Abū al-Faḍl Aḥmad
d. 448

11
Abū al-Ḥasan ᶜAlī
aṣ-Ṣandalī
d. 484

III

13
Abū al-Ḥasan Muḥammad = d.
d. 517

IV

18
Abū Ṭālib al-Qāsim
d. 491

19
Abū ᶜAbd Allāh al-Ḥusain
d. 488

V

VI

VII

VIII

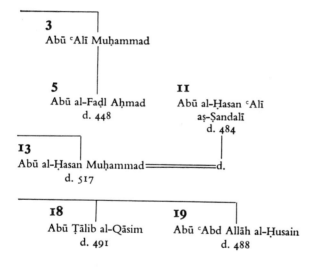

22. Abū Muḥammad Hibat Allāh al-Basṭāmī	See Basṭāmī Genealogical Key #9.
23. Abū al-Qāsim Zaid	Fārisī II, f66a–b.
24. Abū al-Qāsim Zaid	Al-Amīn, *A^cyān ash-Shī^ca*, XXXII, 390–391; I. Athīr, XI, 234–236, 271.

Appendices / Bibliography / Indices

Appendix I — *The Madrasa*

Although, as has already been pointed out, the history of the origin and development of the institution known as the madrasa is not central to the educational history of Nishapur or to the social organization and functioning of the city's patriciate, it is nevertheless a topic that has excited a great deal of debate and speculation among other historians of Islamic education. Since there is a great deal of information concerning the madrasas of Nishapur which is germane to this on-going debate, it would be cavalier to ignore the subject altogether simply because the author's notions on educational history do not coincide with those of others. The purpose of this appendix is to present in summary form the data available on the madrasas of Nishapur along with the references to that data. The order is roughly chronological.

1. *Madrasa Miyān Dahiya:* The earliest evidence of a madrasa in Nishapur is al-Ḥākim's notice on the life of Abū Isḥāq Ibrāhīm b. Maḥmūd b. Ḥamza known as al-Qaṭṭān contained in the section of his work covering people who died between roughly 270 and 314. The text reads: "His mosque and his madrasa are known as Miyān Dahiya. After him there was no *mudarris* for the Mālikī madhhab in Nishapur." Assuming no corruption in the text, it is clear from this that there was a Mālikī madrasa in operation in Nishapur before the end of the third century and that it was distinct from a mosque. Since Abū Isḥāq was a jurist, it is more than likely that what he taught in the madrasa was law. The fact that this is in the biography of the last Mālikī mudarris in Nishapur carries with it the strong implication that there had been earlier Mālikī mudarris', presumably with madrasas, and that there were at the same time mudarris' of other madhhabs, again presumably with madrasas. The name Miyān Dahiya is Persian and means "middle of the village" suggesting a nonurban location. It should be noted that chronologically this madrasa antedates both al-Azhar in Cairo and the flourishing of the Karrāmiya sect, both of which have been suggested as models of the Sunni madrasas.
Reference: Ḥākim, f19a.

2. *Madrasa Abū al-Ḥasan ᶜAlī aṣ-Ṣibghī:* Samᶜānī gives the date of death of this man as 305, but al-Ḥākim who studied under him was not born until 321. Hence, he probably died in the alternative year 350. He succeeded his father, however, in writing legal opinions in a madrasa, and this pushes the date of the madrasa well back toward the third century.
Reference: Samᶜānī, f349b.

3. *Madrasa Abū al-Walīd al-Qurashī:* Abū al-Walīd was a Shāfiᶜī and died in 349. One reference to studying law in his madrasa is dated 341. The other pertains to a different teacher in the same institution.
References: (Abū al-Walīd) Subkī, III, 226–229; Samᶜānī, f446b. (Madrasa) Samᶜānī, I, 231; II, 17.

4. *Madrasa Abū Isḥāq al-Basṭāmī:* Al-Ḥākim says, "He lived in Nishapur in the Garden of the Rāzīs (Bāgh ar-Rāziyīn), and he had there his madrasa and his palace (*dār*) which he built for the People of Tradition." No direct relation can be traced between this man, who died between 314

and 335, and the later Shāfiᶜī Basṭāmī family. However, the phrase People of Tradition (Ahl al-Ḥadīth) usually applies to the Shāfiᶜīs in Nishapur. Abū Isḥāq bore the title raᵓīs.
Reference: Ḥākim, f30a–b.

5. *Madrasa Ibn Fūrak:* At the behest of the Shāfiᶜī party in Nishapur, the Sīmjūrid governor Nāṣir ad-Dawla Abū al-Ḥasan Muḥammad invited the famous Ashᶜarī Ibn Fūrak from Rayy to Nishapur and built for him a palace (dār) and a madrasa out of an old convent (*khāngāh*) named for Abū al-Ḥasan al-Būshanjī. Nāṣir ad-Dawla was out of power after 372 so his act of patronage must have taken place before then.
Reference: Subkī, IV, 128.

6. *Dār as-Sunna* or *Madrasa aṣ-Ṣibghī:* This was the madrasa of which al-Ḥākim was director, but it was founded by and named for al-Ḥākim's teacher, Abū Bakr Aḥmad aṣ-Ṣibghī who lived from 258 to 342. He was no relation of the Ṣibghī mentioned under section 2. The name Dār as-Sunna suggests that the study of ḥadīth was the purpose for which the madrasa was founded, and that impression is corroborated by the several instances of ḥadīth teaching that are known to have taken place there. The madrasa was located at the gate of the Old Congregational Mosque which may explain why it is not mentioned after the early part of the fifth century. The madrasa was a Shāfiᶜī institution, and the mosque was increasingly becoming a Ḥanafī stronghold during that period.
References: (Ṣibghī) Subkī, III, 9–12. (Madrasa) Subkī, IV, 159; Fārisī II, f1b–2a, 26b; Samᶜānī, II, 105; V, 125.

7. *Madrasa Abū ᶜAlī ad-Daqqāq* or *Madrasa al-Qushairī:* This madrasa was built in 391 by Abū ᶜAlī who was a famous Sufi. After his death it seems to have been under the control of his young daughter Fāṭima until her marriage with the even more famous Sufi Abū al-Qāsim al-Qushairī after which it became known as the Qushairī madrasa. It remained in the charge of the Qushairī family thereafter. It was located in the quarter of the ᶜAzra Gate on a street also named for Abū ᶜAlī. Despite the Shāfiᶜī allegiance of its directors, the madrasa seems to have been more a Sufi institution than a school of law. One Mālikī is known to have lived in it. Sessions of preaching in the madrasa are mentioned, as well as specifically Sufi activities, but not law classes or legal disputations.
References: Fārisī I, f5b, 82b; II, f123a, 36a, 106a–b, 69a, 135b, 121b.

8. *Madrasa Abū Manṣūr al-Ḥamshādī:* Abū Manṣūr was a Shāfiᶜī and had both a mosque and a madrasa. He died in 388.
Reference: Subkī, III, 179–181.

9. *Madrasa aṣ-Ṣāᶜidī:* This was the foremost Ḥanafī madrasa in Nishapur founded by Naṣr b. Sabuktakīn, the brother of Maḥmūd of Ghazna, for Abū al-ᶜAlāᵓ Ṣāᶜid, the patriarch of the Ṣāᶜidī family. The year of its founding was 390. There is no question but that the Ṣāᶜidī madrasa was first and foremost a school of law. It was located on the Street of the Fullers (Sikka al-Qaṣ-ṣārīn) where the Ṣāᶜidī family also had its mausoleum. It seems quite likely that this madrasa was

the pattern for the later Niẓāmiya, which would help to explain why the Niẓāmiyas were all primarily schools of law instead of some other type of madrasa.
References: Fārisī I, f36a, 79b, 83a, 87b, 92a; II, 80b, 136b; Subkī, IV, 314.

10. *Madrasa Abū Isḥāq al-Isfarāʾinī:* Abū Isḥāq was counted with Ibn Fūrak and al-Bāqillānī as one of the greatest Ashʿarī theologians of his time. The madrasa that was built for him in Nishapur is described as being unparalleled by any earlier construction, but it would be a mistake to read any great significance into this rather standard bit of hyperbole. He taught law in the madrasa and ḥadīth in the ʿAqīl Mosque.
References: Subkī, IV, 256–262, 314; Samʿānī, I, 296.

11. *Madrasa al-Baihaqī* or *Madrasa Kūyi Sayyār:* There is some confusion as to exactly which man named Abū al-Ḥasan al-Baihaqī built the Baihaqī madrasa. The two candidates are Abū al-Ḥasan Muḥammad b. Shuʿaib al-Baihaqī, a prominent Shāfiʿī jurist who died in 324, and Abū al-Ḥasan ʿAlī b. al-Ḥusain al-Baihaqī, who was also a Shāfiʿī but whose talents ran to adab rather than the law. He died in 414. The men do not appear to have been related. Ibn Funduq ascribes the building of the madrasa to the former and says that the latter was simply the director of it. Samʿānī and Subkī say that Abū al-Ḥasan Muḥammad was a mudarris, but do not mention his founding a madrasa. Al-Fārisī says explicitly that the madrasa was built by Abū al-Ḥasan ʿAlī out of his own funds at a cost of many thousand dirhams. To add to the confusion, there is a separate Sayyār Street (Kūyi Sayyār) madrasa in Baihaq which has no connection with the one in Nishapur. Since there is no mention of the Baihaqī madrasa between 324 and 414, it appears likely that Ibn Funduq is wrong and al-Fārisī right and that the madrasa was in fact founded by Abū al-Ḥasan ʿAlī al-Baihaqī who died in 414.

According to Ibn Funduq, Abū al-Ḥasan ʿAlī divided the day in the madrasa into three parts, one for studying law, one for studying ḥadīth, and one for preaching. From other references, however, it appears that one of the primary functions of the institution was as a library of ḥadīth books. Abū Ṣāliḥ al-Muʾadhdhin who succeeded Abū al-Ḥasan al-Baihaqī as director was particularly concerned with the book collection as was his son-in-law Abū al-Qāsim Salmān al-Anṣārī who succeeded to the post after Abū Ṣāliḥ's death in 470. Adding to the impression that legal studies were not the main focus of the institution is the fact that one man who lived there taught law in a mosque on Ḥarb Street. There is a possibility that a Sufi convent (*duwaira* = *khāngāh*) was associated with the madrasa as well.
References: (Abū al-Ḥasan Muḥammad) I. Funduq, p. 158; Subkī, III, 173; Samʿānī, II, 413–414. (Abū al-Ḥasan ʿAlī) I. Funduq, p. 172; Fārisī I, f61a. (Madrasa) Subkī, IV, 314; Fārisī I, f4b–5a, 27a–b, 29b–30a, 46b–47a, 53a, 83a–b; II, f17a, 25a–b, 31a–32a, 94a–b. (Other Kūyi Sayyār madrasa) I. Funduq, p. 236.

12. *Madrasa Abū Saʿd az-Zāhid al-Kharkūshī:* Abū Saʿd al-Kharkūshī was a wealthy, Shāfiʿī-Ashʿarī ascetic who is primarily known for having built a hospital in Nishapur in which he and his followers dedicated themselves to menial nursing chores. However, he also built a madrasa

and a Sufi convent in Kharkūsh Street. The date of his death is variously given as 404, 406, or 407. Two of his successors as director are known.
References: (Abū Saᶜd) Samᶜānī, V, 101–102; Fārisī I, f47a–b; Subkī, III, 369. (Madrasa) Fārisī I, f82b, 86a; II, 24b–25a.

13. *Madrasa Abū Saᶜd al-Astarābādī:* Abū Saᶜd was a Sufi and a Shāfiᶜī who died in 440.
References: Subkī, IV, 293–294, 314.

14. *Madrasa Abū ᶜUthmān aṣ-Ṣābūnī:* The Shaikh al-Islām Abū ᶜUthmān was one of the most important members of the Shāfiᶜī-Ashᶜarī faction in the days before their persecution. He died in 449. Little is known about his madrasa beyond the names of two people who recited ḥadīth there. One man who had a Shāfiᶜī mosque in the quarter of Ramjār at his death made over his palace as an endowment for the Ṣābūniya located in the same quarter. This is presumably the Ṣābūnī madrasa which is otherwise known to have been located on Ḥarb Street.
References: Fārisī I, f85b; II, f14b–15a, 18b–19a, 79b.

15. *Madrasa Sūrī:* This madrasa was in the quarter of Bāb ᶜAzra, the same location as the Qushairī madrasa. Its origin is uncertain, but it was probably named for a son-in-law of Abū ᶜUthmān Ismāᶜīl aṣ-Ṣābūnī named Abū Bakr Muḥammad b. Maḥmud b. Sūra at-Tamīmī. It was a Shāfiᶜī institution, but no clue to its functioning is given. One of its residents during the early stages of the Ashᶜarī persecution was the famous Ashᶜarī Abū Bakr Aḥmad al-Baihaqī.
References: Fārisī I, f4b; II, f12a, 30a, 31a.

16. *Madrasa al-Mushaṭṭī:* Abū al-ᶜAbbās al-Mushaṭṭī for whom this madrasa was named is completely unknown. Several names are associated with it, one of them in the capacity of law teacher. It was probably Shāfiᶜī.
References: Fārisī I, f42a, 91a; II, f14b, 28a, 134b.

17. *Madrasa Sulṭāniya:* This is presumably the madrasa Nāṣir-i Khusraw mentions as being founded by Ṭughril Beg in the year 437 next to the saddlers' market. Ḥanafī law was taught in it.
References: IAW, I, 106, 135; Yāqūt, *Muᶜjam al-Buldān*, I, 517; Nāṣir-i Khusraw, *Safarnāmeh*, p. 3.

18. *Madrasa Sarhang:* If Sarhang is interpreted to mean a military commander, this madrasa was probably founded by some Seljuq official. It was presumably Shāfiᶜī since Ilkiyā al-Harrāsī who later became head of the Niẓāmiyas in Nishapur and Baghdad studied there.
References: Old Subkī, IV, 281–282.

19. *Madrasa Abū al-Ḥasan ᶜAlī aṣ-Ṣandalī (Shāfiᶜī):* This was not the same man as the leader of the persecution of the Ashᶜarīs. He was a Shāfiᶜī student of Abu Muḥammad al-Juwainī. He lived in his madrasa which was situated inside his mosque.
References: Fārisī II, f114a.

20. *Madrasa Abū al-Ḥasan ᶜAlī aṣ-Ṣandalī (Ḥanafī):* This was the Muᶜtazilī preacher who played

a major part in leading the persecution of the Ashᶜarīs. The only reference to his madrasa is when it was burned down in the factional warfare that destroyed the city.

References: (aṣ-Ṣandalī) Fārisī I, f68a–b; IAW, I, 357–359. (Madrasa) I. Athīr, XI, 236.

21. *Madrasa ash-Shaḥḥāmī:* This is almost certainly to be identified with the Ḥaẓīra ash-Shaḥḥāmī (Shaḥḥāmī Garth) which was situated within the Maniᶜī Congregational Mosque and designed for the study of ḥadīth.

References: (Madrasa) Fārisī II, f128a. (Ḥaẓīra) Fārisī II, f13b–14a, 34a, 41b, 47b–48a.

22. *Madrasa Sahl aṣ-Ṣuᶜlūkī:* The namesake of this Shāfiᶜī madrasa Abū aṭ-Ṭayyib Sahl aṣ-Ṣuᶜlūkī died in the first decade of the fifth century, and the madrasa was still operating in 474.

References: Fārisī II, f14a.

23. *Madrasa al-Ḥabīrī:* Ṣāᶜid al-Ḥabīrī was a Karrāmī who had a madrasa in Ramjār quarter.

References: Fārisī II, f75b.

24. *Madrasa al-Khuṭbī:* Abū Ḥātim Muḥammad al-Khuṭbī was a Karrāmī who built a madrasa in the market of the Kirmānīs and taught law and theology in it. He died in 488.

References: Fārisī II, f20b–21a.

25. *Madrasa al-Bīshakī:* Abū Saᶜīd Ṣiddīq al-Bīshakī was also a Karrāmī who had a madrasa. He died in 486.

References: Fārisī I, f87b; II, f75a.

26. *Madrasa Abū al-Ḥasan al-Qaṭṭān:* Abū al-Ḥasan ᶜAlī al-Qaṭṭān was a Ḥanafī-Muᶜtazilī and was khaṭīb of the Old Congregational Mosque prior to Abū ᶜUthmān aṣ-Ṣābūnī. His madrasa, where he taught ḥadīth, was in the market of the Ḥaḍarīs (?).

References: Fārisī I, f63b.

27. *Madrasa al-ᶜImādiya (ᶜAmīdiya):* A member of the Baḥīrī family taught ḥadīth in this institution before moving on to the Maniᶜī Congregational Mosque. It seems likely that the name is spelled wrong and that the founder was Muḥammad b. Manṣūr an-Nasawī known as the ᶜamīd of Khurasan.

References: Fārisī II, f16b, 43b.

28. *Madrasa al-Bushtī:* Abū Bakr Aḥmad al-Bushtī was a Shāfiᶜī who died in 429. He built a madrasa at the gate of his house at the end of Musayyib Street and endowed it with all his wealth. He also taught in the Ṣibghī madrasa (section 6).

References: Fārisī I, f26b; Subkī IV, 80.

29. *Madrasa al-Ḥaddād:* The only known person connected with this madrasa was a Sufi who was "servant of the Sufis (*khādim al-fuqarāᵓ*)" in it. He died in 478. It was obviously a Sufi institution.

References: Fārisī II, f35a.

30. *Madrasa Nāṣiḥ ad-Dawla:* Nāṣiḥ ad-Dawla was the honorific of Abū Muḥammad al-Fandūrjī, one of the lieutenants of Niẓām al-Mulk. One person known to have taught law in his madrasa died in 480, another in 530.
References: (Nāṣiḥ ad-Dawla) Fārisī I, f70a; Sam^{c}ānī, f432a. (Madrasa) Fārisī I, f52b–53a; Subkī, VI, 168.

31. *Madrasa as-Samarqandī:* Abū ^{c}Ali al-Ḥasan as-Samarqandī died in 395.
Reference: Fārisī I, f3a.

32. *Madrasa Aḥmad ath-Tha^{c}ālibī:* Aḥmad ath-Tha^{c}ālibī is not the same as the famous poetry anthologist ^{c}Abd al-Malik ath-Tha^{c}ālibī. A specialist in adab, he was buried in this madrasa in 474.
Reference: Fārisī II, f16a.

33. *Madrasa al-Faryābādī:* Abū Ṣādiq ^{c}Abd al-^{c}Azīz al-Faryābādī had a madrasa and died in the year 428.
Reference: Fārisī II, f100b.

34. *Madrasa al-Matuwiyī:* A madrasa was built for Abū al-Ḥasan ^{c}Alī al-Matuwiyī in which he taught law. He died in 444.
References: Fārisī I, f63b.

35. *Madrasa al-^{c}Abbādī:* Abū al-Ḥusain Ardashīr al-^{c}Abbādī was a Sufi, but he is also entitled amir. He was appointed to the madrasa at the gate of the Manī^{c}ī Congregational Mosque. He died in 497.
References: Fārisī II, f48b.

36. *Madrasa aṣ-Ṣūfiya:* This Sufi madrasa was in Post Street (Sikka al-Barīd). Its one known resident died in 491.
References: Fārisī I, f35b.

37. *Madrasa az-Za^{c}faranī:* Abū ^{c}Uthmān Sa^{c}īd az-Za^{c}faranī was buried in his madrasa in 427.
References: Fārisī I, f22a.

38. *Madrasa Abū Sa^{c}īd al-Basṭāmī:* Abū Sa^{c}īd al-Ḥusain al-Basṭāmī is not known to have been related to the famous Shāfi^{c}ī Basṭāmī family. He died in 430.
References: Fārisī I, f9b.

39. *Madrasa an-Niẓāmiya:* The relation of the Niẓāmiya in Nishapur to the overall political strategy of Niẓām al-Mulk is discussed in chapter 5. Here only information pertaining to the madrasa proper will be given. One general question that should be mentioned, however, is what distinctions can be drawn between the Niẓāmiya and the many madrasas that preceded it in Nishapur. From the available data, the only apparent distinction is a negative one. There are no references to anyone living in the Niẓāmiya while references to residents in other madrasas abound. Whether this is significant or merely coincidental is difficult to say.

The first director of the Niẓāmiya was Imām al-Ḥaramain al-Juwainī who served in the post for about thirty years and died in 478. This puts the foundation date back to the very earliest period of Niẓām al-Mulk's ascendancy in Nishapur in 450. Imām al-Ḥaramain was succeeded as director by his son Abū al-Qāsim Muẓaffar, but only after some dispute. Abū al-Qāsim was killed in 493. The next director was Imām al-Ḥaramain's student Ilkiyā al-Harrāsī. He did not stay long in the post, for around 498 he moved to Baghdad to become director of the Niẓāmiya there. After al-Harrāsī there is a brief gap, and then al-Ghazzālī, the most famous of Imām al-Ḥaramain's students, was lured out of retirement in Ṭūs to take the job in 499. How long he held it before his death in Ṭūs in 505 is not known. Between al-Ghazzālī's final retirement and the destruction of the Niẓāmiya by the Ghuzz in 548, only one director is known. He was Abū Saᶜīd Muḥammad b. Yaḥyā, a student of al-Ghazzālī. He was born in 476 and killed by the Ghuzz in 548. It is possible that this is the complete list of the directors of the Niẓāmiya madrasa, but there were probably one or two others who are unknown.

Two others posts in the Niẓāmiya are spoken of in the sources, that of librarian and that of Qurᵓan reciter. Two incumbents for each position are known. Both of the Qurᵓan readers were trained as grammarians; one of them was the grandson of a raᵓīs of the city. They seem to have exercised their office in a mosque inside the madrasa, and both were personal appointees of Niẓām al-Mulk. As for the two librarians, one was definitely a personal appointee of Niẓām al-Mulk, and the situation of the other is unclear. That Niẓām al-Mulk maintained personal jurisdiction over all appointments seems apparent.

In addition to the office holders already mentioned, there are numerous instances of people reciting ḥadīth in the Niẓāmiya. Exactly how the ḥadīth sessions were organized and who had jurisdiction over them is uncertain. One man, Abū Muḥammad al-Ḥasan as-Samarqandī, appears to have acted as arbiter of ḥadīth teaching. Al-Fārisī says that "he was appointed to sit in the Niẓāmiya and maintain the order of ḥadīth reciting there. He used to be present there every day from noon until evening, and in his presence took place the examinations (*fawāᵓid*) and the pronouncing of ḥadīth." Without corroborating evidence, however, the regular appointment of an official with this duty cannot be affirmed.

References: (Director) Fārisī I, f48b, 72a, 90a; Old Subkī, IV, 197, 281–282; Horst, *Die Staatsverwaltung*, p. 163; EI², II, 1039; Makdisi, "Muslim Institutions," p. 41. (Qurᵓan reader) Fārisī II, f16b, 144a. (Librarian) Fārisī I, f29b, 75b. (As-Samarqandī) Fārisī I, f7a. (Ḥadīth classes) Fārisī I, f43b; II, f14b, 15a, 32b, 40a, 91a, 115b, 132b.

Appendix II *Qāḍīs of Nishapur*

The following is a partial chronological list of the chief qāḍīs of Nishapur. The lacunae are many, particularly prior to the year 913/300, and the order is sometimes conjectural. Moreover, since the distinction between a chief qāḍī and a subordinate qāḍī is not always made, some individuals may not belong on the list at all. Still, even a defective list of the holders of this crucial office is of value in trying to understand the city's history. All known Shāfiʿī office holders are indicated.

Dates in office or death date	*Name and comments*	*References*
1. Died 163	Abū Muʿādh Bakīr ad-Dāmghānī an-Naisābūrī. Died in Damascus.	Samʿānī, V, 291; Ḥākim, f7b; ʿIbar, I, 241.
2. Died 199	Abū ʿUmar Ḥafṣ al-Balkhī an-Naisābūrī. Did not die in office; father held same post.	ʿIbar, I, 329; IAW, I, 221; Ḥākim, f7b–8a.
3. Died 209	Abū ʿAmr Ḥafṣ as-Sulamī an-Naisābūrī. Held office for twenty years.	ʿIbar, I, 357; Ḥākim, f10b.
4. 213–ca. 214	Abū Muḥammad Naṣr an-Naisābūrī. Kufan madhhab. Died 233 or 236.	IAW, II, 193; Ḥākim, f17b.
5.	Abū Saʿīd or Abū Ayyūb Ashraf. Studied under Abū Yūsuf who died in 182.	IAW, I, 162; Ḥākim, f10a.
6.	Abū Muḥammad ʿAbd Allāh b. Maimūn. Father was qāḍī of Balkh and died in 171.	IAW, I, 279; Ḥākim, f12b.
7. Died 244	Abū ʿAlī al-Ḥasan as-Sulamī.	IAW, I, 190–191; Ḥākim, f10a.
8. Died 258	Abū ʿAlī Aḥmad as-Sulamī. Son of #3.	ʿIbar, II, 16.
9. ca. 225	Abū al-ʿAbbās Muḥammad ath-Thaqafī al-Ḥamīrī. Became qāḍī early in Ṭāhirid period.	Samʿānī, III, 141.
10. Died 297	Abū Bakr Mūsā al-Anṣārī al-Khaṭmī. First Shāfiʿī qāḍī. Served in Rayy, Nishapur, and Ahwaz. Died in Ahwaz.	ʿIbar, II, 109; Subkī, II, 345; T. Baghdād, XIII, 52–54.
11. ca. 255–ca. 265	Abū Muḥammad Aḥmad adh-Dhuhlī. Began under Ṭāhirids and ended under Saffārids. Died in prison in Baghdad in 269.	Samʿānī, VI, 22–23.
12. ca. 279–285	Abū Rajāʾ Muḥammad al-Jūzjānī. Kufan	IAW, II, 29;

Dates in office or death date	*Name and comments*	*References*
	madhhab. Qāḍī of Ṣaffārid ᶜAmr b. al-Laith. Died in Jūzjān in 285.	Ḥākim, f25a; Samᶜānī, III, 401.
13. ca. 286–298	Abū Muḥammad ᶜAbd Allāh b. Salma. Ḥanafī chosen to be qāḍī by Shāfiᶜī Ibn Khuzaima at beginning of Sāmānid period. Died in office.	IAW, I, 276; II, 55; Ḥākim, f22b; Samᶜānī, II, 207.
14. Died 309	Abū Saᶜīd ᶜAbd ar-Raḥmān b. al-Ḥusain.	IAW, I, 300; Ḥākim, f23a.
15. ca. 309–315	Abū ᶜAlī al-Ḥusain al-Junābadhī. Died in office.	Samᶜānī, III, 334; Ḥākim, f30b.
16. Died 359	Abū ᶜAlī al-Ḥasan al-Baihaqī. Died in Baihaq.	I. Funduq, p. 127; Ḥākim, f40b, 41a; Samᶜānī, II, 413.
17. ca. 327–337	Abū Muḥammad Yaḥyā al-Jārūdī.	ᶜIbar, II, 293; Ḥākim, f54a; IAW, II, 23.
18. 337–345	Abū Aḥmad Muḥammad al-Marwazī. Died in 353.	IAW, II, 23; Ḥākim, f47a.
19. 345–ca. 351	Abū al-Ḥusain Aḥmad "Qāḍī al-Ḥaramain." Died in 351.	IAW, I, 107–108; ᶜIbar, II, 290; Shadharāt, III, 7–8.
20. ca. 351–ca. 371	Abū Bakr Aḥmad al-Ḥīrī al-Ḥarashī "al-Qāḍī al-Ḥīrī." Second Shāfiᶜī qāḍī. For justification of assigned dates see chapter 5.	See Maḥmī genealogical key #19.
21. Died 378	Abū al-Qāsim Bishr al-Bāhilī.	Samᶜānī, II, 72; Ḥākim, f40b.
22. ca. 375–377	Abū al-Qāsim ᶜAlī b. Aḥmad. Son of #19.	Fārisī, I, f61a; II, f110b.
23. 377–392	Abū al-ᶜAlāᵓ Ṣāᶜid. Beginning of Ṣāᶜidī family domination.	See Ṣāᶜidī genealogical key #1.

Dates in office or death date	*Name and comments*	*References*
24. 388	Abū ʿAmr Muḥammad al-Basṭāmī. Held office for only a few months. Third Shāfiʿī qāḍī.	See Basṭāmī genealogical key #5.
25. 392–405	Abū al-Haitham ʿUtba. Last qāḍī of the Kufan madhhab.	IAW, I, 342–343; Ḥākim, f47a; Fārisī I, f72a–b; II, f117a; Shadharāt, III, 181.
26. Died 433	Abū Saʿīd Muḥammad aṣ-Ṣāʿidī. Son of #23.	See Ṣāʿidī genealogical key #6.
27. Died 427	Abū Saʿd ʿAbd ar-Raḥīm al-Ismāʿīlī "al-Qāḍī al-Mukhtār."	See Ṣāʿidī genealogical key #12.
28. ca. 428	Abū al-Ḥasan Aḥmad b. ʿAlī. Son of #22, grandson of #19. Held office for only a few days. Died in 446.	Fārisī II, f28a.
29. ca. 431–443	Abū al-Ḥasan Ismāʿīl aṣ-Ṣāʿidī. Died in 443. Son of #23, brother of #26.	See Ṣāʿidī genealogical key #5.
30.	ʿAbd al-Wahhāb an-Nasafī. Held the post for two years. Student of Abū al-ʿAlāʾ Ṣāʿid.	IAW, I, 335.
31. Died 470	Abū al-Qāsim Manṣūr aṣ-Ṣāʿidī. Son of #29.	See Ṣāʿidī genealogical key #22.
32. Died 484	Abū Bakr Muḥammad an-Nāṣiḥī. Deposed for corruption.	See Ṣāʿidī genealogical key #11.
33. Died 482	Abū Naṣr Aḥmad aṣ-Ṣāʿidī. Son of #26, grandson of #23.	See Ṣāʿidī genealogical key #24.
34. 482–ca. 527	Abū Saʿīd Muḥammad aṣ-Ṣāʿidī. Son of #33, grandson of #26, great-grandson of #23. Died in 527.	See Ṣāʿidī genealogical key #38.

Dates in office or death date	*Name and comments*	*References*
35. Died 532	Ṣāᶜid aṣ-Ṣāᶜidī. Great-grandson of #29.	See Ṣāᶜidī genealogical #44
36.	Abū ᶜAlī al-Ḥasan aṣ-Ṣāᶜidī. Followed his brother (#35) as qāḍī but served for only four months.	See Ṣāᶜidī genealogical key #45.
37. Died 551	Abū al-Mafākhir ᶜAzīz aṣ-Ṣāᶜidī. Son of #34 grandson of #33, great-grandson of #26, great-great-grandson of #23.	See Ṣāᶜidī genealogical key #46.
38. Died 552	Abū al-Qāsim Manṣūr aṣ-Ṣāᶜidī. Brother of #37.	See Ṣāᶜidī genealogical key #47.
39. Died 554	ᶜAlī aṣ-Ṣāᶜidī. Died in Rayy. Son of #38.	See Ṣāᶜidī genealogical key 49.
40.	Yaḥyā aṣ-Ṣāᶜidī. Contemporary of the poet ᶜAṭṭār.	See Ṣāᶜidī genealogical key #48.

Bibliography

Ahmed, Munir-ud-Din. *Muslim Education and the Scholars' Social Status up to the 5th Century Muslim Era in the Light of the Taʾrīkh Baghdād.* Zurich, Verlag "Der Islam," 1968.

Allard, Michel. *Le Problème des attributs divins dans la doctrine d'al-Ashᶜarī et de ses premiers grands disciples.* Beirut, Imprimerie Catholique, 1965.

Allen, W. E. D. *A History of the Georgian People.* London, K. Paul, Trench, Trubner, 1932.

al-Amīn, Muḥsin. *Aᶜyān ash-Shīᶜa.* 53 vols. Beirut, Maṭbaᶜa al-Anṣāf, 1960–.

al-Baghdādī, ᶜAbd al-Qāhir. *Al-Farq bain al-firaq.* 2 vols. Vol. I trans. K. C. Seelye, New York, Columbia University Press, 1919. Vol. II trans. A. S. Halkin. Tel Aviv, 1935.

Baihaqī, Abū al-Faḍl. *Taʾrīkh-i Baihaqī.* Edited by Q. Ghanī and ᶜA. A. Fayyāḍ. Tehran, Maḥfūẓ Press, 1945. Notes used from edition of Saᶜīd Nafīsī, 3 vols. Tehran, University of Tehran Press, 1940–1953.

al-Bākharzī, Abū al-Ḥasan ᶜAlī. *Dumya al-Qaṣr wa ᶜAṣra Ahl al-ᶜAṣr.* Edited by Muḥammad Rāghib aṭ-Ṭabbākh. Aleppo, ᶜIlmiya Press, 1930.

Barthold, Wilhelm. *Turkestan Down to the Mongol Invasion.* E. J. W. Gibb Memorial Series, n.s. V. 3rd ed. London, Luzac, 1968.

Beaurecueil, Serge de. *Khwādja ᶜAbdullāh Anṣārī.* Beirut, Imprimerie Catholique, 1965.

Bosworth, C. E. *The Ghaznavids: Their Empire in Afghanistan and Eastern Iran 994–1040.* Edinburgh, Edinburgh University Press, 1963.

Bosworth, C. E. "The Rise of the Karāmiyyah in Khurasan." *Muslim World,* 50 (1960), 5–14.

Bowen, Harold. "Notes on Some Early Seljuqid Viziers." *Bulletin of the School of Oriental and African Studies,* 20 (1957), 105–110.

Breebaart, D. A. *The Development and Structure of the Turkish Futuwah Guilds.* Ann Arbor, University Microfilms, 1966.

Brockelmann, Carl. *Geschichte der Arabischen Litteratur.* 2 vols. and 3 supplemental vols. Leiden, E. J. Brill, 1937–1949.

Bulliet, R. W. "A Muᶜtazilite Coin of Maḥmūd of Ghazna." *American Numismatic Society Museum Notes,* 15 (1969), 119–129.

Bulliet, R. W. "A Quantitative Approach to Medieval Muslim Biographical Dictionaries." *Journal of the Economic and Social History of the Orient,* 13 (1970), 195–211.

Cahen, Claude. *Mouvements populaires et autonomisme urbain dans l'Asie musulmane du moyen âge.* Leiden, E. J. Brill, 1959.

The Cambridge History of Iran. Vol. I, *The Land of Iran,* ed. W. B. Fisher. Vol. V, *The Saljuq and Mongol Periods,* ed. J. A. Boyle. Cambridge, Cambridge University Press, 1968.

Dawlatshāh. *Tadhkirat-i Shuᶜarāʾ.* Edited by Muḥammad Ramaḍānī. Tehran, Khāvar Press, 1959.

Dennett, Daniel C. *Conversion and the Poll Tax in Early Islam.* Cambridge, Mass., Harvard University Press, 1950.

adh-Dhahabī, Abū ᶜAbd Allāh Muḥammad. *Al-ᶜIbar fī Khabar man Ghabar.* Edited by Ṣalāḥ ad-Dīn Munajjid and Fuʾād Sayyid. 5 vols. Kuwait, Office of Printing and Publication, 1960–1966.

——— *Al-Mushtabah fī ar-Rijāl*. Edited by al-Bajāwī. 2 vols. Cairo, ʿĪsā al-Bābī al-Ḥalabī, 1962.

——— *Kitāb Tadhkira al-Ḥuffāz*. 4 vols. Hyderabad, Osmania Oriental Publications Bureau, 1955–1958.

——— *Taʾrīkh al-Islām*. Vol. 11. Manuscript, Aya Sofya 3009. Istanbul.

Encyclopaedia of Islam. 1st ed., 4 vols. Leiden, E. J. Brill, 1913–1934. New ed., 2 vols. to date. Leiden, E. J. Brill, 1960–.

Encyclopaedia of Religion and Ethics, ed. J. Hastings. 13 vols. New York, Charles Scribner's Sons, 1908–1927.

Faḍāʾil Balkh. Manuscript in Bibliotheque Nationale, Persian 115. Paris.

Farhang-i Jughrāfyā-yi Īrān. 10 vols. Tehran, Army Geography Office, 1949–1953.

al-Fārisī, Abū al-Ḥasan ʿAbd al-Ghāfir. *Siyāq li-Taʾrīkh Naisābūr*. See Frye, *The Histories of Nishapur*.

Frye, R. N., ed. *The Histories of Nishapur*. Facsimile edition of mss. by Abū al-Ḥasan ʿAbd al-Ghāfir al-Fārisī and Abū ʿAbd Allāh Muḥammad al-Ḥākim an-Naisābūrī. Cambridge, Mass., Harvard University Press, 1965. For further information see Introduction.

Gibb, H. A. R. *Studies on the Civilization of Islam*. Boston, Beacon Press, 1962.

Goblot, Henri. "Dans l'ancien Iran, les techniques de l'eau et la grande histoire." *Annales: Économies, sociétés, civilisations*, 18 (1963), 499–520.

al-Ḥākim an-Naisābūrī, Abū ʿAbd Allāh Muḥammad. *Taʾrīkh Naisābūr*. See Frye, *The Histories of Nishapur*.

Horst, Heribert. *Die Staatsverwaltung der Grossselǧuqen und Horazmšāhs (1038–1231)*. Wiesbaden, Franz Steiner Verlag, 1964.

Hourani, A. H., and S. M. Stern. *The Islamic City*. Oxford, Bruno Cassirer, 1970.

al-Ḥusainī. *Akhbār ʾud-Dawlat ʾis-Saljūqiyya*. Edited by M. Iqbal, Lahore, Punjab College Publications, 1933.

Ibn Abī al-Wafāʾ. *Al-Jawāhir al-muḍiya fī ṭabaqāt al-Ḥanafiya*. 2 vols. Hyderabad, Nizamia Oriental Publications Bureau, 1914.

Ibn al-Athīr, Abū al-Ḥasan ʿAlī. *Al-Kāmil fī at-Taʾrīkh*. 13 vols. Beirut, Dar Sader, 1965–1967.

Ibn al-Athīr, Abū al-Ḥasan ʿAlī. *Al-Lubāb fī tahdhīb al-ansāb*. 3 vols. Cairo, Maktaba al-Qudsī 1938.

Ibn Funduq. *Taʾrīkh-i Baihaq*. Edited by A. Bahmaniyār. Tehran, Islamiya Press, 1938.

Ibn al-ʿImād, Abū al-Falāḥ ʿAbd al-Ḥayy. *Shadharāt adh-Dhahab fī Akhbār man Dhahab*. 8 vols. Cairo, Maktaba al-Qudsī, 1931–1932.

Ibn al-Jauzī, Abū al-Faraj ʿAbd ar-Raḥmān. *Al-Muntaẓam fī taʾrīkh al-mulūk wa al-umam*. 5 vols. numbered 5–10. Hyderabad, Osmania Oriental Publishing Bureau, 1938–1939.

Ibn Khallikān, Abū al-ᶜAbbās Aḥmad. *Wafayāt al-Aᶜyān wa Anbā᾽ Abnā᾽ az-Zamān*. Edited by Muḥammad ᶜAbd al-Ḥamīd. 6 vols. Cairo, Maktaba an-Nahḍa, 1948–1949.

Ibn Mākūlā. *Al-Ikmāl fī rafᶜ al-irtiyāb ᶜan al-mu᾽talaf wa al-mukhtalaf min al-ismā᾽ wa al-kunā wa al-ansāb*. 6 vols. to date. Hyderabad, Osmania Oriental Publishing Bureau, 1962–1967.

Ibn al-Qaisarānī. *Ziyāda ᶜalā Kitāb al-Ansāb al-Muttafaqa*. Edited by P. DeJong. Leiden, E. J. Brill, 1865.

Iqbāl, ᶜAbbās. "Jāmiᶜ-yi Manīᶜī-yi Nīshābūr." *Mihr*, 3 (1936), 1089–94.

Jackson, A. V. W. *From Constantinople to the Home of Omar Khayyam*. New York, Macmillan, 1911.

The Jewish Encyclopedia. 12 vols. New York, Funk and Wagnalls, 1901–1906.

Juvainī, ᶜAta-Malik. *The History of the World Conqueror*. Translated by J. A. Boyle. 2 vols. Cambridge, Mass., Harvard University Press, 1958.

al-Khaṭīb al-Baghdādī, Abū Bakr Aḥmad. *Ta᾽rīkh Baghdād*. 14 vols. Beirut, Dār al-Kitāb al-Arabī, n.d.

Lane, E. W. *An Arabic-English Lexicon*. 8 vols. London, Williams and Norgate, 1863–1893.

Lapidus, I. M. *Muslim Cities in the Later Middle Ages*. Cambridge, Mass., Harvard University Press, 1967.

Laufer, Berthold. "Geophagy." *Field Museum of Natural History Anthropology Series*, 18 (1930), 101–198.

Makdisi, George. "Autograph Diary of an Eleventh-Century Historian of Baghdād." *Bulletin of the School of Oriental and African Studies*, 18 (1956), 9–31, 239–260; 19 (1957), 13–48, 281–303, 426–443.

Makdisi, George. *Ibn ᶜAqīl et la résurgence de l'Islam traditionaliste au XIᵉ siècle*. Damascus, Imprimerie Catholique, 1963.

Makdisi, George. "Muslim Institutions of Learning in Eleventh-Century Baghdad." *Bulletin of the School of Oriental and African Studies*, 24 (1961), 1–56.

al-Maqdisī. *Aḥsan at-taqāsīm fī maᶜrifa al-aqālīm*. Edited by M. J. de Goeje. In *Bibliotheca Geographorum Arabicorum*. 2nd ed. III. Leiden, E. J. Brill, 1906.

Markow, A. K. *Inventarny katalog musulmanskich monet*. St. Petersburg, 1896.

Nāṣir-i Khusraw. *Safarnāmeh*. Edited by Muḥammad Dabīr Siyāqī. Tehran, Zavvār Bookstore, 1956.

Nicholson, Reynold A. *Studies in Islamic Mysticism*. Cambridge, Cambridge University Press, 1921.

Pritsak, Omeljan. "Āl-i Burhān." *Der Islam*, 30 (1952), 81–96.

ar-Rāwandī, Muḥammad. *Rāḥat aṣ-ṣudūr wa āyat as-surūr: Being a History of the Seljūqs*. Edited by M. Iqbāl. E. J. W. Gibb Memorial Series, n.s. II. London, Luzac, 1921.

Russell, J. C. "Late Ancient and Medieval Populations." *Transactions of the American Philosophical Society*, vol. 48, no. 3 (1958).

Ṣafā, Zabīh Allāh. *Ta'rīkh-i Adabiyāt dar Īrān*. 2 vols. Tehran, Ibn Sina, 1956–1957.
as-Sahmī, Ḥamza. *Ta'rīkh Jurjān*. Hyderabad, Osmania Oriental Publications Bureau, 1950.
as-Samᶜānī, ᶜAbd al-Karīm. *Kitāb al-Ansāb*. Edited by ᶜAbd ar-Raḥmān al-Yamānī. 6 vols. to date. Hyderabad, Osmania Oriental Publications Bureau, 1962–. Old facsimile edition edited by D. Margoliouth, E. J. W. Gibb Memorial Series, vol. XX. London, Luzac, 1912.
Schacht, Joseph. *An Introduction to Islamic Law*. Oxford, Clarendon Press, 1964.
as-Subkī, Abū Naṣr ᶜAbd al-Wahhāb. *Ṭabaqāt ash-Shāfiᶜiya al-Kubrā*. 6 vols. Cairo, al-Maṭbaᶜa al-Ḥasaniya al-Miṣriya, 1905–1906. New edition edited by M. aṭ-Ṭanāḥī and ᶜAbd al-Fatāḥ al-Ḥalū, 6 vols. to date. Cairo, ᶜĪsā al-Bābī al-Ḥalabī, 1964–.
as-Sulamī, Abū ᶜAbd ar-Raḥmān Muḥammad. *Ṭabaqāt aṣ-Ṣūfiya*. Edited by Nūr ad-Dīn Sharība. Cairo, Dār al-Kitāb al-ᶜArabī, 1953.
Sykes, P. M. "A Sixth Journey in Persia." *The Geographical Journal*, 37 (1911), 1–19, 149–165.
aṭ-Ṭabarī, Abū Jaᶜfar Muḥammad. *Ta'rīkh ar-Rusul wa al-Mulūk*. Edited by Muḥammad Abū al-Faḍl Ibrāhīm. 9 vols. to date. Cairo, Dār al-Maᶜārif bi Miṣr, 1960–.
Ta'rīkh Samarqand. Manuscript in the Bibliothèque Nationale, Arabic 6,248. Paris.
Thaᶜālibī. *Yatīma ad-Dahr*. 4 vols. Cairo, Maktaba al-Ḥusainiya, 1934.
Thābatī, M. *Ta'rīkh-i Nīshābūr*. Tehran, Ministry of Roads, 1956.
Tibawi, A. "Origin and Character of *al-Madrasah*." *Bulletin of the School of Oriental and African Studies*, 25 (1962), 225–238.
Torres Balbas, Leopoldo. "Extension y demografia de las ciudades hispanomusulmanas." *Studia Islamica*, 3 (1955), 35–59.
ᶜUtbī. *Kitab-i-Yamini*. Translated by J. Reynolds. London, Oriental Translation Fund, 1858.
Weber, Max. *The City*. Translated by Martingale and Neuwirth. New York, Collier Books, 1962.
Wilkinson, C. K. "The Īrānian Expedition, 1936." *Bulletin of the Metropolitan Museum of Art*, 32 (1937), section II.
Wilkinson, C. K. "The Īrānian Expedition, 1937." *Bulletin of the Metropolitan Museum of Art*, 33 (1938).
Wulff, H. E. "The Qanats of Iran." *Scientific American*, 218 (1968), 94–105.
Yāqūt, Abū ᶜAbd Allāh. *Irshād al-arīb ilā maᶜrifa al-adīb; or Dictionary of Learned Men of Yāqūt*. Edited by D. S. Margoliouth. 7 vols. E. J. W. Gibb Memorial Series, Vol. 6. Leiden, E. J. Brill, 1907–1927.
Yāqūt, Abū ᶜAbd Allāh. *Muᶜjam al-Buldān*. 5 vols. Beirut, Dar Sader-Dar Beyrouth, 1955–1957.
Zambaur, E. de. *Manuel de généalogie et de chronologie pour l'histoire de l'Islam*. Hannover, Heinz Lafaire, 1927.

Index of Names

In alphabetization the following elements of the name have been ignored: Abū — "father of"; Ibn, b. — "son (or daughter) of"; Umm — "mother of"; al-, at-, as-, etc. — the Arabic definite article. Individuals with identical names have been distinguished by Roman numerals according to chronological precedence.

ᶜAmīd Khurāsān, Muḥammad b. Manṣūr an-Nasawī. *See* Muḥammad
ᶜAmīd al-Mulk, Abū Naṣr Manṣūr al-Kundurī. *See* Manṣūr (Abū Naṣr)
al-ᶜAmmārī, ᶜAbd ar-Raḥmān. *See* ᶜAbd ar-Raḥmān
ᶜAmr (Abū ᶜAbd ar-Raḥmān) b. Muḥammad al-Baḥīrī, 193–195, 197, 199
ᶜAmr b. al-Laith aṣ-Ṣaffār, 69, 257
al-Anṣārī, Abū Bakr Mūsā al-Khaṭmī. *See* Mūsā (Abū Bakr)
al-Anṣārī, Abū Ismāᶜīl ᶜAbd Allāh. *See* ᶜAbd Allāh (Abū Ismāᶜīl)
al-Anṣārī, Abū al-Qāsim Salmān b. Nāṣir. *See* Salmān (Abū al-Qāsim)
Ardashīr (Abū al-Ḥusain) al-ᶜAbbādī, 254
Asᶜad (Abū al-Maᶜālī) b. Ṣāᶜid aṣ-Ṣāᶜidī, 215, 223, 226
Asᶜad b. Muḥammad ar-Rawaqī, 162, 186
al-Aṣamm, Abū al-ᶜAbbās Muḥammad b. Yaᶜqūb. *See* Muḥammad (Abū al-ᶜAbbās)
al-Ashᶜarī, Abū al-Ḥasan. *See* Abū al-Ḥasan
Ashraf, Abū Saᶜīd (Abū Ayyūb), 256
al-Astarābādī, Abū Saᶜd. *See* Abū Saᶜd
ᶜAṭṭār, 215, 259
al-ᶜAwwālī, Aḥmad b. ᶜAlī. *See* Aḥmad
Ay Abah al-Muʾayyad, 77–80, 127
al-ᶜAyyār, Nūḥ. *See* Nūḥ
al-Ayyūbī, Abū al-Ḥasan ᶜAlī b. Muḥammad. *See* ᶜAlī (Abū al-Ḥasan)
ᶜAzīz (Abū al-Mafākhir) b. Muḥammad aṣ-Ṣāᶜidī, 215, 223, 226, 259

al-Baghdādī, Abū Manṣūr ᶜAbd al-Qāhir b. Ṭāhir. *See* ᶜAbd al-Qāhir (Abū Manṣūr)
al-Bāhilī, 159
al-Bāhilī, Abū al-Qāsim Bishr. *See* Bishr (Abū al-Qāsim)
Baḥīr (Abū Ḥāmid) b. Muḥammad al-Baḥīrī, 193, 195, 197–198
Baḥīr b. Nūḥ, 192, 199
al-Baḥīrī. *See* chapter 12 and names of individual family members
al-Baihaqī, Abū ᶜAlī al-Ḥasan. *See* al-Ḥasan (Abū ᶜAlī)
al-Baihaqī, Abū Bakr Aḥmad b. al-Ḥusain. *See* Aḥmad (Abū Bakr)
al-Baihaqī, Abū al-Ḥasan ᶜAlī b. al-Ḥusain. *See* ᶜAlī (Abū al-Ḥasan)
al-Baihaqī, Abū al-Ḥasan Muḥammad b. Shuᶜaib. *See* Muḥammad (Abū al-Ḥasan)
al-Baihaqī, Abū Muḥammad al-Muᶜallā. *See* al-Muᶜallā (Abū Muḥammad)
al-Bākharzī, Abū al-Ḥasan ᶜAlī. *See* ᶜAlī (Abū al-Ḥasan)
Bakīr (Abū Muᶜādh) ad-Damghānī, 256
Abū Bakr, 30
Bakr b. Wajīh ash-Shaḥḥāmī, 172, 177, 191
al-Balᶜamī, Abū al-Faḍl. *See* Abū al-Faḍl
al-Bālawī. *See* chapter 7 and names of individual family members
al-Balkhī, Abū ᶜUmar Ḥafṣ. *See* Ḥafṣ (Abū ᶜUmar)

Abū Saᶜd al-Astarābādī, 252
Abū Saᶜd al-Kharkūshī, 251
Saᶜd b. Muḥammad al-Isfarāᵓinī al-Iskāf, 230–231, 233
Abū Saᶜd az-Zāhid, 134
aṣ-Ṣaffār. *See* chapter 11 and names of individual family members
aṣ-Ṣaffār, ᶜAmr b. al-Laith. *See* ᶜAmr
Ṣāḥib b. al-ᶜAbbād, 115
Sahl (Abū al-Qāsim) b. ᶜAlī an-Nāṣiḥī, 211, 221, 225
Sahl b. Abī Sahl, 160, 186
Sahl (Abū aṭ-Ṭayyib) b. Ismāᶜīl al-Basṭāmī, 118, 131–132
Sahl (Abū aṭ-Ṭayyib) b. Muḥammad aṣ-Ṣuᶜlūkī, 117–118, 120–121, 129, 132, 135–136, 236, 239, 241–242, 253
Sahl (Abū aṭ-Ṭayyib) as-Sarrājī, 229, 231, 233
Sahl (Abū ᶜUmar) b. ᶜUmar al-Basṭāmī, 123, 125, 130, 133
as-Sahmī, Abū al-Qāsim Ḥamza b. Yūsuf. *See* Ḥamza (Abū al-Qāsim)
Saᶜīd (Abū ᶜAbd Allāh) b. Muḥammad al-Furātī al-Khūjānī, 142, 144, 148
Ṣāᶜid b. ᶜAbd al-Malik aṣ-Ṣāᶜidī, 78, 214–215, 222, 225
Saᶜīd b. ᶜAbd ar-Raḥmān al-Bālawī, 98, 103
Saᶜīd b. ᶜAbd ar-Raḥmān al-Ḥarashī, 90, 101
Ṣāᶜid (Abū al-ᶜAlāᵓ) b. Manṣūr aṣ-Ṣāᶜidī, 212–214, 223, 225
Ṣāᶜid (Abū al-ᶜAlāᵓ) b. al-Muᶜallā aṣ-Ṣāᶜidī, 63, 67, 70–71, 73, 94, 118, 140, 159–160, 201–205, 208–209, 211, 217, 223, 229, 238, 250, 257–258
Saᶜīd b. Baḥīr al-Baḥīrī, 192, 198
Saᶜīd (Abū al-Barakāt) b. Asᶜad ar-Rawaqī, 162, 186, 189
Ṣāᶜid al-Ḥabīrī, 253
Ṣāᶜid b. al-Ḥusain aṣ-Ṣāᶜidī, 215–216, 224, 226, 259
Saᶜīd b. Masᶜūd al-Ḥadhdhāᵓ, 230–232
Abū Saᶜīd b. Muḥammad al-Bālawī, 96, 102, 105
Saᶜīd (Abū Naṣr) b. ᶜAbd ar-Raḥīm al-Ismāᶜīlī as-Sarrājī, 207, 217–218
Saᶜīd (Abū Saᶜd) b. Ismāᶜīl aṣ-Ṣābūnī, 139, 143, 145
Ṣāᶜid (Abū Saᶜīd) b. ᶜUbaid Allāh al-Ḥaskānī al-Ḥadhdhāᵓ, 230–232
Saᶜīd (Abū ᶜUmar) b. Hibat Allāh al-Basṭāmī, 123, 130, 133
Saᶜīd b. ᶜUthmān, 89
Saᶜīd (Abū ᶜUthmān) b. Muḥammad al-Baḥīrī al-Mūlqābādī, 194, 196–198
Saᶜīd (Abū ᶜUthmān) az-Zaᶜfarānī, 254
Saᶜīda b. Zāhir ash-Shaḥḥāmī, 171, 178, 191
aṣ-Ṣāᶜidī. *See* chapter 13 and names of individual family members
aṣ-Ṣāᶜidī, Abū ᶜAbd Allāh Muḥammad b. al-Faḍl al-Furāwī. *See* Muḥammad (Abū ᶜAbd Allāh)
aṣ-Ṣāᶜidī, Abū al-Barakāt ᶜAbd Allāh b. Muḥammad al-Furāwī. *See* ᶜAbd Allāh (Abū al-Barakāt)
aṣ-Ṣāᶜidī, Abū Muḥammad al-Faḍl b. Aḥmad al-Furāwī. *See* al-Faḍl (Abū Muḥammad)

General Index

Harvard Middle Eastern Studies

Out of print titles are omitted.

2. *Middle Eastern Capitalism: Nine Essays.* By A. J. Meyer. 1959.
3. *The Idea of the Jewish State.* By Ben Halpern. 1961. (Second edition, 1969.)
4. *The Agricultural Policy of Muhammad ᶜAli in Egypt.* By Helen Anne B. Rivlin. 1961.
5. *Egypt in Search of Political Community: An Analysis of the Intellectual and Political Evolution of Egypt, 1804–1952.* By Nadav Safran. 1961 (also a Harvard Political Study).
6. *The Economy of Cyprus.* By A. J. Meyer, with Simos Vassiliou. 1962.*
7. *Entrepreneurs of Lebanon: The Role of the Business Leader in a Developing Economy.* By Yusif A. Sayigh. 1962.*
8. *The Opening of South Lebanon, 1788–1840: A Study of the Impact of the West on the Middle East.* By William R. Polk. 1963.
9. *The First Turkish Republic: A Case Study in National Development.* By Richard D. Robinson. 1963.
10. *The Armenian Communities in Syria under Ottoman Dominion.* By Avedis K. Sanjian. 1965.
11. *Muslim Cities in the Later Middle Ages.* By Ira Marvin Lapidus. 1967.†
12. *Tripoli: A Modern Arab City.* By John Gulick. 1967.
13. *Pioneers East: The Early American Experience in the Middle East.* By David H. Finnie. 1967.
14. *Shaykh and Effendi: Changing Patterns of Authority Among the El Shabana of Southern Iraq.* By Robert A. Fernea. 1970.
15. *Between Old and New: The Ottoman Empire under Sultan Selim III, 1789–1807.* By Stanford J. Shaw. 1971.
16. *The Patricians of Nishapur: A Study in Medieval Islamic Social History.* By Richard W. Bulliet. 1972.

* Published jointly by the Center for International Affairs and the Center for Middle Eastern Studies.

† Published jointly by the Center for Middle Eastern Studies and the Joint Center for Urban Studies.